SECOND EDITION

Daytrips

SPAIN *and* PORTUGAL

SECOND EDITION

Daytrips

SPAIN *and* PORTUGAL

50 *one day adventures by car, rail or ferry including 51 maps*

NORMAN P.T. RENOUF

HASTINGS HOUSE
Book Publishers
Fern Park, Florida

For Kathy:
No longer an "Absent Friend;" now an ever-loving and supportive wife, without whom this guide, or anything else I do, would not be possible. And a special mention to Mike "Segundo Piso" Kelly, who was instrumental in introducing us all those years ago, and who assists me in some of my travels.

Edited by Earl Steinbicker, creator of the DAYTRIPS series.

Copyright© 2001 by Norman P.T. Renouf.

ISBN: 0-8038-2012-7

Cover design and book layout by Mark Salore.
Printed in the United States of America.

10 9 8 7 6 5 4 3 2

Comments?   Ideas?
We'd love to hear from you. Ideas from our readers have resulted in many improvements in the past, and will continue to do so. And, if your suggestions are used, we'll gladly send you a complimentary copy of any book in the series. Please send your thoughts to Hastings House, Book Publishers, 2601 Wells Ave., Suite 161. Fern Park, FL 32730, e-mail to Hhousebks@aol.com. Visit us at www.DaytripsBooks.com

Contents

Introduction

Visitors to Spain and Portugal can choose from an enormous range of experiences. There are magnificent cities and medieval towns to be explored, mountains to be climbed, history to be relived and exotic food and a wide range of wonderful wines to be tasted. Few places can match the Iberian Peninsula's glorious history, enriched with a kaleidoscopic array of social customs, architecture, art, and music. Its geographic features are equally varied; numerous mountain ranges, arid plains, a real desert, lush valleys and, of course, any type of beach you care to seek.

It is, though, a huge place, and as a consequence Daytrips Spain & Portugal is not meant to be a comprehensive guide to these two countries. It focuses, instead, on Madrid, Barcelona and Seville in Spain, and Lisbon and Oporto in Portugal — which are not only places of important tourist interest in their own right, but make the most logical base for daytrips in the region. There are, however, many other cities, most particularly in Spain, that are simply too far from the major centers to be visited on a daytrip. Important in their own right, these have individual chapters dedicated to them, and often have more than one suggested tour and perhaps a daytrip or two.

Daytrips have many advantages over the usual point-to-point touring, especially for short-term visitors. You can sample a far greater range in the same time by seeing only those places that really interest you instead of "doing" the region town by town. This can lead to a more varied diet of sights, and allow you to change the attractions on a day-by-day basis. Daytrips are also ideal for business travelers with a free day or so interspersed between meetings.

The benefits of staying in one hotel for a while are obvious. Weekly rates are often more economical than overnight stays, especially in conjunction with airline package plans. You also gain a sense of place, of having established a temporary home-away-from-home in a city where you can get to know the restaurants and enjoy the nightlife. Then, too, you won't waste time searching for a hotel room every night. Your luggage remains in one place while you go out on carefree daytrips. There is no need to pre-plan every moment of your vacation since with daytrips you are always free to venture wherever you please. Caught in Madrid on a Monday when many of the museums are closed? Well, why not head for Ávila to see the majestic walls? Is rain predicted for the entire day? You certainly won't want to be outdoors, so why not try the wonderful museums and churches. The operative word here is flexibility; the freedom of not being tied to a schedule or route.

All of the daytrips in this book may be taken by train, bus or car. Full information for doing this is given in the "Getting There" section of each trip. A suggested do-it-yourself walking tour is outlined in both the text and on the street map. Practical considerations such as time and weather are included, along with price-keyed hotel and restaurant recommendations and background information.

Destinations were chosen to appeal to a wide variety of interests, and include fresh discoveries along with proven favorites. In addition to the usual cathedrals, castles, and museums there are Roman ruins, great seaports, numerous places of compelling historical interest, and even hot-air balloon trips over the Pyrennes. Most of the attractions have an entrance fee; in many instances these are nominal although in some places (especially Barcelona), they are more expensive and can quickly add up. Cathedrals and churches will appreciate a few coins in the collection box to help with their maintenance costs.

Finally, a gentle disclaimer. Places have a way of changing without warning, and errors do creep into print. If your heart is absolutely set on a particular sight, you should check first to make sure that the opening times are still valid. Phone numbers of the local tourist information offices are included for this purpose.

One last thought — it isn't really necessary to see everything at a given destination. Be selective. Your one-day adventures in Spain and Portugal should be fun, not an endurance test. If it starts becoming that, just stroll to the nearest bar, order your favorite beverage, and sit down and relax. There will always be another day.

Happy Daytripping!

Section I

DAYTRIP STRATEGIES

The word "Daytrip" may not have made it into dictionaries yet, but for experienced independent travelers it represents the easiest, most natural, and often the least expensive approach to exploring European countries. The strategy is that you base yourself in a central city, and explore the surrounding areas on a series of one-day excursions from there. This works very well in the major cities such as Madrid, Barcelona and Seville in Spain, and Lisbon and Oporto in Portugal. The Iberian Peninsula, though, covers huge distances, and several places of great interest cannot be reached on daytrips from these bases, most particularly in Spain. Therefore, some cities are either covered as entities on their own, with one or more Suggested Tours, and also sometimes with a daytrip to a nearby town.

ADVANTAGES:

While not the answer to every travel situation, daytrips offer significant advantages over point-to-point touring following a set plan. The following are some reasons for considering the daytrip approach:

1. Freedom from the constraints of a fixed itinerary. You can go wherever you feel like going whenever the mood strikes.
2. Freedom from the burden of luggage. Your bags remain in your hotel room while you run around with only a guidebook and camera.
3. Freedom from the anxiety of reservation foul-ups. You don't have to worry each day about whether that night's lodging will actually materialize.
4. The flexibility of making last-minute changes to allow for unexpected weather, serendipitous discoveries, changing interests, new-found passions, etc.
5. The flexibility to take breaks from sightseeing whenever you feel tired or bored, without upsetting a planned itinerary. Why not sleep late in your base city for a change?
6. The opportunity to sample different travel experiences without committing more than a day to them.

7. The opportunity to become a "temporary resident" of your base city. By staying there for a few days, or more, you can get to know it in depth, becoming familiar with the local restaurants, shops, theaters, nightlife and other attractions etc. — enjoying them as a native would.

8. The convenience of not having to hunt for a hotel each day, along with the peace of mind that comes from knowing that a familiar room is waiting back in your base city.

9. The convenience of not having to pack and unpack your bags each day. Your clothes can straighten themselves out hanging in a closet, or even be sent out for cleaning.

10. The convenience, and security, of having a fixed address in your base city, where friends, relatives and business associates can reach you in an emergency. It is exceedingly difficult to contact anyone who changes hotels daily.

11. The economy of staying at one hotel on a discounted longer-term basis, especially with airline package plans. You can make reservations for your base city without sacrificing any flexibility at all.

12. Above all, daytrips ease the transition from tourist to accomplished traveler. Even if this is your first trip abroad, you can probably handle an uncomplicated one-day excursion on your own. The confidence thus gained will help immensely when you tackle more complex destinations, freeing you from the limitations of guided tours and putting you in complete control of your own trip.

DISADVANTAGES:

For all of its attractions, the daytrip concept does have certain restrictions. The size of the Iberian Peninsula has been mentioned above, and another disadvantage is that travelers forego the pleasures of staying in different, usually smaller, towns. To alleviate this I have recommended hotels in every town, which allows travelers the option of using daytrips part of the time and touring the rest.

GETTING THERE

Any number of airlines fly across the North Atlantic to Spain and Portugal, offering fares, schedules and package deals that constantly change to meet the competition. The two national airlines are obvious possibilities: **IBERIA**, ☎ 1-800-772-4642 and www.iberia.com, the national airline of Spain, has direct flights to Madrid from Chicago, Los Angeles, Miami, and New York City in the USA, and Montreal, Canada. **TAP**, ☎ 1-800-221-7370 in the USA, is the national airline of Portugal, and has direct flights to Lisbon from New York City and Newark, New Jersey, and from Boston, via the Azores. Two other companies that specialize in Spain are: **air europa**, ☎ 718-244-7055 and www.air-europa.com, that has flights from New York

JFK to Madrid, and **Spanair**, ☎ 888-545-5757 or www.spanair, who, offering an alternative for those preferring not to fly through New York, have services from Washington Dulles to Madrid. Both of these last two also have internal services in Spain, and those planning on flying around that country should seriously consider purchasing a **Spanair Spain Pass**. From either Madrid or Lisbon airports there are special bus services to the downtown areas.

GETTING AROUND

BY RAIL: EURAILPASS

Without doubt the most popular way of traveling around not just Spain and Portugal, but Europe as well, is by train. And equally without doubt the best method of doing this is by purchasing one of the range of passes issued by **Rail Europe**, ☎ 1-800-4-EURAIL in the USA or ☎ 1-800-361-RAIL in Canada, or www.raileurope.com on the Internet, before you leave for Europe. The web site also contains useful rail trip planning information, especially the section on Fares and Schedules. There are any number of variations on the theme, from the general **Eurailpass** that allows unlimited travel in and between the following seventeen countries: Austria, Belgium, Denmark, Finland, France, Germany, Greece, Hungary, Italy, Luxembourg, Netherlands, Norway, Portugal, Republic of Ireland, Spain, Sweden, and Switzerland. These generally offer a choice of either 15 or 21 days, or 1, 2, or 3 months, of unlimited travel. There are also general **EurailDrive** passes. These allow you to travel on any 6 days out of 2 months, four of which are on the national rail networks of the 17 Eurailpass countries, and the other 2 in a car from either Avis or Hertz. Those planning to travel in only a few countries will want to consider the **Europass**. This allows you either 5, 6, 8, 10 or 15 days in a 2-month period for travel in and between France, Germany, Italy, Spain, and Switzerland. And as far as readers of this guide are concerned an associate country, including Portugal, can be added for a small extra charge.

Those planning to visit just Spain or Portugal also have options. The **Spain Flexipass** allows any 3 days of unlimited travel, 1st or 2nd class, starting at US$155 (2nd class); and additional days of train travel can be added at US$30 (2nd class) and US$35 (1st class) each. The **Spain Rail'n Drive** plan allows 3 days unlimited train travel and 2 days car rental with unlimited mileage, with up to 2 months to complete your travel. Prices depend upon class of rail travel and car category (four categories are available) and start at US$255 per person for two traveling together. The **Portuguese Railpass** allows any 4 days unlimited train travel, 1st class, in a 15-day period and costs US$105. Those planning on traveling in both countries might well consider the **Iberic Railpass**, this allows any 3 days unlimited 1st class train travel in a 2-month period. This costs US$205 and up to 7 additional days train travel can be purchased at US$45 a day.

BY RAIL: INDEPENDENTLY

Those wanting to plan their train journeys can now do it from home themselves, providing they have access to the World Wide Web. **RENFE** has a site of its own, www.renfe.es, which although it is in Spanish is not too difficult to naviagate around. The Portuguese railway **CP** also has a site, www.cp.pt, with English translations.

BY RAIL: SPAIN - RED NATIONAL DE LOS FERROCARRILES ESPANOLES (RENFE)

THE NETWORK AND SERVICES:

RENFE has an extensive network throughout Spain that, with the principal exceptions of coastal regions in the north (Atlantic side) and the far south, has direct connections between most major cities. There are several junctions, otherwise rather obscure places, but located at strategic points in the network, of which travelers should be aware as there may be long stops while waiting for ongoing connections, or for trains to be joined together, or you may even have to change trains. The most important, in alphabetical order, are Bobadilla, Espeluy, Medina del Campo, Monforte and Venta de Baños. Of these, most travelers will encounter Bobadilla as it connects Algeciras, Cádiz Córdoba, Granada, Málaga, and Seville.

The rationale behind the services is rather complicated, but nevertheless logical, and is as follows: **Nucleo de Madrid:** These are services originating from, and returning to, Madrid and whose destinations are every other important city in the country. **Nucleo de Barcelona:** These are services originating from, and returning to, Barcelona and whose destinations are many other important cities throughout the country. **Nucleo de Pais Vasco:** These are services originating from, and returning to, the Pais Vasco region and whose destinations are, with the exception of Valencia, Alicante and Andalucía, cities in the north of the country. **Lineas del Grupos:** These are services between cities and regions that are grouped geographically. The lineas del grupos connect cities already served by the above Nucleos, as well as many others. **Cercanías:** These are local trains that operate only from the following stations or areas: Asturias, Barcelona, Bilbao, Cádiz, Madrid, Málaga, Murcia, San Sebastián, Santander, Seville and Valencia.

TICKETS:

Tickets are available from railway stations and travel agencies, and seat reservations must be made in advance, or just prior to boarding, for all long-distance journeys.

THE TRAINS:

There are many different train types, with a variety of facilities and different names. With the exception of AVE trains, most run on broad-gauge tracks. As with the services there is a logic to it — and the first thing to understand is that the trains fall within the following four categories:

Alta Velocidad Española—AVE:

These very high-speed trains, inaugurated in April 1992, run on spe-cially-built standard-gauge track between Madrid, Ciudad Real, Puertollano, Córdoba and Seville, with the minimum journey time being only 2.5 hours between Madrid and Seville. They have their own system of classification and services throughout the day are divided into four types, but only the following three will be of interest to most travelers. ***Tren punta*** run at times of the day when most people are likely to be traveling, ***Tren valle*** run at times of the day when fewest people are likely to be trav-eling, and ***Tren Llano*** run at times between the two. There are three differ-ent classes: ***Turista, Preferente*** and ***Club***, in ascending order, and the pric-ing schedule is such that the more popular the train classification, the higher the fare. The facilities on these trains are excellent; for all classes there is a bar/cafeteria, telephone, drinks machine, seats for babies and games, as well as audiovisual entertainment. In Preferente and Club, food is served to your seat, with a free drink in Club, and free daily newspapers are also distributed.

Largo Recorrido (Long-distance) Trains:

These trains are further sub-divided depending upon whether they run during the day or at night. There are three types of daytime trains:

Talgo (red and white trains) and ***Talgo pendular*** (blue and white trains): These offer the highest level of service on the longest, and most impor-tant, of the daytime routes. They have first- and second-class seats, restau-rant and cafeteria, air-conditioning, audiovisual entertainment, plus stew-ardesses and free daily newspapers in first class. They leave either in the morning or early afternoon, and sometimes both.

Euromed: These are new high-speed trains running between Barcelona, Tarragona, Castellón, Valencia and Alicante.

Alaris: This is another new, high-speed, service betwen Madrid, Albacete, Xátiva and Valencia.

Diurnos: These also operate on the longest of the daytime routes, and scheduled to depart in the morning and arrive at their destination in the evening. They are much slower than the Talgos, offer a lower level of ser-vice, and the trains are not so comfortable.

InterCity—IC: These are different from the other trains. They are very fast, generally only have three coaches—one first- and two second-class—and do not operate on that many routes. The level or service is also high: cafeteria/bar, air-conditioning and the audiovisual entertainment in all classes with stewardesses and free daily newspapers in first class.

Night trains:

Tren-Hotel: These are of the very highest standard and operate with-in Spain only on the most important routes. The *gran clase* cabins have their own individual telephones, toilets, washbasins and showers with towels, soap and shampoo included. You even get a morning call allowing you time to shower and breakfast before reaching your destination. There are also single-, double- and four-bed compartments but the latter are "single-sex" except when booked by a family group. These also have a restaurant and a bar.

Talgo Camas: These are the same as the tren-hotel but without the *gran clase* facilities, and they operate on more routes.

Estrellas: Literally "Stars", these are the night-time equivalent of the *diurnos*, offering beds (first- and second-class), couchettes (second class only) and regular seating. There are few facilities, generally only a restaurant, cafeteria or bar—depending upon departure time. Also they are very slow; the departure time is often early evening and the planned arrival is usually around 8.00 a.m. the next day.

Regional Trains:

Their rationale is to connect, over medium distances, capitals or urban centers of administrative, commercial or academic importance.

Regional expres: These have fewer stops, first- and second-class seating, are air-conditioned and usually have a automatic drinks machine.

Regional: These generally only have second-class seating, stop at more stations, are often planned to have connections with other trains and are essential transport between small and medium size towns.

Cercanías—Local Trains:

These are painted red and white, are second-class only and have no facilities. They only operate from the cities already previously detailed.

International Services and Trains:

There are not that many of these and they operate between the following cities: Madrid and Lisboa; Madrid and Paris; Barcelona and Paris; Barcelona and Zurich and Barcelona and Milano.

BY RAIL: PORTUGAL - CAMINHOS DE FERRO PORTUGUESES (CP)

THE NETWORK:

The Portuguese railway system is run by Caminhos de Ferro Portugueses, which has an extensive network throughout the country. The majority of visitors with rail passes will, however, be concerned mainly with the lines between Portugal and Spain and, internally, those lines connecting Lisbon with Oporto and the Algarve, and it is on these that this section concentrates. That is not to say that other lines are not worth exploring—quite the reverse; simply, they are outside the scope of this guide.

TICKETS:

Tickets are available from railway stations and travel agencies, and must be purchased in advance, or you may incur a substantial fine. Seats, too, must be reserved in advance on international and express trains, and certain others.

THE TRAINS:

Alfa:

The Alfa trains linking Lisbon with Oporto are actually French CORAIL trains, and stop only at Coimbra. There are first- and second-class carriages, both air-conditioned, breakfast is served to passengers' seats and there is a bar. There are also Alfa Club facilities for frequent travelers.

Intercidades (Intercity):
The Intercidades between Lisbon and Oporto and Faro are also French CORAIL trains, with first- and second-class air-conditioned carriages and a bar or mini-bar. They make more stops than an Alfa on the run to Oporto. On other routes there are non-air-conditioned first- and second-class carriages with a bar or mini-bar, and trains stop only at the most important stations.

Inter-Regional:
These have non-air-conditioned first- and second-class carriages, with a bar or minibar depending upon the length of the journey, and they make more frequent stops than the Intercidades.

Regional:
These trains stop at all stations. They have non-air-conditioned first- and second-class carriages, and no refreshment facilities.

CROSSING BETWEEN PORTUGAL AND SPAIN:

There are four crossing points by train between Portugal and Spain. They are detailed below in clockwise order, starting with the most northerly:

Tui/Valença do Minho:
This is the crossing point for Inter-Regional trains between Vigo and Oporto. It is most probably the least-used route between the two countries, but is convenient for those going to, or from, Santiago de Compostela.

Vilar Formoso/Fuentes d'Oñoro:
This is the border crossing point for the Lisbon/Paris/Lisbon Surexpreso, and estrella with one service daily in each direction. The journey time is very long. The train leaves Lisbon early in the afternoon and arrives in Paris the next evening. It has single-, double- and four-bed compartments, couchettes in second class and first- and second-class seating. The route takes it across northwest Spain, passing through Salamanca, Valladolid, Burgos, San Sebastián and Irún.

Marvão-Beirã/Valencia de Alcántara:
This is the border crossing point for the Madrid-to-Lisbon line.

Vila Real de Santo António/Ayamonte:
The complications of this, the most southerly crossing point between Spain and Portugal, are often underestimated by travelers. The problems start where the RENFE network ends, at Huelva. Taxi drivers wait at the station offering to take travelers on to Ayamonte, but this is an unnecessary expense of many thousands of pesetas. Instead make for the new *Estación de Autobuses*, from where there are frequent, and inexpensive, bus services. Once at Ayamonte, ignore any taxi drivers offering to take you to

Vila Real, but walk straight ahead to the river, and take the small ferry boat across to Vila Real de Santo Antonio. The train station used to be less than 100 yards from the quay, but that, inexplicably, has recently been closed and it is now necessary to travel to the Town Station, a short taxi ride but long walk away.

INTERNAL LINES:
Lisbon/Oporto/Lisbon:

This is the most important line in Portugal and, as a consequence, it has its own special service, the *Alfa,* as well as a special *Intercidades* and the *Inter-Regional* trains.

Lisbon/Vila Real de Santo António/Lisbon:

This line connects Lisbon with the Algarve and southern Spain and is served by the *Intercidades,* which end at Faro where a transfer to a Regional service onto Vila Real is necessary.

BY BUS:

Traveling by bus in Spain and Portugal is considerably more compli-cated than by train, both because of the vast distances concerned and the proliferation of privately-owned bus companies. Unless it is your specific choice, therefore, buses are best used only as specified in the individual chapters.

BY CAR:

There are any number of car rental companies, both international and national, throughout Spain and Portugal, so there is no problem with availability. Unless, that is, you require an automatic transmission; these are few and far between, and exorbitantly expensive. Even standard-trans-mission cars are expensive when rented in these countries. It is much wiser, and cheaper to decide on your requirements before leaving home and pre-book through a reputable company. One that I would recom-mend is **auto europe**, ☎ 1-800-223-555 or fax 800-235-6321 from the USA and Canada. All weekly rates are in US Dollars and include unlimited mileage; they guarantee to give you the best rate, and if you find a better one they'll beat it; they have no cancellation charges and have hotel deliv-ery available and free drop off within each country. They also offer an extremely wide range of automobiles, from the smallest mini up to a Ferrari sports car.

ACCOMMODATIONS

A selection of accommodations has been included for every destination, all of which are known by the author. All cities, often in the downtown area or around the railroad stations, have many more places at the lower end of the scale, *pensión* in Spain, *pensão* in Portugal. These are general-ly inexpensive, but tend to be rather basic and, more often than not, don't have a private bathroom.

The price scale is as follows:

SPAIN:

$$$	=	Over 20,000 ptas, EUR 120.20
$$	=	Between 10,000 ptas and 20,000 ptas, EUR 60.10 and 120.20
$	=	Under 10,000 ptas, EUR 60.10

PORTUGAL:

$$$	=	Over 20,000$00, EUR 99.76
$$	=	Between 10,000$00 and 20,000$00, EUR 49.88 and 99.76
$	=	Under 10,000$00, EUR 49.88

CULTURE

THE BULLFIGHT:

No one can visit the Iberian Peninsula and avoid, in some way or another, bullfighting; even if it is just seeing the posters *(carteles)* stuck all over the walls. And it's certainly a controversial topic, even among the citizens themselves. Even though there are bullfights in Portugal, they are not as common and are different from those in Spain; most notably in that the bull is not killed. Although this concept may appeal to foreigners, those seriously interested in the topic think it flawed. The following comments, then, are applicable to the Spanish bullfight *(corrida de toros)*.

There are many misconceptions regarding bullfighting, and two of the most common are that they are held in every Spanish town every Sunday, and that it is a sport. First, they are only held on a weekly basis in Madrid and Barcelona; every other town has them at irregular intervals or on special holidays, and during the latter they are held daily for the duration of the holiday. Non-Spanish often think of it as a sport, and as the bull is invariably killed consequently think of it as unfair. The Spanish consider it something between sport and an art form, often sections between which it is reported upon in the newspapers, and don't even think about notions of fairness. If travelers to Spain go to a *corrida*, in any of its various forms, they are best advised to put any pre-conceptions behind them and view it for what it is, not what they think it should be. In any event those seeing one for the first time will not, naturally, understand many of the nuances and technicalities. It is better to just sit back and enjoy the spectacle, and particularly the way the crowd interacts with the events.

Don't expect passivity; they are never slow to give praise, and can be particularly volatile with their displeasure. What you will see is truly a colorful and dramatic event, the only one of its kind in the world where men pit their brains and reflexes against a far more powerful, and wild, animal. Make no mistake about it, the *toreros* lives are at stake every time they approach the bull! And it is enhanced by the rather curious combination of the certainty of very rigid ceremonial regulations, and the absolute uncertainty of what will happen when man meets the bull *(toro)*. You may be confused by some of the events, some of them won't appear to have any logic, but you certainly won't be bored. Don't, though, expect it to be a pretty sight. There will always be much blood flowing from the bull and, at times, its death can be painfully slow. And a *torero* impaled on a bull's horns, on occasion mortally so, is an emotional sight indeed. Emotion, though, is what a *corrida* is all about. Whether it is good, bad or indifferent it always generates emotion. For some the spectacle will be too much, and they will leave appalled. The majority will enjoy it for what it is, be glad they have been, but never wish to go again. Others, though, will be absolutely fascinated, and for a few the emotions generated by both the corrida and Spain will become inextricably linked. And it is likely to spark a love affair with Spain that will last a lifetime.

LANGUAGE:

In Spain, Castillian Spanish is the official language, but since Franco's death and the granting of (limited) autonomy to many regions, traditional languages are now equal to, and in some places more popular than, Castillian. So much so, in fact, that over 40% of the population lives in regions that are bi-lingual. This can cause confusion to travelers as station signs, for example, can be in both languages, but street addresses only in the local language. An obvious example is the word for street: in Castillian it is *Calle;* in Catalan it is *Carrer* and in Galician it is *Rúa.* The latter language, incidentally, closely reflects that of its near neighbor, Portugal. The most unusual of these languages is the Basque *Euskara,* an unpronounceable and unintelligible collection of X's and Z's. It's not surprising that no one knows its origin! And to complicate matters even further there are the regional dialects of Castillian. Most prominent of these is found in Andalucía. In Andaluz all the S's, except those at the beginning of the word, are dropped. Hence *adiós* becomes *adio,* and *beunos días* becomes *beuna día.*

SPAIN AND PORTUGAL:

First-time visitors to the Iberian Peninsula might readily assume that Spain and Portugal would, in many instances, be similar. But that would be a wrong assumption. In fact there are few similarities, and it is always a fascinating matter of conjecture as to how two countries so close together can be so different. The differences in the languages are reflective of other matters: many common words — but often with a different pronunciation; but many more that are strikingly different. And, generally, the national character couldn't be more different, either. The Spanish are loud, noisy, extremely gregarious and prefer to relax very late at night and into the early hours. The Portuguese, on the other hand, are much less demonstrative, and are often ending their evening out before the Spanish have even left home! Socially, too, there are obvious differences. Portugal is a multi-ethnic and multi-cultural, and this can be seen anywhere in the country. In Spain, however, apart from obvious tourists, you will rarely see anyone who isn't indigenously Spanish.

FOOD AND DRINK

As with places of accommodation, a selection of restaurants has been included for each destination. Their approximate price range, based on the least expensive complete meal offered, appears as:

$ = Inexpensive
$$ = Reasonable
$$$ = Luxurious and expensive

In Spain, however, travelers may well want, sometimes, to forego a formal restaurant and bar-hop to partake of that delightful Spanish creation; the *tapa*. These free delights are served, on a small plate with a piece of French bread, when you order a beer or glass of wine. They can consist of almost anything, but the most popular are made of potatoes *(patatas)*, various meats *(carnes)*, small fish *(pescado)*, and even octopus *(pulpo)*. Unfortunately, some bars treat foreigners differently than locals and do not serve tapas automatically, and more and more are actually charging for them. The best response is not to frequent those particular bars again.

PRACTICALITIES

HOLIDAYS:
Legal holidays in **Spain** are:
- New Year's Day (January 1)
- Epiphany
- Maundy Thursday (Thursday before Easter)
- Labor Day (May 1)
- Corpus Christi
- St. James's Day (July 25)
- Ascension Day (August 15)
- Columbus Day (October 12)
- All Saint's Day
- Constitution Day (December 6)
- Immaculate Conception
- Christmas Day

Legal holidays in **Portugal** are:
- New Year's Day (January 1)
- Good Friday
- Liberty Day (April 25)
- Labor Day (May 1)

- Corpus Christi
- Portugal's and Camões Day (June 10)
- Assumption Day (August 15)
- Republic Day (October 5)
- All Saint's Day
- Restoration of Independence Day (December 1)
- Immaculate Conception
- Christmas Eve
- Christmas Day

The dates of certain religious holidays change annually. Certain autonomous regions, and many communities—no matter how small—have their own holidays.

MONEY MATTERS:

Traveler's checks are the safest way to protect your money while abroad. Often, though, you'll be charged service fees both when purchasing and converting them. An alternative, depending upon the fluctuating exchange rates, is to purchase checks in the currency of the country you are visiting. This, again, has its problems and, in any case, you'll likely to be charged extra for this service. Storefront money changers *(cambios)* abound and compete for your business with local banks. And as almost all of them offer different rates, some with and some without commission to complicate matters, it presents travelers with a bewildering choice of options. Really, there is only one certainty in this process; whether changing travelers checks and/or cash, or using ATM's or your credit card, every time you change money you are going to lose a percentage of it in fees and poor exchange rates. That's upsetting, but a fact of life. Changing relatively large sums at one time, though, will save you some money.

Automated Teller Machines (ATMs) are probably the most convenient way of changing money, and are used as you would at home, although they are not always the least expensive. As at home they are available 24 hours a day, and are conveniently located at almost any bank you pass, and at airports and stations etc. For some reason or another I have never been able to get my card to work in Portugal, and no one at my bank has been able to ascertain why. So if you intend to use your card there, check with the bank before you leave.

Credit Cards are widely accepted throughout both Spain and Portugal, but rarely by budget hotels and restaurants.

EUROS will become legal tender on January 1st 2002 in both Spain and Portugal, and in mid-2002 the Peseta and Escudo become history. Between now and then it is possible to pay in EUROS by credit card and check and, as a consequence, every price is shown in the local currency and EUROS.

TELEPHONES:

Public telephones in both Spain and Portugal accept coins, either coins or a pre-paid phone card, or just a pre-paid phone card. Both countries are divided into area **codes**, and these codes are always shown in the **PRACTICALITIES** section of each tour.

Care needs to be taken when making **international calls** from these countries. Be aware that placing a call from your hotel room is, no matter how convenient, by far the most costly way. Almost every hotel places a very heavy surcharge on any call made from the room, let alone an international one. And using a calling card from your regular long-distance service back home isn't too much cheaper either. In Spain look for the sign **Telefonica**; in these places, run by the telephone company, you are assigned a booth and pay (anything over 500 ptas with a credit card if desired) when you have finished the call. A recent innovation are pre-paid cards that can be bought at home and used abroad. These appear (I haven't used one yet) to be the cheapest and most convenient way of making calls home. Providing, of course, they work in the country you're going to.

Another recent method is the use of calling cards isued by your local long-distance supplier, e.g. AT&T or MCI. Remember, though, to ask for the toll free number for each country before you leave, as sometimes it is difficult to obtain in Spain and Portugal.

WEATHER:

Most travelers to the Iberian Peninsula will expect it to be hot in July and August; many, though, won't realize quite how hot! The area bordered by Madrid, Portugal to the southwest and Seville and Granada to the south can be excruciatingly hot, with temperatures of well over 100 degrees F. In fact the triangle between Granada, Córdoba and Seville is recognized as being one of the hottest areas in Europe. Seville itself has known temperatures of around 120 degrees, while 110 is almost commonplace. So pack accordingly, and remember to drink plenty of water. Conversely, the vast majority of travelers will not be aware that winter in the Iberian Peninsula can be very long, and very harsh. The continental-type climate, except around the narrow coastal plains, can leave much of the central plateau bitterly cold, with many of the higher sections inundated with snow. So much so, in fact, that skiing is a popular sport in many areas!

SUGGESTED TOURS

The do-it-yourself walking tours in this guide are relatively short and easy to follow. They generally begin, and end, at the main square in each town. Suggested routes are shown by colored lines on the maps, while circled numbers refer to major attractions or points of reference along the way, with corresponding numbers in the text. Remember that the tour routes are only suggestions—you may prefer to wander off on your own using the maps as guides. You can estimate the amount of time that any segment of a walking tour will take by looking at the scaled map, and figuring that the average person covers about 100 yards in one minute.

Trying to see everything in any given town could easily become an exhausting marathon. You will certainly enjoy yourself more by being selective and passing up anything that doesn't catch your fancy; in favor of a friendly bar, perhaps. Not all museums will interest you, and forgiveness will be granted if you don't visit *every* church.

Practical information, such as the opening times of various attractions, is as accurate as was possible at the time of writing, but everything is subject to change. You should always check with the local tourist information office if seeing a particular sight is crucially important.

* OUTSTANDING ATTRACTIONS:

An * asterisk before any attraction denotes a special treat that, in the author's opinion, should not be missed.

TOURIST INFORMATION

Each daytrip destination has its own **tourist office** information listed in the **PRACTICALITIES** section, and has the location marked on the appropriate map with the word "info" or the symbol **i**.

ADVANCE PLANNING INFORMATION:

The **Tourist Office of Spain** has branches throughout the world to help you plan your trip. In North America these are:

666 Fifth Avenue, 35th Floor, **New York**, NY, 10103
☎ 212-265-8822, FAX 212-265-8864
e-mail buzon.oficial@nuevayork.oet.mcx.es

San Vicente Plaza Building, 8383 Wilshire Boulevard, Suite 960
Beverly Hills, California, 90211
☎ 213-658-7188, FAX 213-658-1061
e-mail buzon.oficial@losangeles.oet.mcx.es

845 N. Michigan Avenue, **Chicago**, Illinois, 60611
☎ 312-642-1992, FAX 312-642-9817
e-mail buzon.oficial@chicago.oet.mcx.es

1221 Brickell Avenue, Suite 1850, **Miami**, Florida, 33131
☎ 305-358-1992, FAX 305-358-8223
e-mail buzon.oficial@miami.oet.mcx.es

102 Bloor Street West, 14th Floor, **Toronto**, Ontario, MSS1M8, Canada
☎ 416-961-3131, FAX 416-961-1992
e-mail spainto@globalserve.net

The **Portuguese National Tourist Office** has branches throughout the world to help you plan your trip. In North America these are:

590 Fifth Avenue, 4th Floor, **New York**, NY, 10036
☎ 212-354-4403, FAX 212-764-6137

60 Bloor Street West, Suite 1005, **Toronto**, Ontario, M4W3B8, Canada
☎ 416-921-7376, FAX 416-921-1353

Section II

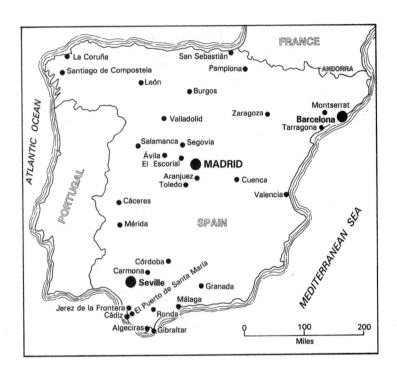

DAYTRIPS IN
SPAIN

The most convenient bases for exploring Spain are Madrid, Barcelona, and Seville. Beyond that, you'll find Granada, San Sebastián, Valencia, Santiago de Compostela, Salamanca, and Cáceres to be workable bases for their specific regions. Also included are tours of Burgos, Cuenca, León, Málaga, Valladolid, and Zaragoza—six towns that really don't work as daytrips, but that are too compelling to miss. For those staying overnight, hotel recommendations as well as restaurant choices are given for each destination.

Madrid:
The Old Town

Although with a long history—prehistoric remains have been found closeby—Madrid didn't attain any real importance until the middle of the 16th century. Colonized by the Romans in the 2nd Century BC, it was occupied by the Moors in 711 who, under Mohammed I in 865, fortified the town and made it a walled city. It wasn't until three centuries later, in 1083, that it was reconquered by King Alfonso VI. Fernando IV summoned the Courts of the Kingdom in 1309, the Catholic Monarchs ordered the de-fortification of the city's walls and gates in 1476 and, in 1561, Felipe II moved the court from Toledo, thus making Madrid capital of a vast empire.

The city then began to grow, and early in the next century, during the Hapsburg era, saw the very important addition of the Plaza Mayor. The House of Bourbon succeeded the Hapsburgs, and it was this dynasty that was responsible for many of the grand, and attractive, buildings and monuments that adorn the city today. Among these are the Royal Palace, completed in 1764; the Alcalá gate, raised in 1778 to honor Carlos III's entry into the city as king, and the Prado Museum constructed between 1785 and 1819.

On May 2, 1808, the citizens rose up against the occupying French army and more than a thousand people died. This event was immortalized by Goya whose paintings, *El Dos de Mayo* and *El Tres de Mayo*, hang proudly in the Prado. During the Spanish Civil War the city was subject to a three-year siege, from November 1936 to March 1939, by the Nationalist forces, whose eventual entry into Madrid ended hostilities. From then the city's population grew dramatically, rising from 1.3 million to over 3 million in 1980.

Today, Madrid is the largest city in Spain and, at an elevation of 655 meters (2,100 ft.), the highest capital in Europe. The ambiance of this hustling, bustling modern city reflects an intriguing blend of old and new.

GETTING THERE:

Madrid is, literally, located at the center of Spain and all distance measurements originate from the *Puerta del Sol* which, fittingly, is the social center of the city. The city is, consequently, the communications hub of the country, with the main railroad lines and highways radiating from the city like spokes from a wheel. Therefore, it is easily accessible by **train**, **bus**, **car**, or **air** from anywhere in Spain.

PRACTICALITIES:

Contrary to what might be expected, "sights" and "monuments" are relatively few in Madrid. There are, however, literally dozens of museums that cater to almost every interest imaginable. The majority of these are closed on Monday, but many offer free admission on Saturday afternoon and/or Sunday. Madrid has a continental-type climate which gives it very hot summers and cold, often long winters that can leave the city snow-covered as late as April.

The comprehensive **Metro** system offers clean, comfortable trains that run from 6 a.m. to 1:30 a.m. A single ticket costs 135 ptas (EUR .81), but if you are planning to be in Madrid anytime at all buy one that allows you ten rides for just 705 ptas (EUR 4.24). This is much more economical, and can even be used by more than one person. The Metro is a considerably quicker way of getting around the city than using buses, as these have to struggle to negotiate the perpetually traffic-filled roads.

The **Dialing Code** is 91.

There are **tourist offices** at *Barajas Airport, Chamartín Railway Station,* and in the *Torre de Madrid* at the *Plaza de España,* but the most convenient is centrally located at *Plaza Mayor,* 3, ☎ 366-54-77, and is open Monday to Friday 10 a.m. to 8 p.m. and on Saturday from 10 a.m. to 2 p.m. Information about Madrid can be found at **www.munimadrid.es** on the World Wide Web and E-Mail enquiries can be sent to **Infomadrid@munimadrid.es**.

ACCOMMODATION:

The choice here is so vast as to be bewildering. The selections below, chosen for location, style and price, have all been personally researched by the author.

The **Ritz** *******GL**, ☎ 521-28-57 or fax 532-87-76, Plaza de la Lealtad, 5, is unquestionably **THE** hotel of choice in Madrid. Opened in 1910 by King Alfonso XIII, it is situated within its own delightful gardens just off the Paseo de Recoletos, in the heart of Madrid. Gracious, elegant, it is adorned by tasteful antiques and offers a harmonious mix of old-fashioned values and traditions, with up-to-date modern comforts. $$$

The **Hotel Villa Real** *****, ☎ 420-37-67, fax 420-25-47 or e-mail info@derbyhotels.es, Plaza de las Cortes, 10, has a delightful location close to the most attractions in Madrid. Behind a traditional façade and with a decor enhanced by Roman mosaics, genuine 19th-century furniture, French drapes, marble and Swedish wood, there are 115 wonderfully modern, yet traditionally styled rooms. For those who really want to splash out, the Imperial Suite, with its silk carpets, jacuzzi and sauna, is the room of choice. $$$

The **Hotel Wellington** *****, ☎ 575-44-00 or fax 576-41-64, Velázquez, 8, is a grand hotel with the ambiance of a private mansion. Located close to the Prado Museum and The Puerta de Alcalá, this offers 275 rooms and 25 luxury suites, all of which decorated in a classically functional style, and equipped with all modern facilities. Look, also, for the impressive El Fogón restaurant, the Bar Inglés for cocktails and a cafeteria. $$$

The **Hotel Santo Domingo** ****, ☎ 547-98-00 or fax 547-59-95, Plaza de Santo Domingo, 13, is found in a quiet location just a few minutes walk from the Puerta del Sol. It has 120 rooms that have each been personalized and are so different from each other in decor and style, but not quality, that eleven pages of photographs of them have been published in *House & Garden*, Spain's most prestigious magazine of decorating style. In fact, no two are alike. $$$

The **Hotel Sanvy** ****, ☎ 576-08-00 or fax 575-24-43, Goya, 3, has 135 modern rooms. Although located some distance from the Puerta del Sol it is conveniently next to the Plaza de Colón, where the terminal for the airport bus is found. $$

The **Gran Hotel Reina Victoria** ****, ☎ 531-45-00 or fax 522- 03-07, Plaza de Santa Ana, 14, is strategically located in the heart of Madrid, faces a pleasing park and is just a couple of minutes walk from the Puerta del Sol. Built over the ancient palace of the Counts of Teba it has a striking façade, large comfortable rooms and its own garage. It is distinguished by its bull-fighting traditions and events. $$

The **Crowne Plaza Madrid City Center** ****, ☎ 454-85-00, fax 548-23-89 or e-mail reservas@crowneplaza.es, Plaza de España, s/n, is an impressively large hotel in a very central location, as the name implies. On its 17 floors there are 306 rooms, including 41 suites, some of which are handicapped accessible and others for non-smokers. Elegantly decorated, these really do have every expected amenity and more, including tea and coffee makers and modem connections. Many, also, have spectacular views over the Plaza de España and the Royal Palace. Look, also, for the fully equipped Business Corner, with all manner of communications and copiers etc. $$$

The **Hotel Opera** ***, ☎ 541-28-00, fax 541-69-23, Cuesta de Santo Domingo, 2, is, as the name implies, very close to the Opera House and the Royal Palace. Within a modern structure you will find 79 very well appointed rooms, some of which have balconies overlooking this historical quarter of Madrid. Keeping to the musical theme, the waiters and waitresses entertain you with operatic tunes in the El Café de La Opera . $$

The **Hotel Carlos V** ***, ☎ 531-41-00 or fax 531-37-61, Maestro Victoria, 5, is found in a very central, but peaceful, location between the Gran Vía and the Puerta del Sol. There are 67 rooms, all entirely renovated in 1996, with every modern facility and, helpfully, a safe. There is also a shuttle bus service to and from the airport. $$

The **Hotel París** **, ☎ 521-64-96 or fax 531-01-88, with its wonderful façade just couldn't be anymore central, overlooking the Puerta del Sol. Inside it combines comfort with a gentle, old-fashioned ambiance. $$

There are literally hundreds of *Hostals* and *Pensións* to be found in the back streets that radiate from the Puerta del Sol and, in reality, there often isn't much difference between them. Choosing one becomes somewhat of a Hobson's Choice, and once you find one you like it is best to stick with it. My choice would always be:

The **Hostal Residencia Las Brisas** *, ☎ 531-44-03, Calle Cruz, 8. Just two-minutes walk from the Puerta del Sol this offers basic, but very comfortable, rooms each with a private bathroom and telephone. Be sure, though, to request a quiet *sin ruido* room, one at the back away from the street. $

FOOD AND DRINK:

Restaurants are generally an even more subjective topic than accommodation. This is compounded in Madrid by the sheer number of restaurants, more than 3,000, in fact. And that doesn't even include the 15,000, more or less, bars and taverns etc. The following recommendations, therefore, are by necessity quite selective.

Goya Restaurant and Terrace (Plaza de la Lealtad, 5) reflects all the grandeur of the Ritz Hotel, within which it is located. Inaugurated by King Alfonso XIII in 1910, it has through the subsequent decades hosted an endless list of the highest ranking national and international royalty, political and other celebrities. Originally the menu was mainly International, recently though it has specialized in a more traditional Spanish-style cuisine. Dining out on the Terrace, overlooking fountains and gardens in the center of Madrid, is one of Madrid's most delightful experiences. ☎ 701-67-67, Ext. 4241 or fax 701-67-76. $$$

Restaurante La Gastroteca de Stéphane y Arturo (Plaza de Chueca, 8) reflects the characters of its proprietors, Stéphane and Arturo, in its esotericness. Here, expect the unexpected; dazzlingly prepared dishes such as Oyster Salad with Baby Eel Mousse; Snails with Nettles or even Duck Breast Hamburgers. One house dish, the *Cocido de Oro*, is a stew that must be contracted for, not simply pre-ordered. ☎ 532-25-64. X: Sat. lunch, holidays, and Aug. $$$

Taberna del Alabardero (Felipe V, 6) is close to the Royal Palace. This was originally the Guardia de Alabarderos tavern, and was named after the guards that used to march by and, later, return to it. The owner, Luis de Lezama, a former priest and delightfully charming host, has fashioned here a wonderful restaurant that has sisters, of the same name, in Peurto Banus, Sevilla and Washington D.C. ☎ 247-25-77 or fax 547-77-07. $$$

Casa Santa Cruz (Calle de la Bolsa, 12), located between the Plaza Mayor and the Puerta del Sol, has an unusual history. Originally a 15th-century church, it subsequently served as the headquarters of the city's first Stock Exchange and is now a very beautiful restaurant which is distinguished by its fine cuisine and exemplary service. ☎ 521-86-23 or fax 522-22-25. $$$

Mesón Rincón de la Cava (Calle Cava de San Miguel, 17), is one of the typical restaurants to be found in the **Caves** (*Cuevas*) under the Plaza Mayor. Enjoy hearty, traditional dishes served in a friendly environment while being serenaded by troubadours. ☎ 366-58-30 $

The streets bounded by the triangle between Carretas, Cruz and San

Jerónimo, just to the south-east of the Puerta del Sol, hold numerous small bars and restaurants. In recent years this has become a really trendy area, and a visit here on a Saturday night late in the evening will find every bar and restaurant full to bursting. The *Patatas Bravas* chain whose name derives from its signature dish, plates of baked potatoes covered with a spicy sauce, also offer wonderful, and inexpensive, dishes of *Pulpo Gallego*, Octopus Galician style. At the corner of Cruz and Victoria you'll find the ancient *El Abuelo*, The Grandfather. No seats here, just a bar where you'll stand and enjoy steaming hot *Gambas en Ajillo* or *Gambas a la Plancha*, shrimps cooked in a boiling pot of garlic and oil or shrimps on a skewer grilled over a hot plate, washed down by the house's rare sweet red wine. An insiders tip; be sure to ask for a voucher that will entitle you to another, complimentary, glass at the branch around the corner. Just down Cruz, at number 6, on the junction of the first, tiny, street on the left is a restaurante/bar named *Nueva Galicia,* ☎ 522-52-89, that is a real favorite of mine. It is run by brothers and their wives, who originate from Galicia. There is nothing fancy here, just solid food at a marvelous price — under 1,000 ptas (EUR 6.01) for a three-course meal, bread and a litre of wine, and friendly, courteous service. Back on San Jerónimo, towards the Puerta del Sol, is a branch of the *Museo del Jamon* chain. An intriguing mix of grocery store and bar where, at the latter, a ham sandwich costs just 210 ptas (EUR 1.26).

SUGGESTED WALKING TOUR:

Numbers in parentheses correspond to numbers on the map.

Start in the center of the **Puerta del Sol** (1), under the equestrian statue of King Carlos III. Nearby is the plaque "Kilometre 0", and it is from here that all distances in Spain are measured. The building opposite, the largest in the square, is the infamous old police station and, immediately behind you stands a statue of the symbol of Madrid, a bear climbing a tree stump. Begin walking away from the bear, towards the narrow side of this irregularly shaped square, and turn right into the very next street, Calle Preciados. This begins with two branches of the *El Cortes Ingles* department store, the one on the left selling records and electrical equipment and the other books. This wide, shop-lined, pedestrian walkway eventually leads up and through to the Gran Via. But, at the first corner, by the entrance to the main *El Cortes Ingles* store, turn left into the much smaller Calle de Tetuan. In truth this is a rather inconspicuous street, but it is home to some interesting contradictions. A charming and most characterful restaurante/bar, the *Casa Libra*, founded in 1860, is soon followed by chairs and tables belonging to a similar establishment which originated on another continent, and a century later, Burger King. And in case anyone is confused by the reference to a bar in Burger King, no, this is not a mistake. All fast-food outlets in Spain, including McDonalds, sell beer as a matter of course.

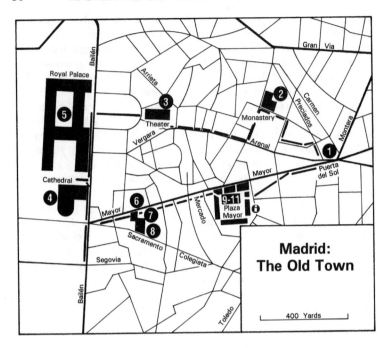

Madrid:
The Old Town

400 Yards

A right turn at the end on Calle del Maestro Victoria brings you up to the rear entrance to *El Cortes Ingles*. This is directly across from one of the better bookstores in Madrid, the *Casa de Libro*. Alongside this runs the Calle de Misericordia, which leads into the Plaza de Descalzas where, on the left side, are two small statues honoring Francisco Piquer y Rudilla (1666–1739) and the Marqués de Pontejos (1790–1840). But it is the building on the right that will command your attraction. Its ancient beauty is only enhanced by the incongruity of the architectural relationship with its considerably more modern, and vastly blander, neighbors. It was Juana de Austria, daughter of Carlos V, born here in 1536, who 23 years later founded the *Royal Descalzas Monastery (Descalzas Reales Monasterio)* (2), ☎ 559-74- 02. This then became a retreat for the kings of Castile and, today, it is an extremely dignified museum housing many important works of art that have been accumulated since its foundation. So much so that in 1987 it was named "European Museum of the Year." *Visiting is not easy, however. There are highly irregular hours; 10:30 a.m. to 12:45 p.m. and 4 p.m. to 5:45 p.m. on Tuesday, Wednesday, Thursday and Saturday; 10:30 a.m. to 12:45 p.m. on Friday and 11 a.m. to 1:30 p.m. on Sundays and holidays, and there are only organized tours lasting about 45 minutes.*

Exit the plaza by way of the facing Calle San Martín. The pleasing façade to the right now belongs to the *Caja de Madrid*—a savings bank, and at the bottom, on the opposite corner of the much busier Arenal, is the strikingly tall rectangular tower, topped by a tiled spire, of the Austrian-styled church San Ginés. In all honesty there is not much else to inspire, with the possible exception of a permanent open-air bookshop, in this stretch of Arenal until, having turned right from San Martín, a grey silver-colored lead-topped building, housing the **Theater Royal** *(Teatro Real)* (3), beckons.

The tiny Calle de Carlos III, just past it, will lead into the pretty Plaza Oriente, which has as its backdrop the most magnificent of palaces. Cross through the park and follow, to the left, the Calle de Bailén alongside the walls of the palace until you reach the open plaza. Here, to the left, is the **Our Lady of Almudena Cathedral** *(Catedral de Nuestra Señora de la Almudena)* (4), ☎ 542-22-00, a towering 19th century Gothic-style structure whose interior decorations and chapels are modern, and quite incongruous to the façade. *Open Monday to Sunday 10 a.m. to 1 p.m. and 5 p.m. to 8 p.m. Entrance free.* Then follow the plaza to the railings at the end for a panoramic view over the southern part of the city, and the countryside stretching away to the horizon, behind a huge fountain.

It's now time to explore the palace, stretching around three sides of the imposing courtyard to the left. In fact, it is much more than just a royal palace; the ***Royal Palace**, **Royal Armory Museum** and **Royal Pharmacy** *(Palacio Real, Museo de la Real Armería y Real Farmacia)* (5), ☎ 542-00-59, is truly a triple delight. Construction of the Royal Palace began in 1738 under the guidance of Felipe V and was completed 26 years later by Carlos III. With its 2,800 rooms this huge seven-level building is the second-largest in Europe, eclipsed only by the Hermitage in St. Petersburg. The last monarch to reside here was Alfonso XIII, the grandfather of the present king, Juan Carlos, who prefers to live in the more modest Zarzuela Palace on the city's outskirts. The Royal Palace is still used for state occasions when, of course, it is closed to the public. The interior is truly palatial; numerous works of art, tapestries, wonderfully painted ceilings and shimmering crystal chandeliers abound. A limited number of rooms may be visited, and tours of them are available in several different languages. The Throne Room, in its anachronistic splendor, holds a special fascination. The **Royal Armory**, founded by Felipe II, has been located on this site since 1893 and its collection, one of the best in the world, will appeal to children of all ages. Exhibited are the belongings of such historic legends as Boabdil, the last Moorish leader of Granada and Spain; the Catholic Monarchs; Maximilian of Austria and many other Spanish monarchs. In addition to armor fashioned for horses, men, children and even dogs there are numerous mementos of famous battles. The **Royal Pharmacy**, a reproduction of a 17th-century laboratory, has cupboard after cupboard full of original porcelain jars and strangely shaped glass vessels, will be of least interest to the majority of visitors. *This complex is open in April Monday to Saturday 9:30 a.m. to 5:30 p.m. and Sunday and holidays 9 a.m. to 2 p.m. and every other month Monday to Saturday 9 a.m. to 6 p.m. and*

Sunday and holidays 9 a.m. to 3 p.m. Entrance with guided visits (in a variety of languages) 950 ptas (EUR 5.71) and 850 ptas (EUR 5.11) unguided, free on Wednesday.

Back out to the main road, turn right and follow Bailén to the bridge, but don't expect the view down to include water. Madrid is one of the few major cities in the world that doesn't have a significant river running through it. Turn back for about 100 yards and make a right into Calle Mayor, where it becomes immediately obvious that this is an area of some importance. Note, as you pass, the heavily armed guards protecting the *Capitánia General*, the early 17th-century Uceda palace and the dignified tower of the church next door. After a short distance you'll arrive in the historical **Plaza de la Villa** (6). On its right, with towers flanking each end, is the **City Hall** *(Casa de la Villa)* (7). Construction on this started in 1644 and was completed in 1690, but the façade facing the street took another 100 years to finish. Next, and also connected to the former, is the broken brick exterior of the early 16th-century **Casa de Cisneros** (8). Restored early in this century, it now houses offices of the Madrid City Council. The plaque outside indicates it is at an elevation of 646.4 meters above sea level. A peek through the metal grille gate reveals a rather pretty wooden beamed and tiled ceiling in the archway. On the final side of the plaza, at number 3, is a house with an unusual archway; this, dating from the 15th century, is the oldest civic building in Madrid.

Continue back up, literally, Calle Mayor and pass the Plaza de San Miguel and its traditional-style **Food Market** *(Mercado)*. Here take the pedestrian walkway, the Calle de Ciudad Rodrigo, which will lead you diagonally through to the delightfully symmetric **Plaza Mayor* (9), the social center of the city. Constructed between 1617 and 1619 by Felipe III, whose equestrian statue stands proudly in the center, it is of huge proportions, 200 yards long and 100 yards wide. Rebuilt after the fire of 1790, today its porticoed ground floor supports three upper levels. The plaza's two most famous houses are the **Bakers' Guild** *(Casa de la Panadería)* (10), which holds some of the city archives, and the **Butchers' Guild** *(Casa de la Carnicería)* (11), whose façades today are decorated with a series of vibrant, and in some instances mildly erotic, paintings. The original 136 houses that surrounded the plaza offered a front-seat view of a wealth of public spectacles, anything from bullfights to executions. Today the events, although no less varied, are of a considerably gentler nature. On Sunday mornings it hosts a coin and stamp market, and the antique postcards sold here make a delightful souvenir. Christmas time traditionally brings stalls where vendors sell a strange combination of religious decorations and practical jokes—which says much about the Spanish character. Book and print markets are also frequent visitors and, during the city's own fair in May, dedicated to San Isidro, a huge stage is erected and the crowds are treated to free concerts, ranging in style from traditional folk music and dancing to ear-splitting modern bands. Even when nothing else is happening, though, this is a marvelous place to be. Sit at a sidewalk café, or lounge on a concrete bench, and be amused and fascinated by the passers-by; have your portrait drawn by a street artist or dine at one of the many restaurants. Few will resist the enticement of artistically arranged displays of food in their windows. Madrid is far from the sea but that doesn't stop it having the second-largest (Tokyo's is first) central fish market *(Mercamadrid)* in the world. Seafood of every conceivable type predominates, but rare is the restaurant which doesn't display a huge octopus *(pulpo)*. Be sure to return in the evening when, particularly on Saturday and Sunday, the plaza really comes to life. In the southwest corner, steps lead down to the Arcos de Cuchilleros and the intriguing cave *(cuevas)* bars built into, and under, the plaza. Bursting to the seams and echoing to the sound of Sevillianas, Andalucian flamenco-type dances that are currently the rage of Spain, these are busy until the early morning hours. Back in the plaza itself there is one bar that will be of special interest to aficionados of bullfighting, and unhesitatingly fascinating to others. The *Bar del Oro,* on the Calle Mayor side of the plaza, is something of a museum; bulls heads, posters and even "suits of lights" cover the walls along with hundreds of photos, some of which are a little gory to say the least. Depart the plaza via the Calle de las Postas, immediately opposite your entrance point. This winds down back to Mayor, past the seemingly irrepressible McDonalds, towards the Puerta del Sol.

Trip 2

Madrid: Puerta del Sol to the Prado

This walk continues your exploration of Madrid.

GETTING THERE:
PRACTICALITIES:
FOOD AND DRINK:
See pages 25-29 for all of the above.

SUGGESTED WALKING TOUR:
Numbers in parentheses correspond to numbers on the map.

Again, begin under the statue of Carlos III in the **Puerta del Sol** (1) but, this time, look for a huge TIO PEPE advertisement, which actually sits atop the aforementioned Hotel París, and head for the street immediately beneath it to the left, the Calle Alcalá. Probably three hundred yards farther on, and again to the left at number 13, you'll find the neo-classical outline of the **San Fernando Museum and Royal Academy of Fine Arts** *(Museo de la Real Academia de Bellas Artes de San Fernando)* (2), ☎ 522-00-46. This academy has an interesting history. It was first opened by Ferdinand VI on June 13, 1752, and initially lodged in the Casa de la Panadería on the Plaza Mayor. In 1773 Carlos III, Ferdinand's half brother, signed an order purchasing the city residence of the Count of Saceda, its present home. This is a traditional-style museum that exhibits a large and varied collection of art spanning many eras, including works by Goya, Rubens and El Greco. *The opening hours are unusual, Tuesday to Friday 9 a.m. to 7 p.m. and Saturday, Sunday, Monday, and holidays from 9 a.m. to 2 p.m. Entrance 300 ptas (EUR 1.80), free on the weekend.*

Continue up Alcalá and your attention will most surely be drawn towards the huge statue of a chariot being led by three horses, which sits, virtually suspended in air, on top of the *Banco de Bilbao y Viscaya* building. From here the road slopes gently down and passes some government offices and the Teatro Alcázar, before its junction with the Gran Via. Cross by here, and take a break for a cool drink under the surprisingly out-of-place canvas awning of the *Circulo de Bellas Artes*.

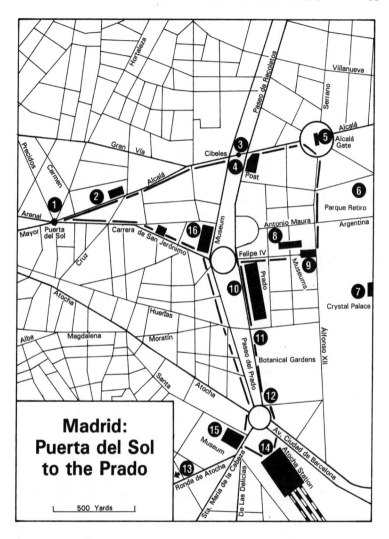

Madrid:
Puerta del Sol
to the Prado

500 Yards

As you continue down what has now become a steeper incline it may be of future use to note that the office on the next corner is that of RENFE, the state railroad company, and that it is only open on weekdays between 9:30 a.m. and 8 p.m. Approaching the bottom of the hill it is impossible to miss, on the left, the verdant gardens of the *Cortel General de Ejercito,* the residence of the commander of the army. Look more carefully and you'll notice the heavily-armed guards who patrol behind the bushes. In the center of this busy junction is a large, circular fountain whose bursts of water encircle a marble statue of the goddess **Cibeles** (3), a passenger in a chariot being hauled by two massive lions. This hasn't always been located here, nor monumental. It dates from the late 18th century, and was located at the beginning of the Paseo de Recoletos. At that time, the waters were actually used by the citizens as drinking water. It wasn't until 1862 that this ceased and, before the end of that century, it was moved to its present site.

Directly behind the fountain is the huge edifice of the Palace of Communications, that houses among other things the **Post Office** *(Correos y Telegrafos)* (4). The easiest way to cross this very busy intersection is to use the underpass, then continue, upwards this time, along Alcalá to the puerta of the same name at the Plaza de la Independencia. One of the most distinctive of Madrid's monuments, the **Alacalá Gate** *(Puerta de Alacalá)* (5) has five entrances, three central arches, and two flanking lateral ones. This was constructed in 1778 as a memorial to Carlos III's entry into the city as King of Spain. The damage clearly evident on this monument, the old entrance to the Aragón road, was inflicted by French cannon balls during the Wars of Independence.

Here, also, is the entrance to the fittingly named **Retreat Park** *(Parque Retiro)* (6), which was commissioned by Felipe IV. Covering 143 hectares of prime city land, it is surrounded by decorative railings and entered by a choice of twelve gates. Inside it is truly a haven. Numerous monuments, fountains and formal gardens surround the huge equestrian statue of Alfonso XII that stands high above the ornamental boating lake *estanque*. One of the park's most attractive features is the **Crystal Palace** *(Palacio de Cristal)* (7), a greenhouse constructed of iron and glass in 1887 to hold exotic plants during the Philippines Exhibition, and now a cultural exhibition center. Take time here to relax like the Madrileños do, especially on weekends, when, with their natural exuberance, they noisily let their hair down.

If your choice is to explore the park a little, be sure to leave by way of the second exit along Alfonso XII, that runs due south of the Puerta de Alcalá. If not, then follow the park along Alfonso XII and turn right into Calle Méndez Núñez, where another option awaits. The typically Austrian-styled building at number 1, the King's Hall of the former Buen Retiro Palace, is the **Army Museum** *(Museo Ejercito)* (8), ☎ 522-06-28. The exhibits here include El Cid's Tizona sword and a portion of the cross Christopher Colombus (Cristobal Colón in Spanish) carried when he landed in the New World. *Open Tuesday to Sunday 10 a.m. to 2 p.m.* One block further along Alfonso XII, at number 28 and immediately across from the park's second gate, is the **El Casón del Buen Retiro** (9). An integral part of the **Prado Museum**, with which it shares the same opening hours and a joint admission ticket, this once held many of Picasso's famous works. These have now been transferred to the **National Museum and Queen Sofía Art Center**, however, and its exhibits now include 19th-century Spanish art and paintings with works from the likes of Zuloaga, Valentín de Zubiaurre and Eduardo Chicharro.

Continue away from the Casón for two blocks and then turn right on to the Calle de la Academia. Pass the Los Jeronimos church and take the footsteps down to the entrance of the ***Prado National Museum** *(Museu Nacional del Prado)* (10), ☎ 330-28-00 or www.mcu.es/prado, which is the most-visited monument in all Spain. At the time this grand building was constructed, in 1785, it was the intended home of the Natural Science Museum. Just a few decades later, in 1819, though, it was inaugurated as the Prado Museum to house the royal collection donated by its founder, Ferdinand VII. Recognized as one of the world's greatest museums, it has a vast collection of over 6,000 paintings, although not all of these are on display. Sections for Spanish, Flemish, Dutch, Italian, French and German schools are complemented by sculpture and salons designated for temporary exhibitions. It is the Goya (1746–1828) collection, though, that is probably the most famous. Begun with just three paintings, which were a part of the original royal collection, it has been added to, substantially, over the years. Helpfully, the Prado has for sale, at a minimal price, comprehensive guides to each collection. *The Prado is open Tuesday to Saturday from 9 a.m. to 7 p.m. and Sundays and holidays from 9 a.m. to 2 p.m. Entrance 500 ptas (EUR 3.01), free Saturday after 2 p.m. and Sunday.*

Exit the Prado to the wide, tree-lined, Paseo del Prado that sweeps down along the main façade. The next stop, in the Plaza de Murillo, just beyond the Prado itself, has attractions of a more three-dimensional kind. Well over two hundred years ago, in October 1751, Fernando VI ordered the construction of the **Royal Botanical Gardens of Madrid** *(Real Jardín Botánico de Madrid)* (11), ☎ 420-30-17, but it wasn't until 1774 that Carlos III had it transferred here. Today, it has blossomed into a tranquil garden graced with over 30,000 different species of plants, right in the heart of a modern, bustling city. The opening hours here are complicated indeed. *Although always opening at 10 a.m. its closing time varies according to the season, changing from 6 p.m., to 7 p.m., 8:30 p.m. and 9 p.m. Entrance 250 ptas (EUR 1.50).*

Outside, continue back down the paseo and, to the left at the junction with the Plaza Emperador Carlos V, you'll find a small **Book Market** *(Mercado del Libro)* (12), which is joined on Sunday mornings by an impromptu, small **Flea Market** *(Rastro)*. Interesting, yes, but it's nothing when compared to the famous real **Rastro** (13), which is centered around the relatively nearby Calle de Ribera de Curtidores. This has been operating, on Sunday mornings and Bank Holidays, for over five hundred years and stretches through numerous adjoining side streets.

Across the Plaza del Emperador Carlos V a shiny new glass structure reflects a greeting. Though train stations do not often rank high on the sightseeing lists, this one is a brilliant exception. Many years ago, when some Spanish trains still resembled those seen in Wild West movies, I remember this as a typically dour old terminal. When the authorities decided to build the principle station at Chamartín, in the north of the city, a new station was built here, **Atocha Cercanías**, to connect to it and allow trains to pass directly through the city to the north or south, thus alleviating the need for a terminal. With the advent of the new high-speed line linking Madrid to Seville, clever planners saw potential in the old terminal building, but not for the trains which now stop just outside the original building, under a new roof. The original platform area has now been transformed into a wonderful concourse. Here, under the original glass roof a veritable forest of huge palm trees, watered by unusual fountains emitting a very fine spray, thrive in this huge, natural glasshouse. You'll certainly leave from this station, the **Puerta de Atocha** (14), relaxed and soothed, whether on a train or to continue your sightseeing walk.

Talking of sightseeing, it's now time to return to the perpetually busy plaza. Cross, at a ninety-degree angle to the Prado, before heading up the Calle de Santa Isabel towards the modern glass elevators that are, quite extraordinarily, attached to the exterior of a late 18th-century building that was once the Hospital General de Madrid. Since 1986, though, this has been the home of the ***National Museum and Queen Sofía Art Center** *(Museo Nacional "Centro de Arte Reina Sofía")* (15), ☎ 467-50-62, which specializes in exhibiting 20th century art by both Spanish and foreign artists. All of Picasso's works, once found in the Casón del Buen Retiro, are now on view here. *Open Monday to Saturday 10 a.m. to 9 p.m. and Sunday from 10 a.m. to 2:30 p.m., closed Tuesday. Entrance 500 ptas (EUR 3.01), free after 2:30 p.m. on Saturday and Sunday.*

It's time now for the last leg of the trip. Return up the Paseo del Prado to the Plaza Cánovas del Castillo but, before continuing on, stop for a drink under the magnificent crystal dome of the Rotunda of the **Palace Hotel**. Once refreshed, continue on to your final destination, the Villahermosa Palace, home of the ***Thyssen-Bornemiza Museum** *(Museo Thyssen-Bornemiza)* (16), ☎ 369-01-51, fax 420-27-80, e-mail inform@museothyssen.org and www.museothyssen.org. Baron Hans Heinrich Thyssen-Bornemisza, who owned one of the world's most impressive private collections of art, including works from the 13th century to date, bequeathed them to Spain. And the early 18th-century *Palacio de Villahermosa*, at Paseo del Prado, 8, has been especially converted to show, to their best effect, nearly 800 works of art by many of the great masters. There are also regular temporary exhibitions. *Open Tuesday to Sunday 10 a.m. to 7 p.m. Entrance to permanent collection 700 ptas (EUR 4.21), temporary exhibition 500 ptas (EUR 3.01), combined ticket 900 ptas EUR 5.41. These tickets can be boked in advance at the ticket office, e-mail taquilla@museothyssen.org.*

To return to the Puerta del Sol go back to the Plaza Cánovas del Castillo, where a right turn will take you up past the **Parliament** *(Cortes)*, along the way.

*Toledo

The history of this fascinating and intriguing city is as long and diverse as that of Spain itself. As far back as 193 BC the Romans conquered the city, named it *Toletum*, and made it one of their strategic strongholds. In the 5th century AD the Visigoths overran the Vandals and established Toledo as their political and religious capital. After the Moors invaded Spain, in AD 711, the city was incorporated into the Córdoba Emirate and, after that disintegrated in 1012, it became the capital of an independent kingdom.

Seventy-three years later King Alfonso VI, of León, re-conquered Toledo under the Christian banner and made it his capital. By the early 13th century the Jews became a major influence but just a century and half later, following a period of strife during the reign of Pedro I (The Cruel), his half-brother led a revolt in which the king was killed and much of the Jewish population massacred. In the 15th century, under the rule of the Trastamara's, the Moors, Jews, and Christians coexisted peacefully and Toledo blossomed into a major cultural center. In 1469 Isabella of Castile and León, of the Trastamara dynasty, wed Ferdinand of Aragón, Catalonia, Sicily, and Naples, thus uniting all these regions into one kingdom.

In 1561 Felipe II, grandson of the Holy Roman Emperor Carlos V, moved the capital to what was then just a small provincial town, Madrid. This event marked the beginning of the decline of the importance of Toledo, even though it remained the seat of the Primate of Spain.

The first sight of this imperial city will surely take your breath away. The River Tajo has succeeded in cutting a deep ravine through the hills, wrapping itself around a steep promontory where, protected by fortified gates, a maze of narrow streets, lanes and plazas combine to form a dramatically beautiful city. Designated a National Monument, Toledo is home to some of the most important monuments in Spain. Of course, there are numerous tourist shops as well. Most of these sell a wide variety of objects, from jewelry and small knives to complete suits of armor, of the city's most famous product—steel. The most popular of these are of the Damascene variety, black steel inlaid with gold, silver and copper wire.

GETTING THERE:

Trains leave from Madrid's Atocha Station, and return from Toledo, basically every two hours between approximately 8 a.m. and 8 p.m., with the journey taking about 75 minutes. RENFE operates the new, air-conditioned, Regional trains on this service.

Buses are not recommended for this daytrip.

By car, Toledo is 44 miles south of Madrid, and is reached by taking the N401 that directly connects both cities.

PRACTICALITIES:

There is so much to see in Toledo that one day barely gives time to scratch its surface, especially taking into account that most the monuments are closed for rather long periods in the middle of the day. It should be noted, also, that the monuments here are designated either "Private" or "State," with the latter closed on Sunday afternoon and all day Monday. Toledo's **Dialing code** is 925. The main **Tourist Office**, ☎ 22-08-43 or fax 25-26-48 is at the Puerta de Bisagra, s/n, and is open Monday to Friday from 9 a.m. to 6 p.m., Saturday from 9 a.m. to 7 p.m. and Sunday and holidays 9 a.m. to 3 p.m. Alternatively, there is also a kiosk in the Plaza de Zocodover with a similar opening schedule. As Toledo is such a difficult city to find one's way around, it is highly recommended that visitors stop by one of these offices to pick up a copy of the **Tourist Plan of Toledo**, an excellent map/guide available (in different languages) at no charge. Toledo has a **population** of about 65,000 and is capital of the province of the same name, one of five belonging to the autonomous region of **Castilla—La Mancha**.

ACCOMMODATION:

Surprisingly, especially given the number of visitors, there is a paucity of accommodation in Toledo, and most of that is in the middle- to upper-price range.

The **Parador Conde de Orgaz** ****, ☎ 22-18-50 or fax 22-51- 66, Cerro del Emperador, s/n, has all the normal classy attributes of a parador, and much, much more. Located high on the hill on the other side of the Tajo it offers a spectacular view of Toledo, especially when floodlit at night. Truly, a sight that will live in your memory forever. $$

The **Hotel Doménico** ****, ☎ 25-00-40 or fax 25-28-77, Cerro del Emperador, s/n, found close by the parador, is a modern hotel of traditional design. It has fifty well-appointed rooms, pool, and a terrace restaurant with views back over the city. $$

The **Hotel Alfonso VI** ****, ☎ 22-26-00 or fax 21-44-58, General Moscardó 2, is located in the heart of the city just a hundred yards or so from the Plaza Zocodover and in the shadow of the towering Alcázar. $$

The **Pintor El Greco** ***, ☎ 21-42-50 or fax 21-58-19, Alamillos del Tránsito, 13, is housed in a delightful 17th-century house that offers all modern comforts, as well as easy parking. It is located in a charming part of the old town, just a few yards from any of the most important monuments, and five minutes walk from the cathedral. $$

FOOD AND DRINK:

Its location between three regions, Castilla y León, Castilla—La

Mancha, and Extremadura ensures that a wide variety of dishes can be found here. The indigenous cuisine of Toledo, though, is based around small game such as partridge, quail, and hare. Specialities include **Partridge** *(perdiz)*, **Beans and Partridge** *(Judías con Perdiz)* and, by way of change, *El Cuchifrito*, which consists of lamb, tomatoes, eggs, saffron, and white wine. The cheese of La Mancha *(Queso Manchego)* is always popular and, for those with a sweet tooth, almonds are used to make delicious **Marzipan** *(mazapán)* pastries. The local wines, both red and white, are rich and full-bodied.

Asador Adolfo (two entrances at Granada, 6 and Hombre de Palo, 7) is one of the most highly rated restaurants in Toledo. Its specialty is the cuisine of La Mancha *(Cocina Manchega)*. ☎ 22-73-21. $$$

Venta de Aires (a block or so away from the Puerta de Bisagra, outside the old walls). Founded in 1891 it retains its traditional style, offers Castillian-style dishes and has had as guests such luminaries as Richard Nixon and the king and queen of Spain. ☎ 22-05-45 or fax 22-45-09. $$$

Restaurante Carlos V (next to the Alcázar at Trastamara, 1). In its Mudéjar-style dining room, you may enjoy a reasonably priced *Menú del Día* that changes frequently. ☎ 22 21 00. $

Hostal-Residencial Pousada (Callejon de San Pedro, almost in the shadow of the cathedral), is fairly basic, as is its restaurant. But the *Menú del Día*, consisting of two plates, bread, and wine is a bargain. ☎ 22 21 00. $

SUGGESTED TOUR:

Numbers in parentheses correspond to numbers on the map.

From just outside the **Train Station** *(Estación de Ferrocarril)* (1) take either bus number 5 or 6, Estación/Plaza Zocodover, to the Plaza de Zocodover to begin the tour. For the energetically inclined it is possible to walk, but it is quite a long way and, for the most part, severely uphill. Difficult enough at the best of times, but much more so during the summer months when temperatures frequently rise above 110°F. Much better to delay this part of the tour until the end of your journey, then you can walk downhill back to the station.

The **Plaza de Zocodover** (2) is irregularly shaped and, although not of much architectural interest, has been the social center of Toledo through the centuries. A market, originated by the Moors, was held here until recently and it has been the site of feasts, tournaments, and executions. Popular legend has it that King Ferdinand III "The Saint" listened to citizens complaints and dispensed justice while seated on his throne in the square.

A short walk up the Cuesta de Carlos V will draw you towards the immense features of the **Fortress** *(Alcázar)* (3), ☎ 22-30-38, a structure situated on the highest part of, and absolutely dominating, the city. There have been fortifications on this site since the 3rd century, and the present building has been completely rebuilt following its destruction during the Spanish Civil War. It also houses a very interesting **Army Museum** *(Museo*

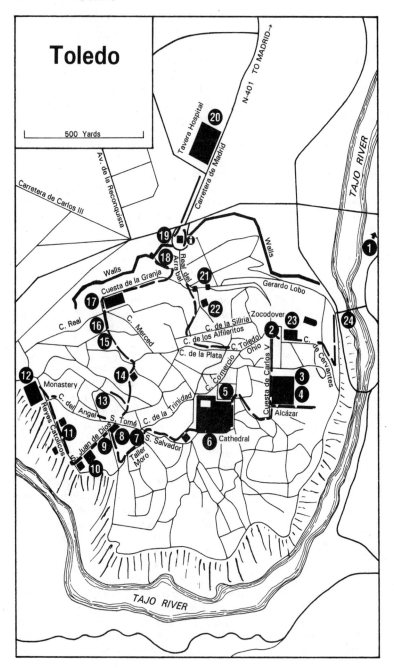

de Ejercito) (4), but it is the events surrounding the Civil War that are of paramount interest here. The most famous of these took place in July 1936 when the commander, Colonel Moscardó, was faced with an agonizing decision—either surrendering or seeing his son executed by the besieging forces. He didn't, his son was killed and the colonel's office remains exactly as it was at the end of the siege; ceiling hanging down, riddled with bullet holes and furniture torn to shreds. Kept as a shrine, the incongruity between this and the rest of the carefully restored Alcázar gives it even greater impact. *It is open Tuesday to Sunday from 9:30 a.m. to 2:30 p.m., entrance 200 ptas (EUR 1.20).*

Before leaving, take a walk around the outside of the Alcázar and enjoy the wonderful views over the Tajo ravine. Retrace your steps down the double staircase turning left back into the Cuesta de Carlos V (towards the Hotel Alfonso VI) where, to its right, a narrow little pedestrian-only street with steps, the Calle Uno de los Pizochos, beckons. At the bottom take a steep right turn through narrow lanes and ancient houses until, at the Calle Cuesta de los Pasquales, a stupendous view of the cathedral tower fills the skyline.

Pasquales leads into the Calle del Colleoso where, at the end, stands the rather attractive **Market** *(Mercado)* and the **Rojas Theatre** *(Teatro Rojas)*. Turn left around the market to the Calle de Sixto Ramón Perro and then follow around the huge cathedral walls past, on the left, the Posada de la Hermanidad. Ramón Perro then turns into Cardenal Cisneros, which continues on around the Cathedral to join the Plaza del Ayuntamiento.

The double-towered façade of the **Town Hall** *(Ayuntamiento)* is impressive enough, but it is dwarfed in both size and beauty by that of the *****Cathedral** *(Catedral)* (5), ☎ 22-22-41 or fax 25-34- 00, whose main entrance is just under the **Palace Arch** *(Arco de Palacio). It is open, daily, free of charge from 10:30 a.m. to Midday and 4 p.m. to 6 p.m.* The seat of the Primate of Spain, this is unquestionably the most important monument in the city, and one that mustn't be missed. The first Cathedral on this site was built by the Visigoth King Recaredo I and the first Bishop of Toledo, San Eugenio. That was converted into a mosque by the Moors, and it was not until 1227 that King Ferdinand III "The Saint" began construction of the present building. Doubt exists as to when it was finally completed, some say the end of the 15th century and others the end of the 16th. There is, however, no doubt that it incorporates numerous architectural styles, so much so that it is often referred to as the "Museum Cathedral".

This really is a most magnificent example of its genre, and besides over twenty side chapels it contains a very fine **Museum of Cathedral Treasure** *(Museo Tesoro Catedralicio)* (6). *Open Monday to Saturday 10:30 a.m. to 6 p.m. and Sunday and holidays 2 p.m. to 6 p.m., entrance 500 ptas (EUR 3.01).* Here you can see a fabulous collection of sacred art, books, tapestries and other exhibits including Enrique de Arfe's Monstrance. Made of solid silver and gold, it has over 5,600 individual parts and weighs in at 430 pounds. Incredibly, more of these, made by Enrique and his brother, are on display in Córdoba, Ávila, and Valladolid. Note also the indications of a curious tradition here. Strange-looking hats hang precariously from the ceiling; if you look closer, you'll notice they are suspended over plaques which indicate tombs of primates buried below. Each of these hats belonged to the respective primate and when they fall, and it could be days or centuries later, the tomb is then removed to the vaults.

The path to the next stop is a little tricky. First head back left under the Palace Arch and down the side of the Town Hall square. Built into the wall here is a **Fountain** *(Fuente)*, an ideal place to replenish your by-now near-empty bottle of water. Then go around the back of the Town Hall following Calle San Salvador and, at the end, around into Calle del Taller del Moro where 100 yards or so ahead, and on the right, is the museum of the same name. The **Moor's Workshop** *(Museo de Taller de Moro)* (7), ☎ 22-71-15, is housed in a 14th-century building, and this small dignified and elegant museum has particularly fine examples of Moorish ornamental plasterwork as well as ceramics and wooden items. *Being a "State" museum it closes Sunday afternoon and Monday but is open at all other times from 10 a.m. to 2 p.m. and 4 p.m. to 6:30 p.m. Entrance 100 ptas (EUR .60).*

Continue to the end of the street, and as the main road runs straight ahead turn right into the Travesia de las Descalos. Just past the Palacio de Fuensalida (where the wife, Isabel, of Emperor Carlos V, lived and died and which is now the home of the Junta de Communes Casa de La Mancha Presidencia) is the splendid Mudéjar tower of the **St. Tomé Church** *(Iglesia de Santo Tomé)* (8), ☎ 25-60-98 or fax 25-12-32. This structure, though, isn't the main attraction here. Inside is one of El Greco's most famous paintings, **The Burial of Conde de Orgaz** *(El Entierro del Conde de Orgaz)*, which was painted in 1583, 271 years after the Count was buried on the actual site. In his will he bequeathed a considerable sum of money to be used for the upkeep of the church and impoverished parishioners. This provision was contested by the heirs and others, however, and it took 270 years to decide the matter in the church's favor. The church then commissioned El Greco to paint a memorial depiction of the burial, which is now on display. The young boy attending upon the saints is considered to be a likeness of El Greco's son, and on a handkerchief dangling from the boy's pocket he signed his name, Doménico Theotokopouli, and the date. *The church is open daily from 10 a.m. to 5:45 p.m. (6:45 in summer). Entrance 200 ptas (EUR 1.20).*

Nearby, in fact just down Calle San Juan de los Reyes and on Samuel Levi to the left, is another place dedicated to El Greco. **El Greco's House and Museum** *(Casa y Museo del Greco)* (9), ☎ 22-40-06 or fax 22-45-59, *is open Tuesday to Saturday 10 a.m. to 2 p.m and 4 p.m. to 6 p.m., and on Sunday from 10 a.m. to 2 p.m. Entrance 400 ptas (EUR 2.40).* El Greco reputedly lived and worked in this charming old house, whose furnishings give a glimpse of life during that era. Besides an attractive garden and patio there are examples of his work in both the house and small gallery.

A little farther on, at the junction with the much larger Reyes

Católicos, is the interesting **Transito Synagogue and Sephardic Museum** *(El Tránsito Sinagoga y Museo Sefardi)* (10), ☎ 22-36-65 or fax 21-58-31. This was built in 1365 by the treasurer and minister of finance to Pedro I "The Cruel", Samuel Halevi, to whom it was dedicated. The main room is fascinating with its beamed wooden ceiling and cornice inscribed with Hebrew inscriptions and verses from the Psalms. The eastern wall, where the Torah's sacred rolls were kept, is embellished with beautiful hand-carved stucco, and the south wall contains the women's gallery. It was later taken over by the Christians and used by the Monks of St. Benedict and the Knights of Calatrava. *Open Tuesday to Saturday 10 a.m. to 2 p.m. and 4 p.m. to 6 p.m. and Sunday 10 a.m. to 2 p.m. Entrance 400 ptas (EUR 2.40).*

Now it's time to turn right onto Reyes Católicos and, on the right, just beyond the Plaza de Barrio Nuevo, is another ancient synagogue, this one dating from the 12th century. Set in a small, secluded garden, the interior of the **St. Mary the White Synagogue** *(Santa María la Blanca Sinagoga)* (11), ☎ 22-72-57, resembles that of a mosque, and its simplicity of style enhances its charm. It was used as a synagogue until 1405, when it was taken over for Christian use. During the 16th century it served as a hostel for repentant fallen women and, later, came under the patronage of St. Mary, who was known as the "White One" after a chapel in Rome, and utilized as a hermitage. *Open daily 10 a.m. to 2 p.m. and 3:30 p.m. to 6 p.m. (7 in summer), entrance 200 ptas (EUR 1.20).*

Literally a stone's throw away the much larger, and very differently styled, **Monastery of St. John of the Kings** *(San Juan de los Reyes)* (12), ☎ 22-38-02, has an interesting story to tell. The Catholic Monarchs commissioned Juan Guas to build a combination church, cloister, and monastery to celebrate victory at the Battle of Toro in 1476, which confirmed Isabella as Queen of Castile. Financed by their private funds, it was originally intended to be their burial place. After conquering Granada, however, they were so captivated by it that they commissioned the construction of a **Royal Chapel** *(Capilla Real)* built there for that purpose. Considered a classic example of Gothic architecture this, unusually for Spain, has a light and airy ambiance within. Note that on either side of the altar are the emblems of the different realms combined by the Catholic Monarchs: Aragón, Catalonia, and Naples for Ferdinand and Castile and León for Isabella. It is now hard to imagine, but the lovely cloister suffered much damage during the Wars of Independence and, in 1810, was even used as a stable by Napoleon's troops. The monastery is famous for its connection with its first novice, Cardinal Cisneros, who died in 1517. *Visit daily from 10 a.m. to 1:45 p.m. and 3:30 p.m. to 5:45 p.m. (6:45 in summer), entrance 200 ptas (EUR 1.20).*

Leave to the right by way of Reyes Católicos and take a sharp left fork into Calle del Angel, for another upward grind. Interestingly, the buildings here, as well as the side streets, get more interesting the higher you get. Across from the Mudéjar tower look for the signpost to the *Museo San Román* and follow, again uphill, a narrow and windy old road to its junction with Calle de las Bulas at the Plaza de Valdecaleros. Not far down Bulas, at numbers 13 and 15, is the **Contemporary Art Museum** *(Museo de Arte Contemporaneo)* (13), ☎ 22-78-71. The *Casa de las Cadenas* is an intricate 16th century house that was tastefully restored in 1973, and its centerpiece is a wooden tri-level patio known as the **Womens Patio** *(Patio de Mujeres)*, around which are displayed exhibits of contemporary paintings and sculptures. *These can be viewed between 10 a.m. and 2 p.m. and 4 p.m. to 6:30 p.m. but, being a "State" museum, it is closed on Sunday afternoon and Monday. Entrance 100 ptas (EUR .60).*

Retrace your steps to the Plaza de Valdcaleros and follow signs guiding you to the left, up narrow cobblestoned lanes to the fascinating *San Román* church, which is home to the **Museum of the Councils and Visigothic Culture** *(Museo de los Concilios y Cultura Visigótica)* (14), ☎ 22-78-72. This strange little museum doesn't have too many exhibits of interest other than Romanesque paintings on the wall, but the building itself is worth the visit. The design of one half resembles a regular church, and the other is reminiscent of a mosque; an intriguing combination indeed. The opening hours here are the same as the Contemporary Art Museum, as is the entrance fee.

Once outside the museum turn left into a narrow alleyway which, after a very short distance, opens into the Plaza de Padilla. In the middle of the plaza you'll find some steps descending into a very narrow and cobblestoned lane. Take these and, at the bottom, make an immediate right here around to another plaza, this time the Plaza de Santa Domingo de Antiguo. Directly in front of you will be the **Cistercian Convent of Santo Domingo de Silos** *(Monasterio Cisterciense de Santo Domingo de Silos)* (15), ☎ 22-29-30. Founded in 1085 by King Alfonso VI, this is the oldest monastery in Toledo. El Greco's first commission in Spain was to paint the *reredos* here; the original contract is actually on display and he and his family are also interned here. The interior of the Renaissance-style church is in stark contrast to the other half where, behind a metal grille, there are unusual exhibits and, of course, paintings by El Greco. *Open Monday to Saturday 11 a.m. to 1:30 p.m. and 4 p.m. to 7 p.m., and Sunday afternoon. During November to March it is open only on weekends, although weekday visits may be arranged in advance at the Nunnery porter's office. Entrance 150 ptas (EUR .90).* As you leave you'll note another church which appears to be, but is not, a part of the monastery. The **Iglesia de la Santa Leocadia** (16) dates from the 12th century, was modified in the 13th century and restored in 1966.

Next, follow the Calle de Santa Leocadia down to an overlapping terrace and the **Miro de la Granja** (17), which allows views over the surrounding countryside. Note the large building to the right, it's the *Hospital de la Talavera* and will be visited soon. In the meantime climb up the small hill and then down the cobblestone lane to the busy Calle Real del Arrabal. A left turn reveals the *Mudéjar* church of **Santiago del Arrabal** (18); the original construction most probably dates from the times of Alfonso

VI, and was reconstructed in the 13th century.

Beyond it, to the right, stands the wonderful "new" gate, the **Puerta Nueva de Bisagra** (19). This has a delightful inner patio flanked by bell towers on either side, and is topped by a magnificent coat of arms. Cross the busy road and, for a change of scenery, walk for about 400 yards along the charming Paseo de Merchan through the park behind the Tourist Office and towards the impressive **Tavera Hospital** *(Hospital de la Tavera)* (20), ☎ 22-04-51. Construction was commissioned by Cardinal Tavera, after whom it was named, in 1541, and his remains now rest in the chapel. The large and ornate patio is bisected by a most unusual covered walkway. On the left side is the private residence of the Duke of Lerma where many works of artistic value, including a magnificent collection of paintings by El Greco, are on display. *This is open daily from 10 a.m. to 1:30 p.m. and 3:30 p.m. to 6 p.m, entrance 500 ptas (EUR 3.01).*

Stroll back through the park, cross back through the Puerta de Bisagra and walk up the Calle Real del Arrabal. As you round a bend keep your eye open for a small tobacco shop, where you will turn right into the Calle de Cristo de la Luz. This leads up to the elegant and unusual 14th-century archway of the **Puerta de Sol** (21). Immediately behind this is an even older and quite curious monument. The **Christ of the Light** *(El Cristo de la Luz)* (22) dates from the 10th century, and is the only building in the city from that era which has been preserved in its original condition. Copied from the La Mezquita in Córdoba, this functioned as a mosque until the reconquest. Visiting it, though, presents unusual problems as there are no official opening hours. It is simply left to the discretion of a caretaker to decide as and when he wishes to turn up. Strange; even for Spain.

Exit into the Calle Carmelitas Descalos and follow the steep, cobblestoned streets towards the tower of the *Iglesia de San Vicente,* and then take a left in the plaza of the same name into Calle Plata. Along the way, you will see the **Post Office** *(Correos y Telegrafos).* At the Plaza Roperia this street changes to Calle Toledo Ohio (named after another Toledo!) which will terminate at the Plaza de Zocodover. Before reaching the plaza be sure to check the plaque at number 57, which is a memorial to José Antonio Primo de Rivera, who founded the Falangist Party and whose remains rest with those of Franco in the basilica at the Valley of the Fallen (see page 64).

You could take a bus back to the station from here, but the walk is all downhill and there are some spectacular sights along the way. Cut down the steps along the long, flat side of the plaza and enter Calle de Cervantes and, immediately on the left, is a museum that it would be a shame to miss. The delightful Plateresque façade of the **Santa Cruz Museum** *(Hospital da Santa Cruz de Mendoza)* (23), ☎ 22-10-36 or fax 22-58-62, serves to give you a foretaste of what to expect. Inside, you'll marvel at the intricately carved Renaissance-style staircase that leads to galleries with splendid panelled ceilings that are home to an eclectic array of exhibits. Among these are 20 works by El Greco, 30 Brussels tapestries, and an interesting assortment of carpets, chests, religious memorabilia, small arms and suits of armor, etc. *It is open Monday 10 a.m. to 6:30 p.m., Tuesday to Saturday from 10 a.m. to 6:30 p.m. and Sunday 10 a.m. to 2 p.m. Entrance 200 ptas (EUR 1.20).*

Once outside carry on back down Cervantes to the ramparts over the ravine, which allows a fine view of the castle on the other side of the river and, below you, the **Alcántara Bridge** *(Puente de Alcántara)* (24), with gates guarding either end. Walking down towards the bridge it becomes obvious that the double-doored gate, with a portcullis, on the city side is by far the oldest. This, in fact, originates from the early 13th century, while the gate at the other side—be sure to note the city's coat of arms on the exterior—was built five centuries later. Turn away from the bridge, and after a last look back at this incredible city, turn sharp left and follow the road around and back to the train station.

Aranjuez

The regions south of Madrid, prior to reaching the plain of La Mancha, are known for their aridity. There is, however, one significant exception. About thirty miles south of the city, at the confluence of the rivers *Tajo* and *Jarama*, lies a highly fertile valley, particularly lush in its contrast to the nearby hills. In days gone by this did not escape the notice of royalty, anxious for a respite from the relentless heat of nearby Madrid and Toledo. It was Felipe II who, in the late 16th century, constructed the first of the palaces here; but it wasn't until the early 18th century that Felipe V formally selected Aranjuez as a royal residence. Construction of the present palace was commissioned by the first of the Spanish Bourbon kings in 1744. He and his successors meant it to be in the style of the great palace at Versailles, near Paris. Although it has never reached that scale, either physically or politically, it is well worth a visit, if only as a monument to the intoxicatingly lavish lifestyle of the monarchs of that period. And, as did they, you will find Aranjuez to be the perfect antidote to the heat of Madrid.

GETTING THERE:

Trains depart Madrid's Atocha station for the short journey, less than an hour, to Aranjuez.

Buses need not be considered as the trains are fast and scheduled runs are frequent.

By car, Aranjuez, 30 miles south of Madrid, may be reached via the N-IV.

PRACTICALITIES:

Avoid visiting Aranjuez on a Monday; everything worth seeing is closed. The **Dialing Code** is 91. The **tourist office**, ☎ 891-04-27, fax 891-41-97 or www.aranjuez.org, is located at the Plaza de Santiago Rusiñol. Aranjuez has a **population** of nearly 40,000 and is in the autonomous community of **Madrid**.

ACCOMMODATION:

It is rather unlikely that visitors to Aranjuez will stay the night, however, just in case the mood strikes you, consider the following suggestion.

The **Hotel Las Mercedes** ***, ☎ 892-20-07 or fax 891-04-40, Andalucía, 15, is a pleasant hotel, with private grounds and a pool, conveniently located near to the palace. $

FOOD AND DRINK:

The fertile valley of Aranjuez is known throughout Spain for the production of asparagus and strawberries. In the spring and early summer, numerous stalls selling these delicacies line the roadside and, of course, you will find fresh green asparagus and strawberries and cream featured on every menu.

Restaurante Casa Pablo (Almíbar, 42), is downtown in close proximity to the bus station. Finely prepared Castillian cuisine may be enjoyed either outdoors, or in one of the two dining rooms, which are decorated with bullfighting posters. ☎ 891-14-51. $$$

Restaurante La Rana Verde (Calle Reina, 1), is found alongside the Tajo river, so aim for a riverside table. This establishment, whose name is translated "The Green Frog", is large and somewhat touristy. Bypass the *menú del día* to sample the game and fish specialties. ☎ 891-32-38. $$

SUGGESTED TOUR:

Numbers in parentheses correspond to numbers on the map.

As the majority of visitors will, most probably, arrive by train, this tour begins at the station. Upon exiting, turn right then take a left at the first junction. The ***Royal Palace** *(Palacio Real)* (1) and its extensive grounds lie directly ahead. Felipe II commissioned the first royal palace here, employing the talents of the same architects who designed the El Escorial monastery. Unfortunately, the original structure burned down in the very early 18th century but, soon after, the Bourbon king, Felipe V ordered a replacement. Both this palace and La Granja, which he was building during the same period in the province of Segovia, were constructed with many similarities to the great French palaces of the era.

The clean, elegant, lines of this palace are evident even from a distance and, upon arriving, you will be enchanted by its formal gardens, where visitors are serenaded by the sound of water cascading over the weir. Unfortunately, you are not allowed to wander freely here. Guided tours are available, but the commentaries are in Spanish. Once inside, you will not find a room that is not lavishly furnished. Two in particular are nothing if not idiosyncratic; one is decorated with Chinese tiles, and the other is a virtual reproduction of a room found in the *Casa Real Vieja* in the Alhambra, Granada.

Among the major attractions of Aranjuez are the verdant gardens, something not particularly common in this usually arid part of Spain, of the *Jardín del Príncipe*. And, while wandering through these you will encounter two more surprises. Closest to the palace is the **Sailors House** *(Casa de Marinos)* (2), which exhibits "landlocked" royal river vessels. At the far end of the park, nearly a mile away, is the **Farmer's House** *(Casa del Labrador)* (3). Do not, however, be misled by the name. In actuality this is a small palace built by Carlos IV in 1803, and used as a retreat by subse-

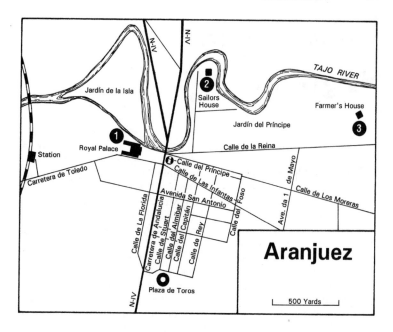

quent kings. It features marvelous marble floors, lavish decor and a private toilet; you've guessed it, decorated as a Throne Room. *The palace and two houses are open Tuesday to Sunday, during the summer from 10 a.m. to 6:15 p.m., and closing an hour earlier during the winter. Entrance for the Royal Palace and Farmer's House is 700 ptas (EUR 4.21) and 300 ptas (EUR 1.80) for the Sailors House. The gardens are open, again on Tuesday to Sunday, in summer from 8 a.m. to 8 p.m., but close one hour earlier in winter.* As these places are quite a distance apart for walking, you might consider a ride on the little "train", *(Chiquitren de Aranjuez)*, that runs between them.

You may conclude, as your visit here comes to an end, that you, indeed, have something in common with past royalty. Namely, a keen appreciation for lovely, interesting and relaxing Aranjuez.

Trip 5
A Daytrip from Madrid

Segovia

S egovia, situated on the northern slopes of the Sierra de Guadarrama mountain chain north of Madrid, was captured by the Romans around 80 BC and served as a valuable strategic military base until the disintegration of the empire. The city was ruled by the Visigoths from that time until they were overrun by the Moors early in the 8th century. It was then reconquered under the banner of Christianity by King Alfonso VI in 1088. Using to full advantage the city's unusual topography, high on a promontory wedged between the Eresma and Clamores rivers, he resettled and fortified the city. Most of the defensive walls, and three of the five gates built during this period, survive to this day.

During the 12th and 13th centuries many Romanesque churches were constructed here, of which eighteen are still standing. Segovia became a royal residence at the end of the 13th century and, in the 15th century, under the court of Trastamara, blossomed into a cultural center. It was on the steps of the original church of San Miguel in the Plaza Mayor that, in 1474, Isabella was proclaimed Queen of Castile. Six years later Segovia became the headquarters of the Inquisitor Torquemada. During this era affluent noblemen built numerous fortified houses throughout the city, many of which were transformed into palaces. These are now renowned for the coats-of-arms proudly carved above their doorways, and Segovia can boast more of these than any other Spanish city. The early 16th century brought turbulence to the town, which was the center of the Communidades Revolt against Carlos V as he attempted to impose absolute rule and raise new taxes. The leaders, Juan de Padilla of Toledo and Juan Bravo of Segovia were ultimately defeated at Villalar in 1521, and their subsequent executions took place in Segovia. In 1986 the city was declared a "World Heritage City" by UNESCO.

GETTING THERE:
Trains depart the underground level of Madrid's Atocha Station, then Chamartín fourteen minutes later, for the scenic two-hour trip to Segovia. No reservations are necessary as the trains are all second-class-only, departing approximately every two hours from around 6 a.m. to 8 p.m.

Buses are actually a slightly faster, and definitely more frequent, way to reach Segovia. These depart from Madrid's La Sepulvedana terminal at Paseo de la Florida, 11, which is just across the road from the Norté train station.

By car, Segovia is about 55 miles northwest of Madrid. Take the A-6 autopista to the Collado-Villalba exit, then proceed on the N-601 north to Segovia.

PRACTICALITIES:

If possible, avoid visiting Segovia on summer weekends, when it is overrun with tourists. The major attractions are open daily all year round, but a few of the more minor sights are closed on Sundays and/or Mondays. The **Dialing Code** is 921. There is a **Tourist Office**, ☎ 46-29-14 or fax 46-04-92, in the Plaza del Azoguejo (next to the Aqueduct), open daily 10 a.m. to 8 p.m. Another one, ☎ 46-03-34 or fax 46-03-30, is at Plaza Mayor, 10, and is open daily from 10 a.m. to 2 p.m. and 5 p.m. to 8 p.m. Segovia has a **population** of about 60,000 and is the capital of the province of the same name, one of nine belonging to the autonomous region of **Castilla y León**.

ACCOMMODATION:

The **Parador de Segovia** ****, ☎ 44-37-37 or fax 43-73-62, Carretera de Valladolid, s/n, is located on the outskirts of the city and is known as the "Viewpoint of Segovia" because it offers incomparable views of the old town. It also has a heated pool and a fine restaurant. $$

The **Hostería Ayala Berganza** ****, ☎ 46-04-48 or fax 46-23- 77, Carreteras, 5, is found in the 16th-century typically Castillian palace owned by the family of the same name, and now declared a Monument of Cultural Interest. A small charming hotel—three singles, 13 rooms with a salon and two suites—it has all modern facilities including a restaurant, bar, room service and private parking. $$

The **Hotel-Residencia Los Linajes** ***, ☎ 46-04-75 or fax 46- 04-79, Dr. Velasco, 9, is housed in a delightful 17th-century building, located just two minutes walk from the Plaza Mayor. It is situated on the edge of the city and affords guests wonderful views over the surrounding countryside. Most rooms have a private terrace, and the cafeteria and bar boast a large one of their own. $$

The **Hotel Infanta Isabel** ***, ☎ 44-31-05 or fax 43-32-40, Isabel la Católica, 1, has a beautiful façade and an elegant mixture of classical style and modern facilities. Ask for a room that overlooks the Plaza Mayor and Cathedral. $$

FOOD AND DRINK:

Segovia is known for its excellent restaurants, which attract diners from Madrid in all seasons. The local signature dish is *Cochinillo Asado* (roast suckling pig), while other specialties include *Cordero Lechal* (roast suckling lamb), *Cochifrito* (lambstew), and *Sopa Castellana* (soup of ham, paprika, and poached egg). Out of an embarrassment of riches, a few choice restaurants are:

Mesón de Cándido (Plaza de Azoguejo, 5, by the Aqueduct), is a national institution, and one of Spain's oldest and best restaurants. It specializes in local cuisine, most notably cochinillo, and reservations are suggested on weekends, ☎ 42-81-03. $$$

Restaurante José María (Cronista Lecea, 11, just off the Plaza Mayor) offers a wide-ranging menu (copies in English are available) of classical regional cuisine. You'll also be treated to a great wine cellar, crisp friendly service and a wonderfully eclectic array of decorations and antiques in the dining room. Collectively, these create a delightful ambiance. ☎ 46-11-11 or fax 46-02-73. $$

Mesón Duque (Calle Cervantes, 12, two blocks west of the Aqueduct) is a friendly old place with colorful decor, that specializes in cochinillo and various other local meat dishes. Reservations are suggested on weekends. ☎ 43-05-37. $$

Mesón del Campesino (Calle de Infanta Isabel, 12, a block southeast of the Plaza Mayor) offers local specialties at very reasonable prices. $

SUGGESTED TOUR:
Numbers in parentheses correspond to numbers on the map.

Leave the **train station** or the **bus terminal** and take either a bus, number 3, or a taxi to the **Plaza Mayor** (1). Don't though, attempt the walk; it is a long and arduous one. Wonderfully old-fashioned and quite impressive, the plaza is surrounded by porticoed buildings whose lower levels contain an array of cafés and bars, the **Town Hall** *(Ayuntamiento)*, tourist office, and the church of San Miguel. In one corner is the towering Cathedral.

Leave the plaza by way of Isabel la Católica. Initially, this is just an ordinary pedestrian shopping street but soon, after passing through the Plaza del Corpus, it transforms into the Calle Juan Bravo. After a short distance this opens out to two plazas, those of **San Martín** and **Las Sirenas** (2), which are joined by steps and are home to numerous interesting buildings. At the first corner is the **Old Prison** *(Carcel Vieja)* (3), that functioned as such until well into the last century and now houses the library and city archives.

Immediately behind this is the most dominant structure in the plaza, the church of **San Martín** (4). This dates from the 12th century, and houses fine examples of paintings and sculpture. Surrounding a statue of, who else, Juan Bravo, leader of the Communidades Revolt, are some really beautiful old mansions. The most prominent of these is the **Torreón de Lozoya** (5), ☎ 46-24-61, built in the 14th century and displaying the coat-of-arms of one of its previous owners, the Aguila family. *It opens July to September. Monday to Friday, 7 p.m. to 9:30 p.m.; and Saturday, Sunday and holidays midday to 2 p.m. and 7 p.m. to 9:30 p.m. The rest of the year it opens Monday to Friday 6:30 p.m. to 9 p.m. and Saturday, Sunday and holidays midday to 2 p.m. and 6:30 p.m. to 9 p.m. Entrance free.* Other buildings of note are the 15th-century *Casa del Siglo* and the *Casas de las Condes de Bornos, de Soller* and *de las Mexia-Tovar.* In the background sits the much larger **Torre de Arias Dávila** (6), an interesting example of a forti-

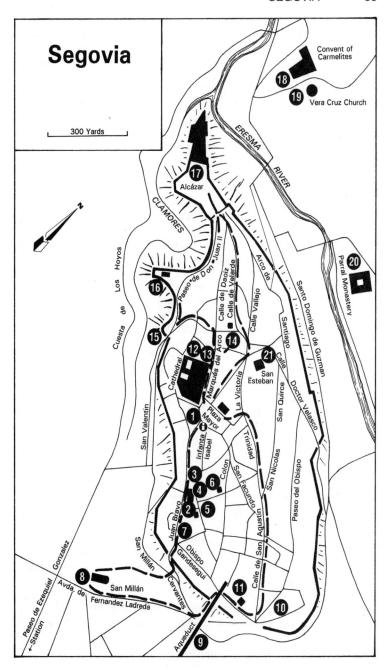

Segovia

300 Yards

Convent of Carmelites
18
19 Vera Cruz Church

ERESMA RIVER

CLAMORES

17 Alcázar

Cuesta de Los Hoyos

Paseo de D on • Juan II

Calle de Daoiz
Calle de Velarde

Arco de

Santo Domingo de Guzman

Parral Monastery
20

16

15

Calle Vallejo

Santiago

Cathedral

Marqués del Arco

12 13

14

21 San Esteban

Calle Doctor Velasco

San Valentin

1

Plaza Mayor

Infanta Isabel

La Victoria

San Quirce

3
4 6
Colon

2
5

Trinidad

San Facundo

San Nicolas

Paseo del Obispo

Juan Bravo

7

Obispo Gandesegui

San Millán

Cervantes

Paseo de Ezequiel Gonzalez

Avda. de Fernandez Ladreda

8 San Millán

Calle de San Agustin

Station

11

10

Aqueduct

9

fied house with ramparts towards the top of the tower.

Continue down Juan Bravo and sneak a glance right, down Calle de la Alhóndiga, towards the lovely old building which is now used as an art gallery. Just past this is a most unusual house indeed. The **Casa de los Picos** (7), ☎ 46-26-74, dating from the 15th century, has a strange exterior decorated with diamond-shaped stones. *Open Monday to Friday, midday to 2 p.m. and 7 p.m. to 9 p.m., and on Saturday and Sunday only in the afternoon.* In fact there is only one other house of this type on the Iberian peninsula, the *Casa dos Bicos* in Lisbon. Follow Juan Bravo again and, as you round a bend, the buildings on the right give way to a panoramic view of the lower part of town, with the mountains in the background. Rest here for a while where, in the mornings and evenings, you'll be entertained by swallows and storks cavorting overhead.

A look below gives a preview of your next destination, the **Iglesia de San Millán** (8). Be patient, though, the route there is both tedious and bland. Follow the steps down and make a sharp right into Arturo Merino, then go on Caraleja across the Plaza del Dr. Gila into the winding Calle de los Carros, left once again for the Calle de Carretas and then a final right on Escultor Marinas to the church. The grounds surrounding it are rather unkept, to say the least, but that doesn't take anything away from what is considered to be the most beautiful Romanesque church in Segovia. Constructed over a Mozarabic structure, of which only a remodelled tower remains, in the early 12th century, it features two 13th-century porches with elaborate capitals on its exterior. There are, also, marvelous views back to the Cathedral, which sits proudly atop the hill.

Follow the Avenida de Fernández Ladreda left, back towards the town and, although rather busy, it is quite an interesting street. Colonnaded on either side, wonderful five-armed lampposts down its center, another Romanesque church—the *San Clemente*—to the right and, as you round a slight curve into the Plaza de Azoguejo at the end, the towering outline of the magnificent *Aqueduct *(Acueducto Romano)* (9). Dating from the 1st or 2nd century AD this, one of the finest aqueducts still in existence, has 165 arches spread over its 728 meter (2,392 ft) length and, at its highest in the plaza, is 28 metres (92 ft) tall. Most amazingly, the granite stones of this symmetrically pleasing structure, which is best viewed in the early morning or early evening, are held together by nothing more than their own gravity.

Now continue the tour by taking the steps up the city side of the aqueduct, actually quite a demanding climb, to reach the walls of the city. Here you can reach out and almost touch the aqueduct, and will have a wonderful perspective of the surrounding countryside, which shows just how rural a town is Segovia. Next take a little pathway, which actually runs parallel to the aqueduct, turn immediately right under the arch and take the steps leading up to the ramparts. Although there is no actual access to the ramparts, this does give you a slightly higher perspective, one of equal height with the top layer of the aqueduct.

Retrace your footsteps and take the Calle de San Sebastián to the right, passing a couple of unusual churches on the way to the *Plaza del Conde de Cheste,* and the junction with the main road. This area was once the home of knights and noblemen, a fact that is reflected in the buildings that flank the tiny rectangular park. The **Casa del Conde de Cheste** (10) is notable for its size, occupying the whole of the southern side, and the **Casa del Marqués de Quintanar** (11) features an ornate doorway with an archway of eleven helmets that is topped by the coat-of-arms of the Heredia-Peraltas. Turn right into San Agustín and bear right at the first fork into Trinidad. Before the road splits again note the interesting colonnaded building, with wooden beams to your right. Keep left on Trinidad, and after passing a group of historic buildings at the Plaza de la Trinidad, turn left at the end before continuing up to the Plaza Mayor.

Directly across the Plaza Mayor is the **Cathedral** *(Catedral)* (12), ☎ 46-22-05. The original cathedral, Santa María, actually located much closer to the Alcázar, was destroyed during the Communidades War. Acting on a royal decree from Carlos V, work on this structure began in 1525. Construction continued, however, for the better part of two centuries, making this one of the last Gothic churches to be completed in Spain. The cloister was moved piece-by-piece from the previous cathedral and the **Cathedral Museum** *(Museo Catedralicio)* (13) is located in several rooms around it. Perhaps the museum's most intriguing exhibit is the 18th-century carriage used today to carry the silver monstrance during the Corpus Christi celebrations. *It is open daily in the spring and summer from 10 a.m. to 7 p.m., closing an hour earlier in autumn and winter. Entrance 400 ptas (EUR 2.40), free for EC citizens.* Come out of the cathedral and turn left into Marqués del Arco. Here gypsies will be hawking their wares on the railings, and tourist shops abound on the other side. A little way down a slight diversion into Desamprados will take you to the **House/Museum of Antonio Machado** *(Casa-Museo de Antonio Machado)* (14), ☎ 46-03-77, at number 5. Machado was a poet who resided in Segovia from 1919 to 1932, and the furniture and other exhibits in this small museum illustrate how modestly he lived. *Closed on Monday and Tuesday, it opens the rest of the week between 11 a.m. to 2 p.m. and 4:30 p.m. to 7:30 p.m. Entrance 200 ptas (EUR 1.20), free on Wednesday.*

Marqués del Arco changes to Daoiz, which is soon enhanced by a charming park in the Plaza de la Merced. This is graced by a traditional fountain, trees, the usual children's playground, and is also home to the Iglesia de San Andrés. The latter gives its name to one of the gates in the city walls, which will be visited next. Get there by taking the steps in the corner of the plaza, which lead steeply down through the old **Jewish Quarter** *(Judería Nueva)* to the Plaza del Socorro and the **Puerta de San Andrés** (15). This has two very formidable towers, one polygonal and the other square. The royal coat-of-arms above the lower of the double arches of this gate was restored in the reign of Carlos V, and is the best preserved in the city. Of interest too, back on the city side, is a very old house with floors and walls which are supported by wooden beams, and with a private chapel built right into it.

Next, follow Calle Zocorro along a rather bland section until, at a curve on the river side, a small road leads to the *Casa del Sol*. This authentic fortress, once a part of the defensive walls, is now home to the **Segovia Museum** *(Museo de Segovia)* (16). It contains a mix of paintings, sculpture, ceramics and archeological exhibits, as well as locally-found coins. Past this point it is actually possible to walk on the ramparts.

Directly ahead of you are glorious views of the next stopping point, the **Alcázar* (17), ☎ 46-07-59, sitting defiantly upon the promontory high above the Clamores river. Enter through the grand iron grille gates, and the small grass park ahead provides a colorful introduction to the façade of what must be everyone's idea of a fairytale castle. Although parts of the structure date from the 12th and 13th centuries, the main portion was built a hundred years later, and was remodelled in the next century. It became a favorite haunt of monarchs; Isabella left from here to be proclaimed queen, and Carlos III founded the Royal Artillery School here in 1762. A century later, in 1862, a fire destroyed the roofs and after its restoration, six years later, the General Military Archives were moved here. Today it provides a suitable home for an interesting ten-room museum, and a highly informative brochure is included in the admission price. Energetic visitors may climb the 152 steps to the top of the tower of St. John where the view, of both city and countryside, is spectacular. *Open daily in the spring and summer between 10 a.m. and 7 p.m., it closes an hour earlier the rest of the year. Entrance 400 ptas (EUR 2.40), free on Tuesday for EC citizens.*

Back outside the Alcázar visitors are faced with a decision. Immediately, but far below and across the river are three monuments easily visible, but not so easily reached. Truthfully, the only realistic option is on foot. This may, however, be a little too much for many, especially in the searing summer heat.

If you opt to brave this side trip, head to the left where, beside a main road, you'll find the **Convent of Carmelites** *(Convento de las Carmelitas Descalzos)* (18), ☎ 43-13-49, founded by St. John, who actually participated in its construction between 1588 and 1591. Upon his death in 1593 he was, as a plaque describes, initially buried here, though his remains were moved to an elaborate sepulchre after his beatification in 1675. *Visit daily from 10 a.m. to 1:30 p.m. and 4:30 p.m. to 8 p.m., closed Monday morning. Entrance by voluntary contribution.* Very close to the convent is a church of an entirely different character. The **Vera Cruz Church** *(Iglesia de la Vera Cruz)* (19), ☎ 43-14-75, dates from the 13th century and is constructed in a twelve-sided shape that is unique in Spain. Small, charming, and unostentatious, it is thought to have been founded by the Knights Templar, as the style is similar to other examples churches they built in Portugal and Italy. *It is open in the spring and summer from 10:30 a.m. to 1:30 p.m. and 3:30 p.m. to 7 p.m., at other times of the year it closes an hour earlier. Closed Monday and November. Entrance 200 ptas (EUR 1.20).*

Some distance away from both is the much larger **Parral Monastery** *(Monasterio del Parral)* (20), ☎ 43-12-98. Founded in 1445 by Enrique IV, and sponsored by the Marqués of Villena, it passed into the hands of the Jerónimos Brotherhood before falling into disrepair after the monasteries were sacked in 1835. Declared a National Monument in 1914, it has an interesting mix of styles and an elaborate sepulchre containing the remains of the Marqués. *It can be visited in the spring, autumn and winter, Monday to Saturday 4 p.m. to 6 p.m. and Sunday and holidays 10 a.m. to 11:30 a.m. A Mass with Gregorian chants is held Monday to Saturday at Midday and on Sunday at 1 p.m. Entrance by voluntary contribution.*

Back outside the iron gates of the Alcázar, carry on straight ahead, then take a left fork into Calle de Velarde Pozuelo. Soon, just past an archway, is another pleasant park of the type that are are spread throughout this city, from which you'll enjoy impressive views out over the countryside. The seriously modern apartments around it are offset by a delightful wooden beamed house to the left. In the rear it has a wooden balcony overhanging a magnificent, and very tempting, swimming pool. Back along Pozuelo, at its junction with Vallejo, is a statue honoring San Juan de la Cruz. Straight ahead, and dominating the skyline, is the particularly unusual tower, sometimes called "the Queen of the Byzantine Towers" of the **Iglesia de San Esteban** (21), a national monument since 1896. Five floors rise from its base, the first two having blocked windows, and the four corners of the tower form bevels and have columns running their entire length. From here it is just a short walk up the Calle de Escuderos, to end the trip back in the Plaza Mayor.

*El Escorial and the Valley of the Fallen
(San Lorenzo de El Escorial y El Valle de los Caidos)

S an Lorenzo de El Escorial, on the foothills of the Sierra de Guadarrama northwest of Madrid, lazed in relative obscurity until 1557, when Felipe II commissioned the construction of a monastery here. This was designed to commemorate his victory over Henri II of France at the Battle of San Quentín, an event that took place on August 10, the Holy Day of Saint Lawrence *(San Lorenzo)*—hence the choice of name. This, however, evolved into more than a monastery as, over the centuries, the Spanish monarchs spent an increasing amount of time here, especially during the summer months to escape the oppressive heat of Madrid. It also became a favorite hunting retreat and, in the 18th century, Carlos III added a number of buildings to house his hunting companions. In the 19th century, the railroad made it possible for the more well-to-do families of Madrid to use San Lorenzo as a vacation site, joining the grand summer court of the monarchs. In 1971 the city was declared a Historical and Artistic Monument and, in 1984, it was recognized by UNESCO as a Monument of World Interest.

Following the Spanish Civil War Generalísimo Franco was searching for a site on which to build a monument to those who died during the hostilities. The place he chose was only a short distance away from El Escorial, in a V-shaped valley of the Sierra de Guadarrama known as Cuelgamuros. It is known today as the Valley of the Fallen *(Valle de los Caidos)*.

Really, neither of these should be missed, and I would list them in a place of high priority on any proposed itinerary. Fortunately, it is doubly convenient that they are close to both Madrid and to each other.

GETTING THERE:
Trains run through San Lorenzo de El Escorial on the main line from Madrid to Ávila and beyond, although there are, naturally, many more local trains from Madrid Atocha, via Chamartín. Unfortunately, the train station at San Lorenzo de El Escorial is some distance from the town, and it is necessary to either take a bus or to make a long and arduous, uphill

walk between the two.

Buses depart, frequently, in the mornings from the combined Metro and bus station at *Moncloa.* Numbers 661 and 664, operated by *Autocares Herranz,* depart from platform 3 and, following a short journey time of approximately one hour, deposit you in the center of San Lorenzo de El Escorial right next to the monastery. *Herranz* also operates a one-a-day service, but not on Monday, to the Valle de los Caidos, leaving at 3:15 p.m. and returning at 5:30 p.m.

By car, San Lorenzo de El Escorial, some 32.5 miles northwest of Madrid, is reached by taking the N-VI *autopista* toll road to Majahondas and then the C-505 to San Lorenzo. The entrance to the *Valle de los Caidos* is 5 miles due north of San Lorenzo de El Escorial, along the road to the town of Guadarrama.

PRACTICALITIES:

Plan this trip for any day except Monday, when both the monastery and *Valle de los Caidos* are closed. Remember, also, this is a mountainous area and, while the weather in Madrid may be balmy, it could be cold, windy and rainy here; so come prepared. The **Dialing Code** is 91. The **tourist office** *(Oficina de Turismo)*, ☎ 890-15-54, Floridablanca, 10, is open Monday to Friday 10 a.m. to 2 p.m. and 3 p.m. to 5 p.m., and on Saturday from 10 a.m. to 2 p.m. San Lorenzo de El Escorial has a **population** of less than 10,000 and is in the autonomous region of **Madrid**.

ACCOMMODATION:

The **Hotel Victoria Palace ******, ☎ 890-15-11 or fax 890-12-48, Juan de Toledo, 4, is a highly elegant yet very comfortable hotel set in its own charming gardens which feature a tempting pool. It is a leisurely couple of minutes' walk from the monastery. $$

The **Hotel Florida ****, ☎ 890-17-21 or fax 890-17-15, Floridablanca, 12, is one very short block from the main entrance to the monastery. The rooms are clean and comfortable. It has a restaurant on site and features, under the hotel, an art gallery. $

FOOD AND DRINK:

Hotel Victoria Palace (Juan de Toledo, 4), an excellent and tastefully decorated restaurant, serves a variety dishes highlighting the cuisines of various Spanish regions. The menu changes daily. ☎ 890-15-11 or fax 890-12-48. $

Restaurante El Cenador de Salvador (Avda. de España, 30, Moralzarzal) is found in the small town of Moralzarzal just a short drive northeast of El Escorial, and it is well worth the effort to get there. Set in a wonderful old manor house in the mountains, it is the brainchild of Salvador Gallego, who is continuing a family tradition of innovative cooking. Certainly not inexpensive, but an experience to relish. ☎ 857-77-22 or fax 857-77-80. $$$

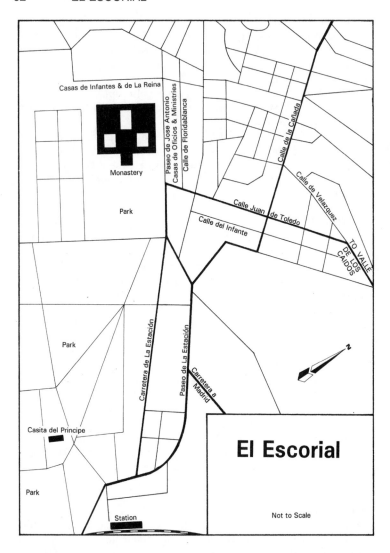

Casas de Infantes & de La Reina

Paseo de Jose Antonio
Casas de Oficios & Ministries
Calle de Floridablanca

Calle de la Cañada

Calle de Velazquez

Monastery

Park

Calle Juan de Toledo

Calle del Infante

TO VALLE DE LOS CAIDOS

Park

Carretera de la Estación

Paseo de La Estación

Carretera a Madrid

Casita del Principe

El Escorial

Park

Station

Not to Scale

Restaurante Tavolata Reale (Plaza de las Animas, 3), is a centrally locat-ed Italian restaurant with a *menú del dia* priced at an affordable price. They also prepare pizzas to go. ☎ 890-45-91. $

Restaurante Chino Hong Kong (San Antón, 6) is, obviously, a Chinese restaurant. The *menú del dia,* on offer Monday to Friday, costs only 600 ptas (EUR 3.61) and includes a drink and dessert. ☎ 896-18-94. $.

SUGGESTED TOUR:
Numbers in parentheses correspond to numbers on the map.

If you plan to visit both of these outstanding monuments in the same day, and for those traveling by public transport that would be the logical plan, you will need to depart Madrid early. It is preferable to arrive in San Lorenzo de El Escorial at or around 10 a.m., when the monastery opens for the day.

Regardless of your method of transportation, this huge structure, built between 1563 and 1584 and nestled, at an elevation of 3,494 feet, on the foothills of the Sierra de Guadarrama, is impossible to miss. It will be visible from miles away. In fact, it is much more than a monastery, and visitors will want to allow plenty of time to explore it thoroughly. The complex is so vast and so fascinating that, in truth, a guide such as this can do little more than skim the surface of El Escorial's intriguing history. I would highly recommend that you purchase a copy of the very informative, and beautifully illustrated, "Visitor's Guide." This is available in many languages and, besides enhancing your tour, will be a memorable souvenir.

Inside, you will find more than enough to capture your interest. First, there is a **Museum of Architecture**, which also includes a gallery of weaponry. The **Gallery of Battles** is 55 yards long, and has frescos depicting war scenes. The **Museum of Art**, which would be a gallery of note in any location, exhibits numerous paintings from the royal collection that were not transferred to the Prado Museum. The **Patio of Masks** is dominated by the adjacent façade of the Basilica and derives its name from the two fountains in the eastern wall. The king's residence, the **Hapsburg's Palace**, lavish in both furnishings and decor, surprisingly, comes across as a rather austere ambiance. Of peculiar interest, the king's bed was positioned within his bed chamber so that it looked directly down into his Chapel with a view of the Basilica's high altar.

El Escorial was intended, also, to be the burial place for Spanish Monarchs and the two **Pantheons**, of totally contrasting styles, are most intriguing. The 17th-century, Baroque style, **Pantheons of the Kings** is accessed via a narrow, metal grilled door leading down into a circular chamber. This is divided into eight sections housing, in chronological order, layers of sepulchres containing the remains of kings and the wives that bore their children, from Carlos I to Alfonso XIII, spanning over a four-hundred-year period of the Spanish Monarchy. The nearby **Pantheon of the Infantes**, dating from the late 19th century, is considerably less ornate in style.

Also of significance are the **Chapter Houses**, designed for the assemblies of monks that lived in the monastery. The **Main Cloister**, embellished with magnificent frescos, is connected, through the Procession Door, to the huge classically-styled **Basilica**, the heart of the monastery's existence. This is, in reality, comprised of not one, but two, churches—the *Sotocoro*, people's church, and the monastic church and Royal Chapel.

One of the more pleasant surprises, however, is found in the **Library**.

In keeping with the uniformity of the entire complex, the façade is relatively plain, but it conceals a highly intricate and beautifully painted interior. The Baroque-styled arched ceiling, adorned with a series of magnificent frescos by Tibaldi, is particularly spectacular. Although a catastrophic fire in 1671 destroyed a portion of the collection, the Library nevertheless still houses in excess of 40,000 volumes. *The Monastery complex,* ☎ *890-59-03, opens Tuesday to Sunday, 10 a.m. to 5 p.m., and admission costs 900 ptas (EUR 5.41).*

You should be aware that, next to the monastery is the **House of the Queen and Children** *(Casita de Infantes y de la Reina)* and, farther away in the grounds, is the **Lower Cottage** *(Casita del Príncipe).* But, as the former is only open on Easter holidays and during August, and the latter indefinitely closed, it is superfluous to describe them here. In any event, if you are going on to visit the *Valle de los Caidos* you will, no doubt, be pressed for time.

The *Autocares Herranz* ticket office is within a strange little bar at Calle Reina Victoria, 3. The only bus leaves, from just around the corner, at 3:15 p.m., except on Mondays. Rather than risk having a problem at the last moment, it is wise to buy your ticket as soon as you reach town. If, by chance, the bus is full the only other option is an expensive (3,800 ptas or EUR 22.84 each way) taxi ride. In comparison, the bus seems a bargain at 870 ptas (EUR 5.23) return, and that includes admission.

The **Valley of the Fallen** *(Valle de los Caidos),* ☎ 890-56-11, features two totally different attractions, each massive in scale. Clearly, Franco wanted to leave behind a memorial of the Civil War that would be a powerful reminder, to future generations, of the sacrifices made by the Spanish people during those calamitous times. Although maybe not its original intention, upon completion it was dedicated in honor of all the men and women, on both sides, who had lost their lives in the course of that conflict. And the huge cross is visible from miles around. It is set upon the summit of a small mountain and stands 492 feet high with a width of 150 feet. On weekends and holidays a funicular will take you to the base of the cross where you may investigate the plinth adorned by four enormous figures depicting the evangelists and their attributes: the bull, the angel, the eagle and the lion. From this vantage point, the size of the cross is overwhelming, and the views back down the valley are worth the trip in their own right.

The **Basilica** is no less spectacular, having been carved 262 yards deep into the granite mountain. It begins as just a tunnel, but opens out into a giant dome that is almost directly under the cross outside. There are small chapels dedicated to various virgins who serve as patrons of various military institutions. Other attractions are a series of Flemish tapestries dating from 1553 and, in prominent positions, the tombstones of Franco and José Antonio Primo de Rivera, founder of the Falangist Party. In the crypt, but closed to the public, are ossuaries containing the remains of tens of thousands of the dead, of both sides, from the Civil War. *Open Tuesday to Sunday 10 a.m. to 5 p.m., entrance 700 ptas (EUR 4.21).*

Do not lose track of time. The bus returns to San Lorenzo de El Escorial at 5:30 p.m., and it's a very pretty ride. From there you may connect with either a bus or train back to Madrid.

Ávila

L
ocated on the plateau *(meseta)* west of Madrid, at an elevation of
1,128 meters (3,700 ft.), Ávila holds the distinction of being the highest city in Spain. Of Celtic-Iberian origins, it was Christianized in the
1st century AD, ruled by the Moors beginning in the the 8th century and
reconquered by King Alfonso VI in 1085. Today, Ávila is famed for things
temporal and spiritual, and it was from this period that the former originated. After the reconquest the city was repopulated by Christian knights
who began work on what is unquestionably Ávila's most dominant feature; its Walls *(Las Murallas)*. Construction of these began in the latter part
of the 11th century, supervised by Count Don Ramón de Borgona, son-in-
law of King Alfonso VI. During the ensuing years various noblemen were
charged with the responsibility of defending a particular section of the
wall and, consequently, many elegant, fortified mansions were built near
or, in some cases, as an integral part of the walls. Many of these still exist
today.

Spiritual influence is equally dominant here, and can be directly
traced to the pervasive presence of Santa Teresa. She was born here in
1515 and her legacy, in the shape of churches, convents and statues, is evident throughout the city. This Catholic visionary and advocate of
Carmelite thought, with her work given impetus by the advances of the
Reformation, founded no less than seventeen convents throughout Spain
and wrote prolifically. For these efforts she was beatified on March 12,
1622.

During the 16th century, Carlos V established his court in Toledo and
drew many of the noblemen there. As a result, Ávila's political and social
import was diminished, beginning a decline that continued into the early
17th century when, after the expulsion of the Muslims, the city's population dropped dramatically. Today, designated a World Heritage City, it is a
quiet provincial capital that has not allowed the demands of tourism to
spoil its natural charms.

GETTING THERE:

Trains of every class depart from both of Madrid's railway stations,
Atocha and Chamartin, on a frequent basis throughout the day. The fastest
service, the InterCity, takes a little over an 75 minutes.

Buses are not a particularly good way to get to Ávila as service is infrequent.

By car, Ávila, 76 miles northwest of Madrid, is best reached by taking the A-6 Autopista superhighway to the junction of the N-501 at Villacastín. From here, Ávila is 19 miles to the southwest.

PRACTICALITIES:

Unusual for Spain, all of Ávila's sights, with the sole exception of the Provincial Museum, are open daily. Ávila's **Dialing code** is 920. The local **Tourist Office** *(Oficina de Turismo de Ávila)*, ☎ 21-13-87 or fax 25-37-17, may be found at Plaza de la Catedral, 4, opposite the Cathedral. Ávila has a **population** of 45,000 and is the capital of the province of the same name, one of nine belonging to the autonomous region of **Castilla y León**.

ACCOMMODATION:

The **Melía Palacio de las Velada** ****, ☎ 25-51-00, fax 25-49-00, Plaza de la Catedral, 10, combines beautifully the grace and ambiance of the 16th-century palace in which it is located and the facilities sought by modern-day travelers. A lovely example of this marriage of antiquity and innovation may be seen in the glass-roofed three-storied central patio, with its beamed ceilings and intricate decorative carvings. Also noted for its unusual square tower, this establishment, once owned by Gomez Dávila, has played host over the years to numerous monarchs. $$

The **Parador Raimundo de Borgoña** ***, ☎ 21-13-40 or fax 22-61-66, Marqués Canales de Chozas, 2, offers visitors the chance to lodge in a typical example of a 16th-century nobleman's home. This backs onto the city walls and, as you would expect in such a setting, is reflective of the charm and character of that bygone era. $$

The **Gran Hotel La Hostería de Bracamonte** **, ☎ 25-12-80, Bracamonte, 6, also housed in one of the city's historic buildings, is of a more modest scale than the preceding two. A restoration in 1989 integrated the necessary updates into this 16th century mansion, but this was, happily, accomplished without disturbing its character. Exposed brickwork and numerous antiques arranged in an intimate and unique fashion in the public rooms create a most pleasing ambiance. A taurine bar completes the package. $

The **Hostal Casa Felipe** **, ☎ 21-39-24, Plaza de la Victoria, 12, is a modest but friendly and clean establishment in a central location in the Old City's main square, offering a good value for money spent. $

FOOD AND DRINK:

The cuisine of Ávila is very much based on the produce of the region; steaks, roast suckling pig, roast lamb and local trout are all highly popular, as are stews. For the sweet-toothed, *Yemas de Santa Teresa* candy made of egg yoke, should not be missed.

Parador Raimundo de Borgoña (Marqués Canales de Chozas, 2), serves in its charismatic restaurant delightfully prepared specialities of the region. ☎ 21-13-40 or fax 22-61-66. $$$

Es Tostado (Plaza de la Catedral, 10), found in the new Meliá Palacio de los Velada hotel, offers a mix of the region's traditional dishes and innovative chef's suggestions, in a simple but elegant environment. ☎ 25-51-00, fax 25-49-00. $$$

Mesón del Rastro (Plaza del Rastro, 4), is found in a traditional old inn built onto the Walls by the Puerta del Rastro. Full of character, it serves typical Castillian cuisine. ☎ 21-12-18. $

Gran Hotel La Hostería de Bracamonte (Bracamonte, 6), has, probably, the most delightful restaurant in town. Its ambiance is enhanced by the typical plates of the region it serves. ☎ 25-12-80. $

Hostal Casa Felipe (Plaza de la Victoria, 12), has a cheap and cheerful restaurant that serves hearty food, and has a good supply of tapas. ☎ 21-39-24. $

SUGGESTED TOUR:

Numbers in parentheses correspond to numbers on the map.

From the **train station** it is a fairly long, but easy, walk to the Old Town. Some may want to conserve their energy, taking a Line 1 bus, or a taxi.

Our tour begins at the **Tourist Office** *(Oficina de Turismo de Ávila)* (1), directly across from the main entrance to the Cathedral. Be sure to stop here and pick up a copy of the informative brochure **Ávila Plan-Guide** *(Ávila Plano-Guía)*, available free of charge. Cross the street to the *Cathedral* *(Catedral)* (2), ☎ 21-16-41, constructed between the 12th and 14th centuries and considered to be one of the earliest Gothic cathedrals. It had the dual roles of church and fortress, and the most noticeable feature of the latter is the fortified head *Cimorro*, built into and protruding from the Walls. The exterior **Door of the Apostles** *(Puerta de las Apostoles)*, at the northern end and dating from the 14th century, is of particular import. This was a part of the the main façade until the 15th century when Juan Guas redesigned the main entrance, moving this door in the process. Inside, in addition to many important works of art and the sepulchres of prominent citizens (most notably that of Don Alonso de Madrigal, El Tostado, a 15th-century bishop of Ávila), the high altar, retrochoir, and choir are of particular interest.

The **Cathedral Museum** *(Museo Catedral)* (3) occupies several rooms and the exhibits are definitely worth a look. Besides the expected religious art, you will find an El Greco portrait of Don García Ibañez, massive books of music manuscripts protected by elaborately embellished covers and, the most precious of these objects, a huge, 1.7 metere (5 ft. 8 in.) tall, silver monstrance crafted by Juan de Arfe in the 16th century. *The museum is open Monday to Friday from 10 a.m. to 1 p.m. and 3:30 p.m. to 5 p.m., Saturday 10:30 a.m. to 1:30 p.m. and 3:30 p.m. to 6 p.m., and Sunday and holidays midday to 1:30 p.m. and 3:30 p.m. to 6 p.m. Entrance 250 ptas (EUR 1.50).*

Before leaving the Cathedral plaza, take a moment to admire the beautiful buildings that surround it. To the left of the Cathedral is the 16th-

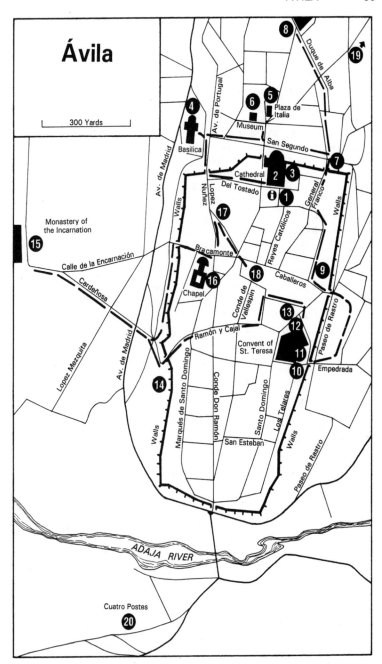

Ávila

300 Yards

Av. de Portugal

8

19

Duque de Alba

5

6

Plaza de Italia

4

Museum

San Segundo

Basilica

Av. de Madrid

Walls

Cathedral

2 3

7

Del Tostado

Nuñez

Lopez

1

General Franco

Walls

Reyes Católicos

17

Monastery of the Incarnation

15

Bracamonte

Calle de la Encarnación

16

18

Caballeros

9

Cardeñosa

Chapel

Conde de Vallespín

13

López Mezquita

Av. de Madrid

Ramón y Cajal

12

Paseo de Rastro

14

Convent of St. Teresa

11

10

Empedrada

Marqués de Santo Domingo

Conde Don Ramón

Santo Domingo

Los Telares

San Esteban

Walls

Paseo de Rastro

ADAJA RIVER

Cuatro Postes

20

century *Palacio de Valderrabanos;* once owned by the chief magistrate of Jerez, Gonzalo Dávila, who played an important role in the conquest of Gibraltar in 1462. Dávila's impressive coat-of-arms adorns the main door to what is today a hotel. Immediately to the right is what must be considered one of the most beautiful **Post Offices** *(Correos y Telegrafos)* in Spain. Next to that is the **Palace of the Boy King** *(Palacio del Rey Niño),* parts of which date from the 13th century. The name derives from the fact that King Alfonso XI, who was only one year of age when he inherited the throne from his father, Ferdinand IV, grew up here. For centuries afterwards it was used as a residence by the local bishops; today, it functions as the public library. Just across the road is the 16th-century *Palacio de las Velada,* previously described in the "Accomodation" section.

Continue down the street, Del Tostado, which runs between the latter two buildings to the *Puerta de San Vicente,* one of nine gateways set in the walls, and out left to the Basilica of the same name. Construction on **St. Vincent's Basilica** *(Basílica de San Vicente)* (4), ☎ 25-52-30, was begun, in the Romanesque style, during the 12th century but not completed until two centuries later. One of its most highly acclaimed features is the main doorway, considered one of the finest in Spain, which is dedicated to the child martyrs, Saints Vicente, Sabina, and Cristeta, siblings who reportedly died at the location. Their bodies are interred inside in the **Sepulchre de los Niños Santos** (Child Saints); the sepulchre is itself church-shaped and covered by a decorated and tiled roof supported by four columns. *The Basilica is open daily from 10 a.m. to 1:30 p.m. and 4 p.m. to 6:30 p.m. Entrance 200 ptas (EUR 1.20).*

Directly before you as you exit the main door to the Basilica is the Calle de San Segundo. Take this road and walk up an incline past a small park following the walls along to the *Puerta del Peso de la Harina,* where a left turn by the old-fashioned Hotel Jardin into Leales leads to the interesting double plazas of *Nalvillos* and *Italia.* Ahead is the 12th-century **Santo Tome el Viejo** (5) church which, unfortunately, is not open to the public, and to the left is the **Provincial Museum of Ávila** *(Museo Provincial de Ávila)* (6), ☎ 21-10-03. Housed in a typical 16th-century mansion, once home to the deans of the Cathedral, the *Casa de los Deanes,* this offers a wide range of archaeological, popular and fine arts exhibits displayed throughout nine rooms located on two floors. *It is open Tuesday to Saturday from 10 a.m. to 2:30 p.m. and 4:30 p.m. to 7:30 p.m., and in the morning only on Sunday. Entrance 200 ptas (EUR 1.20).*

Head back onto San Segundo, where the unmistakable bulge of the *Cimorro* of the Cathedral faces you on the left. Walk another particularly attractive stretch of the walls, and adjunting a plaza stands the most important gate in the city, the **Puerta del Alcázar** (7), that stands guard over the oldest section of the walls. Its small archway, adorned by the coat of arms of the Catholic Monarchs overhead, is flanked by two huge towers. The adjacent *Plaza de Santa Teresa,* the social center of the city, has a sandy playground which connects the Puerta to the *Iglesia de San Pedro* (a national monument) at the other end.

As an optional diversion, visit **Saint Teresa's Museum** *(Museo Teresiano)* (8), the entrance to which is found on the Calle de las Madres, just two blocks along the Duque de Alba from the left-hand side of the Iglesia de San Pedro. Located next to the Convento de San José (inaugurated in August 1562 and the first founded by Saint Teresa) this strangely-designed museum houses relics and memorabila of the Saint. Displayed in a series of rooms along the walls and protected by both glass and bars, are letters, books, an "authentic" replica of her cell, and even her coffin. *Regular hours are daily from 10 a.m. to 2 p.m. and 4 p.m. to 7 p.m., entrance 300 ptas (EUR 1.80).*

Just inside the Puerto del Alcázar, to the left, is the small Plaza Calvo Sotelo, where you'll find a charming little garden, the entrance to the ramparts and examples of the stone pigs indiginous to this area. Take Franco, a typical shopping street, down to the next plaza where a left will bring you to the huge edifice of the Episcopal Palace, which, strangely, is not designated as a tourist sight on the city plan! Next, follow down Calle Piá y Deniel and at the end, on the left, in the Plaza Pedro Dávila, stands the magnificent **Dávila Palace** *(Palacio de los Dávila)* (9). In actuality, this is a combination of four exceptionally attractive buildings of varying architectural styles, Romanesque, Mudéjar, and Renaissance, each reflective of its period of construction, between the 13th to 15th centuries.

Exercise caution as you make a left turn into the very narrow (one-way for motor vehicles) lane which leads through another gate, the *Puerta del Rastro,* into a wide paseo and little park of the same name. The *Paseo del Rastro* runs along the side of the walls and is a very popular place for Ávilans to take a leisurely stroll. From here you'll enjoy an interesting perspective of the walls snaking their way downhill, the modern town below and, in the background across the Ambles Valley, the peaks (5,250 feet high and often snow covered) of the Sierra de Ávila.

At the end of the paseo enter back into the Old City through yet another gate, the *Puerta de Santa Teresa,* where you'll be greeted by yet another collection of historic buildings. Just to the left is the 16th-century **Nuñez Vela Palace** *(Palacio de los Nuñez Vela)* (10), built in the Renaissance style by Blasco Nuñez de Vela, who later became Viceroy of Peru. Now home to the Law Courts, this building features an elegant two-story patio, and the entrance and surrounding windows reside behind columns decorated with the family coat-of-arms.

To its right is the **Convent of Saint Teresa** *(Convento de Santa Teresa)* (11), ☎ 21-10-30, dating from 1635. The façade of this Carmelitas Descalzas convent is emblazoned with the coats-of-arms of numerous families. The rather elaborate interior contains memorabilia and various images of the Saint as well as, reputedly, the exact site of her birth. *It is open daily from 9:30 a.m. to 1:30 p.m. and 3:30 p.m. to 9 p.m., but closes a half-hour earlier in winter.*

Next take Madre Soledad up to the left. The unusual building to the right with the double round towers is the *Delegación de Hacienda,* local government offices. Immediately opposite this are two excellent examples of 16th-century Renaissance architecture, the **Palacio de los Almarza** and **Mansión de los Superunda** (12) Amble on to the next corner where you'll find another 16th-century structure, the **Guzman Tower** *(Torreón de Guzman)* (13). This fascinating tower was designed with fortification in mind, with outlook posts situated at each corner and overhanging battlements protecting the front entrance. Note that the coat-of-arms of every family that has owned it are displayed on its exterior.

Leaving this area by way of the now-familiar Sancho Dávila, pass the imposing, and seemingly modern for this area, *Diputación Provincial* before turning left at the end, by the *Iglesia de San Juan.* Follow Blasco Jimeno to a "T" junction and take a right onto the seemingly bland Jimena Blásquez. This, in turn, leads into Ramón y Cajal where, at the end, you'll find a wonderful parador. Along the way, a quick detour left into Calle de Vallespin reveals an attractive 16th-century bulding whose ornate doorway is lavishly decorated with coats-of-arms, shields, eagles and various other motifs. Until recently it served as a military academy, but it does not appear to be in use at present. Make your way back past the parador to the Plaza Concepción Arenal which leads to the *Puerta del Carmen.* Here, built into the walls, is a huge tower with three arches, topped by the inevitable stork's nest.

A walk through to the other side of the gate affords an impressive view of the heavily fortified *Walls (14) which snake proudly up and down the contours of the city's boundaries. These are an average of over 4 yards high and 9ft. thick. Built into their nearly 3,000-yard length are 90 towers and 9 gateways.

Nestled in the valley, with mountains sitting grandly on the horizon, is the rather large **Monastery of the Incarnation** *(Monasterio de la Encarnación)* (15), ☎ 21-12-12. The journey there, though, is quite a walk and some may prefer to take a bus (the U, Green Line) from the Plaza de Santa Teresa. Construction on this structure began in 1513 and, totally coincidentally, the date of its inauguration coincided with the baptism of Teresa de Ahumada in April, 1515. Saint Teresa entered this monastery in 1536, where she resided for the next 30 years, 27 fulfilling her vows as a nun and the final three as its prioress. In sparse, cell-like rooms she developed her ideas of Carmelite Reform, and planned trips around Spain during which she founded new monasteries. *Open daily 9:30 a.m. to 1:30 p.m. and 3:30 p.m. to 6 p.m., entrance 150 ptas (EUR .90).*

Return back to the walls and follow this exceptionally impressive stretch back up to the *Puerta del Mariscal.* Pass through into the Plaza Fuente El Sol, and take note of unusual stone cross standing in its center. To the left is the Palacio de Bracamonte and, straight ahead, the irregular outline of the **Mósen Rubi Chapel** *(Capilla de Mósen Rubi)* (16), ☎ 21-15-87. Begun during the 16th century under the patronage of the Herrera and Bracamonte families, it was completed by Mósen Rubi whose father,

Diego de Bracamonte, was tried in 1592 for refusing to pay taxes to support Felipe II's wars. *Open daily 5 p.m. to 7 p.m., entrance free.* An immediate left, past the appropriately named Hotel Bracamonte on the corner, leads up Lopez Nuñez and to two excellent examples of noblemen's fortified houses, the **Mansións de los Aguila** and **de los Verdugo** (17). These date from the late 15th and early 16th centuries. Backtrack down Esteban Domingo to the **Victoria Square** *(Plaza de la Victoria)* (18), also known as the Plaza of the Little Market *(Plaza del Mercado Chico)*, after the traditional market held there every Friday. This fine example of a typical central square is flanked at one end by the **Town Hall** *(Ayuntamiento)* and at the other by the *Iglesia de San Juan*, the site of Santa Teresa's baptism in April, 1515.

Before ending your trip back at the Cathedral square, just two or three blocks away up from the right hand side of the Town hall, hop on the Number 3, Blue Line bus (following a circular route through the city) to a monument that really should not be missed; the **Royal Monastery of Saint Thomas and Oriental Art Museum* *(Real Monasterio de Santo Tomás y Museo de Arte Oriental)* (19), ☎ 22-04-00. From 1482, when construction began, the building has been managed by the Dominican Order. Once the seat of the university, it was also used frequently by the Catholic Monarchs as a summer residence. And it is in the church, dominating the center, that you can see the very impressive sepulchre of Prince Don Juan, eldest son and heir of Isabella and Ferdinand, who died at the young age of 19. The three connected cloisters, contrasting and somewhat in disrepair, are still charmingly dignified. The rooms of the Royal Palace are to be found around the last, the King's Cloister. It is here, also, that you will find the entrance to the Oriental Art Museum. Although, at first glance, it is seemingly incongruous with its surroundings, its presence here is, in actuality, totally logical. It was, after all, the Dominican missionaries who collected these exhibits, over the centuries, during their travels through the Far East. A similar such museum exists in Valladolid. *Open daily 10 a.m. to 1 p.m. and 4 p.m. to 8 p.m.. Entrance cloisters 100 ptas, museum 200 ptas (EUR 1.20).*

Before leaving Ávila, there is one more, very special place that should be visited, ideally at night. It's best to take a taxi to the **Cuatro Postes** (20), which is a short distance outside of the city walls on a hill overlooking the River Adaja. The monument in itself is curious. It consists of four Doric columns connected by cornices, each of which is decorated with the city's coats-of-arms. In the center stands a stone cross. Besides the obvious religious significance, it affords sweeping panoramic views of ancient Ávila encircled and protected by its comforting walls. Impressive enough by day, but absolutely breathtaking when illuminated by floodlights—which seem to propel the city out of the enveloping darkness of the night.

Barcelona:
An Introduction

Don't be deceived by modern, ultra-progressive Barcelona. Like most Spanish cities, it has a long and glorious history. Justifiably proud of its reputation for culture and art, Barcelona has combined her past glories with a keen focus on the future. This attitude transformed Barcelona into an outward looking and dynamic city. Since the death of Franco in the mid-1970s, the Catálan culture, suppressed over the centuries by the central government in Madrid, has once again flourished—a resurgence most apparent in the language. With Catálan becoming the speech of choice, Barcelona has something it has dearly wished for—a style and atmosphere not found elsewhere in Spain. This can be confusing to tourists who will, most certainly, leave with a misleading impression of the country should they visit only Barcelona.

In spite of its Phoenician origins, the city prospered under the Romans. The remains of portions of the walls constructed during that period are still visible in the Gothic Quarter, and extensive excavations of the Roman town are on display in the City History Museum. The period of Visigothic rule saw a decline in the city's importance. The Moors, in their subsequent sweep across the Iberian peninsula, were not able to keep control of this area for long. In 801, following its recapture by the Franks, the city was incorporated into Charlemagne's empire as the capital of the Earldom of Barcelona, the most dominant of the Catálan earldom's. During the 12th century it was united with the kingdom of Aragón. It was during this period that the city's flourishing maritime trade propelled it to prominence once again. Soon, Barcelona was regarded as one of the most important ports on the Mediterranean. For nearly 500 years, while the greater portion of Spain was still under Moorish rule, Barcelona and Catalunya remained Christian and, as a consequence, maintained open connections with the rest of Europe. These combined influences, naturally, endowed this region with an entirely different character from the rest of Spain.

With the wedding of Ferdinand and Isabella in 1469, the kingdoms of Castile and Aragón united to form the country of Spain as it exists today. The newly formed government, in the process of centralization, attempted to suppress the well-entrenched Catálan independent institutions. Throughout the next several centuries, indeed until Franco's death in 1975, Barcelona, struggling to maintain its unique identity, repeatedly tried to gain independence. Unsuccessful in these efforts, and having most often allied itself with the enemies of the central government, Barcelona reaped the wrath of the status quo in increased control and harsher restrictions. During the Spanish Civil War it served as the capital of the Republican forces, and was one of the last cities to succumb to Franco in 1939. The dictator sought revenge, tightening the central government's grip on the city as never before.

It wasn't until after his death that a new constitution, enacted in 1978, allowed the region limited autonomy. At this time the regional parliament was restored and Catálan was, once again, declared the official language. From that date the city and region have not looked back; the economy has boomed, the Catálans have held the balance of power in the central parliament, and the world became enamored with the charms of Barcelona when it hosted the 1992 Olympics.

GETTING THERE:

By air, Barcelona's El Prat airport receives international flights from major European cities, and flights directly and via Madrid from North America. Domestic flight service is available to and from the more important Spanish cities.

Trains depart from the modern Sants station or the recently renovated terminal of França. There are domestic services to Madrid via Zaragoza or Valencia; to Andalucia via Madrid or Valencia; to Cáceres via Madrid; to northwestern Spain via Zaragoza, Burgos and León; and to País Vasco via Zaragoza. International service is available to Paris, and Geneva via Avignon.

Buses are not recommended. Long distances are generally involved, and the trains offer more selection.

By car, Barcelona is about 390 miles from Madrid, which can be reached by taking the N-II for the duration or by traveling the A-2 autopista toll road to Zaragoza, and the N-II on from there. The A-7 autopista toll road links Barcelona to France in the north via Gerona, and Valencia in the south via Tarragona and Castellon.

GETTING AROUND BARCELONA:

By Subway: There are two different subway systems in Barcelona.

TMB *(METRO)*, ☎ 318-70-74 or 010, the regular subway, is signified by a white **M** in a red diamond. It has five color-coded lines that run in the city itself on Monday to Thursday between 5 a.m. to 11 p.m., Friday and Saturday and on the eve of Public Holidays from 5 a.m. to 1 a.m. and Sunday 6 a.m. to Midnight. Individual ticket 145 ptas (EUR .87).

FGC *(Ferrocarrils de la Generalitat de Catalunya)*, ☎ 205-15-15 or 010, has two lines in the city and four more that go to nearby towns and operate on Monday to Thursday from 5 a.m. to 11 p.m. and Saturday and Sunday from 5:55 a.m. to 00:39 a.m. Individual ticket 145 ptas (EUR .87).

By Bus and Nite Bus:

Daytime buses operate daily from 4:30 a.m. to 10 p.m., with an individual ticket costing 145 ptas (EUR .87), and Nite Buses run daily from 11 p.m. to 4 a.m., with an individual ticket costing 150 ptas (EUR .90).

Multi-trip Passes:

Many visitors to Barcelona will be staying for more than one day and, in that case, it makes economical and practical sense to purchase a multi-trip pass.

The **T1 travelcard** allows for 10 trips on any combination of the Metro, FGC or bus and costs 720 ptas (EUR 4.33).

The **T2 travelcard** allows for 10 trips on the Metro only, and costs 720 ptas (EUR 4.33).

The **T-Dia 1** is good for one day on any combination of Metro, FGC and bus, and costs 600 ptas (EUR 3.61).

The **T-Dia 2** is good for two days on any combination of Metro, FGC and bus, and costs 1,450 ptas (EUR 8.72).

The **T-Dia 3** is good for three days on any combination of Metro, FGC and bus, and costs 2,150 ptas (EUR 12.92).

To and From the Airport *(Aeropuerto):*

By Bus, ☎ 010: Airport/Plaça Catalunya/Airport departures every 15-minutes on Monday to Friday 5:30 a.m. to 10:15 p.m. and Saturday, Sunday and holidays 6 a.m. to 10:20 p.m., fare 465 ptas (EUR 2.80).

By Taxi: Approximately a 30-minute trip that should cost between 2 to 3,000 ptas (EUR 12.02 to 18.03), with an additional airport surcharge of 300 ptas (EUR 1.80).

By Train, ☎ 490-02-02: Airport/Plaça Catalunya/Airport departures every half hour, daily, from 6:08 a.m. to 10:08 p.m. A 20-minute trip that costs 305 ptas (EUR 1.83) on regular days and 350 ptas (EUR 2.10) on holidays.

PRACTICALITIES:

There are literally dozens of museums in Barcelona and, though opening hours may vary, it is safe to assume that most will be closed on Monday. It should be noted that entrance fees to museums here are generally much more expensive than elsewhere in Spain.

Barcelona's **Dialing Code** is 93. Tourist information is readily available in Barcelona. Permanent **Tourist Information Offices** are situated at convenient locations throughout the city: **Gran Vía Corts Cátalanes**, 658. ☎ 301-74-43 or fax 412-25-70, is open Monday to Friday 9 a.m. to 7 p.m. and Saturday 9 a.m. to 2 p.m. **Estació Barcelona Sants**, which offers information on the city of Barcelona only, is open during the summer daily from 8 a.m. to 8 p.m. and the rest of the year Monday to Friday 8 a.m. to 8 p.m. and Saturday, Sunday and holidays from 8 a.m. to 2 p.m. Closed Christmas and New Year's Day. **El Prat Airport Terminal A International arrivals**, ☎ 478-47-04, is open Monday to Saturday from 9:30 a.m. to 3 p.m. and **Terminal B National arrivals**, ☎ 478-05-65, is open Monday to Saturday 9:30 a.m. to 8 p.m. and Sunday and holidays from 9:30 a.m. to 3 p.m. **Barcelona Tourist Information Office**, Plaça de Catalunya, 17, basement. ☎ 906 30- 12-82, open daily, except Christmas and New Year's Day, 9 a.m. to 9 p.m. Located on the subterranean level of the Plaça de Catalunya, offers comprehensive information about places of interest in Barcelona, money exchange, hotels and shopping. The **Palau de la Virreina**, La Rambla, 99, ☎ 301-77-75, open Monday to Saturday 11 a.m. to 2 p.m. **Barcelona City Council**, Plaça Sant Jaume, 1, open Monday to Saturday 8 a.m. to 8 p.m. and Sunday 8 a.m. to 2 p.m. During the busy summer months there is an office at the **Estació de França**, open Monday to Saturday from 9:30 a.m. to 8 p.m., and Sunday from 9:30 a.m. to 3 p.m., as well as mobile booths in the main sightseeing areas between late June and late September from 10 a.m. to 8 p.m. and young information officers working in pairs in the same areas and at the same times. For more information ☎ 010 for Barcelona Information.

The **Barcelona Card**, on sale at the Barcelona information offices at Plaça Catalunya, Plaça Sant Jaume and Sants Railway Station, costs 2,500 ptas (EUR 15.03) for 24-hours, 3,000 ptas (EUR 18.03) for 48-hours and 3,500 ptas (EUR 21.04) for 72-hours and allows for a hefty range of discounts for transport, museums, entertainment, restaurants, leisure and shopping.

As you might have guessed, forward-looking Barcelona is well represented on the **World Wide Web**. The most informative—and multiligual sites, are www.barcelona-on-line.es, www.bcn.es and www.barcelonaturisme.com. Barcelona has a metropolitan **population** of over 3,000,000 and is the capital of the province of the same name, one of four belonging to the autonomous region of **Catalunya**.

Barcelona Bus Turístic, ☎ 304-31-35 or 010: This tour, which takes you past 17 of Barcelona's most interesting places, runs between the end of March and the beginning of January. The buses leave the Plaça de Catalunya between 9 a.m. and 9:30 p.m. and the journey, if uninterrupted, lasts for approximately two hours. You may, however, get on and off any number of times, perhaps for a closer inspection of the highlights. The next bus will be by in 15 to 30 minutes. As an added bonus, there is a tourist information officer on each bus. Tickets, which may be purchased on the bus, are valid for the day of purchase only, but the accompanying discounts for many of Barcelona's main attractions are valid until the end of the season. In 2000 the cost was 1,400 ptas (EUR 8.41) for a one-day ticket, or 1,800 ptas (EUR 10.82) for a ticket valid on two consecutive days.

ACCOMMODATION:

The **Hotel Claris *****, ☎ 487-62-62, fax 215-79-70, e-mail info@derby hotels or www.derbyhotels.es, Paris, 201, in the city center, is one of the most eclectic and unique hotels—not just in Barcelona but Spain as well. From its base as a neoclassical 19th-century palace it has been amazingly transformed into a highly unusual, but very attractive, hotel. It has sixty different types of rooms, all of which are furnished in a combination of classical 18th-century style, English and modern. Look, also, for the Japanese garden,museum on the 1st floor and the rooftop pool and terrace. $$$

The **Hotel Arts** *****, ☎ 221-10-00, fax 221-10-70 or www.hart.es, Marina, 19-21, is housed in a masive, and architecturally emblematic, tower next to the Olympic Marina. It is the first property that the famous Ritz-Carlton group opened in Europe and, as such, you can expect all the attendant luxuries expected of these hotels. All of the rooms are decorated in a style that combines the latest fashions, Gaudi patterns and high-tech facilities including Bang & Oluffson audiovisual equipment. It also offers tremendous views over the city and the Mediterranean. $$$

The **Husa Palace** ***** GL, ☎ 318-52-00 or fax 318-01-48, Gran Vía Corts Catálanes, 668, formerly known as the Ritz, is one of Barcelona's most esteemed hotels. In a prestigious location and with a marvellous façade, this hotel originally opened in 1919, but has recently undergone a complete renovation. It offers refined public rooms and huge, fully appointed and classically furnished bedrooms. It also features a fine restaurant, and private parking. $$$

The **Hotel Gran Derby** ****, ☎ 322-20-62, fax 419-68-20 or www.derby hotels.es, Loreto, 28, is located in a quiet area a short distance outside of the city center. It consists of 40 ultra contemporary duplexes and junior suites, all completely soundproofed, with background music, individual safes and many other interesting extras. There is also a coffee shop and bar, and garage parking. $$$

The **Hotel Derby** ****, ☎ 322-32-15, fax 410-08-62 or www.derby hotels.es, Loreto 21-25, is just across the road from its sister hotel. Larger, with 111 rooms, it is little less modern in style, but the sizeable rooms share all the same luxury features. $$$

The **Hotel Astoria** ***, ☎ 209-83-11, fax 202-30-08 or www.derby hotels.es, Paris, 203, just off the Av. Diagonal, a few minutes walk from the Plaça de Catalunya, is housed in a building typical of those in this eclectic area, and has been opened nearly fifty years. Now a part of the small Derby Collection of hotels, the 117 guest and public rooms share all the high standards of that group. Parking 50 yards away. $$

The **Hotel Balmes** ***, ☎ 451-19-14, fax 451-00-49 or www.derby hotels.es, Mallorca, 216, is a real "boutique" style hotel that belies its 3-star rating. Not only is the ambiance very modern, and the 100 rooms equipped to the highest standads, but it also features a restaurant, garden, bar and pool. $$

The **Hotel San Agustín** *(Sant Agustí)* ***, ☎ 318-16-58 or fax 317-29-28, Plaza San Agustín, 3, is tucked away in a fairly quiet plaza just two minutes away from the center of La Rambla and the Liceu Metro station. Each room has a private bath, air conditioning, satellite TV and a private safe. This is really good value for money. $

The **Hotel Mesón Castilla** **, ☎ 318-21-82 or fax 412-40-20, Valldoncella, 5, is a dignified hotel on the quiet Plaça Castilla, just a hundred yards or so from the Plaça de Catalunya. There are 56 rooms, each with private bath and TV. The public rooms are particulary elegant, and it has parking facilities. $

FOOD AND DRINK:

Catalán cuisine, by its nature more international in scope than Castillian, shows heavy French and Italian influences. *Fidueà,* similar to paella but made with noodles; *Pa amb tomáquet,* bread soaked with olive oil and spread with tomato; *Amanida catalana,* a salad with Catalán pork meat and sausages; *Bacallà a la Llauna,* salted cod baked in garlic, tomato, paprika and wine and *Perdius amb farcellets de col,* partridge with stuffed cabbage leaves are just a sprinkling of the favorite local dishes. There are also many ethnic eateries in Barcelona. Indian restaurants are common in the ancient *El Raval* quarter.

Many of the favored wines come from the *Penédes* region, in the south of Catalunya. This area is famous for its *cava,* a bubbly champagne-style drink, a fact that accounts for the popularity, in Barcelona, of *xampanyerias* champagne bars.

Restaurant can costa (Passeig Joan de Borbó, 70), in the traditional seafaring quarter of Barceloneta has for over 70 years dished up its specialties, *paellas, fideuà,* fish and shellfish. ☎ 221-59-03. $$

El Born (Passeig del Born, 26), in the old Ribera Quarter near the Santa María del Mar church, was once operated as a fish house but now specializes in fondues and raclettes. ☎ 319-53-33. $$

Gambrinus (Moll de la Fusta, 12), is easily found. Just look for the tremendous model prawn residing on its roof, which should give you a clue about what type of food to expect. Over 28 varieties of seafood tapa are served, as well as the customary *paella, fideuà* and grilled seafood. Only open for lunch, and closed on Wednesdays. ☎ 221-96-07. $

Restaurant La Fonda Escudellers (Carrer dels Escudellers 10), is located about three quarters of the way down La Rambla, and off to the left. This really popular restaurant features modern decor, excellent food and reasonable prices. ☎ 318-87-92. $

Restaurant Els Tres Bots (Carrer Sant Pau, 42), typical of those in the area, is found about 200 yards off La Rambla, near the Liceu Theatre. Don't expect anything fancy, and make your choice from a wide ranging menu chalked up on a huge board. ☎ 317-10-42. $

Pollo Rico (Carrer Sant Pau, 31), just past the Els Tres Bots, specializes in chicken roasted on a spit. Eat downstairs at the bar, if you can find a seat, or pay a little extra for a table upstairs. ☎ 441-31-84. $

Trip 8

Barcelona: La Rambla to the Old Port

This colorful walk explores the heart of Barcelona.

GETTING THERE:
PRACTICALITIES:
FOOD AND DRINK:
   See pages 75-79 for all of the above.

SUGGESTED TOUR:
   Numbers in parentheses correspond to numbers on the map.
   The large square known as **Plaça de Catalunya** (1) is the hub of the city, separating its old and new quarters. Surrounded by large buildings, it's a place where people come to sit on the grass banks or park benches, by the cooling rush of huge fountains, to relax and "people watch", a popular pastime here. And to feed the pigeons. In one corner there is a strange-looking obelisk and, on closer view, a statue of a nude woman and a fountain.
   Follow the crowds and cross the road into a wide, tree-lined median, separated from the buildings that flank it by two busy roads. The first glance, which takes in a variety of American-based fast-food joints to the right, reveals nothing particularly spectacular, but that will follow. Each of the world's major cities has its famous streets. Paris has the Champs-Élysées, New York has Broadway and Fifth Avenue, and London has Pall Mall—but none of them pack the character and excitement of *La Rambla (2). On this street, which forms an axis between the Plaça de Catalunya and the Port, it is not grand buildings that are the attraction, although there are some of those; it's not the proliferation of theaters, although it is home to a famous one; and it's not grand shops and department stores that draw visitors, though there are many of both. The magnetic force of La Rambla is other people, and that is exactly what makes it so different. Perhaps only Nevsky Prospekt in St. Petersburg, Russia, has an ambiance approaching the one found here but, of course, that lacks the special fla-

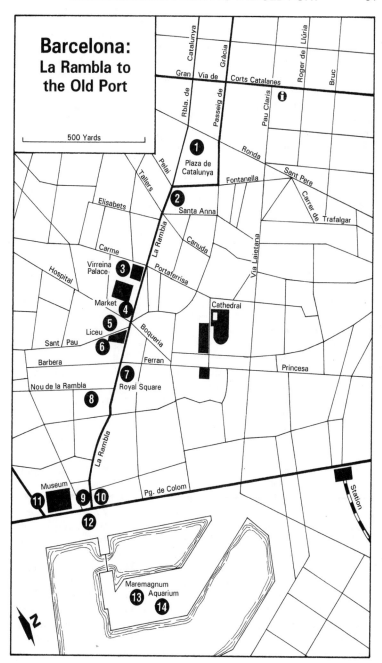

Barcelona:
La Rambla to
the Old Port

500 Yards

Catalunya
Gràcia
Roger de Llúria
Bruc
Gran Via de Corts Catalanes
Rbla. de
Passeig de
Pau Claris
Ronda
Pelai
Tallers
Plaza de
Catalunya
Fontanella
Sant Pere
Santa Anna
Elisabets
Carrer de Trafalgar
Canuda
La Rambla
Carme
Via Laietana
Hospital
Virreina
Palace
Portaferrisa
Market
Cathedral
Liceu
Boqueria
Sant / Pau
Barbera
Ferran
Princesa
Nou de la Rambla
Royal Square
La Rambla
Museum
Pg. de Colom
Station
Maremagnum
Aquarium

vor found only along the Mediterranean.

No matter the time of day, and often into the early hours of the morning on weekends, La Rambla is filled with people strolling its length, or simply sitting at the outdoor tables watching the world go by. This is as fascinating a sight for me now as it was 39 years ago, when as a wide-eyed sixteen-year-old I was traveling alone and visiting Spain for the first time. Sitting on this street, sipping a beer at 1:30 a.m., I fell inextricably under the enchantment of both Barcelona and the country. And, the freedoms that the people have won for the Catalan culture since that time make the atmosphere still more exhilarating. You might be deceived, though, as you enter the street. Rows of chairs line the sides and people, usually the elderly, will be reading or dozing there. If you are in need of a rest, beware; the seats aren't free. Once seated it won't be long before an eagle-eyed attendant will idle up and expect the fee.

Newspaper kiosks are everywhere, and as you press on you'll find stalls, on either side, selling all manner of birds, chickens and small animals such as cats and mice, not to mention aquariums full of fresh-water fish. By now you will certainly have become aware of the street performers, who delight in treating passers-by to all manner of artistic endeavors. You may come upon girls dancing, dogs jumping through hoops or men throwing them through the same, a children's ballet performance, jugglers, knife throwers, or even flame-throwing artistes. Name it, it's here. As you'll soon discover, all of the acts have one thing in common; each closes with a similar curtain call—the customary collection for the performers.

A fairly recent phenomenon are the "Living Statues", a unique way of earning money that's common throughout Spain. Impersonating a celebrity or famous historical personality, or posing in a re-enactment of a well-known event or local custom, and often wearing luminous paint on the face and hands, the "statue(s)" position themselves on a platform and strike a series of poses. Sometimes the pose will change with each contribution, and it is amusing to watch the surprise and delight on the faces of children who bring the statue "to life" by placing a few coins in the inevitable hat. The cleverest of these take advantage of their surroundings and dress accordingly, as you will see.

Nearby is the **Virreina Palace** *(Palau Virreina)* (3), ☎ 301-77-75, which is to the right and now used as a cultural center. *Open Tuesday to Saturday 11 a.m. to 8:30 p.m. and Sunday 11 a.m. to 2:30 p.m., entrance free.* It is also the home of a tourist office for information on Barcelona (see above for details). Here the birds and small animals give way to a series of flower stalls, selling every type of flower imaginable and painting La Rambla with their palette of vibrantly colorful blooms. Just past the palace there is another place, the type of which plays a vital role in the daily lives of people throughout the whole of Spain. Though supermarkets have made daily food shopping redundant throughout most of the U.S.A., that is not the case here. In Spain most women would not pass a day without a visit to their local *Mercado* where, instead of settling for the sterility of plastic-wrapped date-stamped meat, chicken or fish, they inspect a variety of fresh goods, make their selection and usually leave it to the vendor to gut the fish and cut the legs and head off a chicken under their careful supervision. Indeed such markets are common, and an integral part of each Spanish city. It is, however, the location of the **Boqueria Market** *(Mercat Boqueria)* (4), slap bang in the middle of one the most important streets of the second-largest city in Spain, that makes this different. It is architecturally impressive as well, and few will be able to resist a stroll through.

It's time for a short diversion. Two blocks down, turn right onto Hospital, and then take a left at the Plaça de Sant Agustí. Here you'll find two interesting, but very dissimilar, places. To the right is an unusual sight, a façade that appears to have been ripped open leaving three towers exposed. This is the old *Sant Agustí* church. Immediately opposite is one of the most colorful bars you are likely to find, and it doesn't even have a bar! The **Bodega Montse** (5) is as old-fashioned as you get; just one room with a couple of tables surrounded by a large number of the establishment's venerable barrels. In agreeable weather you may choose to have a seat at one of the rickety outdoor tables, savor a glass of wine, and ponder how the façade opposite came to be so intriguing.

Back on your way, turn left again at the bottom of Arc de Sant Agustí and follow Sant Pau back to the La Rambla. It is here that the street begins another transformation. Now, outdoor bars and restaurants separate the newspaper kiosks, providing a fine place to sit and drink in all that surrounds you. To the right is the famous **Liceu Opera House** *(Gran Teatre del Liceu)* (6), www.licieubarcelona.com, considered the most decorative and important in the world when it was built in 1847. It has, however, had a propensity for disaster, having burned to the ground first in 1861 and again on January 31st 1994. The site takes up nearly a half a city block, and numerous commercial organizations combined resources to rebuild it yet again. And their efforts were well rewarded when, on October 7th, 1999, 2,367 luminaries were invited to watch *Turandot* being performed in yet another grand opening. *It is possible, daily, to take an unguided tour of the Licieu between 9:45 a.m. and 11 a.m. (With the last admission being 10:15 a.m.) for 500 ptas (EUR 3.01). Guided tours (in Catalan, Spanish, English or French), arranged in advance* ☎ *485-99-00, fax 485-99-18 or e-mail visites@licieubarcelona.com, can be taken during the same hours but only from Friday to Monday, for 800 ptas (EUR 4.81).* Next door is the *Hotel Oriente,* built in 1882 and a stylish building in its own right.

Cross the street now, and pass through the narrow Carrer, the Catálan word for *Calle,* named Colón into a gracefully symmetrical five-storied, porticoed plaza that was built as a result of an entry in a competition held in 1848. The **Royal Square** *(Plaça Reial)* (7) is adorned by a central fountain and iron lanterns, both designed by Gaudí, and no less than 35 palm trees. These days, however, the charm of the surroundings is not always matched by that of those who hang out here. Meanwhile, back across the road, just down the Nou de la Rambla, is another example of the work of the great eccentric. At numbers 3 to 5 is the *Palau Güell* which was originally constructed as a home for the Count Güell, and now houses the **Performing Arts Museum and Theater Institute** *(Museu de les Arts de l'Espectacle Institut del Teatre)* (8). It is the research, documentation and distribution centre for the Theater Institute, and houses exhibits relating to the world of performing arts as well as a library.

Continuing down La Rambla, its chameleon character shows itself again. It widens out some, allowing street artists an arena in which to pursue their trade. This is a good place to get your image permanently, and perhaps a little irrelevantly, transposed to paper. Deceptive images, too, impact the street's character by here. Those beautiful women you see strolling imperiously, and usually a little too over—well, often under—dressed may not be what they seem. Those passing near enough to become privy to their conversation will get a deep-throated clue that this is a particularly favorite haunt for transvestites. The sexuality of the other women, similarly dressed, who frequent this section of La Rambla will not be a matter of doubt. One of the city's "Red Light" areas is centered around the narrow, and rather seedy, collection of streets to the right, and many of their more conspicuous occupants prefer to solicit here for prospective clients. Move a little farther on and the character changes yet again. This time, positioned appropriately across from the modern *Centre d'Art Santa Monica,* are double lines of stalls selling a wide variety of handicrafts.

As you come to the end of La Rambla, the 150-foot-tall iron column of the **Columbus Monument** *(Monument a Colón)* (9), ☎ 302- 52-24, built for the 1888 World Exhibition, dominates the skyline. This serves to memorialize and to celebrate his first voyage to the Americas, from which he was welcomed home by the Catholic Monarchs in, of course, Barcelona. An elevator transports visitors to an observation platform situated inside a globe that supports a statue of the explorer. The views afforded makes this a worthwhile stop on your tour. *It is open between June 1st and September 24th, daily from 9 a.m. to 8:30 p.m.; between April 1st to May 31st on Monday to Friday 10 a.m. to 2 p.m. and 3:30 p.m. to 7:30 p.m.; and between September 25th and March 30th on Monday to Friday from 10 a.m. to 2 p.m. and 3:30 p.m. to 6:30 p.m. and Saturday, Sunday and holidays 10 a.m. to 6:30 p.m. Entrance 250 ptas (EUR 1.50).* As you approach the monument, if you are lucky, you may have an opportunity to visit with the man himself. Well, at least a passable re-incarnation by a very commercially minded "human statue."

To either side are two museums of an entirely different caste. The **Wax Museum** *(Museu de Cera)* (10), ☎ 317-26-49 or fax 318-53-46, is in an interesting building housing 360 reproductions enhanced by audio and visual effects. *In summer it is open daily from 10 a.m. to 8 p.m. and, during the other seasons, Monday to Friday between 10 a.m. and 1:30 p.m. and 4 p.m. to 7:30 p.m., and on Saturday, Sunday and holidays from 10 a.m. to 1:30 p.m. and 4:30-8 p.m.* On the other, right hand side, you will see, in the

Royal Shipyards and Maritime Museum *(Reial Drassanes / Museu Marítim)* (11), ☎ 342-99-20 or fax 318-78-76, the most complete, and important, medieval dockyards still in existence. The seven bays closest to La Rambla were originally constructed in the 14th century, with the others added in the 17th century. The exhibits include a life-size replica of the galley used by Juan de Austria. *The museum is open Monday to Sunday from 10 a.m. to 7 p.m.; entrance 800 ptas (EUR 4.81), free on the first Sunday of each month.*

Seeing all of these boats may have you daydreaming about life at sea. Fortunately, just across the road, on the edge of the harbor, you have a choice of two short voyages. The **Golondrinas** (12), ☎ 442-31-06, will take you from the **Old Port** *(Port Vell)* to the **Breakwater** *(l'Escollera)*, at the end of the harbor, *fare 440 ptas (EUR 2.64)*. Alternatively, the **Escua** (12) offers a much longer voyage between the **Old Port** and the **Olympic Port** *(Port Olimpic)*, well past the harbor limits, *fare 1,250 ptas (EUR 7.51)*.

On the left, a wooden bridge passes over the water to the middle of the harbor and the new complex of **Maremagnum** (13), www.mare magnum.es, on the *Moll Espanya*. Basically, this contains a modern American-style shopping mall and food court, a multi-movie house and the recently constructed **Aquarium** *(L'Aquarium)* (14), ☎ 221-74-74, fax 221-92-26, e-mail info@aquariumbcn.com or www.aquariumbcn.com. The latter is one of the largest in Europe and features an underwater tunnel where you may observe sharks swimming around you. *Open Monday to Friday 9:30 a.m. to 9 p.m., weekends and June and September it closes at 10:30 p.m. and in July and August it closes at 11 p.m. Entrance 1,450 ptas (EUR 8.72) adults and 950 ptas (EUR 5.71) children.* Look for the IMAX, featuring a seven-story-high OMNIMAX screen that, utilizing IMAX 3D technology, produces the most realistic sensations ever seen in a movie.

End this tour with a walk along the Moll back to the city, and a stroll along the palm-tree-lined promenade to the Columbus Monument to return along La Rambla to the Plaça de Catalunya.

Trip 9

Barcelona:
To the Gothic Quarter

This walk leads you through some of the oldest parts of the ancient city.

GETTING THERE:
PRACTICALITIES:
FOOD AND DRINK:
See pages 75-79 for all of the above.

SUGGESTED TOUR:
Numbers in parentheses correspond to numbers on the map.

Begin, again, at the **Plaça de Catalunya** (1), but this time walk away from La Rambla around the El Cortes Ingles department store to the smaller Plaça Urquinaona, and note the strangely-shaped apartment buildings there. Continue along the Ronda de Sant Pere where, until the end is reached, the modern apartments and shops are only interrupted by a small monument to Casanova half-way along. It is a surprise, though, to see the archway of the **Arc del Triomf** (2) which, although not as impressive as its Parisian counterpart, is still imposing. This is the beginning of the attractive palm-tree-lined Passeig de Lluís Companys, which is enhanced by graceful lanterns and, along the side, the **Palace of Justice** *(Palau Justíca).* Attention will inevitably be drawn to the highly unusual structure at the end. Resembling a fortress, with red brick crenellations, three square gold-topped towers and a glass room in another octagonal tower, this was built by Domenech i Montaner as the café/restaurant for the 1888 Universal Exhibition. It is now the **Zoology Museum** *(Museu de Zoologia)* (3), ☎ 319-69-50 or fax 310-49-99, and houses entomological, malacological, vertebrate and other zoological specimens. *It is open Tuesday to Sunday from 10 a.m. to 2 p.m.*

This museum is just inside one of the main gates to the **Parc de la Ciutadella** (4), which comes about its name, "Park of the Citadel", because it is on the site of the fort built by Felipe V in the early 18th century. That was demolished to make way for the 1888 Universal Exhibition. Only a few of the original structures still survive, the most important of which are the Governor's Palace and Arsenal, now the residence of the Catálan

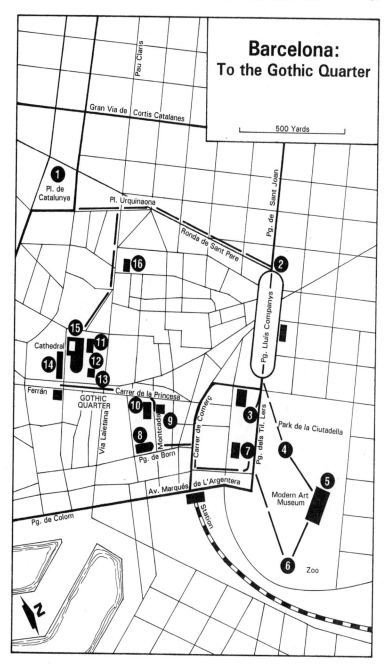

Parliament and Museum of Modern Art. Although not as centrally located as the Retiro Park in Madrid, this serves the same social purpose for the citizens of Barcelona. It is a wonderful place to just wander around through the gardens, with their eclectic collection of old and new statues, fountains and trees whose names, conveniently, are explained in English.

Once through the gate, head to the left towards the ornamental lake that has, as a backdrop, a huge monumental archway topped by a statue. The walk between this and the lake ahead takes you past a life-size model of a Mammoth which, when combined with the surrounding noise and odor will give you a clue to what else is found in the park. Next, you will come upon the Plaça d'Armes in front of the old Governor's Palace, which now serves as the **Museum of Modern Art** *(Museu d'Art Modern)* (5), ☎ 319-57-28 or fax 319-59-65. It has a collection of mainly Catálan paintings, engravings, drawings, furniture, and sculptures from the 19th and 20th centuries. *Hours are Tuesday to Saturday 10 a.m. to 7 p.m. and Sunday 10 a.m. to 2:30 p.m. Entrance 400 ptas (EUR 2.40).*

Just beyond this the suspicions aroused by the noise and odor will be confirmed. Here is the entrance to the **Zoo** *(Parc Zoologic)* (6). As zoos go this is a quite a good one, with over 400 species and 7,000 animals. There is one creature, though, who makes it exceptional; and he knows it! **Snowflake** *(Copito de Nieve)* is the only albino gorilla in captivity in the entire world and, living with his two girl friends, has been entertaining his guests for over thirty years. Cut straight across the park from the main entrance to the zoo and, just before the exit, there is another museum that is worth a visit. The **Geology Museum** *(Museu de Geologia)* (7), ☎ 319-68-95 or fax 319-93-12, is one of the oldest in the city, founded in 1878 and opened in 1882. *Its exhibits, large collections of minerals, rocks and fossils, may be viewed Tuesday through Sunday between 10 a.m. to 2 p.m.*

The Avinguda Marquès de l'Argentera leads away from the park. On its left is the traditional façade of the wonderfully renovated train station, *Estació França* and, across from there, is the Carrer del Comerç. Following along to the right is a structure that once housed a traditional local food market, the *Mercado de Born,* but that has now been reborn as an exhibition center. The Passeig del Born, opposite it, is in the heart of the ancient quarter of *Ribera* and, as will become quickly evident, has a somewhat mixed character. Residing incongruously alongside tenement buildings lining the rather seedy alleyways are fashionably trendy bars and restaurants, palaces and, at the end, a church considered to be one of the most beautiful examples of Gothic architecture in the region. From the exterior, the *Iglesia Santa María del Mar** (8) may not look so special, but don't be fooled. Built between 1329 and 1383 to replace its 10th century predecessor, it has tall, very elegant supporting columns and a pleasing lack of ornateness.

Retrace your steps for twenty yards or so and turn left into a narrow, pedestrian passageway that really is a street with a difference. Surrounded by what could be described as slums, the *Carrer Montcada,* a street filled with palaces, is entirely out of character with its near neighbors. These days the palaces have been transformed into a varied collection of museums and art galleries which, combined with the small speciality shops and some characterful bars, make this a street not to be missed. Two of these palaces, the Berenguer Aguilar and Barón de Castellet house one of the city's most visited museums, the *Picasso Museum *(Museu Picasso)* (9), ☎ 319-63-10 or fax 315-01-02. Throughout their wonderfully renovated rooms are works which give testimony to the artist's genius, representative mainly of his early period in Barcelona and Paris. Although these are displayed in chronological order, to appreciate them to the fullest it is recommended that a catalog be purchased in the bookshop. *This is open Tuesday to Saturday and holidays from 10 a.m. to 8 p.m. and on Sundays from 10 a.m. to 3 p.m. Entrance 500 ptas (EUR 3.01), free on the first Sunday of each month.*

Just across the street, at number 12, in the Gothic Marquès de Lló palace is the **Clothing and Textile Museum** *(Museu Tèxtil I d'Indumentàia)* (10), ☎ 319-76-03 or fax 315-01-02. It has a collection of fabrics from the 4th to 20th centuries, and a particularly good period-costume display. *It is open Tuesday to Saturday from 10 a.m. to 5 p.m. and Sundays and holidays 10 a.m. to 2 p.m. Entrance 300 ptas (EUR 1.80), free on the first Sunday of each month.* Before leaving this street, be sure to pop into the *El Xampanyet* bar at number 22 where, besides a tasty collection of tapas, a refreshingly light, sparkling and low alcohol—only 10%—champagne-like *cava* is served.

To reach the **Gothic Quarter** *(Barri Gòtic)*, the oldest part of the city, turn left onto Carrer de la Princesa and, at the end, cut diagonally across the Via Laietana. After passing the old walls in the Plaça de Ramón Berenguer El Gran, take the narrow Tapinería which angles off to the left and then turn again on the left into the even narrower Baixada de la Canonja. This will lead you to the main entrance of the Cathedral in the Plaça de la Seu. Forego that leg of the tour for a moment and, instead, make an immediate left onto the Carrer del Comtes de Barcelona which follows the walls of the Cathedral and other Gothic buildings to the **Frederic Marès Museum** *(Museu Frederic Marès)* (11), ☎ 310-58-00 or fax 319-41-16. As the name implies, this houses the collection of the sculptor Frederic Marès, as well as a variety of religious objects, dating primarily from pre-Roman times to the 20th century. Be sure to investigate the patio which, with its tiny fountain, fishpond and small cafeteria is an absolute delight. *The museum is open Tuesday to Saturday from 10 a.m. to 5 p.m. and on Sunday and holidays from 10 a.m. to 2 p.m. Entrance 300 ptas (EUR 1.80).*

Leaving here, take the first left, Baixada de Santa Clara, to the really impressive **King's Square** *(Plaça del Rei)* (12). It is rather small, but totally prepossessing, surrounded by the most beautiful collection of Gothic architecture in the city. The façade of the former royal palace is topped by a most unusual five-level tower block, that could be considered a 16th-century predecessor to the modern skyscraper. Some of these buildings function as the **City History Museum** *(Museu d'Història de la Ciutat)* (13), ☎ 315-11-11 or fax 315-09-57, which may be accessed by three different entrances on the square. Most interesting are subterranean excavations of the old Roman city. These are well exposed and interconnected, with a comprehensive description in English. *It is open Tuesday to Saturday from 10 a.m. to 8 p.m. and Sunday from 10 a.m. to 2 p.m. Entrance 500 ptas (EUR 3.01), free on the first Sunday of each month.*

Leave the square by way of Veguer and turn right onto Llibreteria, ending in the Plaça de Sant Jaume. To the left is the Town Hall, but it is the **Generalitat Palace** *(Palau de la Generalitat)* (14) opposite that is of greater importance. Construction began during the reign of Jaume II in the 15th century, but it was not completed until two centuries later. This is now the site, as it has been whenever political expediencies have permitted, of the autonomous government of Catalunya. The patio staircase, Chapel of Sant Jordi (Saint George, patron saint of Catalunya) and the Orange Tree patio are well worth seeing, but this may present some difficulty as it is open to visitors only on April 23, St. George's day. The Carrer del Bisbe Irurita, is easily recognizable. A modern, yet Gothic style, covered bridge links the Generalitat to this, the old Canon's residence, which is now home of the Provincial Council President.

Bisbe eventually leads to a small entrance into the Cathedral **Cloister** *(Claustro)* and, as an example of its genre, this cloister has more character than most. Around the perimeter, as expected, are numerous chapels but it is the center, with a pleasant little garden partially occupied by geese and their pond, that adds to its charm. In one of the corners nearest to the Cathedral entrance is a most unusual drinking fountain, topped by a very small, but absolutely enchanting, equestrian statue of Sant Jordi. *The cloister is open daily from 8:45 a.m. to 1:30 p.m. and from 4 p.m. to 7 p.m.*

There has been a ***Cathedral** *(Catedral)* (15) on this site since the 9th century. When the original structure was destroyed in 985, a Romanesque Cathedral, consecrated in 1058, replaced it. Construction on the present Cathedral began at the end of the 13th century, though the main façade was not completed until over 600 years later. Not overly large, its Gothic style, particularly the height and elegance of the colonnades, is similar to that of the *Santa María de la Mar*. This one, however, is considerably more ornate inside. The stained-glass windows are impressive and the choir, where Carlos V met with the Chapter of the Golden Fleece and King Henry VIII of England in 1519, can be visited for a small fee. Beneath the main altar is the sepulcher, carved in 1327, in which rest the remains of the patron saint of the city, Santa Eulalia. *Opening hours are 8 a.m. to 1:30 p.m and 4 p.m. to 7:30 p.m.*

Exit by way of the main door and cross the Plaça de la Seu into the Calle Dr. Joaquim Pou, which leads up into the Via Laietana. Within a couple of hundred yards you will come to a rather inauspicious side street, Sant Pere Més Alt, in which hides a really extreme example of modernist architecture, the **Music Palace** *(Palau de la Música)* (16). Though anyone could be excused for attributing this piece to Gaudí it, in fact, was built by Lluis Domènech I Montaner in 1908. From this point, it is just a short walk back up Via Laietana to the Plaça Urquinaona and back into the Plaça de Catalunya.

Trip 10

Barcelona: North to the Sagrada Família

The name of this, the modern quarter of the city, *L'Eixample* (The Extension), refers to the expansion away from the older part of town between Plaça de Catalunya and the Port during the second half of the 19th century. On this walk don't expect to see much of historical importance; instead expect to be enthralled by the imagination of the modernist architects of that period; especially, of course, Antoni Gaudí.

GETTING THERE:
PRACTICALITIES:
FOOD AND DRINK:
See pages 75-79 for all of the above.

SUGGESTED TOUR:
Numbers in parentheses correspond to numbers on the map.
Start again from the **Plaça de Catalunya** (1). This time head directly away from La Rambla along the left-hand side of the Passeig de Gràcia. The majority of the buildings are occupied by fashionable shops, hotels, restaurants, etc. but, after going two blocks, at number 35 on the corner of Consell de Cent, the first of the unusual houses is found. This one, the **Casa Lleó I Morera** (2), dating from 1905 and done in a floral style, is the work of Lluis Domènech I Montaner. This is, however, merely a precursor of what is to come. At number 41 is the **Casa Amatller** (3), created by Puig I Cadafalch in 1900, and at number 43 is the **Casa Batlló** (4). This dates from 1904, and considering the weird designs, trademark ceramic-tiled roof and mosaic façade, it doesn't take a genius to come to the conclusion that this is a Gaudí eccentricity. Just around the corner, at 255 Aragó, is the **Fundació Tàpies** (5), ☎ 487-03-15 or fax 487-00-09, a starkly modern building topped with decorative coils of wire no less, which has the most complete collection of works by the Catálan artist. *It is open Tuesday to Sunday from 11 a.m. to 8 p.m., closed August. Entrance 500 ptas (EUR 3.01).*

For those with such interests, the **Egyptian Museum** *(Museu Egipci)* (6), ☎ 488-01-88 or fax 487-01-88, just a hundred yards away at Rambla de Catalunya, 57, exhibits one of the best collections of its kind in Spain. *It is*

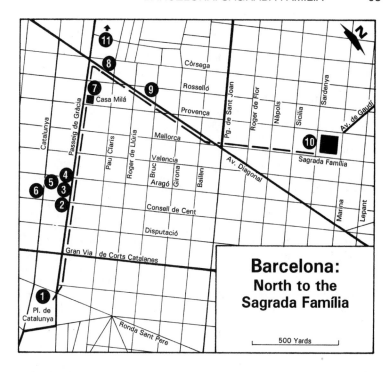

Barcelona:
North to the
Sagrada Família

500 Yards

open Monday to Saturday from 10 a.m. to 2 p.m. and from 4 p.m. to 8 p.m. and Sunday 10 a.m. to 2 p.m. Entrance 700 ptas (EUR 4.21).

The next, last and largest of these intriguing houses is at Passeig de Gràcia, 92, on the opposite side of the street. The pleasing, curvaceous, wrought-iron-balcony covered, façade of the ***Casa Milá** (7), also known as the La Pedrera, is visible from some distance away. It was built in 1905 and has been classified by UNESCO as a World Heritage Site. Its interior is just as ornate but you don't have to take my word for it. This is one of Gaudí's creations that may be visited. From Tuesday to Saturday 30-minute guided tours begin on the hour between 10 a.m. to 1 p.m.

An Egyptian Needle sits in the middle of the Plaça de Joan Carlos I, at the junction of Passeig de Gràcia and the Avinguda Diagonal. Turn right here and the next building of interest will be immediately upon you. Yet another modernist building, this one by Puig I Cadafalch, the **Casa Baró de Quadras** (8) is home to the **Music Museum** (Museu de la Música), ☎ 416-11-57 or fax 217- 11-06. It has instruments from the 16th to the 20th centuries, mostly Spanish and European in origin, and its guitar collection is considered one of the world's finest. Visit Tuesday to Sunday from 10 a.m. to 2 p.m and on Wednesday from 10 a.m. to 2 p.m. and 5 p.m. to 8 p.m. Entrance 300 ptas (EUR 1.80), free on the first Sunday of each month.

A little farther down, this time on the left, is a fort-like structure with two round towers and gargoyles that peer out from their stations on a wooden roof overhanging the elaborate brickwork. On closer inspection it can be identified as the **Casa Terrades** (9), otherwise known as the *Casa de les Punxes*, another invention of Puig I Cadafalch. The ensuing stretch of the Avinguda Diagonal, which follows down to the statue that dominates the Plaça Mossèn Jacint Verdaguer, is of virtually no interest. Once in the plaza, however, the famous spires of Gaudí's greatest landmark, the symbol of Barcelona, come into view, though they are still a full five blocks in the distance on Carrer Mallorca.

The ***Sagrada Família** (10), ☎ 455-02-47 or fax 435-83-35, is, put quite simply, an inimitable monument to the weirdly fertile imagination of its creator, and no number of words can adequately describe its complexity. Construction, which began in 1883, halted upon his death. The models and drawings Gaudí left behind (on display today in the small museum) show exactly how he envisioned the finished project though, believe it or not, it is considerably more intricate than what you will see today. Unfortunately, no plans detailing how he intended to accomplish this end result have been found, and it is ironic that the architectural genius who lies buried in a crypt beneath this work may have taken the secrets necessary to bring the dream to fruition to the grave. Over the past several decades other architects, following his style, have attempted to continue the project but much, much more work remains to be done and, inside, it is not much more than a shell. It is possible, though, either to climb, or to be raised by elevator, to the towers to get different perspectives of the surrounding city. *It opens daily, throughout the year at 9 a.m., and closes during November to February at 6 p.m., during March, September and October at 7 p.m., in April to August 8 p.m. Entrance 800 ptas (EUR 4.81).* Two small parks flank this monument, the *Plaça de la Sagrada Família* to the left, and the rather more pleasant *Plaça de Gaudí* on the other side. These provide ideal places to sit and take in this incredible phenomenon.

Having made such frequent references herein to Gaudí, it would be remiss to end this tour without taking in the **Güell Park** *(Parc Güell)* (11). But there is one problem—it is not the easiest place to reach. A taxi is the best option, and not that expensive, but the more frugal will take the Metro Blue Number 5 line from Sagrada Família to Diagonal and then the Green Number 3 line to Lesseps, from where it is a short uphill walk to the park. This, with its lovely views back over the city, was once intended to be an English-style garden. The house, originally built by Francesc Berenguer, was subsequently purchased by Gaudí who resided here between 1906 and 1925. Today it is a small museum that exhibits his personal effects, furniture, and drawings which, like his inventions, are rather extraordinary. *It is open daily, except Saturday, from 10 a.m. to 2 p.m. and from 4 p.m. to 7 p.m. Entrance 200 ptas (EUR 1.20). Closing time is an hour earlier from October to March.* The English garden has long since been forgotten and, in the park Gaudí allowed his already vivid imagination to run wild. A stroll through it is like wandering through a child's fantasy land of irrelevance.

To complete the tour retrace the route to the Lesseps Metro station, and take a train directly to the Plaça de Catalunya station.

Barcelona: Montjuïc, the Olympic Stadium, and the Spanish Village

A more contemporary side of Barcelona is probed on this enjoyable little excursion.

GETTING THERE:
PRACTICALITIES:
FOOD AND DRINK:
See pages 75-79 for all of the above.

SUGGESTED TOUR:
Numbers in parentheses correspond to numbers on the map.

Starting, as with the other tours, in the **Plaça de Catalunya** (1) this tour proceeds down **La Rambla** (2) to the port, and on to the aerial cable-car station atop the rather rickety-looking **Torre Jaume I** (3), on the Moll Barcelona. This structure, reminiscent of the Eiffel Tower, could use a good lick of paint. That aside, the views from the top, and from the cable car over to Montjuïc, are truly spectacular. *It operates on a 15-minute frequency between midday and 5:45 p.m. on Tuesday to Sunday, closing thirty minutes later on Saturday, and costs 1,200 ptas (EUR 7.21) for a ticket.* Immediately behind the Torre Jaume I is the futuristic **World Trade Center**, designed by the famed architectural compnay Pei, Coob, Fred & Partners. Once back on land stop for a moment to admire the views, then cross through the small park, *Jardins de Miramar,* to the road on the right. At the *Plaça de Carles Ibañez,* take the left fork along the Avinguda de Miramar. The surrounding area is rather pleasant parkland with numerous trees and bushes that help keep it reasonably cool, and it compensates somewhat for the fact that this leg of the journey is an uphill slog. Soon enough, though, the gardens of the **Montjuïc Amusement Park** *(Parc Atraccions Montjuïc)* (4) appear to the left with the entrance being just around the corner. If you are planning a visit, be sure to take note of the unusual opening hours. *All year it's open on Saturday from 6 p.m. to 1 a.m. and*

Sunday and holidays from midday to 11:15 p.m. It is open Tuesday to Friday from 6 p.m. to midnight between the middle of May and the middle of September.

Just a few lengths farther on is the swimming pool where, opinion has it, the most dramatic photograph of the 1992 Olympics was taken. Few will forget the spectacular image of a diver in mid-air, with a panoramic view of the city as the background. Now this pool, in spite of its unparalleled vista, is closed and a little rundown. Perhaps the authorities don't realize what a splash they could make if they pooled their resources to re-open it.

Immediately across the road are two innovative forms of transport, going in opposite directions. The **Montjuïc Cable Car** *(Teleférico de Montjuïc)* (5), ☎ 443-08-59 or 010, *operating Monday to Sunday from 11 a.m. to 2:45 p.m. and 4 p.m. to 7:30 p.m. with a fare of 400 ptas (EUR 2.40),* rises up to the **Montjuïc Castle** *(Castell de Montjuïc)* where, in addition to the ruins and marvelous views, the **Military Museum** *(Museu Militar)* (6), ☎ or fax 329-86-13. This has an usual collection of weapons, lead soldiers, maps, etc., *and is open Tuesday to Sunday and holidays from 9:30 a.m. to 7:30 p.m. Entrance 200 ptas (EUR 1.20).* For the moment ignore the funicular, just opposite the cable car, and continue on up the street, where the futuristic building on the right announces, appropriately, that it is the home of the **Joan Miró Foundation** *(Fundació Joan Miró)* (7), ☎ 329-19-08, fax 329- 86-09, e-mail fjmiro@bcn.fjmiro.es or www.bcn.fjmiro.es. The structure itself, the work of Jose Luis Serp, is worth a visit, but the highlight here is the permanent exhibition of paintings, drawings, sculptures, tapestries and graphics of Joan Miró. It also serves as the center for Contemporary Art. *Open Tuesday to Saturday July to September 10 a.m. to 8 p.m., closing an hour earlier the rest of the year, all year Thursdays until 9:30 p.m., and Sunday and holidays from 10 a.m. to 2:30 p.m. Entrance 800 ptas (EUR 4.81).*

A bit farther up the hill, and on its summit, is the massive **Olympic Stadium** *(Estadi Olímpic)* (8). Although general admission to this impressive stadium is not allowed, you may visit at the mid-level. There is even a small café where you can sip a beer, admire the stadium and dream of what it would like to receive a gold medal in front of over 80,000 cheering spectators. Behind the covered stand there are other, futuristic, attractions. The huge, domed building, **Palau Sant Jordi** (9), is of a Japanese design which has no supporting columns for the roof. Excellent acoustics make it well suited for its current use as a concert hall, with a seating capacity of 17,000. At the end of the same plaza stands the **Torre de Calatrava** (10), a communications tower with an unusual design that became one of the symbols of the 1992 Olympic Games.

Those wishing to investigate, in greater detail, the intricacies of the 1992 games may inspect, below the stadium itself, the **Barcelona Olympic Foundation and Olympic Gallery** *(Fundació Barcelona Olímpica: Galería Olímpica)* (11), ☎ 426-06- 60 or fax 426-92-00. Here visitors find a perma-

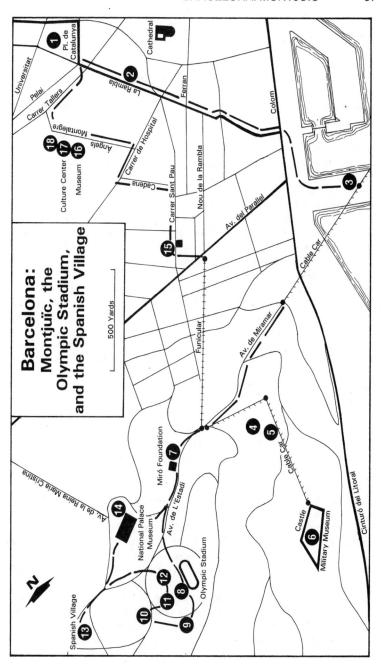

Barcelona:
Montjuïc, the
Olympic Stadium,
and the Spanish Village

N

500 Yards

nent exhibition of the 1992 25th Olympiad and the 9th Paralympic Games, which are enhanced by some interesting multimedia shows. *It is open Tuesday to Saturday from 10 a.m. to 2 p.m. and 4 p.m. to 8 p.m., and on Sunday from 10 a.m. to 2 p.m. Entrance 375 ptas (EUR 2.25).* Before closing the Olympic chapter venture back out into the main road, now suitably named Avinguda Estadi. A couple of hundred yards to the left are more swimming pools, the **Piscines Bernat Picornell** (12), and these (both indoor and outdoor) are open to the public.

Next, for a total change of scenery, cross the road and take the steps down, by the side of a huge ravine and pond. Follow the signs around, passing the riding school along the way, until you come to the Avgda. Marquès de Comillas and the **Spanish Village** *(Poble Espanyol)* (13), ☎ 508-63-30, fax 508-63-33, e-mail info@poble-espanyol.com or www.poble-espanyol.com. This curiously combines many, many different elements. As with several attractions in Montjuïc, it was built for the International Exhibition of 1929, and this with the intent of combining the varied architectural styles found throughout Spain into one "Village". It must have been successful, because walking around this amalgamation of 177 buildings does, indeed, seem like walking throughout Spain itself. Not relegated to being simply museum pieces, the buildings themselves house regional craft and tourist shops and, of course, many restaurants specializing in the various types of regional cuisine. The main entrance, a replica of the Portal de San Vicente in Ávila, has been converted into a popular night club. *Needless to say this, too, has curious opening hours: Monday from 9 a.m. to 8 p.m.; Tuesday to Thursday, the day before public holidays and public holidays from 9 a.m. to 2 a.m.; Saturday from 9 a.m. to 4 a.m. and Sunday from 9 a.m. to midnight. Standard admission, which includes the Barcelona audiovisual show, is 950 pts (EUR 5.71). Entrance is free after 9 p.m.*

Exit by the main gate and walk down the hill until you reach the first set of steps to the right. These, in fact, don't look very enticing and are uphill as well. Persevere, for at the top is a pathway from which an escalator will glide you up to the huge and gracious **National Palace** *(Palau Nacional)* (14) which, with its dome styled after the U.S. Capitol, served as the Spanish Pavilion during the International Exhibition of 1929. It is now home to what is considered to be one of the finest collections of Romanesque art and architecture in the world. Early in this century many of the architectural treasures of Catalunya were being looted. It was decided to move as many of these as possible to the *Museum of Catalán Art (Museu Nacional d'Art de Catalunya (MNAC)),* ☎ 423-71-99 or fax 325-57-73, which has been renovated—to mixed reviews—by the Italian Gae Aulenti, who also oversaw the conversion of the railroad station, Gare d'Orsay, in Paris to a modern museum. Look here for works of art by the likes of El Greco and Zurbarán. *It is open Tuesday to Saturday from 10 a.m. to 7 p.m. and Sunday 10 a.m. to 2:30 p.m. Entrance 500 ptas (EUR 3.01).* Just outside the front of the palace is a terrace with such a spectacular, and varied, view that its attraction is magnetic.

Rows of steps cascade down towards the two Italian-style towers, the great monument and the gushing fountains of the Plaça d'Espanya. In the background are the mountains of *Tibidabo* and the dramatic television communications facilities of *Torre de Collserola*. On weekend evenings there are incredible illuminations here, and you may wish to descend and explore some of the attractive buildings before ending the tour back at the Plaça de Catalunya.

Another unusual attraction in this immediate area is a very spectacular exhibition of horse-riding skills by the Mounted Unit of the Municipal Police. *This lasts 50-minutes and was held only at 9 p.m. on Fridays between June 25th and September 24th (in 1999) at the Pista d'hípica de la Foixarda, Avda. Montanyans, 1, and costs 800 ptas (EUR 4.81).*

Most visitors will prefer, instead, to walk around the palace and taking either the steps or escalator up, past the statue of the Olympian holding aloft a flaming torch, to the Avinguda Estadi. From here you can retrace the path back to the **Funicular de Montjuïc** (15), ☎ 010, that runs on a *daily 15-minute frequency in summer between 10:45 a.m. to 8 p.m. and winter only on Saturday and Sunday during the same hours. Tickets cost 200 ptas (EUR 1.20) each.* This modern train deposits you on the Avinguda Parallel, at the Plaça de Raquel Meller, just across the road from the *Teatro Apollo.* Cut along the side of that and continue on up to the Carrer Sant Pau which leads into one of the oldest areas of the city, *El Raval.* Though lovely monuments reside here, they have, as their very close neighbors, narrow streets filled with tenement slums and one of the city's "red light" streets, Carrer Robador. A certain amount of caution is advisable here. Almost immediately, one of the oldest of the city's monuments faces you, the simple and elegant lines of the church of **Sant Pau del Camp** (15). Discovery of an early 10th-century tomb on the premises has evidenced that this church was built sometime in the 9th century. This is incongruous with its surroundings, but don't expect to gain entrance unless you pass by on a Sunday morning.

Next, take Carrer de la Cadena, to the left, and then make a right on Carrer de Hospital. A couple of blocks farther on you'll come upon a gateway in an impressive old building which leads into the *Jardins de Rubió i Lluch* of the ancient hospital of *Santa Creu.* Pass through to the Carrer Ángels and, at the plaça of the same name, you'll find an ultra-modern three-story building by the architect Richard Meier that is the residence of the **Contemporary Art Museum of Barcelona** *(Museu d'Art Contemporani de Barcelona)* (16), ☎ 412-08-10 or fax 412-46-02. Inside are numerous permanent, as well as temporary, exhibitions of works produced by national and international artists over the last forty years. *It is open Tuesday to Friday from midday until 8 p.m., Saturday 10 a.m. to 8 p.m. and Sunday 10 a.m. to 3 p.m. Entrance 600 ptas (EUR 3.61), 300 ptas (EUR 1.80) on Wednesday.*

Behind this, in Carrer Montalegre, is a restored building that functions as the **Contemporary Culture Center of Barcelona** *(Centre de Cultura*

Contemporànea de Barcelona) (17), ☎ and fax 412-07-81, which has an unusual patio. Three sides are finished in the traditional manner and the other is glassed in. Adjoining it is the 18th-century **Casa de la Caritat** (18) that, besides an elegant patio, has beautiful wooden painted ceilings and a tiled staircase. *Open Tuesday to Saturday 11 a.m. to 2 p.m. and 4 p.m. to 8 p.m.; and Sunday 11 a.m. to 7 p.m. Entrance 600 ptas (EUR 3.61), 400 ptas (EUR 2.40) on Wednesday providing it is not a holiday.*

Montalegre leads into the Plaça de Castilla, from where Carrer Tallers winds through an interesting small shopping area before ending at La Rambla. A left, then, will end the tour back at the Plaça de Catalunya.

Montserrat

Though Montserrat boasts an incredibly spectacular location, set upon a range of uniquely shaped mountain peaks, it is most known for its connection to a relic of the Christian faith, a carved wooden statue of the Virgin Mary known as the *La Moreneta*, the little dark Madonna, which was found nearby. There are, of course, various legends associated with the find. The most popular says that it was made by St. Luke and brought to Spain by St. Peter. Whatever the merits of that story, it was in truth found on these mountains in the 12th century and it, and this place, have been a focal point for pilgrims ever since.

A hermitage that made its home on the mountain prior to the discovery subsequently became a Benedictine monastery and, finally, the home of *La Moreneta*. It is documented that as long ago as the early part of the 13th century, boy singers performed here. These were the predecessors of the now world-famous *Escolania Choir*. At the commencement of the 15th century the monastery gained the status of independent abbey, and at the end of the same century a printing press was installed.

In 1493 one of the hermits of Montserrat sailed with Christopher Columbus, who named one of the islands discovered on that journey in honor of the monastery. Saint Ignatius of Loyola visited in 1522, but the arrival of Napoleon's troops nearly three centuries later wasn't so hospitable. During that encounter, Montserrat was virtually destroyed. A quarter of a century later enactment of the Secularization laws led to its abandonment, but within ten years the monks had returned. The latter part of the century, 1881, saw the Canoninical Coronation of the *La Moreneta*, and she was proclaimed the patroness of Catalunya.

GETTING THERE:

Trains of the **Catalan Railroads** *(F.F.C.C. Generalitat de Catalunya)* depart from the terminal at Barcelona's *Plaça d'Espanya* for the station of Aeri de Montserrat.

Buses depart from Ronda Universitat, 5, in Barcelona.

By car, Montserrat, 32 miles northwest of Barcelona, is reached by taking the N-II to either the exit at km. 591, and then through Abrera and Monistrol; or the exit at km. 578, and then through Els Brucs and Can Maçana. Alternatively, take the A-2 *autopista* toll road to the Martorell exit, then follow the signs to Montserrat.

PRACTICALITIES:

Even in summer it may get quite cool here, so dress accordingly. The **Dialing Code** is 93. Montserrat has a **population** of 2,500 and is in the province of Barcelona, one of four belonging to the autonomous region of **Catalunya**.

ACCOMMODATION:

The **Hotel Abot Cisneros** ***, ☎ 835-02-01 or fax 828-40- 06, Plaza de Montserrat, s/n, the only hotel at Montserrat, offers 41 clean and comfortable rooms. It is located just a few yards from the monastery. $

FOOD AND DRINK:

There are a variety of eateries and bars in Montserrat. Bars are open from 9 a.m. until at least 6 p.m., and later in the summer. A self-service cafeteria is open from 1 p.m. to 5 p.m.; and a restaurant opens from midday to 3 p.m.

SUGGESTED TOUR:

Numbers in parentheses correspond to numbers on the map.

The most dramatic way to visit Montserrat is via train and, for those choosing this option, the tour really begins at the *Plaça d'Espanya* station in Barcelona. From there catch a Catalonian Railroad train to *Aeri de Montserrat*. This takes you, first, through the sprawling suburbs of Barcelona but, after a while, you will notice in the distance a range of mountains distinguished by a most unusual series of closely packed, strangely shaped peaks. It is from the appearance of these that the name Montserrat, meaning serrated peaks, is derived. The highest elevation in the range is reached upon *Sant Jeroni,* at 4,075 ft., and the monastery itself rests at an elevation of 2,393 ft.

As you get nearer to (and into the shadow of) these mountains, you begin to doubt that the train can possibly get to the top. It can't. But don't worry, you won't have to climb on foot. A genuine Swiss-style cable car will raise you to what seems an improbable elevation, where you will find the Montserrat complex. A tip for money-wise travelers: purchase a combined train/cable car ticket at the station in Barcelona. At times, there may be a wait either for a cable car, or for a train back to Barcelona. On these occasions pay a visit to the very tiny bar tucked behind the Barcelona-bound platform. It's nothing fancy but it serves the purpose.

The ride up is nothing if not dramatic, and you may even get some butterflies in your stomach as the cable car rises above an overhanging rock to dock at Montserrat. From first glance it becomes obvious that Montserrat is much more than a simple monastery. Walk up the ramp and stairs to the **Plaça de la Creu** (1) (Square of the Cross), where you'll find a snack bar, quickly followed by the Information Office and a combination Self-Service Restaurant and gift shop. Just past this is another, smaller, square, the *Plaça de l'Abat Oliba* where the buildings around the perime-

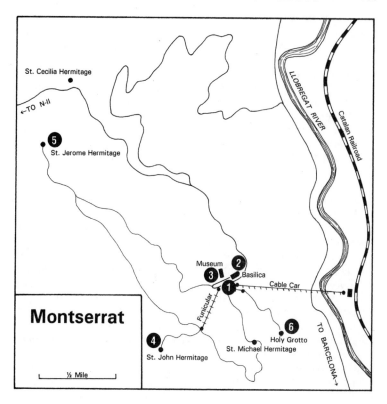

St. Cecilia Hermitage

←TO N-II

LLOBREGAT RIVER

Catalan Railroad

5
St. Jerome Hermitage

Museum
2
3 Basilica
1   Cable Car

Funicular

Montserrat

4
St. John Hermitage

6
Holy Grotto
St. Michael Hermitage

TO BARCELONA→

½ Mile

ter house the pilgrims "cells". Each morning the farmers' wives *(pageses)* bring their produce to a market here. Continue on, following the street around to the right, actually doubling back on the way you came, but at a higher elevation. This takes you to the main square, the Plaça de Santa María. If you would like a little more information on the area, you may want to pay the building to your right a visit. It runs a free audiovisual show, "What is Montserrat?," every thirty minutes.

The structures around the square look fairly unassuming, but it is nevertheless apparent that there is a great attraction here. To the left, and physically the most appealing, are the two wings, dating from 1476, of the Gothic Cloister. Next to these is the monastery itself. The original was destroyed by Napoleon's troops in the early 19th century, and this structure was built to replace it. The unusual design of the façade incorporates three impressive upper balconies, each featuring immense arches, which frame decorative works by the sculptor Joan Rebull. The ground level is adorned by five arched porches through which you will pass to enter the 18th-century atrium of the church. Here you will find a couple of sepulchures among numerous statues and much elegant art work, and the entrances to the 12th-century Romanesque church, the monastery, and the Basilica itself. At this point you have to make a choice of what to visit first. The monastery is not an option. This working monastery is home to approximately eighty Benedictine monks and is, obviously, off-limits to tourists. And access to its library, which contains over 250,000 volumes, is granted to scholars only. So, the question now becomes, the Basilica or the shrine?

The 16th-century **Basilica** (2) is of huge proportions, 225 ft. long and 70 ft. wide with a domed ceiling, built over elegant arches, that reaches a height of 109 ft. The effect, for all its spaciousness, is a little dark and foreboding. Of particular interest are the choir stalls reserved for the community of monks. Try to time your visit (on any day except during July) for 1 p.m. This is the hour when the *Escolania*, reputedly the oldest boys' choir in the world, founded in the 13th century, performs the *Salve* and the *Virolai*—the hymn of Montserrat. Each evening, at 7:10 p.m., after Vespers, they alternate with the monks to sing the *Montserratine Salve*.

Whether pilgrim or tourist, the zenith of a visit to Montserrat lies through a door set in the right-hand wall of the atrium. Follow along, past the side chapels of the Basilica, ascending a heavily-decorated stairway and going through the elaborate doors that lead you to *La Moreneta. The little dark Madonna, a carved wooden statue of the Virgin Mary, resting on a piece of Montserrat rock has become the most revered icon in Catalunya. In fact, a pilgrimage here is considered, among those Spain has to offer, to be second in importance only to Santiago de Compostela. Newlyweds come here by the thousands, believing this will bring a blessing to their marriages. Stairs lead down the opposite side and out into a small courtyard where you may want to observe the custom of lighting a candle before exiting back into the *Plaça de Santa María*. This square is usually a hive of activity, especially on weekends and holidays. You will see many of the "blessed" honeymooners having their photos taken, and you may even be entertained by local folk singers and dancers performing, among other things, the popular *sardanes*. This is also the site of the **Montserrat Museum** (3) *(Museu de Montserrat)*, which exhibits important traditional works of art, a collection of modern Catalan art, and a display of gifts donated to Montserrat.

If you are feeling energetic, you may spend some time exploring the mountains, stopping now and again to investigate the famous hermitages. There are thirteen of these on the mountains, which before the Wars of Independence were occupied by hermits of the monastery. The first one you will come to is that of **Saint John** (4) *(Sant Joan)*, and the seven-minute funicular ride up an incline that reaches 65.5% is worth a try its own right. From the top there are spectacular views almost directly down to the Basilica.

The really adventurous might take the 90-minute walk up and around to the **Saint Jerome** (5) *(Sant Jeroni)* hermitage, which is the highest at 4,075 ft. Not only does this afford even better vistas, to the Pyrenees and even Mallorca weather permitting, but you also catch a glimpse of a number of the other hermitages along the way.

Another funicular offers you the option of visiting the **Holy Grotto** (6) *(Santa Cova)*. This is actually a chapel, dating from the 17th century, constructed in the shape of a cross and topped by a dome. It is particularly revered as legend has it that is the spot where the *La Moreneta* was found.

Before taking the cable car back down and returning to Barcelona, take a walk along the promenade to the large, rectangular, building perched on the edge of the mountain just ahead. Have a seat in the open-air restaurant/cafeteria and admire the views back down the valley.

Tarragona

Tarragona can claim to be one of the oldest cities in Spain, and its strategic position—180 feet above the Mediterranean—was not overlooked by the ancient Iberian tribes. In fact, their fortifications were so secure that the Romans, who landed here in the 3rd century BC, literally built on them to establish their town of *Tarraco* as an important political and military center. Growing to a population of over 30,000 it became, in 27 BC, the capital of the largest Roman province on the peninsula, *Tarraconensis,* and was even allowed to coin its own currency. During this period several emperors, including Augustus and Hadrian, resided here and the city developed into one of the most gracious in Spain. Today, the many surviving monuments from that era are of international interest, attracting visitors from around the world to what otherwise would just be another sleepy provincial town.

GETTING THERE:

Trains depart from Barcelona's centrally-located Passeig de Gracia station, next to the Plaça de Catalunya, or from the main Sants station, one stop to the south. There are numerous trains each day; the journey time depending on the type of train chosen. The slowest are the Cercanías; Talgo and InterCity are the fastest, with the latter taking about an hour.

By car, Tarragona lies about 65 miles south of Barcelona. Take the A-7 *Autopista* to the N-240 exit, then follow signs to the city center.

PRACTICALITIES:

The major attractions are closed on Mondays; on other days the opening hours are usually from 10 a.m. to 1 p.m. and 4-7 p.m. Tarragona's **Dialing Code** is 977. The **Provincial Tourist Office**, ☎ 23-34-15 or fax 24-47-02, is at Carrer de Fortuny, 4, and opens Monday to Friday 9 a.m. to 2 p.m. and 4 p.m. to 7 p.m.; and Saturday 9 a.m. to 2 p.m. The **Municipal Tourist Office**, ☎ 24-52-03, fax 24-55-07, e-mail turisme@tinet.fut.es or www.fut.es/~turisme, at Carrer Major, 39, opens in summer Monday to Friday 9:30 a.m. to 8:30 p.m., Saturday 9:30 a.m. to 2 p.m. and 4 p.m. to 8:30 p.m. and Sunday 10 a.m. to 2 p.m.; and in winter Monday to Friday 10 a.m. to 2 p.m. and 4:30 p.m. to 7 p.m. and Saturday and Sunday 10 a.m. to 2 p.m. In addition, there are several booths located throughout the city. Tarragona has a **population** of about 111,000 and is in the region of **Cataluña.**

ACCOMMODATION:

The **Hotel Imperial Tarraco** ****, ☎ 23-30-40 and fax 21- 65-66, Rambla Vella, 2 is not only the grandest in town but has a marvelous location offering spectacular views. $$

The **Hotel-Residencia España** *, ☎ 20-15-40, Rambla Nova, 49 is a considerably more modest, but still very comfortable establishment, located on the city's main street. $

FOOD AND DRINK:

Seafood, of course, is the main specialty of the region.

Sol Ric (Calle Via Augusta, 227) is probably the most famous in town. Whether eating inside or in the beautiful garden, you can enjoy an unmatched array of seafood dishes. ☎ 23-20-32. $$

Barquet (Calle Gasómetre, 16) is a more modest establishment operated by two brothers with a passion for the cuisine of Tarragona. $

SUGGESTED TOUR:

Numbers in parentheses correspond to numbers on the map.

Turn right out of the **train station** (1) *(Estación de Ferrocarril)* and walk up a small hill towards a traffic circle, across from which are stairs built into a wall, leading up to the Baixada del Toro. Follow this street, with increasingly wide views of the Mediterranean to the right, up another incline towards an imposing monument. The statue of Roger de Llauria, a combination admiral and pirate who conquered Sicily for King Pedro III of Aragón, stands guard over an important junction in the city. To the left is the wide **Rambla Nova**, which we'll explore in greater detail later, and straight ahead is the impressive **Balcó del Mediterrani** (2). This pedestrian walkway is located on a 320-foot-high "balcony" that, when followed around, offers a truly spectacular vista of the coastline and city. Below it lies the **Roman Amphitheater** (3), ☎ 24-25-79, *(Anfiteatro Romano)*, and ruins of the 12th-century **Santa María del Miracle** church. *Open June to September, Tuesday to Saturday 9 a.m. to 9 p.m. and Sunday and holidays 9 a.m. to 3 p.m.; April to May, Tuesday to Saturday 10 a.m. to 1:30 p.m. and 3:30 p.m. to 6:30 p.m. and Sunday and holidays 10 a.m. to 2 p.m.; and October to March, Tuesday to Saturday 10 a.m. to 1:30 p.m. and 3:30 p.m. to 5:30 p.m. and Sunday and holidays 10 a.m. to 2 p.m. Entrance 300 ptas (EUR 1.80).*

Continue along the Balcó past the impressive Imperial Tarraco Hotel and head for the old city walls, just past another traffic circle, and a fort-like structure with an imposing tower. This is the 2,000-year-old **Roman Praetorium** (4) *(Pretori Romà)* which, as Tarragona claims to be the birthplace of Pontius Pilate, is commonly known as the Castle of Pilate. Inside, you'll find the *****Tarragona History Museum** *(Museu de Historia de Tarragona)*, whose displays include a 3rd-century Roman sarcophagus and a 10th-century *mihrab* from Córdoba. The top of the tower offers tremendous views. At the other end, you may wander through the labyrinth of spooky tunnels that once led out to the amphitheater, and which were used as prisons during the Spanish Civil War.

Next door, in the Praça del Rei, is an altogether more modern building that is home to the **National Archaeological Museum** (5) *(Museo Arqueològico Nacional)*, ☎ 23-62-09. Among its impressive exhibits is a collection of Roman mosaics, including the famous **Head of Medusa* with its penetrating stare, sculpture, ceramics, coins, silver, and an unusual jointed ivory doll discovered in a 4th-century grave. *Open June to September, Tuesday to Saturday 10 a.m. to 8 p.m. and Sunday and holidays 10 a.m. to 2 p.m.; and the rest of the year Tuesday to Saturday 10 a.m. to 1:30 p.m. and 4 p.m. to 7 p.m. and Sunday and holidays 10 a.m. to 2 p.m. Entrance 400 ptas (EUR 2.40), includes entry to the Early Christian Necrpopolis and Museum.*

Leaving the Praça del Rei by way of Santa Ana, you'll pass the **Modern Art Museum** (6) *(Museu Arte Moderno)*, ☎ 23-50-32, housed in the Casa Montoliù. *Open Tuesday to Friday 10 a.m. to 8 p.m., Saturday 10 a.m. to 3 p.m. and 5 p.m. to 8 p.m. and Sunday 11 a.m. to 2 p.m.* Next is the Forum, which has a section of the old walls. Turn immediately left into Mercería, a narrow street with a porticoed walkway leading to the cathedral steps. This area of small streets and plazas is of particular interest on Sundays mornings, when it plays host to the lively **Flea Market** *(Rastro)*.

The steps take you up to the highest point in town and to the not especially impressive main façade of the **Cathedral* (7), ☎ 23-86-85. Rather hemmed in by the surrounding streets, this is located on the site of an old mosque and, although construction was begun in 1171 it wasn't consecrated until 1333. As a consequence, it reflects a rather unusual mix of Romanesque and Gothic styles. The inside is dark and gloomy, brightened only somewhat by light filtering through the fine stained-glass windows. Of particular note is the grand 15th-century marble **altarpiece (Retablo de Santa Tecla)*, honoring Tarragona's patron saint. It is the large, magnificent **Cloister**, though, with its beautiful 12th-century sculptures and graceful lines that is the main attraction here. Also of interest is the main exhibit in the small **Cathedral Museum** *(Museu Diocesano)*, a 15th-century tapestry, *La Bona Vida*, depicting life in medieval times. *Open daily mid-March to the end of June 10 a.m. to 1 p.m. and 4 p.m. to 7 p.m.; July to mid-October 10 a.m. to 7 p.m.; mid-October to mid-November 10 a.m. to 12:30 p.m. and 3 p.m. to 5 p.m.; and mid-November to mid-March 10 a.m. to 2 p.m.*

Stepping outside, a walk around the perimeter of the cathedral will give you a true sense of its immense size. In fact, it is the largest in the whole of Catalonia. Return down the steps into Carrer Major, a shopping street that—like the other streets nearby—is graced by elegant wrought-iron lanterns. As this winds down and around its character changes as it becomes the cobblestoned Baixada Misericordia. At the junction of the two streets, to the right, notice the end of one house that has been decorated with a delightful mural. Just before it meets Rambla Vella, turn again to the right, following the block-long *Plaça de la Font* to the elegant **Town**

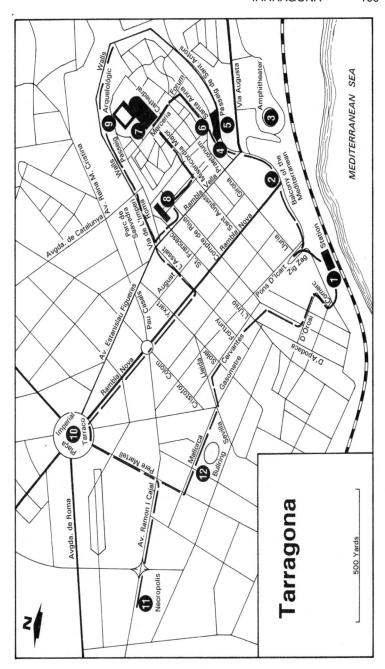

Tarragona

500 Yards

MEDITERRANEAN SEA

Hall (8) *(Ayuntamiento,* or *Ajuntanent* in Catalan), located at the far end.

A left turn there brings you out on the much busier Rambla Vella. Turn right for two blocks, then right again on an incline to the Via de L'Imperi Romà. This is an unusual street indeed. A pedestrian walkway divides it; on the left is the **Parc de Saavedra**, containing some ancient ruins, and on the right are portions of the ancient wall. At its end is the beginning of the **Passeig Arquelológic** (9), ☎ 24-19-52. This is a very interesting half-mile walkway that winds its way back around the cathedral. The upper levels of the ramparts were built by the Romans on top of huge cyclopean boulders, supposedly placed there by Iberian tribes in the 6th century BC. It has, of course, been much changed over the centuries, particularly in medieval times and in the 17th century. *Today it offers many interesting views and is open June to September, Tuesday to Saturday 9 a.m. to 9 p.m. and Sunday and holidays 9 a.m. to 3 p.m.; April to May, Tuesday to Saturday 10 a.m. to 1:30 p.m. and 3:30 p.m. to 6:30 p.m. and Sunday and holidays 10 a.m. to 2 p.m.; and October to March, Tuesday to Saturday 10 a.m. to 1:30 p.m. and 3:30 p.m. to 5:30 p.m. and Sunday and holidays 10 a.m. to 2 p.m. Entrance 300 ptas (EUR 1.80).*

Retrace your steps back to Rambla Vella, cross it into L'Assalt, and pass an elaborately-spired church with its decorative coat-of-arms on your way to the modern city's main street, the **Rambla Nova**. A Rambla by name it may be, but it certainly doesn't match the Rambla of Barcelona, even though it has its own merits. The tree-lined central walkway provides a pleasant place to sit and rest. A little to the right is the monument to the Heroes of 1811, and one block farther on is a charming fountain, the **Fuente del Centenario**. The biggest surprise is farther down the hill at the **Plaça Imperial Tarraco** (10). Here, incongruous in its rather bland surroundings, is quite an unusual little park occupying the center of the traffic circle. It has a fantastic fountain that shoots water 30 to 40 feet into the air, and is flanked by two ponds that are home to an eclectic collection of ducks and geese. At night the scene is illuminated by floodlights sitting atop ethereal metal pylons. On a hot summer's day this spot makes a wonderful respite from ardent sightseeing.

The scenery for the final leg of this trip is not particularly interesting, consisting mainly of apartment blocks. Interspersed among these, though, are a few fascinating places. Follow the map to the ancient ***Roman-Palaeo-Christian Necropolis and Museum** (11) (Museu I Necròpolis Paleocristians),* ☎ 23-62-09, used from the 3rd to the 5th centuries AD. Discovered when constructing the adjacent tobacco factory, this necropolis has proved to be the most extensive yet unearthed in Spain. Many of its best artifacts—dating from Roman to Pagan periods—are on display in the museum. Outside, viewable from the sidewalk, are some of the many crypts that have been excavated. *Open June to September, Tuesday to Saturday 10 a.m. to 8 p.m. and Sunday and holidays 10 a.m. to 2 p.m.; and the rest of the year Tuesday to Saturday 10 a.m. to 1:30 p.m. and 4 p.m. to 7 p.m. and Sunday and holidays 10 a.m. to 2 p.m. Entrance 400 ptas (EUR*

2.40), and includes entry to the Museo Arqueológic.

Retrace your steps and turn right onto Pere Martell for one block. Immediately upon taking a left onto Mallorca the unmistakable outline of the **Bullring** (12) *(Plaza de Toros)* looms from the next corner. The only opportunity to go inside is on the day of a fight. Besides the fact that these are infrequent during the season (March to October), it wouldn't appeal to everyone. But just a little up the hill are some bars that specialize in things taurine; the posters and other artifacts displayed in them are worth seeing to those interested in the bulls.

Continue along Mallorca to Praça Ponent and there make a left onto Lleida. At its junction with Cardenal Cervantes are the remains of of the **Municipal Forum**, where city business was conducted during Roman times. From here follow the map back to the railroad station.

Seville:
(Sevilla)
Royal Fortress, Cathedral, and the Giralda

Seville's long and illustrious history begins, as local legend goes, when Hercules founded a town on this spot and called it *Hispalis*. The more verifiable account has the Phoenicians establishing a trading port here about three thousand years ago. Following an interlude in which the area was controlled by the Carthaginians, the Romans, who were fighting for control of the Iberian Peninsula, won a battle near Seville in 206 BC. Soon after, they built a resort facility for the use of their troops to the north of present day Seville, naming it *Itálica*. This area flourished and, in fact, two Roman emperors, Hadrian and Trajan, were born there. In 45 BC Julius Caesar revitalized Hispalis, naming it *Colonia Julia Romula*, and this city became one of the most affluent in the colony. The decline of Seville's fortunes paralleled that of the Roman Empire and, subsequently, in the first decade of the 5th century the Vandals seized and sacked the city. For a short period, about a century and a quarter, the Visigoths took a turn at ruling the area.

In AD 711, the Moors began their invasion of Spain, and it was just one year later that they captured Seville and transformed it into a center for their culture. In 844 the Vikings made a short-lived attempt at controlling Seville. They were soon driven out, but not before destroying many of the beautiful mosques and other buildings constructed by the Moors. The city bounced back and, by the 10th century, it was considered one of the most important cities in the Caliphate of Córdoba. Early in the 11th century internal warfare caused the breakup of that Caliphate into many smaller kingdoms, among which the taifa of Seville was one of the wealthiest and most renowned under the reign of al-Mutamid. This king lost control of the city in 1091 when it was taken over first by the Almoravids and, in rapid succession, the Almohads. Seville became the capital of Muslim Spain. The caliph of the Almohads built an incredibly beautiful minaret, *La Giralda*. Also built during this period was the famous *Torre de Oro*. These structures are now world-famous symbols of Seville (*Sevilla* in Spanish).

In 1248, following a two-year siege, the Christians re-conquered Seville under King Ferdinand III, "The Saint". The Moorish residents abandoned the city in droves, and it was quickly repopulated by Castillians. In 1401 construction began on the massive new Cathedral, even today the third-largest in the Christian world. Sevilla was the welcome home port for Christopher Columbus following his Voyage of Discovery in 1492. On Palm Sunday in 1493 he (Cristobal Colón) entered the city in triumph. The real boon came in 1503 when the *Casa de Contratación* in Seville was awarded the monopoly for Spanish trade with the Americas. Thus began a period of prosperity that lasted nearly two centuries, leaving as a legacy many beautiful monuments and achievements of note. Magellan departed from here, in 1519, on his successful venture to sail around the world. Seven years later Carlos V married Isabella of Portugal in the Alcázar and was later crowned Holy Roman Emperor. He was succeeded by his son Felipe II in 1556. The inefficiencies of Spain's central government under his leadership, a devastating war at sea against England, and an outbreak of bubonic plage in 1649 (in which half of the population died) was a devastating combination that led to the decline of Seville's commercial importance. It 1680 the Admiralty was transferred to Cádiz, and the *Casa de Contratación* followed in 1717. In 1810, during the Wars of Independence, the French occupied Seville for two long years, finally ousting Napoleon's troops with the help of the Duke of Wellington, who is still considered a hero here today. 1848 saw the first celebrations of the *Fería de Sevilla*, an event that now draws visitors from around the world.

During the Spanish Civil War, Seville was the first city to fall to the rebel forces who used the captured Radio Sevilla to spread their propaganda.

Today, as it has from the city's founding, the River Guadalquivir forms the basis of the city's prosperity; it is the only river port in Spain. With prosperity came the social problems prevalent in most modern urban areas. Both unemployment and crime are higher than in other places you may visit in Spain, and you should exercise caution regarding handbags and camera bags. Local young men are only too happy to relieve you of these, snagging them out of the hands or off the shoulders of visitors while whizzing around on their mopeds. The antidote is to carry them on your side that faces away from the street, especially when traveling through any of the narrow streets and alleyways. Be careful, also, when taking a rest on one of the inviting park benches; valuables left by your side are tempting to fleet-footed thieves. Even in a car your assets are not safe. Never leave bags, valuables, cameras, etc. sitting loose on the seats, and pay particular attention when stopped at traffic signals, when you may be approached by thieves posing as vendors or children begging, or by youngsters on motos.

Don't, however, let these considerations put you off visiting Seville. This is a city of stunning beauty and incredible charm. In fact, when you suggest to a Sevillano that his city is the most beautiful in Spain, you'll most probably get the following response: *"No, en el todo mundo,"* "no, in the whole world."

GETTING THERE:

By air, Seville's San Pablo airport, ☎ 444-90-00, recently built to accommodate the influx of travelers to Expo'92, receives International flights directly from major European cities, and via Madrid from North America. Domestic flights arrive from the more important Spanish cities.

Trains arrive at the city's new station, *Santa Justa,* ☎ 441-41-11, again constructed for Expo'92, from Madrid, on either the AVE high-speed or on regular services, both via Córdoba. Services run from Barcelona or Valencia via Alcázar de San Juan and Córdoba; from Algeciras, Málaga, or Granada via Bobadilla and Utrera; from Cádiz via Utrera; from Huelva and from Cáceres via Mérida and Zafra.

Buses arrive at either the new *Plaza de Armas,* ☎ 490-77-37, or the old *San Sebastián,* ☎ 441-71-11, bus stations from all points in Spain. In fact, they are definitely recommended for travel to and from Algeciras, Cáceres, Granada, Málaga, Mérida and Zafra.

By car, Seville lies 336 miles southwest of Madrid. It is reached (via Córdoba) on the N-IV, a recently updated, fast, divided highway. It is connected to Cádiz, via Jerez de la Frontera, by either the A-4 *autopista* toll road or, alternatively, by a continuation of the N-IV, a stretch that has not been upgraded. Huelva may be reached by taking either the A-49 *autopista* toll road or the N-431 and Zafra, Mérida, and Cáceres by taking the N-630, which although scenic is not a particularly good road.

PRACTICALITIES:

Of the places you'll want to see in Seville many, with the notable exception of the Cathedral, are closed on Mondays. Seville draws visitors from around the world throughout all the seasons of the year and, consequently, in this busy city, accommodation can be difficult to find. This is particularly true in the Spring during **Easter Week** *(Semana Santa)*, and the **April Fair** *(Fería de Abril)*. These two events are so widely acclaimed that accommodation must be booked many, many months in advance. If you are fortunate enough to secure a place, expect to be charged double the normal rate. Be warned, also, that during the months of July and August temperatures of well over 100° F can be a daily occurrence. And it often rises to above 110, or more.

The **dialing code** is 95. The main **Tourist Office**, *Oficina de Turismo,* ☎ 422-14-04 or fax 422-97-53, Avenida de la Constitución, 21, is located a hundred yards or so from the Cathedral and is open Monday to Saturday from 9 a.m. to 7 p.m. and Sunday and holidays from 10 a.m. to 2 p.m. An informative city plan is available for the minimal charge of 100 ptas (EUR .60).

Interesting **Internet** sites for Sevilla are www.sol.com, www.sevilla.org and www.sevillaonline.com.

Seville has a **population** of just over 700,000 and is the capital of the province of the same name, one of eight belonging to the autonomous region of **Andalucía**.

ACCOMMODATION:

The **Hotel Alfonso XIII** ***** **GL**, ☎ 422-28-50 or fax 421-60-33, San Fernando, 2, opened by Alfonso XIII himself, is the jewel in the crown that is Seville. This huge and beautiful structure, located in the center of the city and set in its own lovely gardens, boasts majestic public rooms encircling its large patio. The rooms and suites are of unparalled luxury. Over the years, the Alfonso XIII has played host to royal families, heads of state, and world-renowned personalities from political, artistic, and social circles. It is at its very best during the *Semana Santa* and *Fería de Abril* celebrations. $$$

The **Hotel Tryp Colón** *****, ☎ 422-29-00 or fax 422-09-38, Canalejas, 1, is another classically refined hotel close to the center of the old part of town and near to all the monuments. Behind an imposing façade find 204 rooms and 14 suites all luxuriously furnished and with every modern amenity. Besides the elegant poublic areas, expect the esteemed El Burladero restaurant, the Taberna La Tasca—noted for its Andaluz cuisine and bullfighting momentos and a gymnasium and sauna. $$$

The **Hotel Los Seises** ****, ☎ 422-94-95 or fax 422-43-34, Segovias, 6, is an absolutely delightful 16th-century palace that has been cleverly converted into a small, 43 room, hotel. Here, historic surroundings combine with modern facilities to create an intriguing environment. It is centrally located in the Barrio de Santa Cruz, and has a roof top pool overlooking the nearby Cathedral and *Giralda*. $$$.

The Hotel **Doña María** ****, ☎ 422-49-00 or fax 421-95-46, Don Remondo, 19, is found directly across the road from the *Giralda*. Behind an unusual façade is a hotel of rare style, offering modern amenities but furnished in an ancient style with numerous lovely antiques throughout. Some rooms have four-poster beds and all have a private bath, air conditioning and TV. There's even a roof-top pool with a spectacular view of the *Giralda*. $$

The **Hotel Taberna del Alabardero** ***, ☎ 456-06-37 or fax 456-36-66, Calle Zaragoza, 20, housed in the 19th-century home of romantic poet J. Antonio Cavestany, is a charming small hotel with just 10 rooms set around an inviting patio. Its restaurant, La Taberna del Alabardero, described in the "Food and Drink" section below, is a gastronomic delight. $$

The **Patios de Sevilla: Patio de la Cartuja** ☎ 490-02-00 or fax 490-20-56, Lumbreras, 8-10; and **Patio de la Alameda** ☎ 490-49-99 or fax 490-02-26, Alameda de Hercules, 56. These are two very typical buildings, in a Bohemian district of Sevilla, that have been carefully converted into 56 modern apartments with a bedroom, sitting room with sofa bed, kitchen and bathroom. A big advantage is the private parking. $$

The **Hotel Monte Triana** ***, ☎ 434-31-11 or fax 434-33-28, Clara de

Jesús Montero, 24, is located in the quieter Barrio de Triana, the old Gypsy Quarter. This is across the river and just ten minutes walk from the city center and the main attractions. It has a nice atmosphere and 117 large modern rooms. $$

The **Hotel Simon** *, ☎ 422-66-60 or fax 456-22-41, García de Vinuesa, 19, is located in a side street, just across the Avenida de Constitución from the Cathedral, behind the charming Plaza del Cabildo. Its 31 rooms are in a mansion typical of those built here in the late 18th to early 19th centuries. These and the public areas are filled with antiques, giving it an ambiance of Andalucian romanticism. $

The **Hostal Residencia Nuevo Suiza** **, ☎ 422-91-47, Calle Azofaifo, 7, is in a narrow passageway just off Sierpes, near the theater. Both the decor and the atmosphere are very dignified and three of the floors have beautiful wooden balconies. $

The **Pensión Cruces** *, ☎ 441-34-04, Plaza de la Cruces, 10, offers modest facilities, a fact that is offset by its delightful character. The structure is over 500 years old and has wonderful patios. Long acclaimed for its charm, it has been featured over the past several years in numerous television programs. $

Note: Visitors traveling by car may, in order to avoid the parking problems and the all-pervasive city heat, elect to stay out in the countryside. And there really is a wonderful mix of options; these range from hotels that can hold their own with any in the world, and an esoteric selection of *haciendas* and *cortijos*. These are traditional Andalucian farmhouses that either belonged, or are still part of, estates that raise the esteemed fighting bulls *(toros bravos)*. Some have been turned into exclusive hotels, while others are still working ranches and just have a few rooms. What they offer, besides a style and elegance not often seen, is a chance to see how these places operate and even, for those brave enough, a chance to participate in an amateur bullfight. Any of the following makes for a convenient base from which to explore Sevilla, and each one is less than 30 minutes commute.

The **Hotel Casa Palacio "Casa de Carmona"** ***** **GL**, ☎ 414-30-00, fax 414-37-52 or www.casadecarmona.com, Plaza de Lasso, 1, is to be found in the 15th- to 17th-century Palacio de Lasso de la Vega. This had been allowed to fall into disrepair until the Guardiola Medina family realized its potential. They have now transformed it into a highly luxurious small, just 30 odd rooms, hotel and each of the rooms has its own antique furniture. The public rooms are an equal delight and, in fact, every care is taken to make you feel this really is an extension of your home, not simply a hotel. Those wanting a more detailed explanation of this truly magnificent place should read my article in the April 1996 issue of *Country Inns* magazine. $$

The **Hotel Hacienda Benazuza** *****, ☎ 570-33-44 or fax 570-34-10, Calle Virgen de Las Nieves, s/n, Sanlúcar La Mayor, 41800, Sevilla, reached by either the A-49 autopista or N-431, is located just fifteen minutes west of Seville. Once the home of King Alfonso X, the property subsequently passed to the Knights of the Order of Santiago and, later, to the Counts of Benazuza. In the 19th century it became the residence of a highly prestigious breeder of fighting bulls, Pablo Romero. Still maintaining the charm acquired over its 1,000-year history, it has been luxuriously restored. No comfort is spared in this hotel that offers a highly esoteric option for the discerning traveler. $$$

The **Hotel Cortijo Águila Real** ****, ☎ 578-50-06 or fax 578-43-30, Carretera Guillena to Burgillos, Km. 4, Guillena, 41210, is housed in a traditional farmhouse located off the N-630 highway just 15 minutes north of the city center. The rooms have been masterfully converted, appropriately blending luxurious appointments to compliment the ambiance. The common rooms are far from common and an elegant dining room (complete with silver place settings) and an inviting pool surrounded by palm trees add to the cocktail that make this ancient mansion intoxicating. $$$

The **Cortijo "La Calera"**, ☎ 423-81-32 or fax 461-31-43, is in Gerena just a short distance north of Seville. It is a working farmhouse, breeding the fighting bulls of *Lora Sangran,* and there are five double rooms, all with a private bath, in the main house, and three more, sharing a bathroom, in a second house. You are more than welcome to visit the Cortijo, bullring and corrals, and there is even a possibility of participating in an amateur bullfight and/or horseback riding. Visits to the nearby 16th-century Gongora wine bodega can be arranged, and the *"La Calera"* even lays on courtesy transportation to and from Seville. $$

The **Cortijo "El Esparragal"**, ☎ 578-27-02 or fax 578-27-83, Carretera Mérida, km 21, 41860, Gerena, dates back to the 15th century when it granted by Juan II to the Duke of Medina Sidonia. It has 10 double rooms with private bathrooms, 6 suites with private bathrooms and 6 servants rooms. Among its facilities are a pool, extensive gardens, bullring, chapel, and stables. It is divided into a big game reserve, stockbreeding farm and farmland, and offers guided visits to the horse, cattle, and fighting bull stockbreeding farms as well as, for an extra charge, big and small game hunting and excursions by foot, by horseback, or in a horsedrawn carriage. They will even arrange an amateur bullfight for you to participate in! $$

The **Cortijo "El Triguero"**, ☎ (91) 411-69-74 or fax (91) 561-17-42, is located just ten minutes east of Seville's airport, just outside of Carmona. It is another working bull-breeding ranch and offers 7 double rooms and 2 singles, with 6 bathrooms shared among them. There are lounges, a dining room, swimming pool surrounded by orange trees, and a bullring. In this delightful ambiance you can also enjoy amateur bullfighting, flamenco, or simply enjoy the pleasing countryside. $

FOOD AND DRINK:

Restaurante Real (located within the *Alfonso XIII,* San Fernando, 2) is as charismatic as the hotel in which it resides. The decor is sublime. Its wonderfully carved ceilings and columns, rich tapestries and shimmering chandeliers create a fitting setting for the elegantly presented International "haute cuisine" or Andalucian gastronomy. ☎ 422-28-50, fax 421-60-33. $$$

Taberna del Alabardero (Zaragoza, 20) is found between the Plaza Nueva and the Plaza de Toros, in the hotel which shares its name. In this lovely old palace, which exudes charm and character, Señor Luis Lezama, a former priest, has fashioned a heavenly environment worthy of the extraordinary dining experience to which it plays host. In addition, Señor Lezama is passing the knowledge on to future generations of chefs enrolled in his highly-acclaimed culinary school located here in Seville. After eating here you'll doubtless want to visit his other restaurants, all of the same name, located in Peurto Banus, Madrid and Washington D.C. ☎ 456-06-37 or fax 456-36-66. $$$

Egaña Oriza Restaurante (San Fernando, 41) is located in a traditional style building, across from the Tobacco Factory, on the corner of the Plaza de Don Juan of Austria. Renown for Jose María Egaña's dishes that combine Basque influences with Andalucian traditions. It has a delightfully avant-garde interior. ☎ 422-72-11. $$$

Los Seises (Segovias, 6) located within the hotel of the same name, and part of its decor are Roman and Moorish walls discovered during the excavations. This is an upscale à-la-carte restaurant that specializes in the finest regional cuisine and desserts created using Arabic influences. ☎ 422 94 95. $$$

Restaurante Marea Grande (Diego Angulo Íniguez, 16) is found a short distance out of the city center on a side street by Eduardo Dato, 29. The effort to find it is more than worthwhile. Besides having a delightful décor and ambiance, it offers an absolutely fabulous array of seafood and shellfish dishes (with some meat ones as well for those who, for some reason or another, aren't partial to fishy dishes). Combined with an interesting wine list and extremely attentive and professional service, the Marea Grande offers a fine dining ecperience. ☎ and fax 453-80-00. $$$

Restaurante La Albahaca (Plaza de la Santa Cruz, 12) is located within a lovely plaza in the heart of the Barrio de Santa Cruz. The three dining rooms, fashioned from the rooms of this old mansion, have a warm, inviting ambiance that complements the surprisingly modern International-style cuisine. Diners select from a menu that changes frequently to incorporate seasonal dishes. When the weather is cooperative, meals may also be enjoyed on the patio. ☎ 422-07-14 or fax 456-12-04. $$

Corral del Agua (Callejón del Agua, 6) is found in one of the many charming 17th-century homes that reside in the shadow of the walls of the *Alcázar* in the *Barrio de Santa Cruz*. Typical Andalucian gastronomy is enjoyed either in the rustic dining room or on the classical patio. ☎ 422-07-14 or fax 456-12-04. $S

Casa Robles (Alvarez Quintero, 58) is very close to the Cathedral in an

18th-century mansion. This is a very popular restaurant with locals and visitors, expect to choose from traditional Andalucian stews, seafood dishes and very tasty homemade desserts. Open daily. ☎ 456-32-72. www.arrakis.es/casa.robles/. $$

Mesón Don Raímundo (Argote de Molina, 26) began life as a 14th-century convent, and the interior decor is particularly emblematic of that era. The menu is full of typical Andalucian dishes, with the specialty being large and small game plates and delightful desserts. ☎ 422-33-55, fax 421-89-51. $$

Horacio (Antonio Díaz, 9) this charming restaurant is found close to the Plaza de Toros and it is unusual in that the ambiance here is creatively modern. This transcends itself in the menu, which features Andalucian and International style cuisine. ☎ 422-53-85 or www.andalunet.com-horacio. $$

El Rinconcillo (Gerona 40-42) was first opened in the 17th century, and is one of the oldest and most charismatic bars in Seville. A running account of your bill is chalked up on the wall. ☎ 422-31-83. $

Bodegón Torre del Oro (Santander, 15) is an integral part of Sevillian social life, so much so that it is featured in the second Seville walking tour, below. Tremendous in size, with row after row of unpretentious tables, typically hearty Andalucian food and drink is served up here in a 19th-century type ambiance. ☎ 421-42-41 or fax 421-66-28. $

Cervecería Internacional (Gamazo, 3) is located just off the Plaza Nueva and for those that enjoy a glass of beer it is irresistible. It has one of the largest selections you could possibly hope to find—often served in their respective glasses, and a tasty array of tapas to match. ☎ 421-17-17. $

SUGGESTED TOUR:
Numbers in parentheses correspond to numbers on the map.

Starting at the **Tourist Office** (1), follow the Avenida de la Constitución towards the Cathedral, stopping just short of that destination, on the corner of Santo Tomás, at a low, squarish building of austere Renaissance style. The **General Archives of the Indies** *(Archivo General de Indias)* (2), ☎ 421-12-34, was constructed between 1583 and 1596 by order of Carlos III. The central patio, main marble staircase, and unusual Cuban wood shelves are of interest as well as the exhibits, which consist mainly of period documents relevant to the New World. *It is open to tourists Monday to Friday between 10 a.m. and 1 p.m., and for purposes of study between 8 a.m. and 3 p.m. Entrance free.*

Behind this, in the Plaza del Triunfo, is the entrance to one of Seville's major attractions. As you enter the ***Royal Palaces and Gardens** (Reales Alcázares y Jardínes)* (3), ☎ 450-23- 23 or www.patronato-alcazarsevilla.es, a marvelous oasis in the middle of this bustling city, you will feel transported back through the centuries. The Moorish invaders built the first fortress on this site in 712. In the 9th century a palace, some of the walls of which are still standing, was added by the Emir, Abdel-Rahman II. The

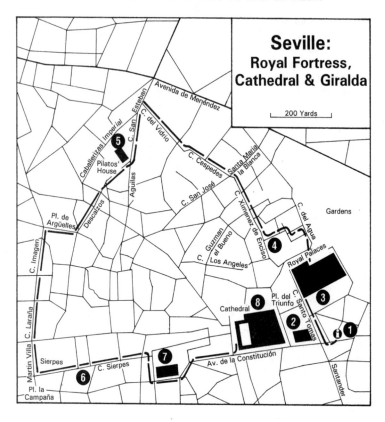

Seville:
Royal Fortress,
Cathedral & Giralda

|___ 200 Yards ___|

Moors built additional palaces, though these were still in the fortress style, and added to the gardens during the 11th and 12th centuries. Following the reconquest in 1248, the Christian monarchs established a court here. King Don Pedro built a luxurious palace on this site in 1364. The same palace was renovated during the 16th century by Carlos V, who made major changes to this structure, which is now recognized to be the oldest royal seat in Spain. The juxtaposition of the contrasting styles resulting from these divergent architectural influences has created a particularly intriguing complex. The examples of Moorish architecture are surpassed only by those found in the *Alhambra,* and the elegantly lush gardens merit a visit in their own right. *Open Tuesday to Saturday from 9:30 a.m. to 7 p.m. and on Sunday and holidays from 9:30 a.m. to 5 p.m. Entrance 700 ptas (EUR 4.21).*

Exit from the Alcázares into the delightful **Patio de Banderas**, a small patio surrounded by interesting houses and filled, as many are here, with orange trees. You will see, above the opposite wall, the tower of the

Giralda rising majestically above the parapets. Time to exit the patio, and you have only two options. Ignore the more inviting one, the gate leading out towards the Cathedral, and take the one in the opposite back corner where a narrow passageway will lead you, passing a small fountain along the way, into the old **Jewish Quarter**, the *Barrio de Santa Cruz*. Calle Judería leads to the Callejón del Agua where the ancient, flower-decked walls of the **Alcázares** provide an imposing contrast to narrow lanes and squares lined with elegant whitewashed houses and their flower-bedecked patios. Among these are sprinkled the inevitable tourist shops and restaurants, but here, thankfully, they don't intrude glaringly on the ambiance. Either Justino de Neve or Pimienta will lead you into the Plaza Venerables where you may be persuaded to take a respite at one of the inviting outdoor cafés or restaurants. Here, too, you will find the **Hospital Venerables** (4), ☎ 456-26-96, founded in 1675 by Justino de Neve. This lovely two-level structure, with its slightly sunken central patio, is considered to be one of the best examples of Baroque architecture in the city. Since 1991 it has served as home to the **Foundation FOCUS** *(Fondo de Cultura de Sevilla). Open daily 10 a.m. to 2 p.m. and 4 p.m. to 8 p.m. Entrance 500 ptas (EUR 3.01).*

On your way to the next attraction you must pass through numerous small streets which, though not particularly interesting in their own right, will give you an insight into the way citizens of this charming city conduct their day-to-day lives. Go around the Hospital Venerables on Jamerdana, then take a right into Ximenez de Enciso where, if you are feeling parched and hungry, a stop at the **Bar Las Terasas** may prove a refreshing diversion. Continue on past the **Santa María la Blanca** church and cross the busier street of like name to Céspedes, where you'll take a right and then a quick left onto Vidrio at the Plaza de las Mercedarias. Follow with another left onto San Esteban. Just past the church of San Esteban is the pathway to one of the classical palaces of Seville, **Pilatos' House (Casa de Pilatos)* (5), ☎ 422-52-98. This extraordinary structure, designated a national monument, was built by the Dukes of Medinaceli at the end of the 15th century, and is popularly considered to be a replica of the home of Pontius Pilate in Jerusalem. The architectural styles evident here range from Mudéjar to Gothic, and the patio is of a classical Renaissance design. There are also wonderful displays of *azulejos*, painted tiles, and a collection of 24 busts of Roman emperors. *Open Monday to Sunday from 9 a.m. to 7:30 p.m. Entrance 1,000 ptas (EUR 6.01).*

Outside again, turn right and take the right fork off Aguilas into Caballerizas, passing through the Plaza de San Ildefonso and into Descalzos which ends in the park of the Plaza del Cristo de Burgos. Take a right and stroll through this charming, rectangular, tree lined park, noticing on your way an odd house at number 17. Soon you'll come upon the very busy Imagen which, on its way to the famous pedestrian shopping street of Sierpes, plays the chameleon changing first to Laraña, then to Martín Villa before it passes the old University to the left. It is difficult to miss the entrance to **Sierpes** (6). Just keep your eye out for a beautiful old building on its corner, home, since 1885, to Campaña, a store that sells absolutely delicious cookies and candy. The suburban shopping mall has replaced the classic downtown department store throughout most of America, and these gigantic sprawls of the retail trade have carved a niche in the Spanish market as well. The mall will be hard pressed, however, to supercede the delightful appeal of shopping streets such as this one. Anything your heart desires will most likely be on sale here in one of the irresistible shops that reside alongside the **Imperial Theater** (Teatro Imperial), and the numerous bars and restaurants. If food is on your agenda, press on towards the end of the street where the most interesting of these establishments, with their quaint outdoor tables, may be found tucked in the narrow passageways near to the Plaza de San Francisco. The façade on the side of the **Town Hall** (Ayuntamiento) (7) facing the plaza dates from the original building, designed in the late 16th century. Its other face, topped by a clock tower, originates from the 19th century and overlooks the Plaza Nueva.

Continue along Avenida de la Constitución where, in the distance, the tower of the **Giralda**, the most visible landmark in Sevilla, beckons you to visit. This and the *Cathedral (Catedral) (8), ☎ 421-49-71, are your next destinations. A mosque was erected on this site in 1172, and twelve years later the Sultan ordered that a minaret be added. The exterior, adorned with typical sebka decoration, is in direct contrast to the blandness of the interior where a series of 35 gently elevated ramps lead visitors to a height of 70 meters (230 ft.), at which point there is an observation platform. This really is the finest vantage point from which to see Seville. Not only are the panoramic views unparalleled but, looking down from this height, the many beautiful patios invisible from street level are unveiled in the patchwork beneath you. The beauty of the minaret is, in fact, responsible for the fact that it survived the reconquest in 1248. When negotiating the terms of their surrender, Muslim rulers, who did not want to see the mosque and minaret under Christian control, asked that they be allowed to destroy them before turning over the city. The Spanish prince, Alfonzo, taken with the beauty of these structures, refused, threatening to put to death anyone who attempted to do so. An earthquake destroyed the tower's original ornamental top in 1356 and it was not until 1558 that it was replaced by the huge bells and revolving weather vane, Giralda in Spanish, that adorn its summit today. With the addition of the weather vane, a statue of a beautiful goddess, representing Faith, by Hernán Ruiz, the total height of the tower was raised to 98 meters (322 ft.).

The huge Almohade mosque was consecrated for Christian use during the period immediately following the reconquest and it was not until the beginning of the 15th century that a decision was made to erect the present Cathedral. Construction took well over a century. The resulting structure is the last, and the largest, of the Gothic cathedrals in Spain. In the entire Christian world it is exceeded in size only by St. Peter's in Rome and St. Paul's in London. It is quite ornate with numerous altars and chapels. The most important of the latter is the **Royal Chapel** *(Capilla Real)*. Contained herein are the tomb of Alfonso X, a museum exhibiting the Cathedral's treasures and, perhaps most popular with tourists, the elaborate tomb of Christopher Columbus *(Cristobal Colón)*, sculpted with four pallbearers representing Aragón, Castile, León, and Navarre, the four kingdoms that together formed Spain at the time of his discoveries. Make note, the dress code is strict here. Shorts, worn by either men or women, are frowned upon. *The Cathedral and Giralda are open Monday to Saturday from 10 a.m. to 5 p.m. and Sunday 2 p.m. to 6 p.m. Entrance 700 ptas (EUR 4.21), free on Sunday.*

Trip 15

Seville:
(Sevilla)

Torre del Oro, Tríana, and the Art Museum

Here's another stroll through old Seville, a delightful excursion into the past.

GETTING THERE:
PRACTICALITIES:
FOOD AND DRINK:
See pages 114-119 for all of the above.

SUGGESTED TOUR:
Numbers in parentheses correspond to numbers on the map.

Begin this tour by crossing the Avenida de la Constitución by the **Tourist Office** (1), taking Rodríguez Jurado, across from the **Archivo de Indias**, then Santander down to the banks of the River Guadalquivir. Along the way you will pass three places of interest. Beneath an archway near Constitución is the old **Royal Mint** *(Real Casa Moneda)*, which now hosts artistic exhibitions. An unusually designed and attractive house stands on the corner of Temprano and Santander. Finally, immediately across from the latter, is the **Bodegón Torre del Oro** (2). Seville has a lion's share of both bars and restaurants, each with its own unique character, but this stands alone in both originality and clientele. Of interest anytime, it is even more so for the hour or so before or after a **Bullfight** *(Corrida)*, when any number of celebrities from the bullfighting *(taurine)* world may put in an appearance.

Now that you have navigated through the constant stream of traffic on the wide and busy Paseo de Cristóbal, and passed across the more peaceful and charming Paseo del Alcade Marqués de Contadero, the gently flowing waters of the River Guadalquivir are sure to delight. Looking across to the opposite bank you'll see the **Barrio de Triana**, not so long ago the traditional Gypsy *(Gitano)* Quarter. Sadly, for those of us who were fortunate enough to have experienced this quarter's unique earthly enchant-

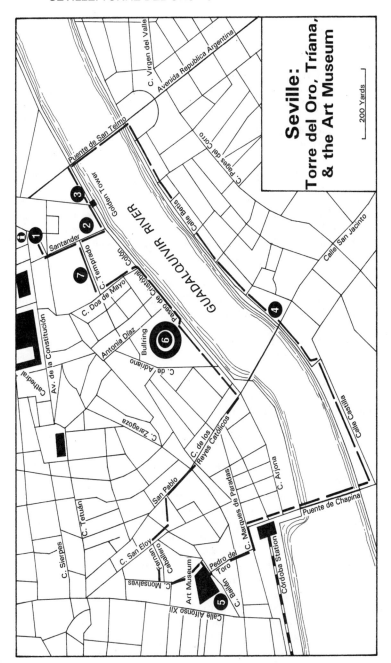

Seville:
Torre del Oro, Tríana,
& the Art Museum

200 Yards

ment, the Gypsies now reside in far less illustrious, in fact boringly bland, apartments that ring the city. The area has, not surprisingly, been "revitalized" and is now filled with all manner of upmarket shops and dining establishments. This, however, you will investigate a little farther on in the tour. Walking along the river you'll no doubt see one or more of the many boats that offer either a trip up and around the Expo'92 site and the theme park **Isla Mágica**, ☎ 902-16-17-16 or www.islamagica.es, or a longer voyage down river to its confluence with the Atlantic Ocean. Of these, **Cruceros Turisticos Torre del Oro**, ☎ 456-16-92, offer the best array of trips. A relaxing alternative is to rent a *pedalo* boat for an hour or so, and guide yourself around the river.

Your gaze will, sooner than later, be drawn to the nearby twelve-sided *Golden Tower (Torre de Oro)* (3), ☎ 422-24-19. A visit here is next on the agenda. Originally constructed in 1220 as a watchtower just outside of the city walls, its name is derived from the golden colored tiles that embellished it at one time. It has served the city in a variety of ways over its lengthy history. During times of potential invasion a metal chain with one end anchored to the tower was hauled across to the other river bank as a barrier to protect the harbor. For a period of time it was used as a vault to store and guard treasures brought to Spain from the Americas, and a less glorious time saw it used as a prison. The structure has undergone some changes over the years as well and, as recently as the middle 18th century, the round top and spire were added. *Today the tower houses a small nautical museum, which may be visited Tuesday to Friday between the hours of 10 a.m. and 2 p.m., and on Saturday, Sunday and holidays between 11 a.m. and 2 p.m. Entrance 100 ptas (EUR .60), free on Tuesday.*

Just beyond the Torre you'll come upon the Puente de San Telmo. As you cross the bridge towards the fountains of the Plaza de Cuba, pause for a moment and take in the marvelous views back to the *Torre de Oro* and the towering *Giralda,* standing proudly in all their splendor. Continue on, turning right into Betis where the terrace of the Restaurante Rio Grande comes into sight. This is another place to enjoy the views, seated now and partaking of your favorite refreshment. And, if seeing those boats on the river is too strong a temptation it is possible, just next door, to hire anything from a rowing boat to a motor boat. You will most likely have realized by this time that you are now in the middle of the upmarket area, formerly the Gypsy Quarter, that you viewed earlier on from across the river. Looking around, one would not have a hint of the scenes that were played out here as recently as thirty years ago. Then, on hot sultry summer nights, the inhabitants would drink and dance, provocatively, together on the river bank. The atmosphere now is certainly more dignified and gentrified, but will leave most visitors less satisfied.

Following Betis to its end, in the Plaza del Altozano, you'll find a **statue** (4) honoring Manolete, a famous local matador. Take the steps down to the riverbank and follow the pathway past a less salubrious neighborhood towards the next bridge, the Puente Cristo de la Expiración. Across the bridge there are two busy junctions. The first, to your left, is home to the new bus station *Estación de Autobuses Plaza de Armas*. On the other side of the street, next to the Plaza de la Legión, is the old train station *Estación de Córdoba*, which was converted into Seville's pavilion, *Pabellon de Sevilla*, for Expo'92. Take a left at the second plaza and the first right onto Pedro del Toro. You'll soon find a peaceful and charming square and, in it, the ***Museum of Fine Art** *(Museo de Bellas Artes)* (5), ☎ 422-07-90, located within in an early-17th-century Baroque building. Before the Spanish government closed many religious orders in 1835, this housed the *Convento de la Merced Calzada*. And, to rub salt into the wounds caused by its closing, many of the exalted exhibits, including works by El Greco, Velázquez, and Valdés Leal were expropriated from this and other closed convents. The gallery is considered to be second, in national importance, only to the Prado and, also one of the most important in Europe. *Open Tuesday 3 p.m. to 8 p.m., Wednesday to Saturday 9 a.m. to 8 p.m., and Sunday 9 a.m. to 2 p.m. Entrance 250 ptas (EUR 1.50), free for EC citizens.*

Ready for a little refreshment, perhaps? Then cross the appropriately named Plaza del Museo and head up Monsalves to its junction on Fernán Caballero. The palace diagonally across to the left is the seat of the President of the Autonomous Region of Andalucia, but the very small bar on the corner may prove the greater attraction. It is a strange little bar indeed—no seats and the other half of it is a grocery store. But it has much character and, of course, the sandwiches are fresh. On your way once again, you'll likely find that the only interesting thing about the next few streets, with the exception of the *Santa María Magdalena* church, are the streets themselves.

Nevertheless, continue on, taking a right into Eloy, at the end of Fernán Caballero, and going around the church into San Pablo which changes its name to Reyes Católicos before ending next to the river, at the Paseo de Cristóbal. After passing through a couple of blocks of bars and shops you'll see, on the left behind an iron grille fence, the now familiar colors of white and mustard. This time, these adorn the walls of the **Bullfighting Museum and Bullring** *(Museo de la Real Maestranza y Plaza de Toros)* (6), ☎ 422-45-77 or www.realmaestranza.com, considered to be the most beautiful in Spain. Work commenced on this plaza in 1761, but it wasn't completed, in its present form, until 1881. Owned by the Knighthood of Real Maestranza, the structure is an important architectural monument in its own right. Also of interest, is the covered bridge that connects the plaza itself with the "social house" for members of the Real Maestranza. For those planning to see just one bullfight *(corrida de toros)*, this is the plaza of choice. The fans *(aficionados)* are so knowledgeable and respectful that they allow the matador to work in perfect silence, and woe to those that break it. Many may be satisfied with a visit to the museum which, though not as good as some (particularly those in Barcelona, Córdoba, Madrid, and Ronda), does allow the opportunity to walk into the ring itself. Once in the middle it seems like a long way back to safety, and there isn't even a bull *(toro bravo)* in sight. Take a look at the deep horn gouges on the gateways *(burladeros)*, the entrance/exit points of the toreros, and you will have some idea of the strength and power of these extraordinary animals. *The museum is open daily 9:30 a.m. to 2 p.m. and 3 p.m. to 6 p.m. Entrance 250 ptas (EUR 1.50).*

A couple of blocks towards to the *Torre de Oro,* still along the city side of the Paseo de Cristóbal, is the ultra modern, totally incongruous, **Palacio de Cultura**. This, yet another of those buildings either constructed or renovated for Expo'92, is home to, among other things, the **Maestranza Theater** *(Teatro de la Maestranza)*, ☎ 422-33-44 or www.maestranza.com. Immediately behind this, on Temprano, is a structure of both temporal and spiritual beauty. The **Charity Hospital** *(Hospital de la Caridad)* (7), ☎ 422-32-32, was built in 1647 and, as it still serves its original purpose, patients are frequently seen convalescing in front of its attractive façade. Inside there is an unusual double patio separated by a double row of columns, and although robbed of many works of art by Napoleon's troops, the chapel still boasts some particularly blood-tingling works by Juan de Valdés Leal. *These may be seen Monday to Saturday between 10 a.m. to 1 p.m. and 3:30 p.m. to 6 p.m, and Sunday 9 a.m. to 1 p.m. Entrance 400 ptas (EUR 2.40).* To finish up this tour take a left at the end of Temprano onto Santander, following this to the Avenida de la Constitución and back to the Tourist Office.

Seville:
(Sevilla)
María Luisa Park and the Plaza España

T his, the last tour in Seville, is the easiest on the mind, the most pleasing on the eye, and certainly the most relaxing.

GETTING THERE:
PRACTICALITIES:
FOOD AND DRINK:
See pages 114-119 for all of the above.

SUGGESTED TOUR:
Numbers in parentheses correspond to numbers on the map.

Again, start at the **Tourist Office** (1), but this time head left towards the fountain that dominates the center of the Puerta de Jerez. Stop for a moment and ponder the row of buildings along the right-hand side. On the surface there seems nothing of interest, but this inauspiciously bland façade camouflages a 17th-century mansion, one of the finest houses in the city, that is owned by one of the most aristocratic families in Andalucía. Walk around the plaza and cross over to the corner of San Fernando and Avenida de Roma. Once again, the wonderful building and gardens you'll see here deserves further investigation. This, you will recognize, is the palatial **Hotel Alfonso XIII** (2) and, even if you are not fortunate enough to be a guest, don't be hesitant about having a look around. The bar in the central patio is also an enchanting place to sit and enjoy a drink.

Just down the Avenida de Roma, as you travel towards the river, is an even grander and more elaborate building with extensive gardens. This, the monumental **Palacio de San Telmo** (3), dates from 17th century. St. Telmo is the patron Saint of sailors and this, as the name may suggest, was originally a Seafarer's University and, during the next century, a Naval Academy. Since that time it has played the chameleon, functioning as the residence of the Dukes of Montpensier, as a seminary and finally, today, behind a most elaborately carved Baroque main archway, as offices for the Government of Andalucía Junta de Andalucia.

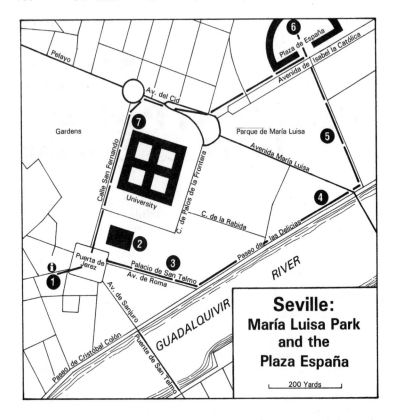

Seville:
**María Luisa Park
and the
Plaza España**

| 200 Yards |

Next, take a leisurely stroll along the riverside promenade that is the Paseo de las Delicias, towards the Glorieta de los Marineros Voluntarios traffic circle. As you approach you'll notice an odd building at the junction on the left-hand side. This, known as **The Queen's Sewing Room** *(Costurero de la Reina)* (4), today has a more mundane task; it functions as a rather isolated city tourist office. Also on Glorieta is one of several entrances to the **María Luisa Park** *(Parque de María Luisa)* (5), a favorite destination for Sevillianos seeking fun and relaxation. This is especially evident on week-ends. Formerly part of the nearby San Telmo gardens, the land was donated to the city by the Duchess of Montpensier in 1893. It is filled with cooling trees and ponds, and graced by lovely fountains and statues. At its eastern end are two pavilions *(pabellons)* constructed for the 1929 Iboamerican Exhibition, which now house the museums of **Archaeology** *(Arqueológico)* and **Popular Arts and Costumes** *(Arte y Costumbres Populares)*.

Continue on, however—the greatest attraction here is directly ahead, just outside of the park itself. The beautiful and intricate **Plaza de España*

(6) is most unusual indeed. Also built for the 1929 Iboamerican Exhibition, it is semi-circular in shape with two immense towers at either end. A slightly less imposing central block is utilized by the Army as offices for the Capitán General. At its base, depicted upon the ever-popular *azulejos*, multi-colored ceramic tiles, are the coats-of-arms and a picture of every Spanish province. Following the curves of the building, and not quite connecting to form a "D" shape, is a narrow ornamental boating lake. The buildings and a central fountain are connected by the ornate bridges which cross the lake.

Exit to the right, and follow the park out to the Glorieta de San Diego, noting on the way a very strangely-shaped house that serves as the Portuguese Consulate. Follow the Avenida del Cid to the fountain of the Plaza de Don Juan de Austria and turn left into San Fernando. Here you cannot but notice an immense, although not very tall, building that is even larger than the Cathedral. It was constructed in the mid-18th century, and by the beginning of the next century the state **Tobacco Factory** *(Fábrica de Tabacos)* (7) employed well over 10,000 women. One of these was the famous Carmen, immortalized by Bizet in his opera of the same name. Today it is part of the University and, if you are young enough or clever enough to masquerade as a student, it is possible to take a look around. Time to end this final tour and, luckily, it is just a short walk from here back to the Tourist Office, via the Puerta de Jerez.

Carmona

Carmona has been coveted, from the beginning of its history that stretches back 5,000 years to the Neolithic period, for its strategic hilltop position overlooking the wide plains nearby. It was instrumental to the defenses of the Tartessans during the 8th century BC and, similarly, to the Carthaginians four centuries later. It was the Roman era, however, that brought to the area prosperity and wealth. Following the Second Punic War, around 206 BC, it is recorded as the Roman town of *Carmo*. Later, during the time of Augustus, a formal town plan was laid out and a main highway, *cardo máximo*, was constructed through town as it ran between, and linked, the gates of Seville *(Hispalis)* to Córdoba *(Córduba)*. By this time, Carmona had emerged as the largest and most powerful town in the region.

The decline of the fortunes of Carmona paralleled that of the Roman Empire but, after a brief period of Visigothic rule, the Moorish invasion of 713 brought a period of renewed growth and prosperity. The Moors governed, under various regimes, for over 500 years until the city was reconquered, in the name of King Ferdinand II, on September 21, 1247. The town was then divided among the victors, with the main beneficiaries being the noble orders of Santiago and Calatrava. Late in the 14th century a period of strife ensued between King Pedro I and Enrique of Trastamara, following which the latter gained control, subsequently imposing severe repression upon citizens in general, and the Jewish population in particular. At the close of the next century Ferdinand and Isabella used Carmona a final base, prior to launching their reconquest of Granada in 1492. Finally, in 1630 Felipe IV brought this repressive period to an end when he granted to Carmona the rights of township. This marked the beginning of a period of sustained growth, during which many of the mansions and palaces which grace the city today were constructed.

Carmona's history is unique in that it was never under the rule of a feudal lord. It was, rather, protected as a "Crown" city. This accounts for the extraordinary number of important homes, palaces, convents and churches found here, which alone make the city worth a visit. It has a quiet, charming atmosphere disturbed by relatively few tourists, and offers a rare opportunity to visit a historically interesting town while experiencing firsthand the delightfully unspoiled lifestyle typical of Andalucía.

GETTING THERE:

Trains do not run to, or offer services that disembark anywhere near, Carmona.

Buses provide the only option of public transport to Carmona. Empresa Casal, S.A., ☎ 499-92-90, operate frequent services from Seville's Avenida de Portugal (just behind the Plaza de España) to the Plaza de Blas Infante (just outside the Alcázar de la Puerta de Sevilla) in Carmona.

By Car, Carmona, just under 20 miles east of Seville (and 345 miles south of Madrid), is reached via the N-IV.

PRACTICALITIES:

One of the main attractions in Carmona, the Necropolis, is closed on Monday. The **Dialing Code** is 95. The **Tourist Office**, ☎ 419-09-55, e-mail car mona@andal.es or www.andal.es/carmona, Arco de la Puerta de Sevilla, is open Monday to Saturday 10 a.m. to 6 p.m. and Sunday and holidays 10 a.m. to 3 p.m. Carmona has a **population** of 25,000 and is in the province of Sevilla, one of eight belonging to the autonomous region of **Andalucía**.

ACCOMMODATION:

The **Hotel Casa Palacio "Casa de Carmona"** ***** **GL**, ☎ 414-30-00, fax 414-37-52 or www.casadecarmona.com, Plaza de Lasso, 1, is housed in the 15th- to 17th-century *Palacio de Lasso de la Vega*. This lovely old structure had fallen into a severe state of disrepair before the matriarch of the Guardiola Medina family transformed it into a highly luxurious small hotel. In each of the 30-odd guest rooms modern amenities are discretely incorporated into lavish traditional decor, embellished with lovely antique furniture. The public rooms are equally delightful, and the service is impeccable. What distinguishes the Casa, however, is its hospitality. Guests are encouraged to relax and treat this lovely palace as their home. Those who would like a more detailed description of this truly magnificent place should read my article in the April 1996 issue of Country Inns magazine. $$

The **Cortijo "El Triguero,"** ☎ (91) 411-69-74 or fax (91) 561-17-42, is located ten minutes east of Seville's airport, just outside of Carmona. This working bull-breeding ranch also offers accommodation; 7 double rooms and 2 single rooms sharing 6 bathrooms between them. Facilities include lounges, a dining room, a delightful swimming pool encircled by orange trees, and a bullring where you may view amateur bullfighting. If that is not to your taste, perhaps you will enjoy the flamenco, or simply the relaxing tenor of the pleasant countryside. $

FOOD AND DRINK:

Among the favorite local dishes are *gazpacho*, a cold soup; *escarolas con pimiento molido,* endives with paprika; and *las patatas en amarillo con bacalao,* potatoes in saffron with cod. For dessert sample a slice of cake, handmade using all natural ingredients in the kitchens of the convents of *Santa Clara* and *Concepción*.

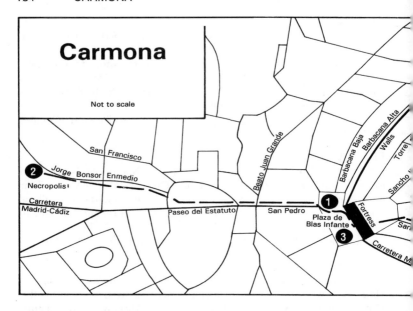

Hotel Casa Palacio "Casa de Carmona" (Plaza de Lasso, 1), true to the standards set by the hotel, boasts an exquisite restaurant, the *El Caballo Blanco*. Amidst an ambiance created by flagstone floors, exposed brick walls and stately columns embellished with frescoes of white horses expect a limited, and very esoteric, menu. If nothing listed tempts your palate then, subject to availability of ingredients, the chef will gladly prepare a favorite dish of your choosing. The service is, as you would expect, impeccable, and carried out in a formal and traditional style where ladies make their selections, without guilt, from a menu with the prices omitted. ☎ 414-30-00, fax 414-37-52 or www.casadecarmona.com. $$$

Restaurante Molina de la Romera (Sor Angela de la Cruz, 8), is a small restaurant serving local dishes in one of the typical side streets of Carmona. ☎ 414-20-00. $

SUGGESTED TOUR:

Numbers in parentheses correspond to numbers on the map.

This tour begins at the main **Plaza de Blas Infante** (1), which separates the old and new sections of Carmona. This is particularly convenient as the plaza actually serves as the bus stop to and from Seville. You will, no doubt, be intrigued by the thought of what lies beyond the ancient gate, but stay your curiosity, turning next onto the irregularly-shaped Paseo del Estauto. At the end the main road carries on to the left, but by taking Jorge Bonsor Enmedio just to its right, very soon you'll come to two fascinating Roman relics. To the right is the old Roman Amphitheatre where, in truth, there is not much left to see. Looking directly across the road, however,

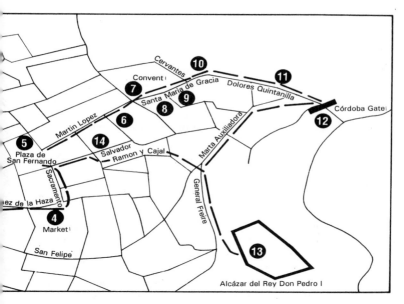

you'll find the *Necropolis and Museum of Carmona* (Museo y Necropolis de Carmona) (2), ☎ 414-08-11 or fax 419-14-76, the largest Roman necropolis standing outside of Rome itself. Within this sprawling complex are over 800 tombs and some, the Tomb of the Elephant and Tomb of Servilia in particular, are absolutely fascinating. *You may visit June 15 to September 15 on Tuesday to Saturday from 9 a.m. to 2 p.m., between September 16 to June 14 it is open Tuesday to Friday 10 a.m. to 5 p.m. and on Saturday, Sunday and holidays from 10 a.m. to 2 p.m. Entrance 250 ptas (EUR 1.50), free for EC citizens.*

Retrace your steps back to the Plaza de Blas Infante and, if you are so inclined, there are any number of small, characterful, bars along the left hand side of the Paseo del Estauto, where you may slake your thirst. And be warned, if you are visiting during the summer, it will most likely be scorchingly hot.

It's time now to turn your attention to what surely must be the most unusual combination of fortress and gateway you are likely to see. The *Fortress and Gate of Seville* (Alcázar de la Puerta de Sevilla) (3), ☎ 419-09-55 or www.andal.es/carmona, stands proudly guarding the entrance to the city from the Seville road. Upon closer inspection it becomes evident that the gate has considerably more depth than width, and that access to the city is attained only by passing through one of the intricate archways on either side. Thus, in its day, it provided a formidable barrier to those who would encroach upon the city's peace. There are traces here that date from the 14th to 12th centuries BC; but it was the Romans, building over

Carthaginian foundations, who fully developed the site between the 3rd and 1st centuries BC. Since that time successive rulers have effected many additions and subtractions, as it has evolved to the structure you see today. As with many of the ancient monuments, this is most impressive early in the morning or at sunset, when the sun overlays the dramatically changing hues of its rays onto the colors of the brickwork. *It is open Monday to Saturday from 10 a.m. to 6 p.m. and Sunday and holidays 10 a.m. to 3 p.m. Entrance 300 ptas (EUR 1.80).*

Pedestrians may enter the old town through either archway, but be aware that cars enter through the much narrower arch on the right-hand side, and leave via the other. After passing through bear around towards the right and into San Bartolome where you'll find, not surprisingly, a church named in honor of the same saint. As you turn left into a deceptively steep street, Calle Domínguez de la Haza, the intriguing house on the right corner is, as the street name has foretold, the Domínguez House. Many Roman remains have been found in this house, including parts of the *cardo máximo*. Near the top of the hill and on the right is a building that bears very few similarities, stylistically, to others in this area. If you are curious, enter through your choice of a limited number of entrances and you will find that this low and long, square building, devoid of windows and decoration, houses the **Mercado** (4). And, inside, this one is quite traditional. As is common in the daily food markets found in towns and villages throughout Spain, all of the activity here takes place before lunch. In the afternoons you'll find only an occasional customer at one of the bars and, maybe, children playing soccer in the spacious central area.

Continue on, taking Sacramento, which runs at a tangent to the market, down to the most interestingly eclectic **Plaza de San Fernando** (5). In the center, palm trees encircle a strange metal column that rests on a stone plinth. Many of the buildings surrounding it, and no two look remotely alike, date from the 16th century. Also known as the Plaza de Arriba, this is where you will find the **Town Hall** *(Ayuntamiento)* which, uniquely to my knowledge, is an adjunct of the San Salvador church. In fact, this functioned as an economic and administrative center during the Roman era. These days, the square is at its most enchanting on a Sunday lunchtime. Just after church services have dismissed, the adults socialize with their friends either inside, or around the outside, of the bars and the air is filled with the delighted squeals of children, dressed in their Sunday best and playing safely in the center.

Exit the plaza by way of Martín Lopez, noting as you look ahead how the houses of this narrow street frame, to perfection, the towering steeple of the **Iglesia de Santa María**. This late-Gothic church was constructed between the 15th and 16th centuries. The interior, though richly endowed with treasures, has a rather dark and foreboding atmosphere, enlivened only by a small patio ornamented with numerous orange trees. Just behind here, on Calle San ildelfonso, is the **Palace of the Marqueses de las Torres** that is home to the small, but interesting, **Museum of Archeology and**

Ethnography *(Museo Arqueológico y Etnográfico)* (6), ☎ 414-01-28. *It is open Monday to Friday 11 a.m. to 7 p.m., but closes at 2 p.m. on Tuesday, entrance 200 ptas EUR (1.20).* Exit, return back to Martin Lopez and carry on to the right where you will be met, in short order, by an multifarious grouping of structures. On the left is the massive and distinctive two-towered façade of the 18th-century **Convent of "Las Descalzas"** *(Convento de las Descalzas)* (7). Opposite this is the **Convent of Santa Clara** *(Convento de Santa Clara)* (8), and some event throughout its history has caused the strange, rectangular, deep cracks in its sides. On the next corner is the 16th-century Charity Hospital and refuge, the **Hospital de la Misericordia** (9), recognized by its attractive clock tower.

Leaving these grand-styled buildings behind, follow Dolores Quintanilla as it winds around to the right and down towards the other of Carmona's famous gates. Along the way are two houses of interest. The first, at **Number 1** (10), was at one time owned by Ruiz Gutiérrez de Hinestrosa. You will have no trouble discerning which is the 18th-century **Casa de las Aguas** (11). Located at number 19, the orange reddish color with which it has been painted makes it easily distinguishable from its neighbors.

Without doubt, however, the dominant structure in this neighborhood is the **Córdoba Gate** *(Puerta de Córdoba)* (12). While not as grand as its counterpart at the other end of ancient Carmona, it is most unusual. A gate has existed on this site since the first century AD, during the height of the Roman Empire, and it was connected to the Puerta de Sevilla by the main Roman road, the *cardo máximo*. Subsequent rulers effected various reconstructions and renovations of the structure, but, most likely, those completed during the 16th, 17th and 18th centuries gave to the central section and arch the relatively modern look you see today. On the other hand, it is apparent that the two octagonal, crenellated, towers on either end originate from a much earlier period. Pass through the gate and take a moment to ponder the view of the extensive plain, known as the *Vega*, which unfolds below, striking in its continuity, and broken only by the traffic hurtling along the modern N-IV highway. You will also see, clearly from this vantage point, that Carmona stands on the last elevated portion of the *Alcores*, and truly dominates the surrounding countryside. In fact, the city is visible for many miles around.

Back inside the gate, retrace your steps up the cobblestone hill for a short distance. Take a left turn into Calatrava which, rising and changing its name along the way, eventually leads to the old **Fortress** *(Alcázar del Rey Don Pedro I)* (13). The walls and ramparts are, for the most part, surprisingly well preserved here, and one corner has become home to the parador hotel. This establishment, situated at the highest point in Carmona, boasts wide-ranging views out over the *Vega* and, perhaps more interestingly, of the rooftops of ancient Carmona which unfold below like a patchwork quilt of color and ever-changing shapes. Leave the grounds of the *Alcázar* the way you came and, on the way back down the hill, you will pass the **Alonso Bernal Escamilla** on the right before making a left at Ramón y Cajal. Here, in quick succession at numbers 8, 9, and 12 you'll find, respectively, the interesting houses of the *Casa de Vila, Casa de Briones* and the *Casa de Marqués de San Martín*. A right, near the end, onto Barrera, brings you face to façade with the imposing **Casa de Rueda** (14). Finally, a left ends the tour back in the Plaza de San Fernando.

As you will most likely have gathered, Carmona has much to offer; and any suggested tour must be considered, to some extent, subjective. Almost without exception, any street you care to wander down is a treasure trove of noteworthy architecture and history. You may, therefore, choose to explore this lovely city at your leisure. And, to do this most effectively, just pop into the tourist office, in the corner of the square, and request a Carmona guide.

The most discerning of visitors will realize that Carmona makes an ideal base from which to explore Seville, which is a convenient thirty minutes or so away when traveling by bus. And, what could possibly be more relaxing than returning each evening to the luxurious, yet unpretentious and hospitable, ambiance of the Hotel Casa Palacio Casa de Carmona?

Jerez de la Frontera

Jerez de la Frontera has a long and kaleidoscopic history, and the most conspicuous of the resulting monuments is the large and impressive *Alcázar*, a memorial of the centuries of Moorish rule. By the 15th century the city had expanded beyond its walls to become one of the most prosperous in Andalucia. It is its geographical location, however—at one point of the triangle formed with El Puerto de Santa María and Sanlucar de Barrameda—that is responsible for its unique climate and *albariza* soil. These attributes, in turn, are the foundation of Jerez's world-wide fame. The Moors brought with their invasion the art of distillation, but it was not until the 18th century that the production and sale of sherry—and of course Brandy—encouraged by the English, grew into the industry that would give the city its identity. Today, the English names emblazoned on the *bodegas*, literally a place where the barrels are stored but more commonly used to identify a particular company, are familiar to everyone.

The city's agricultural connections have led to a love affair with the horse, and visitors to Jerez will not want to miss a stop at the Royal School of Equestrian Art. During May, the city celebrates the annual Horse Fair (*Fería de Caballo*).

Although there are really no monuments of particular note here, what the city does have is a distinctly different, and very charming, ambiance. Consequently, few tourists will be disappointed with a stop in Jerez de la Frontera.

GETTING THERE:

Trains run through Jerez de la Frontera on their way to and from Seville and Cádiz. Services are offered in all categories, ranging from slow local services to major long-distance trains to Madrid.

Buses are best used when travelling from Algeciras and Málaga, cities where there are no convenient train connections.

By car, Jerez de la Frontera, 387 miles south of Madrid, is reached by taking either the N-IV for the entire journey or, alternatively, the N-IV as far as Sevilla and then the A-4 *autopista* toll road.

By air, the airport, nearly 5 miles from the city center, has limited direct International connections and internal flights to most Spanish cities.

PRACTICALITIES:

During the summer months, the heat in Jerez can be really stifling and, although the sea is not that far away, do not presume you will be delivered its cooling breezes. Accommodation may be difficult to find during the city's two festivals; the *Fería de Caballo* in May, and the *Fería de Otoño* in late September/October. The **Dialing Code** is 956. The **Oficina de Turismo**, ☎ 33-11-50, fax 33-17-31 or www.webjerez.com, is found at Larga, 39. It is open from June to September between 9 a.m. to 2 p.m. and 5 p.m. to 8 p.m. and the rest of the year between 9 a.m. to 2 p.m. and 4 p.m. to 7 p.m. Jerez de la Frontera has a **population** of 200,000 and is in the province of Cádiz, one of eight belonging to the autonomous region of **Andalucía**.

ACCOMMODATION:

The **Hotel Royal Sherry Park** ****, ☎ 30-30-11, fax 31-13- 00 or www.travelcom.es/sherry, Álvaro Domecq, 11, is a wonderfully modern hotel, with every expected facility. It is set in its own lovely park-like grounds, and features an inviting pool complex. $$

The **Hotel Guadalete** ****, ☎ 18-22-88, fax 11-22-93 or www.travel com.es/guadalete, Avenida Duque De Abrantes, 50, is a recently constructed hotel set in its own grounds and located just a short distance from the Royal Andalucian School of Equestrian Art. Modern in both style and facilities it, also, has an large and enticing pool. $$

The **Hotel Jerez** ****, ☎ 30-06-00, fax 30-50-01, e-mail jerez@travel com.es or www.travelcom.es/jerez, Avda. Alvaro Domecq, 35. This is a large and impressive hotel at the far end of the Avenida from the center of town. Pleasant rooms, fine facilities and a large garden and pool. $$

The **Hotel La Cueva Park** ****, ☎ 18-91-20 or fax 18-91-21, Ctra. De Arcos de la Frontera. Just a short distance from Jerez, on the road to Arcos, this modern hotel is a delight. Nice rooms, good amenities and an impressive restaurant. $$

The **Hotel Monasterio San Miguel** ****, ☎ 54-04-40, fax 54- 26-04, e-mail monasterio@jale.com or www.jale.com/monasterio, Calle Larga, 27, El Puerto de Santa María. El Puerto is a short fifteen minutes from Jerez by train or car, and the experience of a stay in this hotel, converted from an 18th-century Capuchin convent, is worth the trip in its own right. The former monastic cells have been transformed into comfortable suites and it has a highly acclaimed restaurant, *Las Bóvedas*, which derives its name from its vaults. $$$

The **Hotel Doña Blanca** ***, ☎ 34-87-61 or fax 34-85-86, Bodega, 11, is a charming hotel located in the city center. It is fully air-conditioned, and each room features a color TV, a radio, a minibar and a private safe. $$

The **Hotel El Coloso** *, ☎ 34-90-08 or fax 34-90-08, Pedro Alonso, 13, is a very pleasant hotel, with good facilities, in a quiet location close to the Plaza del Arenal. $

FOOD AND DRINK:

Its proximity to the Atlantic Ocean makes seafood, in particular shell-fish, a great favorite in Jerez de la Frontera. This, of course, is accompanied by sherry *(Fino)* in all its varieties, with the most popular being those of nutty dry type.

Restaurante El Bosque (Avenida Álvaro Domecq, 26), conveniently near to a number of the major hotels and the city center, offers innovative seafood dishes and caters to the city's elite. Reservations recommended, ☎ 30-33-33. X: Mon. $$

Restaurante Tendido 6, as the name indicates, is found next to the *Plaza de Toros*. The decorations are, as you would envision, very much taurine in nature. Patrons enjoy traditional food and lots of it. ☎ 34-48-35. X: Sun. $$

Hotel Royal Sherry Park (Álvaro Domecq, 11), has, as you would expect, a delightful formal restaurant. There is also a surprise. Next to the pool is a terrace cafeteria offering basic, but plentiful and well cooked, dishes at extraordinarily inexpensive prices. And the ambiance is charming. ☎ 30-30-11 or fax 31-13- 00 $

SUGGESTED TOUR:

Numbers in parentheses correspond to numbers on the map.

Jerez de la Frontera is an anomaly within Spain, a rare town whose central plaza is not named *Mayor* or *España*. Here, it is called the **Plaza del Arenal** (1) and, not unusually, is the logical place to begin your tour. Take a moment, though, before you set out. Surrounded by towering palm trees, and under the watchful eye of Don Miguel Primo de Rivera, astride his mount upon a plinth in a fountain adorned pool, this is an ideal place to have a seat, relax and soak up the atmosphere. Leave the plaza by way of Calle San Agustín and take a left into Santa Cecilia. You will soon come to the towering façade of the **Iglesia de San Miguel** (2), ☎ 34-33-47. Dating from the 15th to 16th centuries, its intricate and attractive altar is of particular interest. *Open Monday to Friday between 10:30 a.m. to 11:30 a.m.*

Retrace your steps down Santa Cecilia and, when you come to a small plaza, go straight ahead down Calle Conde Bayona towards the forbidding walls of the **Alcázar and Mosque** (3), ☎ 31-97-98. Following the crenellated walls and towers around to the left, it will soon become apparent that this immense structure is in a state of some disrepair. The **Mosque** *(Mezquita)* (4), is located on the side facing away from Calle Bayona. It is of Almohade design, and this small and dignified structure dates from the 11th century. Also inside is the rather curious **Camera Obscura** *(Cámara oscura)*. Found in the tower of the Baroque Villavicencio Palace, it offers visitors a bird's eye view of the city. *Both of these are open daily between May and September from 10 a.m. to 8 p.m.; and the rest of the year 10 a.m. to 6 p.m. Admission to the Alcazar is 200 ptas (EUR 1.20) and (Camera Obscura) 500 ptas (EUR 3.01).*

Continue on and, at the end of the first stretch of walls, the scenery

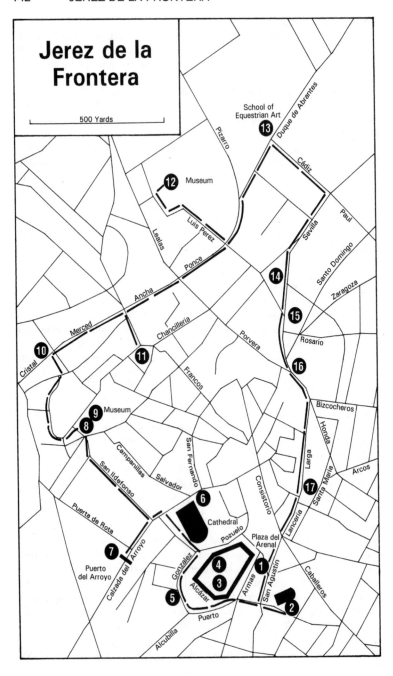

Jerez de la Frontera

500 Yards

changes suddenly and dramatically. An open plaza area, the Alameda Vieja, graced by lovely shade trees and a bandstand, form the foreground with the rolling vineyard covered hills stretching to the horizon. Between the two, and just down some steps, is the sprawling *Gonzalez Byass Bodega complex (5), ☎ 34-00-00, fax 35-70-46 or www.gonzalezbyass.com, easily identifiable by the familiar signs advertising one of its most famous products, *Tio Pepe*. Note the two plaques outside the door, indicating the Vice-Consulancy of Italy and Denmark. Of all the bodegas in Jerez this is my personal favorite. *It may be visited, by advance reservation, Monday to Friday and on Saturday and Sunday morning. Entrance 350 ptas (EUR 2.10) Monday to Friday and 450 ptas (EUR 2.71) on Saturday and Sunday.* In addition to an informative introduction to the intricacies of grape cultivation and the production of famous local wines, there are several interesting surprises that are more appropriately left unexplained here.

Just a short distance around the *Alcázar* from the Gonzalez Byass Bodega is the **Cathedral** *(Catedral)* (6), ☎ 34-84-42. Constructed in the 17th century, over an old mosque, this is an interesting mix of Gothic, Baroque and Neo-Classical styles. It is interesting to note, however, that the main tower is separated from the main structure. *Opening hours are odd as well: Monday to Friday 6 p.m. to 7 p.m. and Saturday, Sunday and holidays from 11 a.m. to 2 p.m.*

Exit the Cathedral by way of the main door and descend the rows of steps. Take the road to your left and follow along until you reach one of the city's ancient gates, the **Puerta del Arroyo** (7), which you will find to be uninspiring—rather plain, and well pock-marked by bullets. Retrace your steps back along the Calzada del Arroyo and make a left onto Espiritu Santo. At the top, you will come to an ancient monastery that precedes the elegant buildings of the **Pedro Domecq Bodegas**. A plaque over the door proclaims it was founded in 1730. You may get a little intoxicated just from the aroma emanating from the bodega.

The road has now changed its name to San Ildefonso. At its end, take your pick from among the narrow streets meandering to the right and into the **Plaza del Mercado** (8). Here you'll find the new, and quite small, **Archaeological Museum** *(Museo Arqueológico)* (9), ☎ 33-33-16, fax 34-13-50 or www.ctv.es/users/jerezmuseoarq/home.htm. *It may be visited Tuesday to Friday from 10 a.m. to 2 p.m. and 4 p.m. to 7 p.m.; and on Saturday, Sunday and holidays between mid-June and the end of August from 10 a.m. to 2:30 p.m. Entrance 250 ptas (EUR 1.50)*. Opposite is the ancient Gothic style church of *San Mateo*. Continue on, following around and through, in turn, the narrow streets of Almendrillo, Alegria, Consolación, and Córdobeses to the rather busier street of Muro and a stretch of the ancient walls. Directly across, and at the back of the Plaza Santa Isabel, is a church, the **Nuestra Señora de la Merced** (10), with an imposing tower and a fascinating doorway. The inside is, likewise, interesting; quite plain but with a spectacular gilded Baroque altar.

Turn left out of the church and follow the reasonably busy Calle

Merced to the Plaza de Santiago, home to the towering church of like name as well as a diminutive fountain and bust of a prominent local figure. Be sure to sneak a peek into the patios of the houses along the way; some are surprisingly elegant indeed. Calle Oliva runs at a tangent to the Plaza de Santiago and, at its end, in the smaller Plaza de San Juan, is the lovely 18th-century **Palace of Pemartín** *(Palacio Pemartín)*. This is the home of the ***Foundation of Andalucian Flamenco** *(Fundación Andaluza de Flamenco)* (11), ☎ 34-92-65, fax 32-11-27, e-mail caf@cica-es and on the Internet at http://caf.cica.es, my favorite place in Jerez. Not only is the palace itself a place of great charm; it houses a wealth of interesting exhibits detailing this fascinating art form. There is an audiovisual demonstration on the hour every hour but, without doubt, the highlight of a visit here is watching the dancers, accompanied by a guitarist, practicing their steps and perfecting their form in the audience of a huge mirror. *It is open Monday to Friday 9 a.m. to 2 p.m., and entrance is free.*

Return to the Plaza de Santiago and, this time, take a right onto Calle Ancha, where you will be greeted by a small park with a couple of modern statues, a fountain and another stretch of the ancient walls. Farther along you will find the **Iglesia de la Victoria**, dating from 1639, and easily recognizable by its round domed top decorated with blue and white tiles. Here, Ancha changes to Ponce. At the next junction, turn left and follow Luis Perez, then Cervantes to the **Clock Museum** *(Museo de Relojes)* (12), ☎ 18-21-00 or fax 31-31-53. This is housed in a neo-classical mansion *La Atalaya*, which is situated amidst beautiful grounds populated by peacocks, black swans, and a variety of other exotic birds. The museum itself, considered one of the best of its kind in the world, displays a collection of over 300 clocks occupying over half of the house. It goes without saying that the best time to visit is just before the hour. *Opening hours are Monday to Saturday 10 a.m. to 2 p.m., and entrance is 400 ptas (EUR 2.40).*

Retrace your steps to the junction with Ponce, making a left onto Pozo del Olivar and then, at the fork, taking Avenida Duque de Abrantes to the right. This will lead, in short order, to Jerez de la Frontera's most acclaimed institution. The ***Royal Andalucian School of Equestrian Art** *(Real Escuela Andaluza del Arte Ecuestre)* (13), Information ☎ 31-11-11, reservations ☎ 30- 77-98, fax 30-99-54 or www.realescuela.org, is set in large private grounds, dominated by an elegant mansion and an indoor stadium that leads to the stable areas. *The world famous "Andalucian Horse Ballet" is performed at midday each Thursday, and at the same time on Tuesday between March and October (except holidays), ticket prices are either 2,500, 2,000 or 1,500 ptas (EUR 15.03, 12.02 or 9.02). There are also special shows during the Fería de Caballo, with all ticket prices being increased 500 ptas (EUR 3.01). On Monday, Wednesday or Friday throughout the year and Tuesday between November and February (with the exception of holidays) all areas, including the stables, are open for inspection and it is possible to watch the horses training in the arena between 11 a.m. and 1 p.m.*

Entrance 500 ptas (EUR 3.01).

Depart via Calle Cádiz, directly across the road. A right, at the end, onto Sevilla, will lead you into the irregularly shaped, and interesting, **Plaza Mamelón** (14). This features a wonderful huge fountain and, fortuitously on a shaded side, there is a characterful bar surrounded, of course, by the inevitable wooden sherry casks. Press on and, just past here, you will find two interesting structures. The first is the **Domecq Palace** *(Palacio de Domecq)* (15), a typically Baroque palace dating from 1778. This is followed, in rapid succession, by the **Convento de Santo Domingo** (16), which dates from the era of the reconquest and is noted for its beautiful cloister. Today it functions as an exhibition hall. It also happens to be directly across from the Tourist Office.

Calle Larga leads from here into a pedestrian shopping area where, if you deserve a break today, you may pay a visit to the inescapable McDonalds. The street ends at its junction with Santa María and a curious round building known as the **El Gallo Azul** (17). Here also is a curious clock set atop a metal tower which, upon best belief, was donated to the city by Pedro Domecq. To the left is the city's food market, **Mercado de Abastos**, and Calle Lanceria, straight ahead, will take you back to the Plaza del Arenal and the end of the tour.

El Puerto de Santa María

E l Puerto de Santa María has signs of settlements that date back to the Inferior Paleolithic age and, currently, excavations are ongoing of a Phoenician town from around the 4th to 3rd centuries BC. Over a millenium later the Moors beat the defending Visigoths at the nearby Battle of Guadalete, beginning their march through Spain. It wasn't until 1260 that King Alfonso X reconquered the city, naming it Santa María de Puerto and giving out land rights. Coming under the rule of the lordship of the Medinacelli family, a period of wealth ensued. It was that family who hosted Christopher Columbus between 1483 and 1486, and assisted him plan his voyages and outfit his vessels. In the 16th and 17th centuries El Puerto de Santa María became the winter quarters and base of the Royal galleys and HQ of the Captaincy General of the Ocean Sea. This, effectively, made it an important base for preparing military naval expeditions. In the early 18th century its status changed when, upon the assumption of the throne of Felipe V it asked to come under, and was given, effective as of May 31st, 1729, the protectorate of the Crown. The 18th century, also, was one of prosperity, but the beginning of the 19th century brought with it problems, as El Puerto became the headquarters of the invading French army besieging Cádiz during the Wars of Independence. Various other changes marked the city during that century and the first part of the next, culminating in the Spanish Civil War in the late 1930s. In the latter half of the 20th century, however, prosperity slowly returned with the development of El Puerto de Santa María, and its environs, as an important resort.

GETTING THERE:

Trains, either local or long distance, run on a frequent basis between Sevilla and Cádiz, stopping at El Puert de Santa María on the way.

Buses operate on a frequent basis from either Cádiz or Sevilla.

By car, use either the A4 *autopista* (toll road) or the slower N-IV from either Sevilla or Cádiz.

PRACTICALITIES:

The **Dialing Code** is 956. The **Oficina de Turismo**, ☎ 54-24-13, fax 54-22-46 or www.elpuertosm.es, Luna, 22, is open Monday to Sunday 10 a.m. to

2 p.m. and 6 p.m. to 8 p.m., and in the afternoons in the winter from 5:30 p.m. to 7:30 p.m. El Puerto de Santa María has a **population** of 70,000, and is in the province of Cádiz, one of eight belonging to the autonomous region of **Andalucía**.

ACCOMMODATION:

The **Hotel Monasterio San Miguel** ****, ☎ 54-04-40 or fax 54-26-04, Calle Larga, 27, has been beautifully converted from an 18th-century Capuchin convent, and a stay here alone merits a trip to El Puerto de Santa María. The former monastic cells have been transformed into comfortable suites, and there is a lovely pool in the gardens. Guests have included the Spanish Royal family. $$$

The **Hotel Meliá El Caballo Blanco** ****, ☎ 56-25-41 or fax 56-27-12, Avenda de Madrid, 1, is found in its own extensive gardens and with a 800 yard frontage on the *Playa* (beach) *de Valdelagrana*. Impressive, in size and taste, this has a variety of rooms and bungalows, all with the latest modern facilities, restaurantsand pools. $$

The **Hotel Los Canteros** ***, ☎ 54-02-40 or fax 54-11-21, Ribera del Marisco, Curva, 6, is pleasant, friendly, hotel in the center of the seafood restaurant part of town. It gets its name from the 17th-century water jugs found in the yard. Select from 39 double rooms, all with a private bath, TV, telephone, mini bar and air conditioning. $

FOOD AND DRINK:

Restaurante Las Bóvedas (Calle Larga, 27), found in, and as distinguished as, the Hotel Monasterio San Miguel, comes by its name for the vaults in which it is located. A very unique restaurant, the specialty here is typical Andalucian cuisine featuring locally cured hams, seafood and shellfish, of course, and even such unlikely treats as Sea Urchins. Fine food, fine wines and fine service. ☎ 54-04-40 or fax 54-26-04. $$$

Restaurante El Faro del Puerto (Ctra. De Rota, Km 0.5), a local favorite, is found just outside the center of town in a charming old house within its own grounds. The cuisine here is acclaimed for its creativity, drawing a fine distinction between traditional and imaginative creations. Whichever you select, you can be sure there will be, from its extensive cellars, a wine to match. ☎ 85-80-03 or fax 54-04-66. $$

Romerijo (Plaza de la Herrería, 1), epitomizes, if not symbolizes, popular seafood and shell restaurants in El Puerto. Open plan, even with a separate fried fish take away Cocedero section, these are not sophisticated in any way with one, albeit very important, exception: the selection of dishes to choose from. These range from a single oyster up to a large plate covered with every type of shellfish and seafood imaginable. ☎ 54-12-54 or fax 54-10-06. $, $$ or $$$ (depending upon tastes and how much you eat).

SUGGESTED TOUR:

Numbers in parentheses correspond to numbers on the map.

As most visitors will be arriving by train the **Railroad Station** *(Estación de Ferrocarril)* (1), is the best place to start. Coming out of there cross, diagonally, the busy N-IV highway and head down the undistinguished Pozos Dulces along the Ribera del Marisco, with the narrow, elongated, Parque Calderón to the left. *Marisco,* of course, is Spanish for Shellfish, and when you combine that with the numerous restaurants along this street it can be deducted, correctly, that in a town famous for its seafood and shellfish this is the place to come for those delicacies. But more about that later. The *parque* and the Ribera culminate at the **Plaza de las Galeras Reales** (2), which gets its name from the fact that the Galeras' Fountain, built to provide water for the vessels sailing to the Indias, was located here.

Continue through this square, along the unusually named Avenida Micaela Aramburu de Mora, where the small street to the left, Luna, is home to the **Oficina de Turismo Tourist Office** (3). El Puerto is renowned for its mansions, many of which date from the 17th and 18th centuries when, after the Chamber of Commerce was transferred to nearby Cádiz from Sevilla, the trade with the Americas brought great wealth to the area. And along this street it is shown in the presence of the *Palacio de Medinaceli* and the Ancient Fish Market, now a restaurant, and the Plaza de Cristobal Colón is so named as it is across from the explorer's own home. Soon, to the right, and improbably so, the silhouette of the **San Marcos Castle**, (4), ☎ 85-17-51, looms. On the site of an old Mosque, it was first fortified after the reconquest of El Puerto by Alfonso X in the middle of the 13th century, and it became the church/fortress of Santa María by the 14th and 15th centuries, and known as the castle of San Marcos. At the end of the latter century extensive transformations were overseen by the then ruler, the duke of Medinacelli. It was the seat of the town council up until 1729, was used as a church until the 19th century and was later converted for housing. In the middle of the 20th century it underwent renovations that saw it resembling its original state. *Open daily 11 a.m. to 1:30 p.m., with a free guide service every 30 minutes, entrance free.*

Although the castle is symbolic of El Puerto's history, the next stop on the itinerary is important in a very different sense for the town. Follow Sol away from the castle and then make a right onto Los Moros and, along that street, you'll pass one of the handful of sherry *bodegas* in and around El Puerto de Santa María. One of the these is certainly worth a visit, not just to learn more about how the precious sherry, and other wines and spirits, are made. but to taste some also. My favorite *bodega* is that of **Osborne**, ☎ 85-52-11, just north of town on the road to Jerez de la Frontera. This is unmistakable, as the huge outline of a ferocious *toro* (bull) graces the grounds. *The bodega opens Monday to Friday with visits, by appointment, in English at 10:30 a.m. Entrance 300 ptas (EUR 1.80).* Another cast of a *toro bravo* stands on a plinth at the end of Sol and, in this instance, it is more

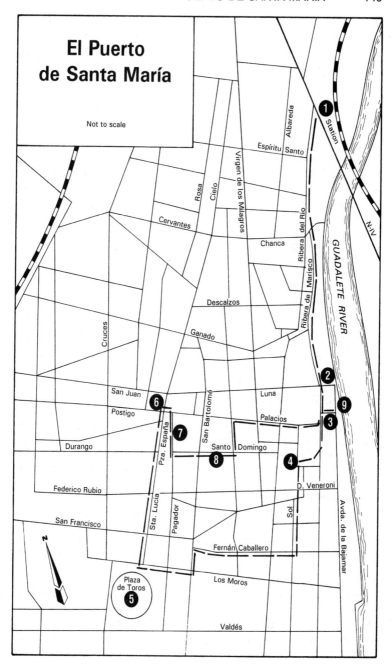

appropriate as it is just outside El Puerto's famed ***Plaza de Toros** (5). Bullfighting has a revered tradition in this town, dating back at least as far as that of Ronda's, but this present *plaza*, considered one of the more emblematic in Spain, was inaugurated on the 5th and 6th of June 1880. Almost every other Spanish city has its own *fería*, of varying length, and bullfights *(corrida de toros)* are held daily. But not so in El Puerto de Santa María. With 22 kms (13.5 miles) of beach El Puerto is a major resort in the summer and, as a consequence, holds its *corridas* on different days throughout the month of August and, sometimes, two in the same evening with the second not beginning until 11:30 p.m. These, more often than not, feature the finest matadors and toros and are a must for *aficionados* of these events. *The plaza is open for inspection from Tuesday to Sunday, except on the days immediately before and open corridas, from 11:30 a.m. to 1:30 p.m. and 5:30 p.m. to 7 p.m. Entrance free.*

Leave the *plaza* by crossing over Los Moros and following Santa Lucia to the Plaza España, the site of El Puerto's main church, the **Iglesia Mayor Priory** (6). Not as prepossessing as many of its kind, but still with an unusually elegant façade, this, as many other important places here, was built under the jurisdictions of the Dukes of Medinacelli. Construction began in the very late 15th century but not being completed, however, until the 18th century. The initial stages of this work were entrusted to a certain Alfonso Rodriguez, who also played a major part in building Sevilla's Cathedral. *Open daily 10 a.m. to midday and 7 p.m. to 8:30 p.m. Entrance free.* Just around the corner, at Pagador, 1, you will find the small, but nevertheless interesting, **Muncicipal Archaeological Museum** *(Museo Arqueológico Municipal)* (7), ☎ 54-27-05. *Open Monday to Saturday, except holidays, 10 a.m. to 2 p.m. Entrance free.* Exit left, and a left at the first street, Santo Domingo, will bring you first to the *Convento de Santo Domingo,* with its Baroque cloisters, and then to the **Rafael Alberti Museum** *(Museo de "Rafael Alberti")* (8), ☎ 85-07-11. Alberti was a famous local poet and artist, and lived in this house when he was a child; today, besides exhibitions of his works, it has other momentoes about his life. *Open Tuesday to Sunday 11 a.m. to 2:30 p.m., entrance 300 ptas (EUR 1.80).*

Time, now, to wander back through town to the Plaza de las Galeras Reales where, depending upon the time of day, and day, more opportunities await you. *At 11 a.m. each Saturday, departing from the Tourist Office, there is a guided walk through town and, in the summer, a sight-seeing train leaves from the square Monday through Sunday from 7 p.m. to 1:30 a.m. This lasts 45 minutes and costs 200 ptas (EUR 1.20).* That it runs until 1:30 a.m. should, very definitely, give you a clue that people keep very late hours here when they are on vacation. In fact, one of the pleasures of visiting El Puerto is walking, late into the evening, along the Ribera del Marisco, and narrow streets behind it, selecting which restaurant to eat in. The whole area is full of life and sound, with large family groups predominating, and the seafood and shellfish is most tempting indeed. Although there are more fancy restaurants, few will want to miss the famous ones operated by Romerijo. Their plastic-coated menus show the widest range of dishes, and relatively inexpensive, but still tasty, wines to match. And if you don't fancy sitting down, or more likely can't find a seat, wander to the Cocedero where you can see the fish frying and purchase what you want to take away with you.

Finally, there is short expedition that no visitor to El Puerto de Santa María should overlook, even though the timing can sometimes be a little difficult. Just across from the Galeras Reales plaza a small steamship sets sail from the **Muelle de Vapor** (9), across the Bay of Cádiz to the enchantingly ancient city of the same name. *Operating Tuesday to Sunday, there are usually four or five sailings, and an extra one on Sundays, with the fare being 275 ptas (EUR 1.65).* However, unless you take the first and return on the last—which makes for a very long day, it won't really leave you enough time to see the most important sights in Cádiz. It may be better, therefore, to consider returning on the train—which has a much more frequent service than the boat.

Cádiz

Cádiz is believed by many to be the oldest city in Spain. It was founded in 1100 BC by the Phoenicians, who were supplanted by the Carthaginians around 500 BC. In 206 BC Cádiz became federally allied with the Romans and it was, subsequently, granted Roman citizenship in 46 BC. Following the demise of the Romans in AD 400, the Visigoths ruled the city for just over 300 years. After the Battle of Guadalete in 711, a long period of Moorish rule began and, in fact, it wasn't until 1262 that the city was finally reconquered by Alfonso X.

The Catholic Monarchs gave Cádiz the rights of monopoly of trade with Africa in 1493 and, on September 25 of the same year, Columbus set sail on the first of his two expeditions that originated from Cádiz. His fourth voyage departed from this port nine years later. During the next century, Cádiz suffered the effects of warfare on more than one occasion. In 1587 Sir Francis Drake attacked the Spanish fleet in Cádiz harbor and, in 1596, an Anglo-Dutch fleet attacked destroying a large part of the city.

Better times were on the horizon, however. In 1717 the *Casa de Contratación*, the rights of monopoly of trade with the Americas (which were previously granted, in 1503, to Seville) was transferred to Cádiz by order of Felipe V, thus beginning a period of economic expansion. Cádiz's most important contribution to recent Spanish history occurred in 1812 while the city was under siege by Napoleon's troops. The national parliament met at the Oratori St. Felipe Neri on March 19 and proclaimed the first Spanish Constitution.

As is evident throughout the city, much of the history of Cádiz is maritime related, due, naturally, to its peculiar geographical location. It lies at the end of a long promontory that curls around from, and runs parallel to, the Spanish mainland. This not only forms a natural harbor but leaves the city very closely surrounded by water on three sides. Although not part of the suggested tour, many visitors will want take to the water. Those so inclined should take the ferry service from the harbor to El Puerto de Santa María, across the bay. El Puerto is truly a place of great charm. Some may even wish to consider using it as a base to explore the surrounding area and, if so, a stay at the Hotel Monasterio San Miguel is highly recommended.

GETTING THERE:

Trains run into the terminal at Cádiz on the line from Seville. Long-distance trains connect Cádiz directly with Madrid and Barcelona, and numerous local services run between the city and El Puerto de Santa María and Seville.

Buses are best used between Cádiz and Algeciras or Málaga, where the rail connections are either cumbersome or nonexistent.

By car, Cádiz, nearly 396 miles south of Madrid, which is reached on the N-IV highway via Jerez de la Frontera, Seville and Córdoba. Alternatively, take the A-4 *autopista* toll road to Seville, and then join the N-IV. Cádiz is also the origination point of the longest road in Spain, the N-340; which runs around the coast all the way to Barcelona, some 750 miles away.

PRACTICALITIES:

Of the limited number of places you can visit in Cádiz, many are closed on Monday. Hence, you may want to schedule your visit here for a different day of the week. The **Dialing Code** is 956. The tourist office **Junta de Andalucía, Oficina de Turismo, ☎** 21-13-13 or fax 22-84-71, Calderón de la Barca, 1, is open Tuesday to Friday 9 a.m. to 7 p.m. and Monday and Saturday 9 a.m. to 2 p.m. Cádiz has a **population** of 160,000 and is the capital of the province of the same name, one of eight belonging to the autonomous region of **Andalucía**.

ACCOMMODATION:

The **Parador Hotel Atlántico** ****, ☎ 22-69-05 or fax 21-45-82, Avenida Duque de Nájera, 9, is a whitewashed modern structure with an enviable location, overlooking the Atlantic Ocean and Bay of Cádiz, at the very end of the city. Guests enjoy classical service in the parador tradition, and parking facilities. $$

The **Hotel Monasterio San Miguel** ****, ☎ 54-04-40 or fax 54-26-04, Calle Larga, 27, El Puerto de Santa María. El Puerto de Santa María is just across the bay from Cádiz and a stay in this hotel, converted from an 18th-century Capuchin convent, alone merits the trip. The former monastic cells have been transformed into comfortable suites and its widely acclaimed restaurant, Las Bóvedas, derives its name from the convent's vaults. $$

The **Hotel Playa Victoria** ****, ☎ 27-54-11 or fax 26-33-00, Glorieta Ingenerio La Cierva, 4, has an interesting modern façade. Located just outside the old city and alongside the Atlantic Ocean, it features totally up-to-date facilities, including jacuzzis in some suites. $$

The **Hotel Puertatierra** ***, ☎ 27-21-11 or fax 25-03-11, Avenida de Andalucia, 34, just outside of the old city, is a new hotel with a particularly elegant façade. It has 100 beautifully appointed rooms, and is only 50 yards from the Atlantic Ocean. $$

The **Hotel Residencia de Francia y Paris** ***, ☎ 21-23-18 or fax 22-24-31, Plaza de San Francisco, 2, is a medium-sized hotel in a very central location. The building is typical of others in the area, and rooms are pleasant, comfortable and reasonably priced. $

FOOD AND DRINK:

Really, there is just one specialty here—seafood, and in all its possible guises. If you are not in the mood for a formal meal, you might choose to pay a visit to one of the several little shops in the area, that are sometimes combined with a small and basic restaurant. Just choose what you fancy and it will be wrapped up for you to take away.

Restaurante El Faro (Calle San Félix, 15), near the southern tip of the La Viña district of the old city, is an institution here. Though renowned for its esoteric range of exotic seafood dishes it, of course, imaginatively prepares the more well-known varieties as well. ☎ 21-10-68 or fax 21-21-88. $$$

Parador Hotel Atlántico (Avenida Duque de Nájera, 9), has a restaurant with enchanting views over the ocean and bay. Favorite dishes here include the traditional fritura gaditana fried fish from Cádiz, as well as sole prepared Cádiz style. ☎ 22-69-05 or fax 21-45-82. $$

Ventorrillo el Chato (Ctra. de Cádiz a San Fernando, Km 687) is found just outside Cádiz on the isthmus connecting Cádiz to San Fernando. Full of character, this restaurant has an attractive Andalucian-style rustic dining room. Andalucian style cuisine too, with very typical stews, fish and meat from the mountains, with mouth watering desserts and fine wines. Closed Sunday. ☎ 25-02-25, fax 25-32-22. $$

Restaurante El Sardinero (Plaza San Juan de Dios, 4), has been delighting diners in Cádiz for many years. It is a good choice if you are looking for a mix of Andaluz and Basque cuisine and, weather permitting, you may dine outdoors. ☎ 28-25-05. $$

SUGGESTED TOUR:

Numbers in parentheses correspond to numbers on the map.

There are many lovely squares in Cádiz, but the one in which you will begin this tour is the irregularly-shaped **Plaza San Juan de Dios** (1). The dominant building here is the **Town Hall** *(Casa de Consistorial)*, but a vast array of bars and restaurants also make their home behind these palm-tree lined sidewalks.

Leave by way of Calle Pelota, to the right as you face the Town Hall. Almost immediately, make another right and follow the much narrower Marqués de Cádiz past a host of small shops, hostals, and pensions, down to Cristobal Colón where you will once again turn right. The most impressive of the buildings here is the *Casa de las Cadenas,* now the home of the **Provincial Historical Archives** *(Archivo Histórico Provincial)* (2). Just across from this is the tiny Calle Cabrera Navares, which will lead into the slightly larger Rosario. The streets in this part of Cádiz are so narrow, and the buildings so steep, that sunlight is effectively shut out for most of the day. A break does come, though, at the Plaza de San Agustín, which is home, not surprisingly, to a church of the same name.

Continue on a little farther up the road, both literally and physically, to the *****Church of Saint Cueva** *(Oratorio de la Santa Cueva)* (3), ☎ 22-36-09,

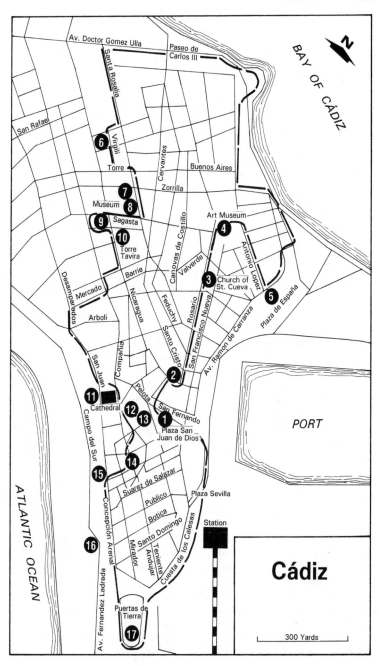

which is the first of the places you should visit. It is a curious and unusual place indeed. The underground chapels date from 1783 and, although they contain many works of artistic interest they are, as basements tend to be, rather damp and dingy. The simple and the ornate mix uneasily in the domed upper chapel, which was added in 1796. The ceiling of the dome is adorned by five spectacular paintings, three of which are by Goya. *If you want to see them, however, you must time your visit carefully as it is only open Monday to Friday between the hours of 10 a.m. and 1 p.m.*

Back outside, a right turn, and following Rosario again, will bring you out to the much larger Plaza de Mina. The gardens in this plaza are lovely, enhanced by fountains and statues, and it is also home to the **Cádiz Museum** *(Museo de Cádiz)* (4), ☎ 21-22-81. This very pleasant and well-presented museum has exhibits relating to local archaeological history on the lower level, and paintings and other art media upstairs. *Opening hours are Tuesday 2:30 p.m. to 8 p.m., Wednesday to Saturday 9 a.m. to 8 p.m. and Sunday 9 a.m. to 2:30 p.m. Entrance 250 ptas (EUR 1.50), free for EC citizens.*

Exit, walking around the plaza and leaving to the right of the museum, by way of Antonio Lopez. A walk down this rather uneventful street will bring you into the much larger **Plaza de España** (5). The dominant building here is the **Diputación Provincial**, but even this is upstaged by the huge semi-circular statue with a towering column dated 1812. Leave the plaza by the corner adjacent to the one through which you entered and continue on through the Plaza Argüelles into Fermin Salvochea. Here you will take a right and follow along Isabel la Católica to the Plaza de los Pozos de la Nieves. Cross over here and follow the promenade for two or three hundred yards. Take this stretch at a leisurely pace, pausing now and again to see if the fishermen have had any luck, and drinking in the glorious views back over the **Bay of Cádiz** *(Bahía de Cádiz)* to the whitewashed towns and villages of the mainland.

Time, again, to turn inland, this time onto Zorrilla, which will soon join Calderon de la Barca back at the Plaza de Mina. This corner is also the site of the Tourist Office. Following Calderon de la Barca you will, after a short while, come to a monument dedicated to the memory of the Marqués de Comillas. The gardens at the end, and running parallel to the bay, are also named in his honor. On the other side of the gardens you will find three more places of interest. On the right, literally jutting into the bay, is the **Museum of the Sea** *(Museo del Mar)*, which has been renovated and today functions as an exhibition center. Across from this are the *Iglesia del Carmen,* and the very elegant headquarters, fittingly bedecked with anchors and cannon balls in the garden, of the **Military Governor** *(Gobierno Militar)*.

Follow the promenade around and, straight ahead, is the seafront Parque Genoves, a very pleasant stretch with the *Hotel Atlántico* visible in the distance. Do not follow this to its end but rather, half-way along, turn back in towards the city onto Santa Rosalia which ends in the unusual double plazas of *Fragela* and *Falla*. The latter is named, appropriately, after an imposing and impressive red brick building that resides there, the **Grand Falla Theatre** *(Gran Teatro Falla)* (6).

From here, take Virgili to its junction with Torre, where a left and a quick right onto Santa Ines brings you to the **Church of Saint Philip Neri** *(Oratorio de San Felipe Neri)* (7), ☎ 21-16-12. Dating from 1679, this structure features a most attractive elliptical design accented by towering columns and an imposing dome. It was here, in 1812, that the parliament sat while composing the country's first constitution. *Visit Monday to Saturday 10 a.m. to 1:30 p.m., entrance 150 ptas (EUR .90).*

Just past there, still within Santa Ines, is the **City History Museum** *(Museo Histórico Municipal)* (8), ☎ 22-17-88. Though small in size, this houses many interesting exhibits. Among these is a large wooden model of the city that may be viewed from above—this really helps to put the city into perspective. *Open Tuesday to Sunday 9 a.m. to 1 p.m and 4 p.m. to 7 p.m., and Saturday and Sunday 9 a.m. to 1 p.m. Entrance free.*

The next stop, the **Women's Hospital** *(Hospital de Mujeres)* (9), ☎ 80-71-45, dates from 1749 and is reached by making a right at the end of Santa Ines into Sagasta and then, after a few blocks, a left into the Calle Hospital de Mujeres. This is easily recognizable, just look for its huge wooden gates. Inside, there is a classic patio and a chapel containing numerous works of art, including a notable El Greco. *Opening hours are Monday to Friday from 10 a.m. to 1 p.m., entrance 100 ptas (EUR .60).*

Take the Calle Rosario Cepeda, directly across from the Hospital, to Nicaragua, where a right will bring you, after a block or so, to its corner with Calle Marqués del Real Tesoro and the unusual **Torre Tavira** (10), ☎ 21-29-10. Constructed as a traditional watchtower, it is now used in a similar, if much more high-tech, fashion. Two exhibition areas display pictures of the city alongside a video and interactive computer demonstration. Its most interesting attraction is at the summit, however, where the Camera Obscura projects a brilliant moving image of the surrounding town. *Opening hours are daily 10 a.m. to 6 p.m., entrance 500 ptas (EUR 3.01).*

There is some distance to go before the next stop on your tour, but it is well worth the hike. Follow Nicaragua, to Londres, where a right leads down the the large rectangular **food market** *(Mercado Central)*, best enjoyed on a Sunday morning when it hosts an intriguing flea and animal market. Take a left in the bottom corner onto Desamparados, which meanders through a much older area and along Calle San Juan before reaching the towering façade of the *****Cathedral** *(Catedral)* (11), ☎ 28-61-54. The exterior is, to say the least, unusual. On either side two round, dome topped, towers reflect two divergent architectural styles, Baroque and Classical, which evidences a prolonged construction period; 1772 to 1838. A recent, and comprehensive, restoration leaves the interior with a feeling of spaciousness and openness uncommon in Spanish cathedrals. The **Cathedral Museum** *(Museo Catedralicio)* is not overly large, but has on display some interesting and valuable religious art, notably a monstrance by Enrique de Arfe. *This is open Tuesday to Saturday from 10 a.m. to 1 p.m., entrance 500* *ptas (EUR 3.01).*

To the right of the Cathedral is a small gateway, the **Arco de la Rosa** (12), which leads into the older, popular, and generally crowded, *Barrio del Populo* of Cádiz. Very soon you'll reach the Plazuela de San Martín, which is adorned by the wonderful façade of the **Casa del Almirante** (13). Take the street directly ahead of you and follow it around to the left into Mesón Nuevo. Go through the double arched **Arco de los Blancos** (14), which leads out to the more modern Obispo Felíz Soto. Take a right here and, when you reach the ocean, another right will bring you to the **Roman Theatre** *(Teatro Romano)* (15), ☎ 21-43-00. While there is not a great deal to see, your imagination will most certainly be catapulted back through the centuries as you stroll among the ruins. *Visit Tuesday through Sunday between the hours of 11 a.m. and 1:30 p.m., entrance free.*

Back onto the main road follow around to the left, noting the elongated building to the right that once served as the **Royal Prison** *(Carcel Real)* (16). Wind along this street as it moves down and away from the Atlantic Ocean until it reaches the back of the **Puertas de Tierra** (17). From this angle the main entranceway to the old city doesn't look very grand, but don't be deceived. A short detour around to the front will show the surrounding fountain, ponds, and gardens in all their splendor. Retrace your steps back inside the walls and, proceeding right towards the bay, the **Law Courts** *(Palacio de Justicia)* will be on the immediate right.

As the street winds down, look off to the right for splendid views of the large docks and two interesting edifices on the other side of the road; the *Iglesia de Santo Domingo* and an old factory, with its chimney still intact, that now serves as the **Congress Hall** *(Palacio de Congresos)*. Just past this, and again to the left, is the entrance to the Plaza San Juan de Dios where you will conclude this tour.

Coto Doñana
National Park

The Guadalquivir River rises in the mountains of southeastern Spain and then makes its way, westwards, across the alluvial Andalucian plain. Passing along its journey the ancient Moorish capital of Córdoba and widening at Sevilla, which it enriched by making it the only river port in Spain, it then turns south and meets the Atlantic Ocean at Sanlúcar de Barrameda. It is unusual for a delta in that it only has one outlet to the sea. This is because, over the centuries, sandbars have developed on its western banks, blocking all other exits. These have been formed into towering dunes by the sea winds which, in turn, protect huge stretches of salt marshes marismas behind them. These two ecosystems, the dunes and marshes, combine with another, scrubland mattoral to form an amazing, and ever changing, natural habitat for a wide array of birds, animals and flora.

This was understood as far back as the 13th century when, in 1262, Alfonso X created a royal hunting preserve for wild boars here. During this era it was a mainly forested area, the way it stayed until the mid-16th century when ground husbandry decimated much of the forests, creating huge ecological changes that foresaw the beginning of the mobile dune system. In the early 14th century, Alfonso's son, King Fernando IV, granted the land to the famed Medina Sidonia family. And it was this combination of family and land usage that gave it its name. The first part *Coto* is actually logical as it means "Game Reserve", the second, though, is more interesting. One of the duchesses of the family, Doña Ana de Silva y Mendoza, built a palace and the area became known as the forest of Doña Ana— *Doñana*.

Since 1969 protective measures have been taken to preserve this area, and in that year the National Park of Coto Doñana was created, and this has been extended in size since and now incorporates over 213,000 acres. It is also the last great wilderness sanctuary in southern Europe, and has been recognized as such by having been granted numerous honors. In 1981 it was created a Biosphere Reserve, the following year it became a member of Ramsar, in 1988 it was made a special bird protection area (ZEPA), having been granted various European Diplomas and named a World Heritage Site in 1994.

GETTING THERE:

Trains do not run to, or offer services that disembark anywhere near Coto Doñana.

Buses provide the only option of public transport to Coto Doñana. Empresa Damas, S.A., ☎ (95) 490-80-40, operate frequent services from Seville's Plaza de Armas bus station to Matalascañas. However, there is no public transport from there to the Vistor's Center at El Acebuche, from where the park tours begin.

By Car, from Seville take the E1/A-49 westwards and then turn south at Bollullos del Condado on to the H-612 and continue on to El Acebuche, which is past El Rocio and a short distance before Matalascañas.

PRACTICALITIES:

The only way to visit the interior of the park is on tours operated by the **Coop. Andaluza Marismas del Rocío**, ☎ (959) 43-04-32, who also own the Hotel Toruño. These leave from the **Centro de Visitantes El Acebuche**, ☎ (959) 44-87-11, and in the summer months it is wise to book ahead of time. Be sure to wear very casual clothes and preferably boots, and expect it to take between 3 and a half to four hours. Be warned, also, that this is a very rough and bumpy ride indeed, and as interesting as it is it is ABSOLUTELY not to be considered by those with such physical problems as artificial hips etc. Also, be aware that once the trip has started there is no way you can get off along the way. There is no guarantee of what wildlife and birds you will see along the way and, in any case, this will vary greatly with the different seasons.

ACCOMMODATION:

The **Hotel Toruño** **, ☎ (959) 44-23-23 or fax 44-23-38, Plaza del Acebuchal, 22, is found in the really unusual small town of El Rocío. Famous for the springtime pilgrimage that attracts hundreds of thousands, it is also the closest thing to an old style Wild West town this side of an old movie. This hotel, modern in style, has a wonderful location overlooking all the animals and birds feeding on the large marshlands behind it. All meals, included in the price, are served in a delightful restaurant across the sanded plaza. Be warned, even if available, rooms during the pilgrimage are frighteningly expensive. $$

SUGGESTED TOUR:

As you pull into the car park at **El Acebuche** it is impossible to ignore the fleet of green, naturally, tall but not very long buses with immense tires. It will cross many peoples minds that these would be difficult to change in case of a flat. And the likelihood is that, during the course of the tour, you will find out just how difficult it is.

Once eveyone is aboard, the bus trundles out to the main road and then follows it towards Matalascañas, a rather inauspicious start. However, before very long it turns into and across, the sand dunes and down onto the beach. And what a beach it is! No other vehicles, except those belonging to the few fishermen who have been allowed to stay here (and live in rather ramshackle looking huts) after the formation of the park, are allowed. Consequently, almost the whole stretch of beach down to its junction with the Guadalquivir is one of the last in Spain to remain in a virgin state. Your only companions besides the occasional other bus are the birds that call this home, most notably terns, gulls and plovers.

Sanlúcar, on the other side of the Guadalquiver, is famous for its Fino sherry and shellfish, a combination that makes for a delicious dish. However, that is for another time, the only time of the year people, in large numbers, pass over here is when they are on the romerío to Rocío. The bus follows the river bank here, and the terrain changes dramatically. Here you are passing through the scrubland area, and it really isn't too pretty. However, a short stop at a collection of **reed houses** within their own compounds, and a visit to a **charcoal pit**, is of interest. Soon after it is time to visit the *marismas*, which are large and intriguing. Of course, it depends upon the time of year as to how wet they are and, and as a consequence, what wildlife and birds you will see. It doesn't help, either, that local agriculture, especially the growing of strawberries and rice, have depleted the water tables in the area. And, another threat to the park are the huge mines someway to the north. In the drier periods the bird count will be much lower, but you will no doubt see cattle, deer and wild boar aplenty. Pay special attention to the *vera*, the ever changing green strip between the dunes and marshes, which is always popular with the wildlife. The array of the latter is amazing; it is known that over 120 species of birds, 28 mammal species, 17 reptiles, 9 amphibians and 8 species of fish breed in the park. Of these, perhaps the rarest are the Spanish Imperial Eagle (a pair of which require nearly 6,500 acres of hunting land in summer, and even more in winter) and the shy lynx. Flamingos, too, are always popular with visitors, and their pinkness is not just a matter of prettiness; it has also to do with the males' sexual attraction. It turns out that the paler the male the less its chances of finding a mate. Interestingly, it comes by that color by its favorite food, shrimp; and the more it eats the brighter it gets. It is also of interest to note that the narrowness of the Straits of Gibraltar is, in part, responsible for the presence of so many birds with large wings. Such creatures are reliant upon the wind currents over land that allows them to glide long distances rather than have to use excess energy flapping their wings. As a consequence, they look for the shortest distances over water in their migratory patterns.

After another stop, the only one with rest rooms and where you are issued a cold bottle of water, the bus heads into the large dune areas behind the beach. Continually evolving, these have been the location for some well known movies that required such a setting. At a short stop it is fascinating to take a closer look at this sand; when picked up and allowed to run through your fingers you will discover that it is, actually, multi-colored and very fine. The bus then retraces its way back along the beach, and to the visitor's center.

Before leaving this area, it really is essential, if you aren't staying there anyway, to pay a visit to the village of **El Rocío**. Without doubt, it is one of the most unusual in Spain. The **church**, and its Virgin, is an essential stop, but the authorities have been clever enough to build a slightly elevated promenade around the side of the *marisma*. For those without the time, or inclination, to take the formal tour, and for those who have taken it and have had their consciousness raised, this offers a great opportunity, and free at that, to view the wildlife.

Córdoba: *Alcázar, Jewish Quarter, and La Mezquita

In the country of Spain, where the long and varied history of most cities gives new meaning to the word ancient, Córdoba is among the most ancient. As long ago as 206 BC it was invaded by the Romans who, in 152 BC, bestowed upon it the title of "Patrician Colony", subsequently making it the capital of the "Roman Ulterior of Spain." Pompeii conquered the city in 45 BC. In 572, after nearly eight centuries of Roman rule, the Visigoth king, Leovigildus, took control of Córdoba. This period was short-lived, however, and in 711 the Moors, crossing from Africa, wrested control of the city in their sweep through the Iberian Peninsula. This proved to be the beginning of three centuries of glittering splendor for this city.

In 756 Abdel-Rahman I, Emir of the Ommiad dynasty, established Córdoba as an independent emirate. Thirty years later construction began on the great Mosque, a journey to which is said to have been comparable to a pilgrimage to Mecca. With its elevation, by Abdel-Rahman III in 929, to the status of Caliphate, the city entered its most important era. Estimates of the population at that time range from 500,000 to as high as 1,000,000; and historians have recorded the number of mosques at anywhere from 700 to 3000, the number of shops at in excess of 80,000 and the number of homes at over 300,000. Not only that, but it was considered to be one of the cultural capitals of the world; a respected center of science and art. Córdoba had the first university in Europe, the first street lighting in Europe, and boasted a library with over 400,000 volumes. In short, it was second in influence, wealth and culture only to Constantinople.

These days of power came to an end, however, when rebellion by the Omeyan Prince Muhammad II in 1009 resulted in the breakup of the Caliphate into separate Moorish kingdoms, precipitating a long decline in the city's fortunes.

By the time Córdoba was reconquered in 1236 by the Castilian/Leónese king, Ferdinand III, known as "The Saint", the city was already in ruins. During the ensuing years it was repopulated by people from the north of Spain. In 1382 Alfonso XI ordered construction of the *Alcázar*, which Queen Isabella made her residence towards the end of the 15th century. It was here that she received Christopher Columbus prior to one of his voyages to the New World and from here, also, that she planned the reconquest of Granada. Her grandson, Carlos V, initiated the construction of the city's Christian cathedral. Oddly enough, he decreed it should be built in the center of the great Mosque; thus creating, by design or accident, one of the world's most incongruous mixtures of architecture and culture.

These days Córdoba is, for the most part, a quiet provincial capital. And, strangely, given its combination of history, fascinating monuments and evident charm, it is often overlooked by tourists who are more familiar with the attractions of its Andalucían neighbors, Sevilla and Granada. Make sure you don't make the same mistake; a visit here is sure to be a highlight of your holiday.

GETTING THERE:

Trains run through Córdoba, on your choice of the new high-speed AVE or the regular tracks, on their way between Madrid and Seville. Trains originating in Madrid, again traveling on either of these tracks, arrive at Córdoba and then continue service on to Málaga on the regular tracks. Services between Barcelona and Seville, via Valencia, also pass through Córdoba. Regional services are available from Córdoba to both Granada and Algeciras, each passing through, and quite often incurring a change at, Bobadilla.

Bus is most probably a better form of transportation when travelling from Granda and, dependent upon the train schedules, may be faster and/or more frequent for this journey as well.

By car, Córdoba, 250 miles south of Madrid, may be reached by taking the N-IV, which also links the city with Seville, 86 miles to its west. Alternative routes are the N-432 to Granada; the N-IV, N-331 or N-321 to Málaga, and the very poor N-432 northwest to Zafra.

PRACTICALITIES:

Although the Mosque/Cathedral is open on Monday, most other monuments and museums are closed. Accommodation is limited in Córdoba, and may be difficult to procure during the summer and autumn months. This problem is exacerbated at Easter *(Semana Santa)* and in May when both the city's annual fair *(Fería de Mayo)* and the biannual Festival of the Patios *(Festival de los Patios Cordobéses)* are held. Visitors, be forewarned that the summer months bring with them overpowering heat, so dress accordingly. The **Dialing Code** is 957. There are two tourist offices, the **Oficina de Turismo de la Junta de Andalucía**, ☎ 47-12-35, open Monday to Friday 10 a.m. to 2 p.m. and 4:30 p.m. to 7:30 p.m., and on Saturday from 10 a.m. to 2 p.m.; and **Patronato Provincial de Turismo**, ☎ 49-16-77, both of which are found near the right-hand side of the Mosque/Cathedral (as you face the river) at Torrijos, 10, in the **Palacio de Congresos y Exposiciones**. Córdoba has a **population** of somewhat over 300,000 and is the capital of the province of the same name, one of eight belonging to the autonomous region of **Andalucía**.

ACCOMMODATION:

The **Hotel Parador de Córdoba** ****, ☎ 27-59-00 or fax 28- 04-09, Avenida de la Arruzafa, s/n, is located in the hills just outside of the city. Built over the ruins of a Moorish summer palace, this is situated in lovely private gardens enhanced by a refreshing pool. The rooms have a decor befitting the style, and guests will enjoy the renowned Parador service. $$

The **Hotel Amistad Córdoba** ****, ☎ 42-03-35 or fax 42-03-65, Plaza de Maimónides, 3, has a marvelous location in the middle of the historical center of Córdoba. It is housed in a building of historical interest that has recently been remodeled into this quality hotel. $$

The **Hotel Conquistador** ****, ☎ 48-11-02 or fax 47-46-77, Magistral González Francés, 15, is a large, beautifully furnished, hotel which offers every possible facility. It is conveniently located directly across from the entrance to La Mezquita. $$

The **Hotel Residencia Maimónides** ***, ☎ 47-15-00 or fax 48-38-03, Torrijos, 4, located across from one corner of the La Mezquita, is a tastefully appointed hotel. The rooms are modern, clean and comfortable. $$

The **Hotel Residencia El Califa** ***, ☎ 29-94-00 or fax 29- 57-16, Lope de Hoces, 14, is in a quiet location sandwiched between the old and new towns, and closeby the popular Paseo de la Victoria. Its 66 rooms are modern and pleasant. All offer the expected facilities, and some feature balconies. Of interest also are its Moorish patios. $$

The **Hotel Boston** *, ☎ 47-41-76 or fax 47-85-23, Calle Málaga, 2, is right on the corner of the busy, but attractive, Plaza de las Tendillas. Traditionally styled rooms with a full range of amenities reside behind an interesting façade. $

The **Pensión Antonio Machado** **, ☎ 29-62-59, Buen Pastor, 4, is an delightful place with a lovely patio, and a convenient location close to the La Mezquita. It offers exceptional good value, as well as an excellent restaurant; but for the use of residents only. $

FOOD AND DRINK:

Hotel Parador de Córdoba (Avenida de la Arruzafa, s/n), has a dining room embellished with a unique combination of Arabic and Andalucían decor. It specializes in local dishes such as *salmorejo cordobés,* cold vegetable soup; *gazpacho blanco de almendras,* cold soup with almonds; or *rabo de toro a la cordobésa,* bull's tail Córdoban style. ☎ 27-59-00 or fax 28-04- 09. $$$

Restaurante El Churrasco (Romero, 16), is found in a delightful 14th-century Jewish home. During the summer months you may choose to enjoy delicious traditional Spanish cuisine around a typical patio. ☎ 29-08-

19 or fax 29-40-81. $$$

Restaurante Almudaina (Campo Santo de los Mártires, 1), is acclaimed for its innovative cuisine, prepared using produce fresh from the local market. It is housed in a beautiful 16th-century mansion. ☎ 47-43-42 or fax 48- 34-94. $$$

Restaurante La Fraqua (just off the Calle Tomás Conde at Callejon del Arco, 2), discretely tucked at the end of an alleyway off the beaten tourist path, offers pleasant first-floor dining around its patio. Guests will enjoy well-presented dishes and fine service. ☎ 48-45-72. $

SUGGESTED TOUR:

Numbers in parentheses correspond to numbers on the map.

Begin your tour at the **Tourist Office** (1), in the *Palacio de Congresos y Exposiciones* at Calle Torrijos, 10, beside *La Mezquita*, where you may pick up a helpful city plan and other useful information. You will also be close to your first destination, the *Diocesan Museum (Museo Diocesano)* (2), ☎ 47-93-75, located in the same complex. Housed in a classically-styled historical building, the exhibits here are displayed over two floors around a majestic patio. On the ground level are numerous ancient Roman artifacts, with paintings and other works of art on view upstairs. *Opening hours are winter Monday to Friday 9:30 a.m. to 1:30 p.m. and 3:30 p.m. to 5:30 p.m., and Saturday 9:30 a.m. to 1:30 p.m.; and summer Monday to Friday 10:30 a.m. to 2 p.m. and 4 p.m. to 6:30 p.m. Entrance 150 ptas (EUR .90).*

Next, take a stroll down Torrijos, in the shadow of the towering walls of *La Mezquita* and under the watchful gaze of the many gargoyles perched upon its roof. These, in fact, are conduits to drain rainwater off the roof. While the need for these may seem ludicrous to those visiting during the full heat of summer, residents and more experienced visitors will verify that, when the rain does come in this region, it literally pours down. During these downpours, the water cascading from the mouths of these gargoyles makes for a surreal sight, indeed.

At the bottom of this street, next to the Guadalquivir river, you'll find a most eclectic grouping of monuments. Dominating the Plaza de Vallinas is the **Gate of the Bridge** *(Puerta del Puente)* (3). This was built in 1572, during the reign of Felipe II, to replace the original structure which dated from Roman times. Nearby is the graceful **Triunfo de San Rafael Column** (4), completed in 1781 at the behest of the Cathedral authorities. It commemorates the rescue of the city from an earthquake by the archangel San Rafael, whose statue adorns the top.

On the opposite side of the river is the impressive outline of the **Calahorra Tower** *(Torre de la Calahorra)* (5), ☎ 29-39-29. It was constructed in 1360 by Enrique II to defend himself from attacks waged by his brother Pedro I; and consists of two parts with the one facing towards the east displaying the royal shield. Today it houses the **Life of Andalucía Museum** *(Museo Vivo de Al-Andalus)*, which presents a cinematic review of

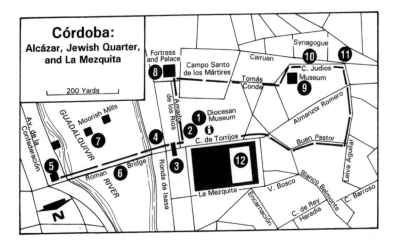

Córdoba:
Alcázar, Jewish Quarter, and La Mezquita

200 Yards

Andalucían life over the centuries. *Visit daily between May 1 and September 30 from 10 a.m. to 2 p.m. and 5:30 p.m. to 8:30 p.m., and the remainder of the year from 10 a.m. to 6 p.m.*

To reach the museum, and then to return to the main road following your visit, you will cross the **Roman Bridge** *(Puente Romano)* (6). While none of the sixteen spans are original, the bridge, one of Córdoba's oldest monuments, dates from the reign of Julius Caesar. Halfway over is yet another memorial to San Rafael, this flanked by elegant lanterns that illuminate and enhance its beauty. Looking out over the river to the small islands in the middle, you'll see the remains of the **Moorish Mills** *(Molinos Arabes)* (7). And, if you happen to have your camera, you'll want to note that this is also an ideal place from which to take pictures of the *La Mezquita.*

Once back on the city side it's time to head for the ***Fortress and Palace of the Christian Kings** *(Alcázar de los Reyes Católicos)* (8), ☎ 42-01-51. The entrance to this is just off the charming square of Campo Santo de los Mártires, best reached by making a left by the *Triunfo de San Rafael* into Amador de los Rios. Built by Alfonso XI in the 14th century over the site of previous Visigoth and Moorish fortresses, it was the home, for numerous subsequent years, of the Catholic Monarchs, who received Columbus and planned the reconquest of Granada here. Following the fall of Granada in 1492, it was first used by the Court of Inquisition, then functioned as a civil jail and military prison. There isn't a great deal to see, but what is here is interesting. The interior is not, as one might anticipate, ostentatious. The highlights are the **Hall of the Mosaics**, featuring ancient Roman mosaics, and a Roman stone sarcophagus that dates from the 2nd or 3rd century.

Back outside, you will note that four towers guard the walls. The tops of those that are open to visitors provide an excellent platform from which to admire the city and surrounding countryside as well as a superb, probably the best, place to take photos of the *La Mezquita*. The extensive gardens of the complex are a peaceful place, the design of which includes a series of rectangular ponds. A number of these have lovely small, arching, fountains along each side; similar to, but not as stunning as, those at the *Generalife* in Granada. *During the months of May to September, opening hours are Tuesday to Saturday 10 a.m. to 2 p.m. and 6 p.m. to 8 p.m. From October through April it is open Tuesday to Saturday 10 a.m. to 2 p.m. and 4:30 p.m. to 6:30 p.m. It is open on Sunday and holidays 9:30 a.m. to 3 p.m. year round. Entrance 425 ptas (EUR 2.55), free on Friday.*

Cross back over the Campo Santo de los Mártires and follow Tomás Conde into the **Jewish Quarter** *(Barrio Judería)*, where the narrow lanes and streets, sloping up and away from the *La Mezquita* in no discernable pattern, are home to some of Córdoba's most attractive patios. In general, throughout the area, patios, which are open courtyards quite often safeguarded by metal grille gates instead of doors, provide a useful, cooling, haven from the searing summer heat of Andalucía. Not content with practicality, though, citizens here compete aesthetically, and the results of their creative endeavors are judged biannually in the Patio Festival *(Festival de los Patios Cordobeses)*. Don't be disappointed, though, if your trip does not coincide with the festival. Among the particular pleasures of a visit to Córdoba is just strolling around this quaint area taking a peek into these patios; and you can be your own judge.

Continuing on, the first place of interest you will come to is in the Plaza de Maimónides. Here, the charming 16th-century **Casa de las Bulas** (9) has two quite disparate attractions. While the larger of these, the **Bullfighting Museum** *(Museo Taurino)*, ☎ 20-10-40, may not be to everyone's taste, it is one of the most comprehensive of its genre in Spain. The normal quota of bulls' heads is complimented by various suits of light *(traje de luces)*, numerous posters *(carteles)*, a large library and permanent exhibitions dedicated to the famous Cordobése *toreros*, Lagartijo, Machaquito, Guerrita and, most famous of all, Manolete. The latter, often considered to be immortal, was eventually killed by a bull in the Plaza de Toros of Linares on August 28, 1947. The other attraction, a crafts market, *El Zoco*, is across the patio and specializes in Cordobése silver and leather work. *The museum opens during the months of May to September, Tuesday to Saturday 10 a.m. to 2 p.m. and 6 p.m. to 8 p.m. From October through April it is open Tuesday to Saturday 10 a.m. to 2 p.m. and 4:30 p.m. to 6:30 p.m. It is open on Sunday and holidays 9:30 a.m. to 3 p.m. year round. Entrance 425 ptas (EUR 2.55), free on Friday.*

Just around the corner, in the narrow Calle Judíos, is the quite old and altogether curious *Synagogue *(Sinagoga)* (10), ☎ 20-29-28. This structure, prefaced by a statue to Maimónides, is one of only three ancient synagogues remaining in Spain, with the other two being in Toledo. Completed around 1315, it is tiny indeed, measuring just 7 meters by 6.5

meters, and features intricate plaster work that is characteristic of Mudéjar art. Following the reconquest of Granada in 1492, and the subsequent expulsion of the Jews from Spain, the synagogue was converted for use first as a hospital and then, in 1588, as a chapel. In 1885 it was declared a national monument. It is open Tuesday to Saturday 10 a.m. to 2 p.m. and 6 p.m. to 8 p.m., and Sunday and holidays 10 a.m. to 1:30 p.m. Entrance free for EC citizens.

If, by now, you're getting a little thirsty, stop by the **Bodega Guzman**, at Judíos, 5. This is an interesting old-style bar with plenty of barrels and other such decorations. And, if your visit is fortuitously timed, you may enjoy one of the photographic exhibitions they occasionally present. Just a little farther up Judíos, on the left, is the **Puerta de Almodovar** (11), which, although renovated in the 19th century, was actually constructed in the 14th century. Today its two towers and narrow arch link the old and new sections of Córdoba.

Opposite the puerta is Calle Fernández, which terminates in the Plaza de Angel Torres. A right here, onto Buen Pastor, will take you down through what begin as several typical narrow streets but become increasing commercialized the closer you get to the *La Mezquita (12), ☎ 47-05-12. The most dominant feature, from this present perspective, is the bell tower, which has its origins in the construction of a 10th-century minaret, the El Alimar. This later served as a model for others, such as the Giralda in Seville, and parts of it are still preserved in the current tower. Construction of La Mezquita, which is built over the site of a Visigothic cathedral, began in 786 at the order of Abdel-Rahman I. The initial design intended that the complex consist of parts; an open courtyard for ablution rituals (Sahm), now known as the Patio of the Orange Trees, and a covered area which would accommodate as many as 10,000 worshipers. Three expansions later, in the 10th century, it was finally completed and, with an area of 23,400 square meters, was for centuries the largest mosque in the Islamic world. Cordoba was reconquered in 1236, and small Christian chapels were added in 1258 and 1260. Nearly three centuries later, in 1523, during the reign of Carlos V, the decision was made to construct a Christian Cathedral in the center of the mosque.

Whether inadvertent or not, the contrasting styles of the mosque and cathedral combine to produce a place of utter fascination, unique in the entire world. In addition, it is the oldest monument in day-to-day use in the Western world. Once inside, you will see hundreds of columns, most supporting double arches. No matter where you rest your gaze, the columns are attended by ever-changing shafts of light and their accompanying shadows; a vista made even more intriguing by the numerous electric lanterns. Upon investigation you will find that, not only are the columns of different colors, they are fashioned from varying materials. Wandering in and out between them becomes mesmerizing. With each step the changing colors and patterns present you with a kaleidoscopic mixture of architecture and light.

Moorish architecture and design is, by nature, intricate and colorful, and both are blended masterfully here. In addition, the Muslim faith does not permit the use of human images. When you reach the Cathedral within, the impact of the absolute contrast in styles is nearly overpowering. In the Cathedral, human images abound, whether in paint, stone or wood, particularly in the form of massive paintings of Christ and the Saints. And, the heavy ornateness and rich colors of the altar, the choir, the pulpit, and the various side chapels, appear less harmonious here.

Along the back, southernmost, wall reside, side by side, two more contrasting expressions of these faiths. The *Mihrab*, a small chamber with a domed roof, was built during the second expansion of the mosque by Al-Hakam II, who was enthroned in 961, and the ornamental plasterwork is simply incredible. Next to it resides the **Cathedral Museum** *(Tesoro Catedralicio)*, which holds all manner of religious art dating from the 15th to 20th centuries. Among its many treasures, there is no doubt which is preeminent. As readers of this guide will have become aware, the Arfe brothers, Enrique and Juan, are renown for their design and crafting of monstrances. One of Enrique's works, weighing over 440 lbs. and fashioned of solid silver, is on display in this museum. It was used for the first time during the Corpus Christi celebrations in 1519.

The entrance to the La Mezquita is from the southeast corner of the peaceful Patio of the Orange Trees. *It is open Monday to Saturday 10 a.m. to 7 p.m. and Sunday and holidays 2 p.m. to 7 p.m. Entrance 750 ptas (EUR 4.33).* As this is a active church, however, it is possible just to walk in earlier or later. Remember, also, to be respectful, both in dress and demeanor. A tip for those who plan to test their photographic skills; as the light here is never really good, a tripod and/or very fast film are most helpful.

Córdoba:
Palace and Museums

T he most magnificent of the monuments and attractions in Córdoba are included on the first tour and, for visitors with a limited amount of time in this city, that is the tour of choice. However, many other attractions in Córdoba are important in their own right, and well worth a visit. These are described in this tour.

GETTING THERE:
PRACTICALITIES:
FOOD AND DRINK:
    See pages 164-166 for all of the above.

SUGGESTED TOUR:
    Numbers in parentheses correspond to numbers on the map.
    Begin in the northwest corner of *La Mezquita* at a tiny little street which, in truth, is not much more than an alleyway. Don't be deceived, however, the **Street of the Flowers** *(Calleja de las Flores)* (1) is one of the most famous in Córdoba for its patios. Next, follow a maze of streets, Encarnación, H. Cristo and M. del Villar until you reach the charming Plaza de San Jerónimo. The dominant building here, a 16th-century palace, houses the **Archaeological Museum** *(Museo Arqueológico)* (2), ☎ 47-10-76, which exhibits important examples of early Christian and Moorish art. *Visit Tuesday 3 p.m. to 8 p.m., Wednesday to Saturday 9 a.m. to 8 p.m., and Sunday and holidays 9 a.m. to 3 p.m. Entrance 250 ptas (EUR 1.50), free for EC citizens.*
    Continue on, taking a steep path to the side and turn left onto the much busier Eulogio Ambrosio de Morales. After a further climb, it ends in another square where you will find the **Town Hall** *(Ayuntamiento)*. Though this is of minimal interest in its own right, to one side there is an interesting, if incongruous, collection of Roman columns. Take Cristina, which runs to the left of the Town Hall and, when you reach the first junction, take a quick look down to the left at the interesting façade of the **Friendship Club** *(Circulo de la Amistad)* (3).
    Cristina now changes to Carbonell y Morand and dead-ends, at which point you will turn into a really unusual, and delightful, plaza. The **Plaza de los Dolores** (4) is the site of the very early 18th-century Convent Hospital of San Jacinto, but the focal point is in the center where, surrounded by

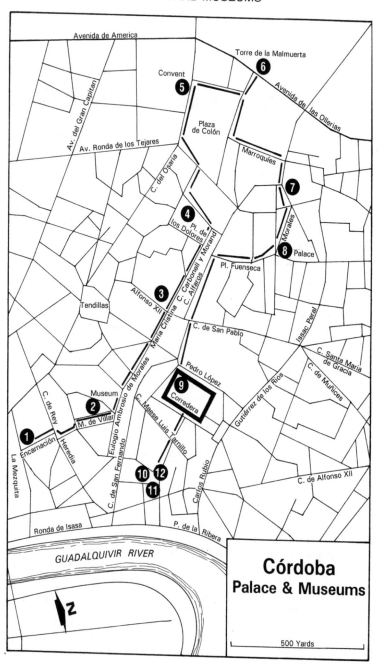

eight lanterns and an iron fence, there is a famous statue of Christ on the Cross. It was erected in 1794 and is known as *Cristo de los Faroles*.

Exit through the other end of the plaza, turn right, and follow Cabrera into the largest square in Córdoba, the Plaza de Colón. In the top left hand corner is the very ornate, and fully restored, **Convento de la Merced** (5), presently used as a local government office. Its claim to fame is that, in the late 15th century, Christopher Columbus *(Cristobal Colón)* stayed here while awaiting an audience with the Catholic Monarchs. Step just outside of the plaza, from the opposite corner, to view a fine example of medieval defensive fortifications, the **Torre de la Malmuerta** (6).

Pass back through the Plaza de Colón following along its long side, and make a left into Marroquíes. Towards the end, and to your right, you will see a tower dominating the scene ahead. Head in that direction and you will find that it belongs to the **Church of Santa Marina** *(Iglesia de Santa Marina)* (7). It is unlikely, unless a service of some kind in is progress, that you will be able to go inside. Nevertheless it is architecturally interesting. There are, in fact, many churches of this type in Córdoba. Following the reconquest, Fernando III founded 14 parishes whose churches, and accompanying squares, add much charm to this city.

Take Morales diagonally away from the church into Plaza de Don Gome and look closely for a hidden jewel. Though it is not easily identifiable, here you will find one of the most delightful 16th-century mansions in the city, the very well preserved ***Palace of the Marquéses of Viana*** *(Palacio de los Marquéses de Viana)* (8), ☎ 48-22-75. It was acquired, in 1980, by a local Savings and Loan Bank, the *Caja Provincial de Ahorros de Córdoba*, who converted it into a museum. As you enter the first patio, note that the corner column has been deliberately omitted to facilitate the entrance of horse-drawn carriages. The house itself boasts a marvelous collection of furniture, tapestries, porcelain, leather and, of course, a library which, in concert, are a testimony to the graciousness of life, at least for some, who lived during that era. The most unusual feature, though, is the incorporation of no less than 13 entirely different and, without exception, charming patios. In 1981 this, though surprisingly one of the lesser-known attractions in Córdoba, was declared a historic and artistic monument of national character. Two years later a subsequent royal decree granted it the status of Artistic Gardens. *Visit daily, with the exception of Wednesday, June 1 through September 30 from 9 a.m. to 2 p.m. And October through May, Monday to Saturday, with the exception of Wednesday, from 10 a.m. to 1 p.m. and 4 p.m. to 6 p.m. and Sunday and holidays 10 a.m. to 2 p.m. Entrance to the house 200 ptas (EUR 1.20) and the patios 100 ptas (EUR .60).*

It's time now to navigate to the next destination. Turn right at the end of the plaza and follow that winding street, which plays at chameleon, changing its name now and again, until you come to the Calle Alfaros. A left will bring you, again, into the Town Hall square where another left descends down a steep hill to a rather unusual façade. Pass through the archway, one of only three entrances into the **Plaza de la Corredera** (9). This and the similar entrance diagonally across in the southeast corner are known as the "High and Low Arches", respectively. The main entrance is located in the south façade, which also houses the food market *(mercado)*. This lovely plaza is rectangular in shape and consists of a lower, colonnaded, level and three upper floors, embellished with galleries and balconies supported by semi-circular arches. Built by the Magistrate Corregidor Ronquillo Briceno, in the late 17th century, this style is unique in Andalucía, though often seen in Castile. In past days it was the site for bullfights and even public executions. 1896 saw the center converted into a covered market but the roof was removed during the 1950s. At present, it hosts a general market from Monday to Saturday, with The Flea Market *(Rastro)* making an appearance on Sunday morning. Shoppers may also treasure-hunt in any number of second-hand junk shops strung along the fringes. In truth, it is a little run down but, oddly, that just serves to accentuate its charms.

Leave via the main entrance in the southern façade, and follow the streets down to the **Plaza del Potro** (10). It derives its name from the fountain in the middle, which dates from 1577, and has a statue of a colt *(Potro)* in its center. This plaza has an entirely different, and even more enticing, ambiance than its neighbors, the effect of which is, unfortunately, spoiled somewhat by the proliferation of tacky tourist vendors.

On one side is a 14th-century inn, the *Posada del Potro*. On another is the 15th-century *Charity Hospital* (Hospital de la Caridad), home to two small, but noteworthy, museums. First, the **Fine Arts Museum** *(Museo de Bellas Artes)* (11), ☎ 47-33-45, exhibits many paintings and sculptures by Cordobése artists. *Open Tuesday 3 p.m. to 8 p.m., Wednesday to Saturday 9 a.m. to 8 p.m. and Sunday ad holidays 9 a.m. to 3 p.m. Entrance 250 ptas (EUR 1.50), free for EC citizens.*

In addition, just across a delightful patio, enhanced with a fountain and busts, is the ever-popular **Julio Romero de Torres Museum** *(Museo de Julio Romero de Torres)* (12), ☎ 49-19-09. The man whom this honors was born nearby and the museum, opened in 1931, contains over fifty works donated by the artist's family. Many are often mildly erotic paintings of Cordobése women. *Visit Tuesday to Saturday from May through September, 10 a.m. to 1:30 p.m. and 6 p.m. to 8 p.m., and on the same days the remainder of the year from 10 a.m. to 2 p.m. and 5 p.m. to 7 p.m. It is open year round on Sunday and holidays from 9:30 a.m. to 3 p.m. Entrance 425 ptas (EUR 2.55), free on Friday.*

To end the tour, leave the plaza and walk towards the river. Upon reaching it make a right and follow along for a few blocks back to the Plaza de Vallinas, where the sight of the rear of *La Mezquita* will, no doubt, draw you in for one more visit before leaving Córdoba.

Córdoba:
*Medina Azahara

Τhis tour has a singular attraction which, unfortunately, is situated such that a visit requires either your own transportation, or the willingness to hire a taxi.

GETTING THERE:
PRACTICALITIES:
FOOD AND DRINK:

See pages 164-166 for all of the above.

SUGGESTED TOUR:

It would be a shame to miss the amazing monument that is the *Medina Azahara, ☎ 32-91-30. In 936 Abdel-Rahman III, reputedly in honor of his favorite concubine Al-Zahra, the Flower, constructed a city/palace in the foothills of the Sierra Morena, just five miles west of Córdoba. And splendid it must have been; detailed records indicate that building materials were brought from such distant places as Constantinople and other locations in North Africa. Despite its grandeur, it had a short life. After the breakup of the Caliphate of Córdoba very early in the 11th century, Medina Azahara was utilized by various factions, then eventually sacked. Many of the materials were, subsequently, used on constructions in Seville and other places and, over the next 900 years, it was allowed to fall into complete disrepair. It was not until 1910 that the arduous work of excavation began. This still continues, but enough of the Medina *Azahara* has been unearthed for visitors to see how incredibly beautiful this city, built on three terraces, must have been. *Opening hours are Tuesday to Saturday from 10 a.m. to 2 p.m. and 6 p.m. to 8:30 p.m., and Sunday and holidays 10 a.m. to 2 p.m. Entrance 250 ptas (EUR 1.50), free for EC citizens.*

Granada:
*The Alhambra
and Generalife

There are few cities in Spain, or in the world for that matter, that evoke such emotions as Granada. Among the many conquerors of this ancient city were the Romans and Visigoths, but it will be most remembered as the Spanish city ruled longer than any other by the Moors. In fact, the Moors dominated Granada for 781 years, between 711 and 1492. By the time it was finally reconquered it had been, by a quarter of a millennium, the sole remaining Muslim kingdom in Spain.

In 711, when the Moors took control of the southern portion of the Iberian Peninsula, Córdoba was established as an independent emirate with Granada as a its provincial capital. Three hundred years later the emirate disintegrated, and the many individual kingdoms which emerged coexisted, but uneasily, through the subsequent two centuries in an atmosphere of turmoil. By 1237 all other cities in Andalucía had been reconquered, but Granada, still under Moorish control, became the capital of the Nasrid kingdom.

And so it remained, for the next 250 years, the final Moorish stronghold, covering 30,000 square kilometers with a population of 400,000. This was a period of social and racial harmony, with Muslims, Jews, and Christians living together in an era of splendor. Nowhere is this legacy more apparent than in the fortress and palaces that combine to form the wondrous Alhambra. With the perpetually snow-covered peaks of the Sierra Nevada providing a dramatic backdrop this, today, is considered one of the wonders of the world.

On January 2, 1492, after many years of struggle, Ferdinand and Isabella finally defeated the last Muslim king, Boabdil, and entered Granada. On his retreat towards the sea Boabdil and his entourage paused upon a hill eight miles south of the city. There, taking his last look at Granada, he began to cry. His mother chided him with the derisory comment, "Don't cry like a woman, for something you couldn't defend as a man." To this day the spot is called *El Suspiro del Moro,* the Sigh of the Moor. The Muslims were banished to the Las Alpujarras, a remote region between the Sierra Nevada and the Mediterranean, and Castilians immigrated in to repopulate the city. Those Muslims that managed to escape exile were forced to profess their faith in Christianity, but, in spite of their conversion, these *Moriscos* were still treated badly.

Though Isabella and Ferdinand had commissioned the construction of *San Juan de los Reyes* church in Toledo as their final resting place, they became so enraptured with Granada that the specially constructed Royal Chapel *(Capilla Real)* in Granada was granted that honor instead. Before this could be completed, however, Isabella died in 1504 followed by Ferdinand twelve years later. Their remains were kept in the San Francisco Convent in the Alhambra (now part of the parador chain), prior to their ceremonious transferral to the *Capilla Real* in 1521.

Upon Ferdinand's death his grandson, Carlos I, succeeded him to the throne and, three years later, following the death of his paternal grandfather, Maximiliano I, he was crowned Carlos V, the Holy Roman Emperor. In 1526 he founded the University of Granada, now the third-largest in Spain, and a year later began building, in the Alhambra complex, a new royal palace, the *Casa Real Nueva.* Unfortunately for posterity, in the process of its construction portions of the Moorish palace were destroyed.

Today, visitors to Granada will find a city divided into three distinct parts. The largest section is situated on relatively flat terrain and, apart from the cathedral, royal chapel, and a handful of other attractions, it is rather modern and nondescript. In contrast, the other two sectors are set dramatically upon the steep hills that rise on either side of the River Darro.

To the left is *Albaicin* which, in its time, was home to the fortresses and palaces of the first Moorish kings, and consists today of narrow streets and twisting lanes lined by charming old houses. Two points are of particular interest here. First, there is Sacramonte, a curious area where gypsies *(gitanos)* make their homes in caves. Some of these have been transformed into *tablaos* for flamenco and the performance of the "typical gypsy marriage ceremony" reenacted for the enjoyment of tourists, at a price.

Second, the *Mirador de San Nicolas,* has world-famous views over the narrow valley to Granada's other, tree covered, hillside sector, the *La Sabica.* There, proudly sits the fabulous *Alhambra* and, at an even higher elevation and to its left, is the *Generalife.* This scene is stunning enough at all times, but most especially when cooperative weather conditions allow the usual haze to dissipate revealing the impressive snow-covered peaks of the Sierra Nevada in the distance. At those times, the magnificent work of nature and the majestic legacy of a civilization combine in a dramatic panorama that will remain forever imprinted upon your memory.

GETTING THERE:

Trains do not serve Granada very well. The line from Madrid uses the non-high-speed tracks via Alcázar de San Juan, Linares, and Moreda. Local services from Córdoba, Málaga, and Seville all pass through, and more often that not incur a change at Bobadilla.

Buses are certainly quicker, and more frequent, from Córdoba and Málaga and, personal preferences aside, most probably a better option from Seville as well.

By car, Granada, 270 miles south of Madrid, may be reached by taking, first, the N-IV to Bailén, and then the N-323 via Jaén. It is connected with Córdoba by the N-432; with Málaga by the N-342 and N-321; with Seville by the N-342 and N-334, and with Motril by the N-323.

PRACTICALITIES:

Most attractions, with the exception of a few museums, are open daily. Granada is a popular destination of tourists from all over the world and, consequently, accommodation isn't always easy to come by. This shortage is exacerbated during the Easter Week *(Semana Santa)* celebrations, and during the city's fair *(fería),* which coincides with *Corpus Christi.* Granada's weather conditions, dramatically affected by the close proximity of the Sierra Nevada mountain range, the highest in Spain with peaks over 11,000 feet, are more variable that those of her Andalucían neighbors. While the summers are blisteringly hot, at other times of the year temperatures may actually be much cooler than those in nearby Córdoba and Málaga.

The **Dialing Code** is 958. There are three tourist offices: the **Oficina de Turismo de la Junta de Andalucía**, ☎ 22-59-90, Corral del Carbón, open Monday to Saturday 9 a.m. to 7 p.m. and Sunday 10 a.m. to 2 p.m.; the **Oficina Municipal de Turismo**, ☎ 22-66-88, Plaza Mariana Pineda, 10, Bajo; and the **Patronato Provincial de Turismo**, ☎ 22-35-27 or fax 22-39-15, Plaza Mariana Pineda, 10, second floor. Granada has a **population** of over 260,000 and is the capital of the province of the same name, one of eight belonging to the autonomous region of **Andalucía**.

ACCOMMODATION:

The **Parador de Granada** ****, ☎ 22-14-40 or fax 22-22-64, Real de la Alhambra, s/n, located within the Alhambra complex, is housed in the old San Francisco convent, which was the temporary resting place for the remains of the Catholic Monarchs. The combination of historical interest, lovely views, exquisite decor and impeccable service makes for an unforgettable stay. $$$

The **Alhambra Palace** ****, ☎ 22-14-68 or fax 22-64-04, Peña Partida, 2, is perched on a cliff at the edge of the Alhambra park complex, overlooking the city below. It offers every comfort and beautiful views of the Sierra Nevada from its terraces. $$

The **Hotel Saray** ****, ☎ 13-00-09 or fax 12-91-61, Paseo Enrique Tierno Galván, s/n, recently opened in 1992, is a large modern hotel located in the city center. Among the 200 rooms, are 4 equipped to accommodate the special needs of handicapped guests. All rooms are furnished with the expected modern amenities, including a private safe. Guests may also enjoy the use of the hotel pool, set in a pleasant garden. $$

The **NH Inglaterra** ***, ☎ 22-15-59 or fax 22-71-00, Cettie Meriem, 4, is a small traditionally styled hotel located conveniently close to the

Cathedral. Its 36 rooms offer all modern facilities, including private parking. $$

The **Hotel Carmen** ****, ☎ 25-83-00 or fax 25-64-62, Acera del Darro, 62. A large, 283 rooms, modern city center hotel central for all the sights. Every expected amenity—including some rooms with terrace and Jacuzzi, restaurant, bar, pool and car park. $$

The **Hotel Palacio de Santa Inés** ***, ☎ 22-23-62 or fax 22-24-65, Cuesta de Santa Inés, 9. This is a magnificent small hotel, just six rooms and six suites, that has been cleverly, and creatively, transformed from a 16th-century palace known as the House of the Eternal Father. Situated in the historic Albaicin area; on the opposite bank of the Darro to the towering Alhambra fortress, it has much ambiance. $$$

The **Maciá Gran Vía** ***, Gran Vía de Colón 25; ☎ 28-54-64 or fax 28-55-91, Gran Vía de Colón 25. A very convenient medium sized hotel, 85 rooms, found in the middle of the city's main street. Just a short walk from the Cathedral, and with a convenient underground garage. $$

The **Hotel Guadalupe** ***, ☎ 22-34-23 or fax 22-37-98, Avda. los Alixares, s/n. A very comfortable medium sized hotel, just 58 rooms, with a Granadino style ambiance located at the top of the hill in the Alhambra complex, very close to the palace itself. $$

FOOD AND DRINK:

Parador de Granada (Real de la Alhambra, s/n, within the Alhambra complex), has a splendid restaurant that specializes in *gazpucho* (cold soup), *Tortilla de Sacromonte* (omelette), and *Piononos de Santa Fe,* (a typically local cake). ☎ 22-14-40 or fax 22-22-64. $$$

Restaurante Sevilla (Oficios, 12), one of the oldest, and most famous, restaurants in the city, is right next to the Cathedral. The speciality here is *Andaluz* and, in particular *Granadino,* cuisine. ☎ 22-12-23 or fax 22- 96-29. $$$

Restaurante Chikito (Plaza Campillo, 9), is a prize-winning restaurant in the city center. And, speaking of food for thought, it also has the reputation as a meeting place for the city's intellectual elite. ☎ 22-33-64 or fax 22-37-55. $$

Las Tinajas (Martínez Campos, 17), is unusual in that it specializes in cuisine in cuisine with natural products, and has a principal dish that is called the "Gastronomic Menu of Granada". A popular meeting place, it also has an amazing collection of over 30,000 bottles of wine from Spain, France and Germany. ☎ 25-43-93, fax. 25-53-35. $$

Cunini (Plaza de la Pescadería), is a dignified and elegant restaurant that is emblamatic of this city. Situated in the very center of town, close to the Capilla Real and Cathedral, since 1955 its speciality is fresh seafood from the Granada coast, including prawns and Norway lobsters from Motril. Look, also, for the *Granadino* style *tapas* and *raciones.* ☎ and fax 25-07-77. $$$

La Trastienda (Cuchilleros, 11, in a small side street just off the Plaza

Nueva), is a delightfully unique establishment. Here, you will make your food selection from a tempting buffet of light fare, mostly hams and cheeses, which are then served up on wooden platters. Add your favorite wine or spirit, retire to the back room—*La Trastienda*—and enjoy. ☎ 22-69-85. $

SUGGESTED TOUR:

Begin the tour at the centrally-located **Plaza de Isabel Católica** (1). From there take a right into Calle Reyes Católicos, following it through to the Plaza Nueva, dominated by the early-16th-century façade of the **Royal Chancery** *(Chancellería Real),* and making another right up the Cuesta de Gomerez. This rather old-fashioned street climbs steeply up towards the most famous monument in the city, indeed in all of Spain, the ***Alhambra and Generalife** (2), ☎ 22-09-12 or www.alhambra-patronato.es. This complex, which draws admiring visitors from throughout the world, is so fascinating, so huge and so intriguing that it merits being the singular attraction on this particular tour.

Halfway up the hill you pass through an ancient gate, the **Torre Bermejas**, one of the oldest parts of the fortress and also known as the "Red Tower." This is your entree to the Alhambra park area, the main entrance is some distance farther on. It must be said here that the Alhambra and Generalife is a place the many facets of which could hardly be described justly in a full book text, let alone in the lines allowed herein. It is highly recommended, therefore, that visitors avail themselves of one, or more, of the many, and beautifully illustrated, guidebooks available in English. Not only will the information it has to offer enhance your visit, but, perhaps in combination with a video, will prove an interesting souvenir.

There has been a fortress, of some nature, on this site since the 9th century, though the first kings of Granada chose the Albaicin hill, on the opposite side of the narrow valley, as the site for palaces and fortifications. It was not until the 13th century, however, that work began on the *Alhambra.* During the next century a number of palaces were added and the combination of fortress and palaces made it, in effect, a small fortified city.

It was in this era, also, that the Nasrid kings constructed, farther up on the hill, the *Generalife,* a recreational palace surrounded by magnificent formal gardens. Following the reconquest the Christian court resided here, during which time Carlos V added a palace, at the expense of some of the intricate Moorish structures, that is totally incongruous with its surroundings. Later, and amazingly, the complex was allowed to fall into decline, sinking so low, in the early 19th century, as to be used as a barracks for Napoleon's troops during the Wars of Independence. Full recognition of the merits of this unique site was not given until 1870, when it was designated a National Monument.

The complex, as it is seen today, is comprised of four basic compo-

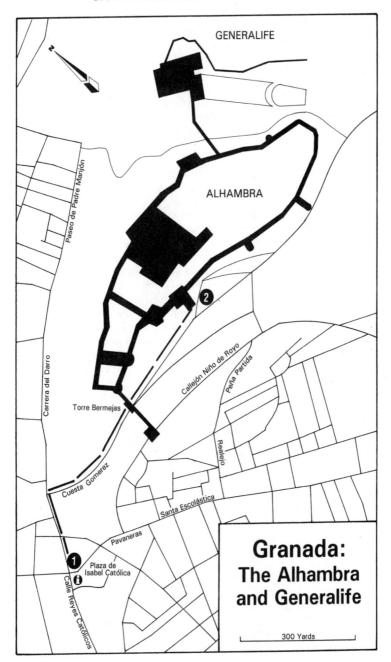

Granada:
The Alhambra
and Generalife

300 Yards

nents:

Alcazaba: This is the fortress, and oldest section, of the Alhambra, with towers dating from as far back as mid-13th century. To sojourn here is like wandering through the ruins of a castle, where the remaining towers show their age and their determination to survive in the large cracks that they bear like so many deep scars. From the top of one, the **Watchtower** *(Torre de la Vela),* is the promise of excellent views over the modern city below, although the almost perpetual smog most often spoils the sight.

*Casa Real Vieja: This, the old Moorish Royal House (or palace), is what most visitors come here to see. It is, in actuality, not a palace but, rather, a simply amazing collection of palaces, each of which has its own patios, often enhanced with fountains and/or pools and various other attendant structures. The intricacy, delicacy and beauty of the designs here create a visual impression that is beyond description. One can easily envision that long-ago time when the courts of kings resided here in splendor, serenaded by the continuous sound of running water, cleverly passing through the rooms in channels, to bring relief from the summer's overpowering heat. There are numerous "must sees" here, including the famous ***Court of the Lions** *(Patio de los Leones);* the **Tower of the Ladies** *(Torre de las Damas),* which boasts five elegant arches and a pool guarded by two, large, decorative lions also serving as fountains; a fascinating series of baths and the carefully terraced gardens. The latter are a cat-lovers paradise, as dozens of them live wild here.

Casa Real Nueva: This might be called the "new" Royal Palace, relatively speaking. Carlos V commissioned its construction as recently as 1527. The exterior of this structure, square in design with various motifs, coats-of-arms, and figures sculpted into the walls, appears rather austere when compared to the surrounding Casa Real Vieja. But it is not without its surprises. Once inside, you will find a large, and very elegant, two-story circular patio supported by impressive columns, which provides a natural theatre that is occasionally used for concerts. This is also home to the **Provincial Fine Arts Museum** *(Museo Provincial de Bellas Artes),* ☎ 22-48-43, which exhibits many paintings and sculptures from the 15th to 20th centuries, and houses a particularly fine collection of the 17th-century Granadino school of art. *Opening hours are Tuesday 2:30 to 8 p.m., Wednesday to Saturday 9 a.m. to 8 p.m. and Sunday 9 a.m. to 2:30 p.m. Entrance 250 ptas (EUR 1.50), free for EC citizens.*

Generalife: Located higher up on the hill and behind the Alhambra, is reached via the interconnecting gardens that are guarded by petite towers along the walls. Oddly, these are only open on certain days and, even then, due to their size, only a limited number of visitors are allowed inside at any one time. This was constructed to function as a recreational palace, providing a haven where kings of that day could escape the pressures of day-to-day life in the Alhambra. The buildings themselves are less opulent, but the wonderful formal gardens, incessantly irrigated by numerous fountains and water channels, in combination with the views to Albaicin and the snow-capped peaks of the Sierra Nevada indeed present an ambiance of serenity and peace.

Without a doubt, you will be reluctant to leave and the charms of Alhambra will, most certainly, beckon you again and again to explore the intricacies of this fascinating place. So allow yourself plenty of time here, and be advised that when touring the *Casa Real Vieja* you are only allowed to go one way around, backtracking is not permitted. *Opening hours are Monday to Sunday 8:30 a.m. to 8 p.m., and night visits to the Palaces only on Tuesday to Saturday from 10 p.m. to 11:30 p.m. Entrance 1,000 ptas (EUR 6.01), but restricted to 7,700 people each day.* When you finally decide to leave, simply retrace your steps back down into the new town to end the tour.

Trip 26

Granada: Cathedral and Royal Chapel

This walking tour explores the Cathedral quarter in the Old Town.

GETTING THERE:
PRACTICALITIES:
ACCOMMODATION:
FOOD AND DRINK:
See pages 177-180 for all of the above.

SUGGESTED TOUR:
Numbers in parentheses correspond to numbers on the map.

Again, begin in the **Plaza de Isabel Católica** (1), where the dominant feature is a towering fountain, and follow the busy Gran Vía de Colón for a hundred yards or so before turning left into the much narrower Oficios. The Cathedral will seem the most obvious destination, but investigate two other attractions first. Immediately to your left is the **Madraza Palace** *(Palacio de la Madraza)* (2). Constructed in 1349, the structure housed a Moorish university until the Catholic Monarchs converted it to a Town Hall, in which capacity it served until the mid-16th century. Today it is owned, as befits its heritage, by the University, who uses it to host meetings and various special events. Farther down Oficios you'll find the ***Royal Chapel** *(Capilla Real)* (3), ☎ 22-92-39. As previously recounted, both Isabella and Ferdinand died prior to its completion, a task which was entrusted to their grandson, Carlos V. The ceremonial transfer of their remains from the Alhambra to this, their final resting place, in 1521, must have been a sight to behold. In their time, other members of the royal family were interred here, but Felipe II had most of them removed to the pantheon in the monastery of El Escorial, leaving only close family members behind. As seen today, the Capilla Real is an intriguing combination of mausoleum, church, and museum, with many personal items of the Catholic Monarchs on display. *Hours are Monday to Saturday from 10:30 a.m. to 1 p.m. and 4 p.m. to 7 p.m., and Sunday and holidays 11 a.m. to 1*

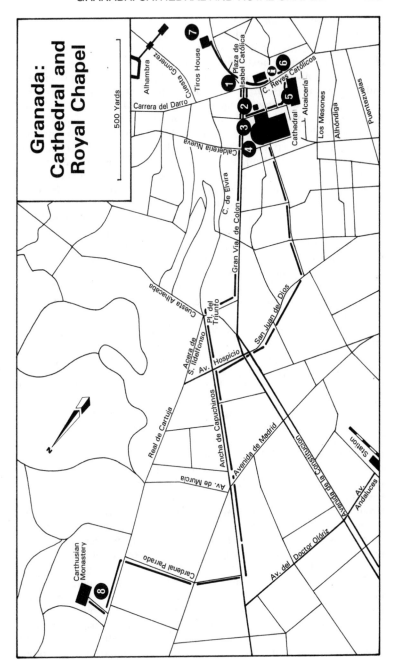

Granada:
Cathedral and
Royal Chapel

500 Yards

p.m. and 4 p.m. to 7 p.m. Entrance 350 ptas (EUR 2.10).

Also in Oficios is the **Cathedral** *(Catedral)* (4), ☎ 22-29-59, considered to be one of the finest Renaissance churches in Spain. Begun in 1518 and completed early in the next century, its interior proportions are gargantuan and, unusually for such places in Spain, the mood is one of openness and light. A small museum exhibits tapestries, paintings and other examples of religious art. *Open Monday to Saturday 10:30 a.m. to 1:30 p.m. and 4 p.m. to 7 p.m., and Sunday 4 p.m. to 7 p.m. Entrance 350 ptas (EUR 2.10).*

Leaving the Cathedral, go back to Oficios and the area of narrow lanes tucked between it and the Plaza Bib-Rambla, which are collectively known as **Alcaicería** (5) Along these, once home to a Moorish market, now reside numerous souvenir shops. Be advised, though, you'll almost certainly be pestered by unrelenting gypsy *(gitano)* women, either begging or wanting to sell you flowers. From here take any lane, running away from the Cathedral, to the busy shopping street of Calle Reyes Católicos. Heading back to the Plaza de Isabel Católica, take a right at Rubio towards the oldest Moorish monument in the city. The **House of Coal** *(Corral del Carbón)* (6), dates from the 12th century and was originally used as a warehouse and lodging place for merchants. After the reconquest it was utilized as a theater, with the surrounding balconies allowing excellent views. Though it is now, and almost always is, undergoing some form of restoration, it presently hosts a government-sponsored market selling typical Granadino arts and crafts. *Open Monday to Saturday 9 a.m. to 7 p.m. and Sunday 10 a.m. to 2 p.m.*

Next, head through the Plaza de Isabel Católica and swing right onto Pavaneras, following along until it reaches the Plaza de Padre Suárez. Here you'll find the 16th-century **Tiros House** *(Casa de los Tiros)* (7). It is adorned by the coat-of-arms of the Grana Venegas family, who constructed it, and five statues of warriors. For those whose interests run in that direction, it now houses the small Museum of History and Handicrafts of Granada.

The next attraction, the **Carthusian Monastery** *(Monasterio de la Cartuja)* (8), ☎ 16-19-32, is over a mile away, and the easiest way of getting there is a number 8 bus which departs from the Plaza de Isabel Católica. If available, take a seat on the right-hand side of the bus. Then you will have an impressive view, along the way, of the huge façade of the **Royal Hospital** *(Hospital Real)*, which sits behind the sloping formal gardens and fountain at the Fuente del Triunfo. As the name would imply, this was founded as a royal hospital in 1504 by the Catholic Monarchs. It has now been fully restored and houses the administrative offices of the University.

Disembark the bus when you reach the monastery, which was founded here in 1506 though construction of the present structure, over a Roman cemetery, did not commence until 1516 and was prolonged for nearly another 300 years. The resulting edifice exhibits some of the most important examples of Spanish Baroque architecture in Spain. The interior is particulary ornate with the sanctuary and sacristy being of particular interest. Look, also, for the numerous paintings, sculptures and other ornaments originating from the 17th and 18th centuries. *Opening hours are Monday to Saturday 10 a.m. to 1 p.m. and 4 p.m. to 8 p.m., and Sunday from 10 a.m. to noon and 4 p.m. to 8 p.m. Entrance 350 ptas (EUR 2.10).*

On your way back to town, before ending the tour, you may wish to disembark at the *Fuente del Triunfo,* and take a stroll down the Calle San Juan de Dios just opposite. This busy shopping street gives a flavor of the day-to-day life in Granada and, a few blocks down, you'll find the massive façade of the church, also named in honor of San Juan, ☎ 27-57-00. *This is open between 7:30 a.m. to 10:30 a.m. and 6 p.m. to 9 p.m.* If you wish to see its impressive collection of paintings, sculptures and sacred art originating from 15th to 20th centuries, and a collection of contemporary art including many works by the Granadino artist Manuel Lopez Vasquez, you'll have to time your visit accordingly. Exit and, just across the road, you will find Calle San Jeronimo which leads back to the Cathedral and then the Plaza de Isabel Católica.

Trip 27

Granada: Sacramonte

This walk is a bit strenuous, but it visits fascinating areas seen by relatively few tourists.

GETTING THERE:
PRACTICALITIES:
ACCOMMODATION:
FOOD AND DRINK:
    See pages 177-180 for all of the above.

SUGGESTED TOUR:
    Once again, depart from the **Plaza de Isabel Católica** (1) and, as you did when following the first tour, head in the direction of the Plaza Nueva. This time, though, carry on right through the square and into the narrow Carrera del Darro where a river, of like name, is on the right. Note, as you go along, the paradox of jumbled lanes and faded houses scattered upon the lower slopes of the huge hill at the summit of which stands, in stark contrast, the majestic presence of the *Alhambra*. Press on and you will soon come to the **El Bañuelo** (2), ☎ 22-23-39, where you'll find Moorish baths dating from the 11th century. Restored in 1928, these are considered to be the best preserved in Spain. *Visit Tuesday to Saturday 10 a.m. to 2 p.m. Entrance 250 ptas EUR (1.50), free for EC citizens.* Just behind this is the exquisite *Casa de Castril*, a Renaissance palace dating from 1539, now home to **Archaeological Museum** *(Museo Arqueológico)* (3), ☎ 22-56-40, where exhibits from Prehistoric, Roman, Visigoth, and Moorish times are on display. *Visit daily 10 a.m. to 2 p.m., entrance 250 ptas (EUR 1.50), free for EC citizens.* An interesting birds-eye view of this house can be had from the rooms of the *Casa Real Vieja*, almost directly above in the *Alhambra*.
    Brace yourself now for a bit of a walk, most of it uphill, to your next, very strange, destination. Following the river away from town along the Paseo del Padre Manjón, turn left up Chapiz and make a right at a large house, the *Casa del Chapiz*. Next take the Camino del Sacromonte continuing along, with the *Generalife* high to your right and sections of the old walls to your left, into the Gypsy *(Gitano)* area of **Sacromonte** (4). The first thing you'll notice here are the houses; which are definitely not of the sort you are used to. Your first clue may come from the strange little chim-

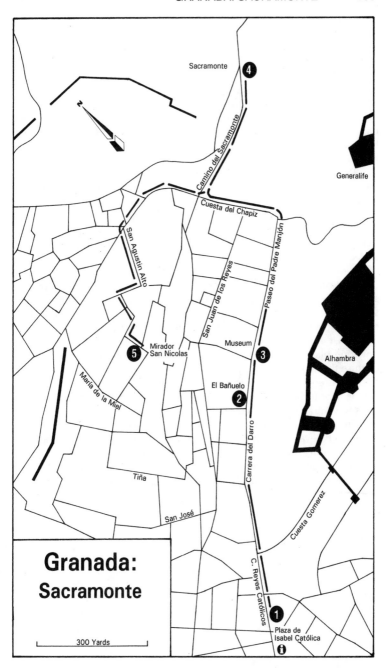

Granada:
Sacramonte

300 Yards

Sacramonte

Camino del Sacramonte

Generalife

Cuesta del Chapiz

San Agustín Alto

San Juan de los Reyes

Paseo del Padre Manjón

Museum

Alhambra

Mirador
San Nicolas

El Bañuelo

María de la Miel

Carrera del Darro

Tiña

San José

Cuesta Gomerez

C. Reyes Católicos

Plaza de
Isabel Católica

neys protruding from the rocks. Yes, these are caves and, in fact, such a lifestyle is not as unusual as you might think. There is a town not too many miles east of Granada, Guadix, that is also famous for its cave dwellers. Notwithstanding that, this still may come as something of a shock. You'll notice, also, a proliferation of *tablaos*. A *tablao* is, literally, the stage upon which flamenco is performed. These days, though, it indicates any place where the same is performed. And, not only do the gypsies make a livelihood from performing that unique Spanish dance, they also reenact Gypsy wedding ceremonies, and offer other tourist attractions. But be forewarned; this would not be considered the safest part of town, so I would not suggest walking back here at night. A taxi would be far safer.

Return to the *Casa del Chapiz*, this time taking a right and following the road around and into the heart of old Albaicin, the Plaza del Abad. If your visit is fortuitously timed there may be a traditional street market here. If not, take a seat at one of the bars, sip a refreshing drink, and let your mind imagine a time long, long ago when this area was graced by any number of Moorish palaces. On your way once again, round the corner and, on the way to the next stop, you'll pass through an 11th-century gate of the Moorish era.

You will have, no doubt, come to realize that the trademark photograph of this city is one of the Alhambra set against the backdrop of the snow-capped peaks of the Sierra Nevada. Not only is it displayed throughout the city on souvenirs of every sort, it is the predominant photograph on tourist literature as well. It will come as a surprise, then, that there is only one place in Granada, the ***Mirador San Nicolas** (5), where you can capture this image with your own camera. That is, of course, if the weather permits and you visit in the afternoon. At that time of the day the sun will be at your back and, if you are very lucky indeed, it will have turned the snow into a rosy pink color.

From here there is no one best way to return down this steep hill to the Plaza Nueva. The better option is to take a leisurely pace through the lanes, admiring the ancient houses and the Alhambra in the distance. And, should you get a little lost, if you just keep going downhill and to your right, sooner rather than later, you cannot fail to find the Plaza Nueva.

San Sebastián

S an Sebastián, called *Donostia* in the Basque *(Euskara)* language, has a long and varied history, but few traces of this heritage are visible in the city today. During the Wars of Independence the city was occupied by the French. Combined Spanish, Portuguese, and British forces instated a blockade, and that effort eventually freed the city. Sadly, during this siege, San Sebastián was completely destroyed by the great fire of August 13, 1813. A century later another conflict, World War I, brought substantial changes to the city; happily, in a less violent fashion. Spain's position of neutrality and San Sebastián's proximity to France, whose border is less that 15 miles away, made it a convenient haven for many wealthy people endeavoring to avoid the hostilities. The gracious social life and upmarket style that developed during that period transformed San Sebastián and adorned it with an ambiance that, still today, is unlike any other in Spain.

This is complemented by its spectacular topography. Beautiful green mountains, the result of a temperate climate, surround the city, culminating in Monte Igueldo to the west and Monte Urgull to the east, which stand like guard towers at either end. The Isla de Santa Clara, in turn, protects the center of San Sebastián's world-famous bay, *La Concha*. This wonderful natural setting is ornamented by solid Victorian buildings which front the promenade around the bay and contrast delightfully with the old-town *(Parte Vieja)* and the harbor which nestles beneath the shadow of Monte Urgull.

It is not surprising, given these many attributes, that San Sebastián is a very popular holiday resort for the Spanish. It is equally predictable that, as a consequence, accommodation is often difficult to find during the most popular months of July and August. The problem is compounded during the week of August 15, when the city's annual Fair *(Fería)*, the Big Week *(Semana Grande)* is held.

GETTING THERE:

Trains arrive at San Sebastián from: Irún, the first stop in Spain; from Madrid directly via Burgos or via Ávila, Valladolid and Burgos; from Barcelona and Madrid via Zaragoza and Pamplona; and from Lisbon/Oporto via Salamanca, Valladolid and Burgos. There is also a narrow-gauge **Coastal Train** *(Tren de la Costa)* that provides service to and from Bilbao.

Buses are probably the best bet if traveling between San Sebastián and Pamplona. For this journey, they are faster and more frequent than the available rail services.

By car, San Sebastián is 295 miles almost due north of Madrid, to which it is joined by the N-1 highway. Alternatively, perhaps a little quicker but much more expensive, take the A-8 *Autopista* toll road to Bilbao and then the A-68 *autopista* to its junction with the A-1 at Miranda de Ebro. The 55-mile journey to Pamplona takes you south on the A-1 to Tolosa, then onto the N-240 east to Pamplona.

PRACTICALITIES:

The opening hours of most of the attractions here are generously long. The **Dialing Code** is 943. There are two permanent tourist offices; the local office, **Centro de Atracción y Turismo**, ☎ 48-11-66, fax 48-12-72, e-mail cat@donostia.org or www.paisvasco.com, located at Calle Reina Regente, just across from the Puente Zurriola. Open June, July, August and September daily 8 a.m. to 8 p.m. and holidays 10 a.m. to 1 p.m.; and the rest of the year Monday to Saturday 9 a.m. to 2 p.m. and 3:30 p.m. to 7 p.m., and holidays 10 a.m. to 1 p.m. During the summer months a small office also operates at the **train station** (*Estación del Norte*). San Sebastián has a **population** of 180,000 and is the capital of the province of Guipúzoca, one of three belonging to the autonomous region of **País Vasco**.

San Sebastián can become estremely crowded in the summer time, especially during the **International Jazz Festival** in July and the **"Big Week"** festivities in August. Some travelers might, therefore, want to consider using BASQUETRAVEL.COM, ☎ 718-638-0190, 1-888-527-0110, Fax 718-638-2988, www.basquetravel.com, a private company based in New York, USA, that offers an array of interesting packages, for a varying number of days, that not only includes accommodation but also gives you the opportunity of obtaining the very best tickets for the events.

ACCOMMODATION:

The **Hotel María Cristina** *****, ☎ 42-49-00 or fax 42-39-14, Paseo República Argentina, 4, is a glorious "Belle Époque" style hotel dating from 1912. It was used as a winter headquarters by King Alfonso XIII and, at various other times, has been chosen as a temporary home by royalty, movie stars and toreros. An extensive renovation in 1987 ensured that the luxurious rooms were equipped with the comforts and conveniences of this age, without sacrificing the style of a more gracious one. $$$

The **Silken Amara Plaza Hotel** ****, ☎ 46-46-00, fax 47-25-48, Plaza Pio XII, 7, is located in a square with a lovely fountain that enhances its own dramatically modern design. All of the 163 rooms are thoroughly modern, sound-proofed and with facilities such as an in-room safe. $$$

The **Hotel NH Aranzazu** ****, ☎ 21-90-77, fax 21-90-50, Vitoria-Gasteiz, 1, is a modern hotel overlooking the Ondarreta beach and just 10-minute's walk away from the center of town. It has 176 rooms and 4 suites, all of which are well equipped and you even get to choose the type of pillow (firm, soft, etc.) you favor. $$$

The **Hotel de Londres y de Inglaterra** ****, ☎ 42-69-89 or fax 42-00-31, at Zubieta, 1, is housed in one of those beautiful Victorian buildings on the promenade, directly overlooking La Concha beach. It offers well-appointed rooms and a genteel ambiance. $$

The **Hotel Orly** ****, ☎ 46-32-00 or fax 45-61-01, Plaza de Zaragoza, s/n. is in a tower block that, although a street or so from La Concha, affords guests truly spectacular views from totally renovated, fully modern rooms located on the upper floors. In 1965 I enjoyed this splendor for less than $2 a night. It costs much more now, but is still good value. It also offers the convenience of private parking. $$

The **Hotel Europa** ***, ☎ 47-08-80 or fax 47-17-30, Calle San Martín, 52, situated in the Romantic Quarter of San Sebastián just two blocks off La Concha, is another structure of the "Belle Époque" style. The ambiance of the interior is reflective of the architecture, harmonious and elegant. $$

The **Hotel Terminus** **, ☎ 29-19-00 or fax 29-19-99, Avenida de Francia, 21, is a few minutes walk away from the town center, and conveniently adjacent to the train station. Obviously convenient to the latter, if sometimes a little noisy, the facilities are clean and comfortable. $

The **Hostal Residencia La Estrella** **, ☎ 42-09-97, Plaza Sarriegui, 1, is in a quiet section of the Parte Vieja. There are 30 large rooms and, overall, it is a little nicer than some of its immediate compatriots. Treble and quadruple rooms are also available. $

FOOD AND DRINK:

Basque cuisine, one of the most acclaimed in the world, is definitely the food of choice. In fact, it is difficult to find anything else. International and regional restaurants, so common in other Spanish cities, are few and far between in San Sebastián. If the local restaurants are judged by the number of acclaimed Michelin stars they have earned, in proportion to the number of inhabitants, San Sebastián easily outshines all other cities in Spain.

Restaurante Arzak (Calle Alto de Miracruz, 21) has a chef, Juan Mari Arzak, who not only has earned for himself a world-wide reputation as one of the creators of the New Basque cuisine, but earned for the restaurant the recognition of three Michelin stars. Obviously, then, this is not inexpensive, but as one of the most renowned restaurants in Spain the Arzak offers an unparalleled dining experience. ☎ 27-84-65, fax 27-27-53. $$$

Restaurante Casa Nicolasa (occupying the first floor of Calle Aldamar, 4), is one of the Haute Cuisine restaurants of San Sebastián. On the edge of the *Parte Vieja,* this restaurant's elegantly simple ambiance is the perfect compliment to the marvelous nouvelle Basque gastronomy of chef and proprietor José Juan Castillo. ☎ 42-17-62 or fax 42-09-57. $$$

Restaurante Salduba (Calle Pescadería, 6), is a restaurant with much character set in the heart of the *Parte Vieja.* A set menu is offered for 3,500 ptas. ☎ 42-56-27. $$

Restaurante La Cueva (Plaza de la Trinidad, s/n), has a wonderful Old World ambiance and specializes in pinchos of meat *(carne)*, kidney *(riñón)*, grilled mushrooms *(champiñón)* and shrimps *(gambas)* — grilled *(a la plancha)* or in boiling garlic *(ajillo)*. ☎ 42-54-37. $

Casa Vergara (Mayor, 21), resides nearly in the shadow of the Iglesia de Santa María. Hams, garlic, and antiques hang from the ceiling and the long bar counters are literally filled with every kind of *pincho* and *banderilla* imaginable. The *Menú del Dia* is very reasonably priced, but go easy with the potent house red wine. ☎ 43-10-73. $

Bar Asador Ganbara (Calle San Jeronimo, 21), also in the *Parte Vieja*, is modern in style and my personal favorite for *pinchos, banderillas* and *tapas*. Especially enchanting on a crowded Saturday evening, when lively patrons just may serenade you with their favorite tunes. ☎ 42-25-75. $

In centuries past cider was the only alcoholic drink accessible to the general public in the Basque Country. It has recently come back into vogue and **Cider Houses** *(Sidrerías)*, also serving a limited menu, dispense the drink from enormous wooden barrels *(kupelas)*. These establishments are enormously popular throughout the area:

Amara-Berri Sidrería *(Plaza de los Marinos)*, located some distance from the center of town and near to the soccer stadium, is a good place to experience the charm of this old Basque custom first hand. ☎ 46-46-84. $

SUGGESTED TOUR:

Numbers in parentheses correspond to numbers on the map.

Begin at the most conspicuous building on the city side of the *La Concha,* and the one that, effectively, divides old and new San Sebastián. Brown in color with twin towers and domed, the **Town Hall** *(Ayuntamiento)* (1) has an intriguing history. In the early 1880s, town authorities donated 7,000 square meters of land with the proviso that "at no time would it be used for anything other than a casino." Such an establishment opened here on July 1, 1887. The casino proceeded to attract high rollers from high society and also offered the chance of winning valuable prizes at the San Sebastián racetrack. Subsequently gambling was outlawed in 1924 and, as a consequence, the building fell into disuse. It was resurrected to serve as the town hall on January 20, 1947.

Before beginning a tour on foot you may want to get a quick overview of what the city has to offer, and an ideal and novel way to do so is to take a thirty-minute train trip around town. Now, the **"Txu-Txu"** (2), which departs from outside the Town Hall at intervals between 11 a.m. and 1 p.m. and 4 p.m. and 9 p.m. in the summer months is not, of course, a real train; but this is one of those times when you should let your imagination ride the rails.

Back at the starting point for the "tour proper", begin by wandering around the seafront, where it becomes immediately evident how *La*

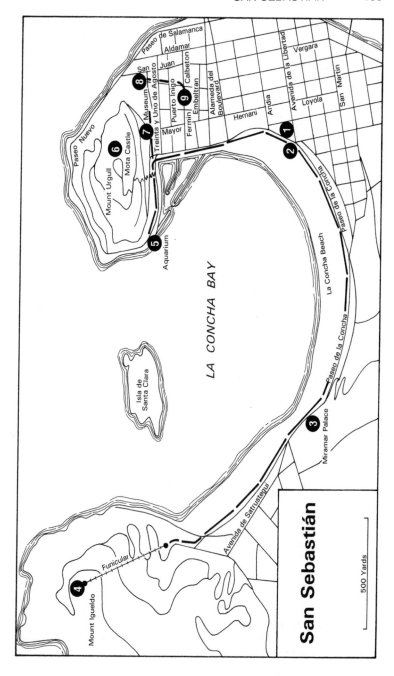

San Sebastián

500 Yards

LA CONCHA BAY

Isla de Santa Clara

Mount Igueldo

Funicular

Avenida de Satrustegui

Miramar Palace

Paseo de la Concha

La Concha Beach

Paseo de la Concha

Aquarium

Mount Urgull

Mota Castle

Paseo Nuevo

Museum

Treinta y Uno de Agosto

Mayor

Fermin

Puerto Inigo

Embeltran

Alameda del Boulevard

Hernani

San Juan

Aldamar

Paseo de Salamanca

Calbeton

Vergara

Avenida de la Libertad

Loyola

Andia

San Martin

Paseo de la Concha

Concha (The Shell), came by its name. Before reaching the promenade, the Paseo de la Concha, pass through a charming small park with a playground for children and chess tables for those who like a challenging respite. The perspective of the beach varies dramatically with the tides. At low tide the sands seem to stretch eternal, while at high tide the beach shrinks so as to be hardly discernable. During the summer months expect the crowds to be so enormous that, often, it is nearly impossible to see where sand ends and water begins. And, don't be surprised to see women, of all ages, sunbathing topless. This is a common practice in Spain, even in conservative San Sebastián. Nudism is allowed, for the more adventurous, on the rocks under Monte Igueldo! Take time to drink in this rare combination of ocean, surrounding green mountains, and sophisticated city life. It is absolutely enchanting.

Wander around, perhaps, as far as the **Miramar Palace** *(Palacio de Miramar)* (3), which is impressive, if rather out of context with its surroundings. Built to resemble a Queen Anne style English cottage, but much grander in scale, it was inaugurated in 1893 as a royal palace for the Regent Queen. It fell into a state of decay, following the death of Queen María Cristina in 1929, until 1971 when it was purchased by the city. Today, the house is used for cultural exhibitions and the gardens serve as a park. From this point on the **La Concha Beach** *(Playa de la Concha)* becomes the **Ondarreta Beach** *(Playa de Ondarreta)* and, in truth, if you are planning a swim, this is a better pushing off point, as more of the beach is left exposed here at high tide. At the end, if you are of such a mind, the funicular rises to the **Fun Fair** *(Parque de Atracciones)* (4), atop Monte Igueldo. Time now to return around the Paseo de la Concha to the *Parte Vieja*, perhaps stopping at the La Perla, an elegant bar/restaurante teetering on the edge of the promenade, where you may enjoy cooling refreshments and a soothing vista.

After passing the town hall, keep to the right of the **Royal Nautical Club** *(Real Club Nautical)* and turn left onto the Paseo del Muelle directly under the Monte Urgull. Along the way it will become increasingly evident that the harbor area is one of much character. Fishing boats pass in and out of the harbor and many restaurants, selling the day's catch, line the quayside. Their customers, seated at quaint outdoor tables, are often entertained by troubadours. Passersby will often be seen feeding the schools of fish that circle hungrily just beneath the surface of the water. Occasionally, a young man or, indeed, girl vies for the prize of admiring glances as they bravely dive the twenty, or so, feet into the murky waters of the harbor.

At the end of the paseo is the **Aquarium** (5), ☎ 44-00-99, e-mail sog@aquariumss.com and www.aquariumss.com, also the headquarters of the Guipúzcoa Oceanographic Society, which was opened in 1928. The inhabitants are specimens of the many species of fish found in local waters, and the exhibits relate to local seafaring traditions. The largest exhibit is the skeleton of a whale captured in 1878, during the days when

San Sebastián was a force to be reckoned with in the whaling industry, and saw her sailors angling for a catch as far away as Newfoundland, Canada. In early 2000 this was undergoing an expansion program that will include a Sharkrium and a 360-degree tunnel that will be unique in Europe. *The Aquarium is open daily from 10 a.m. to 8 p.m. Entrance 1,100 ptas (EUR 6.61) adults and 550 ptas (EUR 3.31) children.* Just a short distance away is a small museum that has on exhibition tools etc., used in traditional shipbuilding and other, similar, maritime themes.

Standing beneath a 95-foot statue of the Sacred Heart at **Mota Castle** *(Castillo de la Mota)* (6), which itself sits upon the summit of Monte Urgull, you may enjoy unparalleled views of the city and surrounding area. Though a visit here is possible, there is one serious drawback; the only way up is on foot. Most visitors, I suspect, will opt for a much less demanding trip on the water. There are two choices during the summer months, a round trip to the Isla de Santa Clara or a short voyage out to the ocean.

To continue the tour walk back around towards the Royal Nautical Club and turn left, through a rather strange double archway with a semi-circular top, into the **Old Town** *(Parte Vieja)*. This is a colorful area indeed. Narrow streets, often no larger than a lane, are full of small shops, numerous bars and restaurants, and an occasional historic building. The first street, Puerto, is fairly typical of what will follow. A left onto Mayor at the first junction will bring you to the façade of the elaborate **St. Mary's Church** *(Iglesia de Santa María)* (7). Baroque in style, and actually situated on the southern slopes of Monte Urgull, the structure was completed in 1764 after 21 years of construction, and is considered San Sebastián's first church.

A left into the Calle Treinta y Uno de Agosto eventually leads to the Plaza de Zuloaga, the home of the **St. Telmo Museum** *(Museo de San Telmo)* (8), ☎ 42-49-70. Along the way, however, take note of the flower-bedecked *Pensión Amaiur*, at Number 44, and the brick walls with wooden beams and numerous barrels belonging to the characterful *Restaurante La Cueva*, in the tiny Plaza de la Trinidad. In the first half of the 16th century, Alonso de Idiaquez, Secretary of State for King Carlos V, and his wife founded San Telmo as a Monastery of the Dominican Order. The building, designed with a lovely Renaissance-style cloister, was used for its intended purpose for three centuries before, in 1836, its fortunes changed dramatically; it became an Artillery barracks. A century later it was designated for use as a museum. From that time it has housed exhibits of archaeological finds as well as traditional, modern and contemporary paintings. Of particular interest is the 590-square-meter mural, by José María Sert, depicting typical Basque scenes and legends. *Open Tuesday to Saturday 10 a.m. to 1 p.m. and 4 p.m. to 8 p.m., and Sunday 10:30 a.m. to 2 p.m. Entrance free.*

Before ending the trip back at the Town Hall, take a few moments to wander through the *Parte Vieja* and, sooner or later, you'll find yourself at its center in the **Plaza de la Constitución** (9). Look overhead and you'll see that the balconies of the houses are all numbered, reflecting their seat positions when the plaza was used as a **Bullring** *(Plaza de Toros)*. In 1974 the authorities demolished the Plaza de Toros to make way for public housing, and it wasn't until the last years of the century that a new, state-of-the-art one, with a retreactable roof was constructed near the football stadium in Anoeta.

Weekend evenings find this old area at its liveliest. While youngsters prefer to frequent those streets with bars that pulsate loudly with whatever musical style is currently in fashion, others bar hop to see where the tastiest titbits can be found. Each bar competes with its neighbors to see which can fill its counter with the most appetizing array of *Banderillas* and *Pinchos*. The variety of these small portions of food, and miniature sandwiches, is incredible and, undoubtedly, enjoyed best when washed down with a glass of frothy beer, or fiery local red wine. Two things you will notice immediately here. The beer glasses are different than those used anywhere else. They are short, fat and filled less than half full. Much more surprisingly, though, payment is handled on the "honor system." No tabs are run and no bill is presented. It is up to you to remember, and recount to the barman, which, and how many of each of the *Banderillas, Pinchos* and drinks you consumed—and no one will question your integrity.

The *Parte Vieja* is also where the **Popular Societies** *(Sociedades Populares)* originated. The first of their type, Union Artesena, was founded in 1870 and, today, there are 22 such gastronomically famous societies. These are, in San Sebastián at least, clubs for men only who take turns cooking the meal of the week for their fellow club members. You can't buy your way into this experience. The meals are free, but unfortunately, only members and their friends are allowed in.

Pamplona

Pamplona, the capital of the autonomous region of Navarra, is a pleasant provincial city that is not without its charms. Yet, for 51 weeks of the year most visitors to Spain decide that there are many cities with more well-known attractions. But the other week, between the 6th and 14th of July each year, tens of thousands of visitors, both from Spain and around the world, descend on Pamplona to experience the *Fería de San Fermín*, an event immortalized by Ernest Hemingway in his 1928 novel, *The Sun Also Rises*.

Apart from the fact that accommodation is impossible to find unless booked many months, if not years, in advance—leaving many of the younger visitors to simply sleep where they drop—the tumultuous, noisy and very alcoholic festivities can be off-putting to potential visitors. And that is beside the fact that independent visitors rarely get an opportunity to do more than skim the surface of the *Fería,* and leave without much more understanding of the complexities of the numerous events than when they arrived.

It came to my attention, however, that there is one way to go to San Fermín and not just have guaranteed, quality, accommodation and the advantage of an English-speaking guide but, also, access to places and things that few foreigners would normally get close to. BASQUETRAVEL.COM, ☎ 718-638-0190, 1-888-527-0110, Fax 718-638-2988, www.basque travel.com, a private company based in New York, USA offers an array of interesting packages, for a varying number of days, that not only includes accommodation but also gives you the opportunity of obtaining the very best views of the morning encierro from a balcony and good tickets for the afternoon's *corrida*. Besides all this BASQUETRAVEL.COM can arrange for dinner reservations, either at a prestigious restaurant or even with a private club *(peña)* of bullfight fans *(aficionados),* and even for admission to a post-bullfight party where you'll have an opportunity to meet matadors and other important personalities involved in the world of bullfighting.

GETTING THERE:

Trains arrive at Pamplona from Madrid either through a limited direct service or, more frequently, via a change at Zaragoza. Another, but longer, option is to take the Madrid-to-San Sebastián train, and get a connection to Pamplona from Vitoria. From Barcelona there are direct services to Pamplona. There are also direct connections from San Sebastián.

Buses are certainly best used between San Sebastián and Pamplona and may well, depending upon the train schedules, be an optimum choice from Zaragoza.

By car, Pamplona is 257 miles north of Madrid, and is reached by taking the N-II north-east to Zaragoza, then the A-68 northwest to its junction with the A-15, which leads north to Pamplona. Pamplona is located less than 60 miles or so due south of San Sebastián, and is reached by taking the N-I and N-240.

PRACTICALITIES:

As will by now have become apparent the week, July 7 to July 14, of San Fermín is the time to be in Pamplona. Hotels rooms really are, though, impossible to obtain then and, it must be reiterated, this is certainly a world-acclaimed festival, but it won't appeal to everyone's tastes and sensibilities. The **Dialing Code** is 948. The **Tourist Office**, ☎ 22-07-41, is found in Calle Duque de Ahumada, s/n, between the Plaza de Toros and Plaza del Castillo. Pamplona has a **population** of 185,000 and is the capital of the autonomous region of Navarra.

ACCOMMODATION:

If you are traveling to Pamplona independently of BASQUE-TRAVEL.COM, don't expect to get a room during San Fermín. For any chance at all of accommodation during this tumultuous week you need to contact your choice of hotel at least six months in advance, and even then you'll have difficulty and pay twice the normal rate. My choice would be from one of the following:

The **Hotel Tres Reyes** *****, ☎ 22-66-00 or fax 22-29-30, Calle Jardines de la Taconera, s/n, has 350 rooms, is centrally located, and is the most famous hotel in Pamplona. It is said that if you sit in the lobby during San Fermín you'll be able to watch the world pass by. $$$

The **Hotel NH Iruña Park** ****, ☎ 19 71 19, fax 17 23 87, Arcadio M. Larraona, 1, considered the second best in the city, is located in a pleasant neighborhood about twenty minutes walk from the city center. Besides very comfortable rooms and suites, expect to find a gastronomic restaurant, café, gymnasium and sauna and private parking. $$$

The **Hotel Reino de Navarra** ***, ☎ 17-75-75 or fax 17-77-78, Calle Acella, 1, is a brand new, and very tastefully modern, hotel. It is located some distance from the center of town, on the other side of the *Parque de la Ciudadela*. An advantage, actually, as you're well away the non-stop noise that goes on all night. $$$

The **Hotel Maisonnave** ***, ☎ 22-26-00 or fax 22-01-66, Calle Nueva, 20, is described in the course of the Suggested Tour.

The **Hotel Avenida** ***, ☎ 24-54-54 or fax 23-23-23, Avenida Zaragoza, 5, part of the Best Western chain, is a charming hotel whose balconies help form an unusual wedge-shaped façade. Located just a short walk from the Plaza de Toros, and around the corner from the Bus Station, this also has a pleasant bar/cafeteria, and tasteful restaurant. $$$

The **Hotel Yoldi** ***, ☎ 22-48-00 or fax 21-20-45, Avenida San Ignacio, 11, is a very pleasant and comfortable medium-size hotel. It has a marvelous location very close to the Plaza de Toros, Plaza del Castillo, and the old town, yet sufficiently far away to be peaceful and quiet. $$

FOOD AND DRINK:

There are any number of restaurants in Pamplona, and some have been mentioned in the Suggested Tour. Most, though, won't find that much time to sit down and eat—there are literally so many other things to do and see. So, eat as many others do; by grabbing some of the delicious *tapas,* and other goodies, on display in every bar.

SUGGESTED TOUR:

To get the maximum advantage of your time in Pamplona it is preferable to arrive there very early in the morning, as this will allow you the opportunity to see one extra *encierro*. The overnight trains from Madrid and Barcelona are ideal for this, as they arrive shortly before 6 a.m. As the train begins to slow down on the approach to Pamplona you'll notice a dramatic heightening of the atmosphere and, as you alight from the train, your senses become attuned to the real sense of electricity, and anticipation, permeating the air.

The RENFE station is some distance from the center of town and some may be tempted to take a taxi to the hotel, but this would be a mistake. The bus that stops just across the station forecourt is not only much less expensive, it is also much more interesting. As people pile on first-time backpackers mix with veteran bullrunners *(corredores)*; those that have come in from neighboring towns and cities and groups of local *peñas*. Don't be surprised if certain members of this particularly strange mix break into song, treating you to versions of the local *jotas*. Although the words most probably won't be understood, these rhythmically catching tunes won't quickly be forgotten either. Time and time again these will echo through the streets of Pamplona and few will want to leave without a CD or cassette that will be played endlessly at home, as both a lively memory of a unique few days and a reminder of the promise that you made yourself—one day San Fermín will be revisited!

As you approach the city center expect to see hundreds of people clad in the traditional white trousers and shirt, a red sash around their waist and a similar colored neck-scarves. Some may be sleeping, others simply milling around and still more sitting at bars drinking; yes, even at this early hour. In fact, before going any further, alcohol is a topic that should be discussed. There are some who have an aversion to drink, in moderation or otherwise, and more who do not like to be around inebriated—to any degree—people. They should think twice before going to Pamplona. The reality of the situation is that, for one week, more people drink more alcohol—of every conceivable type for longer hours than any-

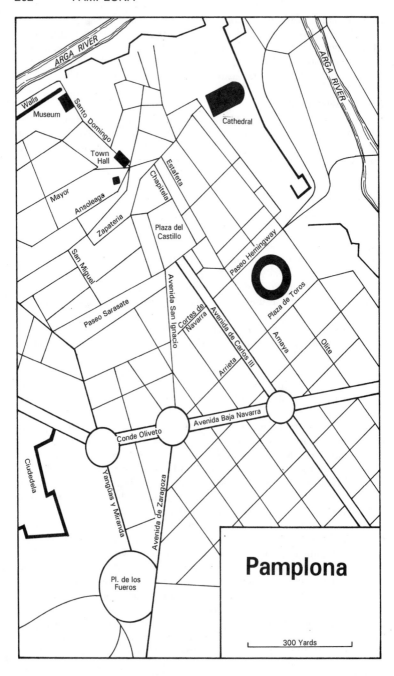

Pamplona

300 Yards

one is likely to see anywhere else in the world. The bars are only obliged to close for two hours a day—usually around 4 a.m. to 6 a.m.—and then only for the purpose of cleaning up what by that time has become a unruly mess. Inevitably, under such circumstances, there are scenes of unpleasantness—albeit, surprisingly very few—and those that are adverse to such things really do need to know in advance what they should expect.

Before arriving at the hotel be aware that, as your reservation is for that night, the room won't be ready for a few hours. So just leave your bags at the reception desk and venture out to savor the ambiance, and prepare for your first *encierro*.

The first place to head for, and it is just around the corner, is the **Plaza Consistorial** which is not only the location of the very attractive and flag bedecked **Town Hall** but also host to the opening and closing ceremonies of San Fermín. On midday of the 6th of July the ceremonies officially begin when a person designated by the city council ignites a *chupinazo* (inauguration rocket) that is fired from the balcony of the Town Hall, beginning 204 hours of festivities. This moment is also the signal for the crowds, that fill every possible inch of the square, to celebrate with a bottle of champagne. In fact Pamplona holds the record for the greatest number of champagne bottles opened and drank per minute/per square meter; the empty bottles when cleaned up weigh thousands of kilos. The closing of the festivities at midnight on the 14th of July brings an entirely more sober—well, dignified ceremony. Again thousands will fill the little square, the darkness is brightened by the candles that everyone holds aloft and, on the stroke of the hour, the singing of the very emotional song *Pobre de Mí* (Poor Me) signals the end of San Fermín for yet another year. At this time of the morning, however, the air is abuzz with expectation as the start time of the *encierro*, which begins just a couple of hundred meters down Calle Santo Domingo, 8 a.m., nears.

If you are not privileged enough to have a balcony view of the *encierro* the reality is that you are unlikely to get much of a view from the streets. One of the sights that is most striking as soon as you approach the Plaza Consistorial are the large wooden posts set in the gaps between the streets. Before the *encierro* can begin cross beams are added to form a double barrier at every junction along the route. Onlookers are only allowed behind the second of these barriers, and even if you claim a place early—at least an hour beforehand—you won't see much unless you are up by the entrance to the *Plaza de Toros* (bullring). These beams and posts each have their very own spot and, if you look closely enough, you'll see they are numbered, in effect forming a gigantic three-dimensional jigsaw puzzle that is erected and taken apart each of the seven mornings. Then, at the end of the *fería*, they are stored away until the next year. An interesting thing to do, in the time remaining before the encierro, is to familiarize yourself with the 800-meter route the bulls will take by walking from the Plaza Consistorial to the *Plaza de Toros*.

Facing away from the Town Hall turn left and shortly you'll see by huge wooden barricades that, effectively, force you into the Calle de Estafeta, the long, narrow, cavernous-like street that leads up a slight incline towards the *Plaza de Toros*. Stop for a moment, though, by the wooden barriers as these feature prominently in almost every *encierro*. As the *toros* struggle to make the sharp right-hand turn into Estafeta they, almost inevitably, slip and slide and crash into these wooden barriers. Like the rest of the *encierro* this makes for dramatic viewing, and it is run and re-run on the national and local TV stations during the day.

Prospective *corredores* need to pay particular attention here and resolve to stay well to the right. It's bad enough getting a horn wound *(cornada)*, as often happens, let alone suffering the indignity of being squashed by half ton of stampeding *toro!* As you proceed up Estafeta the shops and bars will be disgorging their customers onto the street, so the store fronts can be safely barricaded, though some bars allow their special guests to watch from the inside. Then, slowly, the street will become empty as the authorities clear everyone out and into the side streets so the process of preparing the route can begin. This is actually an interesting ritual in its own right, and will be seen more clearly the next morning from a first-floor balcony.

Time now, though, to head for the **Plaza de Toros** itself and, in particular, the *taquilla* ticket office where for just a few hundred pesetas you can purchase a ticket to watch the *encierro*, and the events that surround it, from inside. If you are prepared to be patient and stake out a position on the first-floor outside balcony this will offer a spectacular view as the *encierro* breaks into view and heads down the wide slope to the narrow passageway, right below you, that leads the *corredores* and *toros* out into the plaza itself.

As the procession passes under you it is then possible to move quickly into the seats of the plaza itself, to see the last of the action. On the other hand the entertainment going on inside the plaza is hard to pass up. There, in a circle on the sand, a local band will be playing the tunes that by now are becoming familiar, and many thousands of spectators will be joining in the fun. Frequently, sections of the crowd will break into spontaneous chants and young, slim hipped, lithesome girls, with their dark hair flowing, will stand on the rows of seats swaying sensually to the pulsating rhythms. There are always one or two—usually male of course—youths with a streak of exhibitionism, fueled not a little by copious amounts of alcohol, who jump the barriers and break into an impromptu dance. The response that this brings is immediate, loud and surprising. To the outsider these first glimpses of San Fermín give the impression that it is anarchic chaos; but this is definitely not so, as will become more and more apparent. Actually, it is a very organized chaos; and when considering the potentially combustible combination of unlimited availability of alcohol, youth, and fatigue one understands that this is how it must be. As a consequence anyone who steps out of line is met by an outburst of derision and scorn that is considerably more serious than lighthearted.

Around a half-past seven the band marches off in formation to thunderous applause, plaza attendants make last-minute preparations and medicos begin to take their places as the tension mounts. Each minute seems to take an eternity to pass as the hands on the plaza clock approach the top of the hour. Then all ears are strained for the sound of the rocket that announces that the gates of the Santo Domingo corrals have been opened and, moments later, another signals that all the *toros* have left and the morning's *encierro* has begun.

At this time seven *toros*, all of which are from the same *ganadaria* (ranch)(toros from different *ganaderias* cannot be mixed as they would certainly fight amongst each other) and a handful of *cabestros* (steers with bells around their necks, the likes of which are used to move *toros* around the ranch) are released into the street. The theory is, and this most often happens, that the *cabestros* will—more or less—keep the toros together until they reach the *Plaza de Toros*, eventually running straight through into the corrals there. The *toros* don't have to stop to be dangerous, however, as they'll often lunge at anything in their path, sometimes to murderous effect. *Toros* from different *ganaderias* can often be identified by distinctive characteristics such as horn shape, coloring and general appearance but, interestingly, they also behave differently during *encierros*.

The local newspaper, *Diario de Navarra*—which incidentally makes an excellent souvenir, offers extremely comprehensive coverage, complete with amazing photographs, of both the *encierros* and the *corridas*, and even details how *toros* from that day's *ganadaria* have behaved in past year's *encierros*. If you are planning on running beware of the day when *toros* from the prestigious *Salvador Guardiola ganaderia* make their annual appearance—they have caused more damage and death to *corredores* than any others.

If a *corredor* falls the golden, and absolutely imperative, rule is to cover their head and lay still. A fall may result in a trampling, but trying to get up is sure to make oneself an appealing target to a passing *toro!* An *encierro* becomes most dangerous, though, when one or more *toros* become separated from the others—sometimes even getting turned around and running back against the runners, as opposed to with them. At these times there is mortal danger in the air and *corredores* must do absolutely nothing to attract the *toros* attention. In amongst the runners are men with green arm bands and long firm canes, these *pastores* are used to working with bulls and they have a two-pronged assignment; to try to keep the *toros* on the move and to keep *corredores*, at least those silly enough to try, away from the *toros*. Have no doubt, the canes may be used on the runners, as well as the *toros*.

Meanwhile, back at the plaza itself, the first of the runners will be appearing in the arena and, as the danger is still some distance back, there is no mistaking the cynicism in the applause they receive. The sense of urgency increases, though, as more and more runners arrive, and very soon the first of the *toros* will break into the arena. At this point more or less anything can happen but, most often, runners will make for the wooden *barrera* (barrier) that forms an inner circle around the plaza, preparing to vault to safety if a marauding *toro*, or *toros*, head their way. Sometimes the *toros* will circle around the ring charging at anyone who is foolhardy enough to attract their personal attention. At other times the *toros* will move straight across the arena and through a gate, guarded by *dobladores*—men with *capotes* (capes)—to the corrals. To sweep-up any *toros* left behind, another set of *cabestros* are released a little later, a third rocket notifies everyone that all the *toros* are in the plaza and the *encierro* ends when all the *toros* are safely past the gate, an event that triggers the final rocket of the morning. The longer an *encierro* lasts the greater the danger. Normally, they take around two-and-a-half minutes but, on occasions, can last for much longer.

But don't leave yet, the action has just begun. Within moments the ring will be swarming with youths; attendants will be replacing parts of the wooden *barrera* removed for the *encierro* and another, entirely more light-hearted, air of expectancy pervades. After a few moments a human barricade forms itself about twenty or thirty feet from two small gates in the *barrera*. Directly behind these are two much more formidable gates that guard the toril, the area directly underneath the arena that houses the *chiqueros*, the small concrete pens where the *toros* are kept until they released into the arena, and that leads back out to the *corrales* (corrals) behind the plaza. Soon, an announcement will be made over the public address system and the gates of both the *barrera* and *toril* will be swung back to form a narrow opening into the plaza.

Immediately, a young *vaca* (cow) with blunted and taped horns will tear out and head straight for the human wall; chaos then ensues. The idea, of course, is to get as close as possible without being caught by the horns; and this is what does, generally, happen. As soon as the *vaca* gets too close it is invariably distracted by someone else, and its target escapes. When it sweeps around the perimeter the sight is hilarious, one after the other bodies disappear over the *barrera*—rather like a living wave. Now and again a youth gets caught but usually no damage is done, and after dusting himself off he is usually mobbed by his friends. After a few moments *cabestros* are released into the arena to lead the *vaca* back into the *corrales*, and the whole process repeats itself several times—usually with bigger and bigger *vacas*.

Following this there may well be a *Concurso de Recortadores*; an event similar to what has just been described, but with bigger *vacas* or young *toros*, where a young man—on his own, or with one or two other accomplices, in the ring—attempts to get as close as possible to the horns before swerving, suddenly, away. On one of the days there is a morning *novillada*, a corrida for aspiring *matadors*, and besides the fact that tickets will be freely available at the *taquilla* for this it is also interesting in its own right. And usually a *Corrida Vasco Landesa* is also held; this is an event where French Basques leap over the animals' horns.

For those really interested in seeing what goes on behind the scenes, one more event occurs at midday; the *sorteo* and *apartado*. Tickets for this can be purchased at the *taquilla* from 11 a.m. and although these days they are not inexpensive, 850 ptas in 1996, it is money well spent—at least once anyway. The entrance is around the side of the plaza closest to Estafeta and, on the way, you pass the famous statue of Ernest Hemingway. Once through the large, very sturdy, gates you are led up a flight of stairs to the first level. Here the main point of interest is the rectangular fencing that looks down into a concrete pit, and although it appears nondescript at the moment it really is the most dramatic place to be later. Unfortunately, though, if you choose to stay here and claim a prized front row place, you'll miss the action elsewhere. Best, perhaps, to come two days and see both aspects.

For the moment head up to the second level, and the sight before you is fascinating indeed; whether you are seeing it for your first or hundredth time it never ceases to intrigue. Below is a network of concrete *corrales* with railed walkways atop the walls and gates, that are operated by a complicated pulley system, separating them. Inside many of these will be *toros* awaiting their moments of glory, and some will hold the larger, and considerably less elegant, *cabestros*, the bells around their necks continually clanking.

If you look closely one corral will be the scene of most activity. This will house the *toros* that have completed the mornings *encierro* and are to be fought that afternoon. Each of the *matadores* who will be appearing that day send one their most trusted advisers, and it is their job to agree upon three pairings of two *toros*. Obviously, this is a more subjective than objective task although such visible traits as horn size and weight come into play. Equally significant are any signs of unprovoked aggression, any *toro* showing such a characteristic will want to be avoided if at all possible.

Pay closer attention and you'll see an imposingly featured guy with a flat *sombrero*, tight gray waist jacket, striped pants and cowboy type boots. This is the *mayoral*, the most important person on any *ganaderia* except the owner *(ganadaro)*, and he travels with the *toros* to ensure, not always successfully—and sometimes unfortunately with his compliance, that they are not tampered with before the *corrida*. He is also available to answer any questions from the *matadores'* advisers. When these latter men have come to an agreement about the three pairings, the numbers of the *toros* (these have been branded onto their right flank years ago at the *ganaderia)* are written onto three cigarette papers which are then folded up and placed inside the mayoral's *sombrero*. This, in turn, is covered by a handkerchief and then well shaken up before the *sorteo* draw takes place. Each of the matadores advisers then selects one cigarette paper, and this determines which matador fights which *toros*.

After a short delay, during which the *corrales* area will have been cleared of everyone except authorized plaza personnel, a fascinating event is about to begin. The *apartado* is the process by which the *toros* are moved from the open *corrales* to the small, closed, *chiqueros* directly under the seats. First, the *cabestros* are moved through the pulley-controlled gates into the corral holding the *toros*. Next, one or two *toros* are coaxed by the *cabestros* through the *corrales* to a corral next to the pit previously described. Then a single *toro* is maneuvered into the pit enclosure, giving those who have been patient enough to stay by the barrier on the first-floor area the closest view they are ever likely to get of a *toro*, before another gate slides open, the *toro* disappears, and the gate of a *chiquero* slams shut on him. And the next time he sees daylight will also be the last time.

For those who are not Spanish, or are unfamiliar with Spanish ways, it may appear rather incongruous that an event that is a precursor to an afternoon of much blood and certain death can be a social occasion as well. But that is just what it partially is and, being Spain and San Fermín there are even two bars on hand, and they also have on offer the most delicious *tapas!*

By now fatigue will be becoming as much of a companion as the excitement and it is time to wander back to the hotel, claim your room and partake of that most pleasing of Spanish customs—a siesta. But even this simple task isn't as straightforward as it might seem. There are many temptations along way: numerous shops selling souvenirs; even more numerous bars, with appetizing displays of *bocatas* (sandwiches), *banderillas* (cocktail snacks on a stick) or *pinchos* (mouthwatering pieces of fish or meat on a skewer). And this doesn't take into account the constant, and ever changing, swirl of people thronging the streets and plazas. All you have seen will be replayed over and over in your dreams and you'll sleep contentedly, yet in anticipation of the even more exciting events to come in the evening and night that lies ahead.

But don't allow too much time for sleep, be sure to set your alarm—or have reception call you—for no later than 4:30 p.m. Now it's time to don your white outfit (after all, you wouldn't want to look out of place, would you?), collect your red neck scarf from the reception desk, and head back to the *Plaza de Toros*. On the way, though, take a very short detour for a look at the activity in the **Plaza de Castillo**. This is the social center of town: the sidewalk bars around the perimeter will be full of *aficionados* debating the merits of the coming *corrida* or busily negotiating for tickets, and the center of the plaza a mass of human activity. However, even all of this noise won't disturb those who have simply crashed out on the grass, impervious to their surroundings.

Next, follow the noise of the loud bands and cut through to the neighboring Estafeta to investigate. At 5:30 p.m. the *mulillas,* two teams of three mules, will leave the Plaza Consistorial and march to the *Plaza de Toros* to the accompanying tunes of the municipal band, the *La Pamplonesa.* Hard on their heels will be the *peñas,* and this will be your first real meeting with them. These clubs can be identified by their particular badge that is worn on the backs of the head scarves, and they usually meet in private quarters at the rear of a bar. And it is from there that they march, in loose formation, to the plaza each day. Each *peña* has its own band and the members, loaded down with every kind of alcohol possible and carrying an unbelievable variation of food, dance their way through the streets. At 5:30 p.m. the gates to the plaza open and, very shortly afterwards, half of the arena—the sunny side—is a mass of color, noise and activity.

BASQUETRAVEL.COM will be supplying you with a ticket for the next day, and this will be in the calmer, shady side where you'll be able to see the activity in the ring from a closer and less excitable perspective. Today, though, be prepared to give yourself a culture shock, and join the *peñas* for an afternoon. Every ticket for each *corrida* will have been sold a long time before, but don't let that put you off. Actually, the face value for tickets in Pamplona is much lower than those in most other *Plaza de Toros* in Spain, and this is of considerable help when looking for black market tickets. The trick in this is knowing exactly what you want, looking around until you find a scalper with it and then bargaining him down to an acceptable price.

What you are looking for today is an ANDANADA SOL ticket, and these two words are clearly printed on each ticket. The face value of these were, in 1996, 1,600 ptas, and 2,000 ptas is about the lowest you should expect to pay. Most scalpers are found in the front of the plaza, near the *taquilla,* but these are often the most expensive; best to look about 100 yards or so away at the beginning of Estafeta. Wander around making it obvious you are looking for something, and you are bound to be approached; then simply hold your nerve and let them know you understand what you want, and the price you'll pay for it.

Once in possession of a ticket there is one more decision to make before entering the plaza: what to take to drink? There are bars and vendors in the plaza, but these have less choice and are more expensive than buying outside. You don't have to take much, maybe a bottle of champagne or a six-pack of beer, but you do need enough to share some with those around you—for reasons that will become obvious.

As you enter the plaza take several of the free programs—these, besides being of interest, also make souvenirs; rent a *almohadilla* (cushion) (these are marked Casa de Misericordia, PLAZA DE TOROS, PAMPLONA, and sneaked out hidden in a plastic bag make an exceptional souvenir) then climb the stairs to the top of the plaza. Before entering the seats themselves be forewarned. Immediately as you come into sight of the *peñas* you will be bombarded, usually with fruit that has been soaking in sangria. Remember, this happens to everyone, not just to obvious foreigners so don't take any offense, and certainly don't react angrily; that'll make you a permanent target. Ignore it, smile and then find yourself a front-row seat that'll offer a panoramic view of the plaza. The noise will be deafening, and the sights around you bemusing. Champagne, wine, beer and other, more exotic, drinks will not only be being consumed continually, but they'll also be being poured over everyone's heads as well.

Don't be surprised, either, to see high-powered water pumps being used to soak everyone in range; baking flour used as confetti; people having their hair washed and even fancy dress artists—an imposing and realistic version of Fidel Castro made an appearance one day! Literally anything goes and after a while, when the initial shock subsides, you'll find yourself joining in. Once your neighbors realize this you will be bombarded with hospitality as well. For over two hours every conceivable kind of drink will be pressed into your hands, remember to share yours around as well, and after the third bull is dead dinner is served—sometimes literally. Most often this is in the form of carefully wrapped elaborate sandwiches that are thrown around, unceremoniously, to members of the *peña*, followed by pastries and cakes. It is not uncommon, though, to see pots of wonderful stew being heated and then served with plates, knives and forks. You can be certain that you won't go hungry either, like the drink the food is shared equally.

As for the *corrida* itself: well, actually, this is mostly peripheral to the *peñas*. They acknowledge the entry of the *toreros,* pay some attention to each of the six fights, are prepared to chant sarcastic comments to certain *matadors* and will be happy to be derisory or congratulatory, whichever is in order, of each *matador's* work. During each fight chants, songs and the by now familiar *jotas* are picked up on by all *peñas*, and every time the drinks vendor passes proclaiming his wares *"Cerveza, Coca-Cola, Naranja y Limón"* he'll be met with an echoing *"Oi",* from hundreds of voices. At the death of each *toro* the sunny side of the arena literally erupts with noise. Each *peña's* band starts up, members sing and dance on the spot, and do as much as they can to soak everyone around them. And this routine continues for every bull!

By the end your senses will be numbed by this overpoweringly emotional experience of organized chaos. And like all other events during San Fermín, organized it is. Inevitably, every now and again tempers will flare and individuals will find themselves in an altercation. The response from all around is most surprising, but certainly indicative of the spirit. A chant goes up *"Peña Fuera"* (Peña Out); it is not the individuals that are castigated but the groups they belong to! If you are really lucky, and have struck up a particular friendship you may be invited back to their clubhouse later. You'll be given a sticky backed badge with the symbol of the *peña* on it that should be applied to the shirt breast, and this is your admission not only to a delicious free dinner but, also, to the private world of the *peñas*.

After the *corrida,* perhaps, wander behind the scenes of the plaza to find the open-air butcher's yard for a compelling yet gruesome scene. Here the toros are split open, skinned and gutted and the remaining choice sections of *carne* (meat) are hung from the walls awaiting delivery to the city's restaurants. Most probably you are watching your next day's lunch! Look, also, for the row of decapitated heads, horns still intact, that make a rather surrealistic picture.

Time now to explore the activities of the night, and there are plenty of them; both organized and not. Schedules of events are avilable in the hotel lobby and the daily newspapers. Back at the Hotel Maisonnave, 9:30 p.m. brings the *tertulia*, which is where the *toreros, ganadaros, aficionados* and critics discuss the day's *corrida*, and an hour later this is followed by dinner with the protagonists. At 10 p.m. the *Toro de Fuego* (bull of fire), departs on its journey from the Plaza de Santiago, and this is a great attraction for both adults and children alike. In some towns they actually do have sticks that are set alight and stuck in *toros*; here, though, they are much more civilized. A man with a metal bull's head and sparklers attached runs through the crowded streets.

Eleven p.m. each night is the time for the magnificent *fuegos artificiales* (fireworks) displays that burst into the sky with colors and shapes that resemble nothing less than a kaleidoscopic rainbow. And then, throughout the city, there are any number of open-air concerts and shows. While everyone's attention is distracted by these events the authorities, cleverly, use the time for the *encierillo* (little encierro). This is when, at 11 p.m., the *toros* are run from permanent holding *corrales* to those temporary ones on Santo Domingo, from where they will be released at 8 a.m. the next morning. For nearly a century the holding *corrales* were down the hill and across the river at the *Corrales del Gas*, but these have been replaced by ones on the same side of the river, and much closer to, those on the Santo Domingo. No matter where they are, they make for a hugely interesting visit during the day. For a small fee you get to see *toros* from the different *ganaderias* at the same level and separated only by a sheet of glass.

Without doubt, though, the greatest entertainment at night in Pamplona is to be found in the streets, plazas and bars, all of which are full to bursting point. Here you'll find every aspect of human emotion; discover unusual food and exotic drinks; meet many fresh acquaintances and, perhaps, make new friends. Bar hopping is developed to an art form here; well, as almost every other doorway is the entrance to one it is impossible for it to be otherwise. The whole ambiance is magnetic, and you are continually drawn to see what is around the next corner or what delights the next bar holds. Perhaps you'll meet the *peña* that has a mongoloid as its band conductor. Quite obviously the instructions aren't harmoniously orchestrated but, at the end, he is hugged and loved by every member of the band. A touching occasion by any standards!

Before long, if you aren't careful, time will have become an irrelevance and the morning's *encierro* will be almost upon you. Remember, at 7 a.m. you have to meet your BASQUETRAVEL.COM guide; and you can't be late or Estafeta will be closed and you'll be denied a most fine vantage point. So, be a little wise; drag yourself away for a couple of hours' sleep. And, as compensation, always remember other nights await you.

If you are really lucky the apartment your BASQUETRAVEL.COM

guide takes you to will be an old-fashioned one. A formidably designed front door will protect beamed ceilings, wonderful wooden floors, treasured family antiques and, of course, the living room will boast two balconies overhanging Estafeta. Indeed, there isn't a finer vantage point to be had. Although the *encierro* is still nearly an hour away, there is plenty to occupy your time. Inside coffee and cookies will be provided, the television will always be offering varying perspectives and commentaries and the morning newspaper's photographs never cease to amaze.

But it is what is happening outside that is most fascinating. Slowly the police will be clearing Estafeta of people and then, very surprisingly, the street is cleaned. And this isn't a superficial cleaning either, it's very thorough indeed. Workers with air blowers attack every crack and cranny, and these are followed by other city workmen who spread sand over any obviously slippery sections. From an unruly mess Estafeta is transformed into the cleanest street in the city, and this process is taken so seriously that the *alcade* walks the length of the *encierro* to ensure that it passes his inspection. By now the *medicos* and ambulances will be installed in their places, obviously as close to the street as they can get, the *pastores*, with their green arm bands and long canes, will have passed on their way down to the Santo Domingo *corrales*, and the length of the *encierro* is effectively sealed.

Shortly before 8 a.m. a wall of police officers forms a human barrier to contain a mass of runners that have been allowed forward some distance to avoid overcrowding, and then something really strange happens. Suddenly many of Estafeta's front doors open and the really serious *corredores* emerge. Well known in the community, and often wearing some article of clothing with a very distinctive color so they can be identified easily on TV, these take up their favorite positions along the route. At the sound of the rocket the police quickly disappear into the conveniently located side street, and the first mass of runners head for the plaza. The noise level increases as the proximity of danger nears and, very shortly, you'll hear the clanging of the *cabestros's* bells and, as they round into Estafeta, distinguish the dark shapes and ominous horns of the *toros* between the seething mass of human bodies. As they pass just a few feet underneath you there is so much to see, and in such a short time, that in trying to see it all there is a danger that you may miss most of it. But don't despair; the television instant replays and slow motion shots will more than compensate.

Once they have passed, a common sight is that of an inert *corredor* lying in the street. Within moments, though, the *medicos* will have him strapped to a stretcher and whisked away to the hospital. His injuries will soon become very public knowledge indeed; closeup re-runs on TV, and in the next morning's papers page after page of photographs and even interviews and pictures from the patient's hospital bed. One's personal embarrassments are afforded precious little privacy in Pamplona!

The next place you might go is of an entirely different character. You'll cross Estafeta and pass through the narrow alleyway where, only minutes before, the *medicos* were stationed, enter into the open expanse of the Plaza del Castillo and be led to an inconspicuous doorway on the narrow, right-hand side of the plaza. The first indication that this is someplace special is that of the doorman assiduously checking membership cards, once past him a staircase leads to the first floor and into one of the most attractive of rooms. In fact a room is an understatement; it is really a hall and it runs almost the entire width of the plaza, as can be seen from the equally long balcony. The walls are a mix of the most beautiful wood and mirrors, and the immense beams of the ceiling are supported by elegantly carved, nude women that are illuminated by glittering reflections from the equal, yet rather different beauty, of the shimmering crystal chandeliers.

This is the Casino Principal and it has an ambiance that would not be out of place in Versailles. At this time of the morning all the tables and chairs have been moved to the edge of the room, a local band plays those ever popular *jotas* and, while you breakfast on *churros* (eaten straight from the paper of course) and *chocolata,* the floor bounces with energetic young dancers. People of all ages are here, and it is especially intriguing watching the young girls admiring their teenage counterparts; you can almost see them counting away the years until they can dress so glamourously, and be held so closely! Really, one of the most eclectic of scenes.

Believe it or not, it is almost time to eat again, and this time the surroundings are not so elegant. More likely than not your destination will be one of the small restaurants in the maze of narrow streets that constitute the *Casco Viejo* (Old Town). Remember the way here as, at night, it is one of the liveliest areas in town. Although the restaurant will be a surprise, what you should order certainly shouldn't be. How could you leave Pamplona without sampling *Estofado de Toro* (Stewed Bull's Meat)? This really is delicious, the meat being of a context and color not found in your local supermarket.

It's almost siesta time again, and your BASQUETRAVEL.COM guide will arrange to meet you in the hotel lobby after to take you to the afternoon's *corrida.* This time it will be very different. The ticket is for the *sombra* (shady side), and as you are well away from the *peñas* there's no need to worry about getting dirty. Also, the *corrida* is seen from a more advantageous perspective and, with explanations available from the guide, you will be able to be understand, and thus enjoy, it more easily. After, if you want, your guide will take you to the *tertulia* back at the hotel, and this is always an interesting event. *Tertulia* literally means a get-together, and each night those involved in the bullfighting world, often this includes the *matadors* you have just seen, use it as a forum for discussing the afternoons *corrida.* Being Spain the public is invited too, and it wouldn't be Pamplona (would it?) without a bar and *tapas.* Even non-aficionados will find something for themselves here.

Of course, if you prefer, you can go off on your own to discover the delights you missed the night before, and revisit those you particularly liked. But like every night during San Fermín the morning comes quickly, and your BASQUETRAVEL.COM guide will be awaiting you at 7 a.m. on the dot, to take you to a balcony for that morning's *encierro*. After which you are spoiled for choice. Maybe you want to follow the *Gigantes y Cabezudos*, an institution that has been around for nearly 150 years. These giants and bigheads leave the *Estación de Autobuses* at around 9:30 a.m. in the morning to wander the streets of Pamplona, returning to their base at 2 p.m. The *Plaza de los Fueros*, an open-air theater, is home to folklore festivals such as *aizkolaris* (woodcutters) and *arrijasotzailes* (stone lifters); the Taconera gardens host local *joteros* and *txistularis* (Basque flute players) while the famous Chamber Choir of Pamplona can be found in the Gayarre Theatre.

However, whichever way you choose to go, with BASQUETRAVEL.COM or independently, the Fería de San Fermín will be one of the experiences of your lifetime; and it will always be something you'll be anxious to return to.

Valencia

T his region was occupied by both Greek and Carthaginian settlements before the Romans, calling it *Valentia,* founded their city on
the site in 138 BC. They were supplanted by the Visigoths who, in
turn, were succeeded by the Moors early in the 8th century. Rodrigo Diaz
de Vivar, more commonly known as *El Cid,* gained considerable fame
when he conquered the city in 1094, but that era was short-lived and it was
reclaimed by the Moors just eight years later. They managed to hold
power until Jaime I, *El Conquistador,* finally reconquered the city in 1238.
He proclaimed the Kingdom of Valencia, and signed a charter (Furs) under
which Valencia was governed for over five centuries.

The 15th century began a period of prosperity, during which the population grew from around 4,000 to 80,000. This trend continued until the
beginning of the 17th century, when the Moors and Jews were expelled
from Spain, and Valencia, as a result, lost over one-third of its citizens. This
was the commencement of a prolonged period of decline which acceler-
ated after the loss of the War of Succession at Almansa in 1707. Valencia
had fatefully cast its lot with Archduke Charles of Austria, and a victorious
Felipe V, in retribution, ordered the abolition of the Furs Charter.

Valencia has, since that time, gained a reputation for independent
thinking. During the Wars of Independence the citizens, led by Father
Rico, in 1808 rose up against Napoleon's troops and took control of the
city. The battle was bloody, however, and the victory short-lived. The
French regained control just four days later. At the end of the 19th century and beginning of the 20th century new forms of transport, new indus-
tries, and the demand for traditional citrus fruit products favorably combined to revitalize the city, spurring a period of renewed economic suc-
cess and growth. In 1865, the government, in this progressive state of
mind, sadly demolished the city's 14th century walls as part of a project to
provide jobs to the needy.

Valencia, true to form, however, supported the losing side in Spain's
Civil War, though for a year, between November 1936 and October 1937, it
served as the headquarters for the Republican government. The city fell to
Franco in 1939. In 1982, by which time it had become the third-largest city
in Spain, Valencia became the capital of the autonomous region of the
Communidad Valencia.

Visitors to Valencia, by no means the most well-known tourist destination in Spain, are in for a very pleasant surprise indeed. The major
attractions are well within walking distance of each other and the admis-

sion charges, unlike other towns, are mostly nominal. The city has a very pleasant ambiance, derived from a delightful combination of unpretentiousness and Mediterranean charm.

GETTING THERE:

Trains run through Valencia on the way to and from Barcelona and Murcia. And, although it may seem illogical when looking at a map, the city is a mid-point for the fast InterCity service between Madrid, via Albacete, and Barcelona, via Tarragona. An alternative line to Madrid runs via Cuenca, but the service is of a lower standard and the trains are less frequent and much slower.

Buses are best used between Valencia and Cuenca, but even then the journey time is often not commensurate with the distance. Expect a minimum of around 4 hours, and sometimes much more as the bus route weaves between towns and villages.

By car, Valencia, about 220 miles just southeast of Madrid, is reached on the N-III highway, probably the least developed of all the major roads in Spain. The A-7 *autopista* toll road connects Valencia with Castellon, Tarragona and Barcelona to the north, and with Alicante and Murcia to the south. Valencia also sits astride the N-340 highway, the longest in Spain, that connects Cádiz to Barcelona.

By air, the Valencia airport, Manises, 5 miles west of the city, is served by a limited number of direct international flights, originating from within Europe, as well as flights from other Spanish cities.

PRACTICALITIES:

There are numerous places of interest and museums in Valencia, and most of them are closed on Monday. Also, be aware that many of these have rather irregular hours during the remainder of the week. The world-famous *Las Fallas* festivities take place during the seven-day period culminating on March 19, and it is impossible to get accommodation at that time without booking many months ahead. This fascinating fiesta honors Saint Joseph, the patron saint of carpenters, and has its origins in the Middle Ages when carpenters burnt their accumulated wood shavings in bonfires *(Fallas)*. These days, highly elaborate and colorful papier-mâché and wooden-framed statues, enormous and depicting anything it is possible to imagine, are erected on every street corner. Then, on the night of March 19—beneath showers of loud and colorful fireworks all, except the one judged to be the best (which goes on permanent display in the Las Fallas museum), are put to the torch.

The **Dialing Code** is 96. Valencia is a city better served than many by local tourist offices. The **Municipal Tourist Office**, ☎ 351-04-17, is located within the Town Hall in an office on the main façade fronting the Plaza del Ayuntamiento. It is open Monday to Friday 8:30 a.m. to 2:15 p.m. and 4:15 p.m. to 6:15 p.m.; and Saturday 9:15 a.m. to 12:45 p.m. The **Communitat Valenciana**, (note the spelling, *Valenciano*—the local language is often used here), has two offices. One is found at Calle Paz, 48, ☎ 394-22-22 or fax 394-27-98, and is open Monday to Friday from 10 a.m. to 6 p.m., and on Saturday between 10 a.m. to 2 p.m. The other, in the main railroad terminal, the Estación del Norte, ☎ 352-85-73, opens Monday to Friday from 9 a.m. to 6:30 p.m. The latter also offers for sale an interesting selection of souvenirs from the Valencia Region. Valencia has a **population** of about 750,000 and is the capital of the province of the same name, one of three belonging to the autonomous region of **Communidad Valencia.**

ACCOMMODATION:

The **Hotel Astoria Palace** ****, ☎ 352-67-37 or fax 352-80-78, Plaza Rodrigo Botet, 5, is, without doubt, my favorite in Valencia. Centrally located, thoroughly modern and comfortable, it also offers a very relaxing ambiance, not to mention a delightful rooftop restaurant and an adjacent parking lot. $$

The **Parador de El Saler** ****, ☎ 161-11-86 or fax 162-70-16, Avenida de los Pinares, 151, is ideal for those wanting to enjoy the city, but stay near the sea. Just 10 miles from the center of Valencia, this establishment has some rooms with sea views, and offers a variety of sporting opportunities—most notably golf. $$

The **Hotel Serrano** ***, ☎ 334-78-00 or fax 334-78-01, General Urrutia, 48, is a modern hotel, with 105 well equipped rooms and a restaurant, located in a quiet area of the city, yet not very far from the center. It has private gardens and a pool. $$

The **Hotel Ad Hoc** ***, ☎ 391-91-40 or fax 391-36-67, Boix, 4, is a small hotel, a combination of just 28 rooms, housed in a 19th-century palace located within the historical zone of Valencia, just a few minutes walk from the city center. The combination of classical and modern styles is intriguing. $$

The **Hotel Cónsul del Mar** ***, ☎ 362-54-32 or fax 362-16-25, Avenida del Puerto, 39, is in a very interesting building that has been tastefully converted into a more than comfortable hotel. Recently opened, in 1995, it features every modern facility, including a jacuzzi in each bathroom. Found between the city center and the port, it also has private parking. $$

The **Hostal Residencia Londres** ***, ☎ 351-22-44 or fax 352-15-08, Barcelonina, 1, is on a relatively quiet side street, just a little way off the Plaza del Ayuntamiento. Very pleasant and comfortable, it offers a good value for money spent. $

The **Hostal Residencia Venecia** **, ☎ 352-42-67 or fax 352- 44-21, Plaza del Ayuntamiento, resides behind an imposing façade that overlooks the main square in Valencia. All rooms have air conditioning, full private bath and telephone. $

FOOD AND DRINK:

Restaurante Rías Gallegas (Cirilo Amorós, 4), is found in the typical Valencian neighborhood of Ruzafa, not far from the Plaza de Toros.

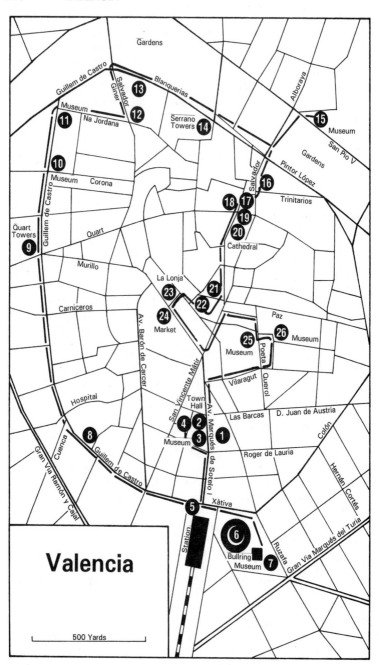

Valencia

Although in the restaurant business for over thirty years, the owners moved to this new location only in 1996. In a dignified ambiance the menu, as the name implies, is totally Galician and is loaded with traditional specialties. Interestingly, it is possible to order half portions of most of the dishes. ☎ 351-21025 or fax 351-99-10. $$$

Restaurante Vinatea (Plaza Rodrigo Botet, 5), is found on the rooftop of the Hotel Astoria Palace. The varied selection of International and regional cuisine is visually complemented by a wonderful panorama of the city. ☎ 352-67-37 or fax 352-80- 78. $$

Restaurante Gargantua (Calle Navarro Reverter, 18), is housed in an early 20th-century mansion, just a few minutes from the city center and near to the Turia riverbed. It is well known for imaginatively prepared Valenciano cuisine. X: Saturday afternoon, Sunday, August. ☎ 334-68-49. $$

Restaurante Viriato (Calle Viriato, 3), is nestled in the maze of narrow streets behind the Serrano Tower. It specializes in Mediterranean cuisine. X: Sun. ☎ 391-11-07. $$

Restaurante La Fondue (Calle Serrano Morales, 11), is located in close proximity to the Gargantua and, as the name proclaims, it specializes in Bourguignone and Savoyard fondues. ☎ 374-74-84. $$

Restaurante Setabis (Plaza del Dr. Collado, 9), just behind La Lonja, offers a delicious, and inexpensive, *menú-del-dia.* ☎ 391-62-92. $

SUGGESTED TOUR:
Numbers in parentheses correspond to numbers on the map.

The **Plaza del Ayuntamiento** (1), colored in the cheerful palette of numerous flower kioscos, is Valencia's main square and the logical place to begin the tour. As its name indicates, the predominant building among those surrounding the perimeter is the **Town Hall** *(Ayuntamiento)* (2). Just to the right of the main entrance is the **Municipal Tourist Office**. Inside, at the top of a most impressive staircase, is the very interesting *Municipal History Museum *(Museo Histórico Municipal)* (3), ☎ 352-54-78. Among the many fascinating exhibits, in addition to the expected selection of paintings and books, you will find the famous Reconquest Banner, the *Senyera;* the sword of the conqueror, Jamie I; and an early-18th-century map of the city. *Opening hours are Monday to Friday 9 a.m. to 2 p.m. Entrance free.*

Exit through the main entrance and make two right turns, into Periodista Azzati, then Arzobispo Mayoral, that lead around the back of the town hall, and to the **Municipal Palaeontology Museum** *(Museo Paleontológico Municipal)* (4), ☎ 352-54-78. Though this has only five rooms, the exhibits, which range from the smallest fossils to dinosaurs, are of interest. Also, there is a curious view through the ceiling into the elaborate Town Hall. *It opens Tuesday to Saturday from 9 a.m. to 1:45 p.m. and Wednesday and Thursday 4:15 p.m. to 7:15 p.m. Entrance free.*

Come out and follow back around to the plaza once again, this time taking a right along Avenida Marqués de Sotelo, where soon you will soon come upon the elaborate façade of the traditional **railroad station** *(Estación del Norte)* (5). It's not overly large, but the hustle and bustle always makes for an interesting sight. Next to the station is the **Bullring** *(Plaza de Toros)* (6), which may be visited Monday to Saturday between 9 a.m. to 2 p.m. and 4 p.m. to 7 p.m. providing, of course, that a bullfight *(corrida)* is not scheduled for that day. Behind the ticket offices *(taquillas)*, in a small covered pedestrian walkway, is the **Bullfighting Museum** *(Museo Taurino)* (7), ☎ 351-18-50, and if you are at all interested in the world of bullfighting, you should definitely add this to your itinerary. Considered to be one of the finest of its genre in the world, it has two floors of fascinating exhibits that may be visited, at no charge, between the hours of 10:30 a.m. and 1:30 p.m. Monday to Friday. Retrace your steps past the Plaza de Toros and the station and turn into the busy Calle Xativa. Once you pass the impressive **Iglesia de San Agustín** the street changes its name to the Avenida Guillem de Castro and, after a couple of hundred yards, on the right hand side, opens up into a quaint little park. Take a respite here in the cooling shade of the trees, surrounded by some interesting statues and lovely fountains. Here also you will find the *Ermita de Santa Lucía* and the **Ancient Hospital of the Innocent Poor** *(Antiguo Hospital de los Pobres Inocentes)* (8), a portion of which houses the **Center for Valencian Arts** *(Centro de Artesanía Communidad de Valencia)*, which displays samples of traditional Valencian dress, silks, fans and various other hand-made objects. However, this was closed in early 2000, with no date given for re-opening.

The next stretch of Guillem de Castro is not particulary inspiring, but don't let this discourage you. Soon the imposing sight of the **Quart Towers** *(Torres de Quart)* (9) appears, dominating the skyline. Constructed during the 15th century as a means of access to the city from the west, these two semi-circular turrets feature double crenellations and massive wooden doors, and are painfully adorned with bullet holes and gouges, a legacy from previous hostilities.

Guillem de Castro now becomes more pleasant, enlivened by a narrow park with fountains and a statue of Cervantes, which stretches to Calle la Corona. Here, on the corner, is an interesting old building, the **Beneficiencia Cultural Center** (10), which houses the **Museums of Ethnology and Domingo Fletcher Prehistory** *(Museos Etnológico y Domingo Fletcher Prehistoria)*, ☎ 388-35-79. *These have the identical opening hours of Tuesday to Saturday 10 a.m. to 2:30 p.m. and 5 p.m. to 8 p.m., and Sunday and holidays 10 a.m. to 8 p.m. Entrance free.* A short distance farther on the unseemly sight of an ultramodern building brings you, at last, to the end of Guillem de Castro. The **Valencian Institute of Modern Art** *(Insituto Valenciano Arte Moderno (IVAM) Centre Julio González)* (11), ☎ 386-30-00, has eight galleries. Two display permanent collections of works by Julio González and Pinazo. Of the six remaining, which exhibit temporary collections of various forms of modern art including photography, one is architecturally interesting in its own right, situated around the remains of the medieval ramparts. *The museum is open Tuesday to Sunday from 11* *a.m. to 8 p.m. Entrance 350 ptas (EUR 2.10).*

Continue on, turning right and following the signs, through a rather peculiar neighborhood of renovated apartments populated by youths expressing their cultural diversity, which lead the way to **IVAM Centro del Carme** (12). The original structure, built in the 13th century, is of architectural interest in its own right, but a wing has been recently added. Its role, under the direction of the Valencian Institute of Modern Art, is to introduce contemporary art, especially the work of local and national artists, to the citizens of Valencia. *These displays may be visited Tuesday to Sunday from noon to 2:30 p.m. and from 4:30 p.m. to 8 p.m.*

Exit right and, at the end of the street, turn right again into Calle San Gines. This leads out to a series of roads running between the historic area and the Turia river bed. In fact, no river flows here at all now, but it has been cleverly transformed into a series of gardens and leisure-and-sports facilities. Make yet another right and follow Calle Blanquerías around to number 23. Artist José Benlliure resided here from 1855 to 1937, and this **House/Museum of José Benlliure** *(Casa-Museo José Benlliure)* (13), ☎ 391-16-62, has, on the ground floor, exhibits that feature his works; those by his brothers, Pepino and Mariano; paintings, ceramics and drawings of other noted Valenciano artists, and fine examples of period furniture. *Opening hours are Tuesday to Friday from 9 a.m. to 1:30 p.m. and 4 p.m. to 6 p.m., and Saturday from 9 a.m. to 1:30 p.m. Entrance free.*

A couple of hundred yards ahead, standing forlornly devoid of its attendant walls, is the second, and more elegant, of the grand medieval gates that once guarded Valencia, the **Serrano Towers** *(Torres de Serranos)* (14). This was constructed in the 14th century and features twin, octagonally shaped, and crenellated towers, with unusual battlements two-thirds of the way up on either side. These are connected by a central fortification with a small gateway at the base.

It is now time to cross the road and follow the river bed along to the third bridge, the *Puente Trinidad,* noting the two statues at the near end. The impressive looking building to the right at the end of the bridge, recognizable by its gleaming domed tower, is the ***Fine Arts Museum** *(Academia Real de Bellas Artes de San Carlos)* (15), ☎ 360-57-93. Originally a convent, this now houses one of the most important galleries in Spain. Exhibits include works by both the Old Masters—Goya, Murillo, Velaquez, and El Greco—and Valenciano artists, as well as a collection of contemporary art, a sculpture pavilion and an archaeological section. *These can be seen Tuesday to Saturday from 10 a.m. to 2 p.m. and 4 p.m. to 6 p.m., and Sunday and holidays from 10 a.m. to 2 p.m.*

Back over the bridge, take the small street, Calle Salvador, directly ahead of you. At first glance this seems quite bland but persevere and, at the end, there are some surprises. The rather plain building to the left, with an overhanging wooden roof is the **Almudín** (16). Built in the 13th century but renovated in the next, this was formerly the city grain store and now functions as an exhibition hall. Directly across, with the dominating towers of the Cathedral and Basilica providing a dramatic background, is the **La Armoina** (17), an open area that seems to have been in a state of perpetual renovation. There are remains from the Republican Roman times, between 173 BC to 75 BC; the Imperial Roman era, between 1st to 3rd centuries; the Visigothic period, between the 6th to 8th centuries; the Islamic occupation, 8th to 13th centuries, and the late Medieval period, from the 13th to 14th centuries.

Turn right and, just a few yards along, the narrow street opens up into the most charming Plaza de la Virgen. Wonderful fountains and statues adorn the center and, straight ahead, is the fascinating 15th-century Gothic building, the **Generalitat Palace** *(Palacio de la Generalitat)* (18). This functioned as the assembly hall of the parliament *(Cortes)* until it was disbanded by a vengeful Felipe V in 1707, and it is currently the seat of the Valencian autonomous government *(La Generalitat)*. As you turn into the plaza the building on the left is the **Basilica of Our Lady of the Forsaken** *(Basilica de la Virgen de los Desamparados)* (19). This precious Baroque building was constructed over the Roman Forum and features a unique elliptic design and a beautifully painted domed ceiling.

Just along from here is the rear of the ***Cathedral** *(Catedral)* (20), the main entrance to which is just past the tower, *El Miguelete,* in the Plaza de la Reina. Construction began in 1262 on what was previously the site of a Roman temple, then a mosque, but the greater part of the structure dates from the 14th and 15th centuries. The interior, which is not overly elaborate, may be visited daily 7:30 a.m. to 1 p.m. and 4:30 p.m. to 8:30 p.m. The attendant **Cathedral Museum** *(Museo de la Catedral)*, ☎ 391-81-27, has an impressive collection of religious art but a rather complicated opening schedule. *For the large part of the year, you will find it open on Monday to Friday between 10 a.m. to 1 p.m. and 4:30 p.m. to 7 p.m., and on Saturday between 10 a.m. to 1 p.m. Entrance 100 ptas (EUR .60).* It is the Cathedral tower, *El Miguelete* that is of most interest; though you must be fit to take full advantage of it. Within this unfinished octagonal, Gothic, tower a narrow and winding concrete staircase comprised of no less than 207 steps ascends to a viewing platform at an altitude of over 210 feet. The vista from this vantage point is spectacular indeed, a bird's-eye view of the city below and the Mediterranean Sea, and mountains upon the horizon. *Opening hours are daily from 10 a.m. to 1 p.m. and 4:30 p.m. to 8 p.m.* If you happen to be in Valencia on a Thursday, then time your visit to the Cathedral for midday. Surrounding Valencia are over 2,300 acres of irrigated land *(huerta)*, watered by canals that, in some instances, are over 2,000 years old. To adjudicate disputes relative thereto the **Water Council** *(Tribunal de Aguas)*, made up of eight men, has met at the Door of the Apostles, on the same day of the week and at the same time of day, for over a thousand years. Business is conducted verbally, in the local language Valenciano, and all decisions are final.

At the end of the Plaza de la Reina you will see, towering high above the rooftops of its neighbors, the intricately designed tower of the **Iglesia**

de Santa Catalina (21). A walk down Sombrería allows closer investigation. Retrace your steps and turn right down the narrow and uneventful Jofrens. Halfway along, a right takes you into the **Plaza de la Redonda** (22), which will certainly not disappoint. Round in shape, it hosts an interesting collection of small shops and enticing bars around its exterior as well as an inner circle of permanent stalls, and proves an interesting place to stop for refreshments, and ponder the contrasts of Valencia.

Return back, and right, into Jofrens taking another right at the bottom into Cerrajeros. This leads to the Plaza del Dr. Collado, an old-fashioned area teeming with characterful shops and bars. Do not be misled by the innocuous façade of the large building to the left; what it conceals merits investigation. Follow one of the small passageways on either side around to the main entrance of the ***La Lonja** (23). Built to house an exchange, at the behest of the city's silk merchants, a prolonged construction spanned the years from 1483 to 1498. It has served a variety of uses since then. Today, it functions as an exhibition hall; but most are as attracted by the exquisite interior as they are by the exhibits. Considered one of the finest civil-Gothic structures in Europe, the focal point is its main hall, the Hall of the Pillars, where a host of delicately crafted helicoidal columns rise gracefully to the ceiling. *With the exception of the months July and August when it is closed on Saturdays, you may visit Tuesday to Saturday from 9:15 a.m. to 2 p.m. and from 4:30 p.m. to 8 p.m., and on Sunday from 9:15 a.m. to 2 p.m.*

Directly across the road from the La Lonja is the equally engaging, though different in both style and purpose, **Central Market** *(Mercado Central)* (24). If you have visited Spain before, or are at all familiar with the culture, you will already understand that within each Spanish community, no matter the size, you will find a local market. While, without doubt, these are all intriguing and enlightening from a social standpoint, most are housed in architecturally nondescript buildings, more intent on function than style. *La Boqueria,* on La Rambla in Barcelona is an exception, as is the *Mercado Central* here. Set within an irregularly shaped, eight-sided Modernistic style building constructed between 1910 to 1926, a surface of over 8,000 square meters earns it the distinction of being one of the largest markets in Europe. Actually, the best perspective of this is seen from the top of the *El Miguelete.* Of course, the best time to experience the market is during working hours, which are before lunch. But during the afternoon numerous little shops around the outside sell a variety of goods, including paella pans and pots, that make excellent souvenirs.

Continuing on, take a left onto the road that runs between the exhibition hall and the market, making another left at the fork and the same again into the much busier Calle de San Vicente Mártir. This will lead back to the Plaza de la Reina but, before reaching there, turn right into Abadia San Martín, which changes to R. Garcia Sanchez before meeting with Poeta Querol. A block or so to the right is the Palace of the Marquis of Dos Aguas, home to the ***National Ceramics Museum** *(Museo de Cerámica*

"Gonzalez Martí") (25). By all accounts this is a truly spectacular museum, but you will be lucky to see that for yourself. It has been undergoing restoration for years and no one can say, definitively, when it will re-open. Just across Poeta Querol, and at the side of a small plaza at Calle de la Nave, 1, is the **Patriach's Museum** *(Museo del Patriarca)* (26), ☎ 351-41-76. Founded by the Patriarch and Viceroy, Saint Juan de Ribera, in the 16th to 17th century, this boasts magnificent Renaissance Cloisters and numerous artistic works of great value by the likes of El Greco and the Flemish Old Masters. *This is open Tuesday to Sunday from 11 a.m. to 1:30 p.m. Entrance 100 ptas (EUR .60).*

From this point return to Poeta Querol and make a diagonal right onto Vilaragut. Follow on through the Plaza Rodrigo Botet and Calle Barcelonina back to the Plaza del Ayuntamiento, and the end of the tour.

Santiago de Compostela

S antiago de Compostela was, at one time, the western boundary of the known world. It claimed no other enduring distinction, however, until early in the 9th century when, in 813, a simple peasant named Pelayo was drawn by brilliant stars to a field where the tomb of the Apostle Saint James (*Santiago* in Spanish) was revealed to him. After verifying its authenticity, Alfonso II had a chapel erected on the spot in 829. Nearly sixty years later Alfonso III replaced this with a far grander church. Possession of that structure had fallen to the Moors by the close of the 10th century.

Whether or not Saint James ever visited Spain has never been substantiated, but this is one instance where it might be said that myth created its own reality. From the earliest days following Pelayo's discovery pilgrims flocked to Compostela, whose name derives from the Spanish for *Campo* (field), and *Estrella* (stars), and Santiago became a symbol in the Christians' struggles to overcome the Moors. Still more myths were created by the tales of Christian Knights who reported visions of St. James leading them in battle against the enemy. He even acquired a nickname; *Matamoros*, killer of Moors, and, naturally enough, he became the Patron Saint of Spain. Following the re-conquest, what had been a steady stream of pilgrims became an ever increasing flow. Although the exact number is not known, figures of up to 2,000,000 a year during the Middle Ages have been proferred. Pilgrims from all over Europe travelled the "Road to Santiago" *(Camino de Santiago)* across northern Spain to this remote corner of the country. With them came the development of churches and inns, and nowhere was this more evident than in Santiago itself. Construction of the massive new Cathedral was started in 1075; in 1189 Alexander III decreed it a Holy City (a status shared only by Rome and Jerusalem), and in the 15th century the exquisite Royal Hospital and Pilgrims' Hostal, now known as the *Hostal de los Reyes Católicos* was built.

The late 16th century added yet another strange twist to the story. In 1589, with Sir Francis Drake attacking nearby La Coruña, the bishop removed and hid the Saint's remains in preparation of a likely attack by the English. He did his job so thoroughly, though, that they were lost for nearly 300 years. It wasn't until 1879 that a Cathedral worker unearthed them, well perhaps not literally, again.

Santiago de Compostela was, in recognition of its many elegant and beautiful buildings, declared a World Heritage Site by UNESCO in 1985. Notwithstanding its relative isolation—a journey here will inevitably take visitors hundreds of miles out of their way—this unique and most charming of cities is not to be missed. Be forewarned, however, to pack your umbrella! This is the rainiest city in Spain.

GETTING THERE:

By Air, Santiago's International airport is at Labacolla, seven miles east of the city. Internal flights are available from many cities in Spain, although not necessarily on a daily basis. International flights arrive directly from some European capitals, and via Madrid when flying from North America.

Trains arrive directly from Madrid, a trip of at least 8 hours; across country on very slow services departing from either Barcelona or País Vasco, with stops at Burgos, León, and Ourense along the way; or from Oporto, Portugal, via a change in Vigo. There are also frequent local services from La Coruña.

Bus, because the distances are so long and the terrain difficult, this option is not recommended.

By car, Santiago de Compostela is 391 miles northwest of Madrid, at the end of the N-VI highway. La Coruña, located due north, is reached using the A-9 *autopista* toll road. The N-550 leads south to Vigo, then continues on to the border with Portugal.

PRACTICALITIES:

Surprisingly, there are few places of interest here that are open to the public. Of those, all (except two museums) are open daily. The important **Holy Year** *(Año Santo)* celebrations, the festival of St. James the Apostle, is held each year during which July 25 falls on a Sunday. At these times the city is even more crowded than normal. You'll notice in Santiago that, among other things, the streets are called *Rua's*, not *Calle's*. As in other autonomous regions, the local *Galician language* is being used more frequently. In many instances this is closer to Portuguese than Castillian Spanish.

The **Dialing Code** is 981. The tourist office **Oficina de Turismo, ☎** 58-40-81, Rúa de Vilar, 43, is open Monday to Friday 9 a.m. to 2 p.m. and 4 p.m. to 6 p.m.; Saturday 10 a.m. to 1 p.m. and 4:30 p.m. to 7 p.m.; and Sunday 10:30 a.m. to 1 p.m.

Santiago de Compostela has a **population** of approximately 90,000 and is in the province of La Coruña, one of four belonging to the autonomous region of **Galicia**.

ACCOMMODATION:

The **Parador Hotel Reyes Católicos** ***** GL, ☎ 58-22-00 or fax 56-30-94, Plaza del Obradoiro, 1, is unquestionably THE hotel of choice in Santiago. It is the oldest, and one of the grandest, hotels in Spain. The original structure was built in the 15th century by the Catholic Monarchs, for use as a

Royal Hospital and Inn for pilgrims. It underwent further extensions in the 17th and 18th centuries. Its location is magnificent also; in one of the most beautiful squares in Spain, and directly under the shadow of the towering façade of the Cathedral. The intricately carved archway over the front door has statues of the Twelve Apostles, as well as figures of Christ and the Catholic Monarchs, whose coats-of-arms adorn either side of the doorway. The inside is equally grand, and it has the traditional parador service to match. $$$

The Hotel **Compostela** ****, ☎ 58-57-00 or fax 56-32-69, Horreo, 1, is located just across the road from the Zona Monumental in the Plaza de Galicia. Behind its traditional-style façade are 99 modernly decorated rooms. $$

The **Hotel Peregrino** ****, ☎ 52-18-50 or fax 52-17-77, Avenida Rosalía de Castro, s/n, is about a 10-minute walk from the Zona Monumental, and the 150 rooms and suites, like the public rooms, are contemporary and elegant. $$

The **Hostal Hogar San Francisco** ***, ☎ 57-25-64 or fax 57-19-16, Campillo del Convento de San Francisco, 3, was founded in the early 13th century by St. Francis of Assisi. Today, however, only Gothic, Renaissance, and Neo-Classical influences are evident. Just 200 yards from the Cathedral, this has 70 simply, yet elegantly furnished habitations and wonderful public rooms, including a most unusual dining room. $$

The **Hotel Residencia Universal** **, ☎ 58-58-00 or fax 58-57- 90, Plaza de Galicia, 2, is a modest, centrally located hotel, with spacious, fully equipped rooms. $

The **Hostal Residencia Miño** **, ☎ 58-03-18, Montero Ríos, 31, is located just off the Plaza de Galicia. The rooms, while comfortable, do not offer guests the luxury of a private bathroom. $

FOOD AND DRINK:

Without doubt, seafood is the specialty here, and the most popular, served in a variety of ways, is Octopus *(Pulpo)*. It is so popular, in fact, that tiny and usually rather basic restaurants, *Pulperías*, dedicated to this creature are sprinkled throughout the city. One of the tastiest dishes is *Pulpo á la Gallega*, octopus grilled with paprika and usually served with boiled potatoes. The appetizer of choice is *Empanada Gallega*, a crusty flat pie filled with either fish, meat or vegetables, and a favorite dessert is *Tarta Compostelana*, made of almonds. In the colder weather a bowl of *Caldo Gallego*, a thick broth filled with all manner of tasty titbits, will surely warm you up. Even the bread here is delightfully unique; dark, heavily crusted and often filled with raisins.

Local *Ribeiro* wines are very popular, and when ordering ordinary table wine in a bar don't be surprised when it is served in a small bowl, instead of a glass.

Parador Hotel Reyes Católicos (Plaza del Obradoiro, 1), boasts the most grand, beautiful and elegant restaurant in the city. What's more, the cuisine is marvelously prepared, and complemented by a selection of fine wines. ☎ 58-22-00 or fax 56-30-94. $$$

Restaurante A Barrola (Rúa Franco, 29), will certainly tempt you with the most wonderful display of fish and shellfish beckoning from the window. The specialty here is a delicious shellfish combination, to be shared by two diners. ☎ 57-79-99. $$

Mesón-Restaurante Casa Elisa (Rúa Franco 36-38), is just down the street from the A Barrola and, having the same owners, shares the same high standards. The range here is wide, but the seafood is very enticing; a house specialty is Octopus in garlic with tiny mussels. ☎ 58-31-12. $$

Restaurante Alameda (Puerta Fajera, 15), is just on the edge of the Zona Monumental and serves local Gallego dishes. ☎ 58-47-96. $$

Restaurante Pulpería O Catro (Rúa de San Pedro, 4), close to the Puerta del Carmen, is one of those very basic restaurants where you only go for the octopus. ☎ 58- 63-92. $

SUGGESTED TOUR:

Numbers in parentheses correspond to numbers on the map.

Begin by entering the **Monumental Zone** *(Zona Monumental)* by way of the **Porte de Mamoa** (1), just off the Plaza de Galicia. Bear right along Calle Las Huérfanes, the Orphans Street, and immediately catch the unusual ambiance of this special town. Granite grey buildings crowd the narrow streets, where many of the shop windows display mouthwatering arrays of local produce. Another right, at Cardenal Payá, leads to the Plaza del Instituto which houses the University, one of the oldest in Spain, and the **Mazarelos Arch** *(Arcos de Mazarelos)* (2) to the right. Although not particularly inspiring visibly, this is the only surviving gate of the old walls.

Pass through it and take the steps down to the busy Calle Calvo Sotelo, and follow it left around the back of the University. Then take the ramp, opposite the large Covento La Enseñana, up to the Plazuela de San Fíz. Before carrying on around the small church of the same name to the **Market** *(Mercado)* (3), stop for a moment to look back. Nestled in the nearby valley is the huge Convento de Belvis, and the verdant hills surrounding it are a reminder of how close Santiago is to the countryside. Markets in Spain are, by their nature, places of color and entertainment, and the one in the Plaza de Abastos is certainly no exception. Four blocks of "formal" interior stalls are ringed by numerous individual traders around the outside. Anything imaginable in the way of fresh fruit, vegetables, meat and fish is available. And there's lots more besides. My favorite vendors, though, are the weatherbeaten farmers and their wives who bring their live chickens, rabbits, and ducks to be sold in the shadow of the walls of the Convento de San Agustín.

Take the steps back down to the main road, which is now called the Calle Virgen de la Cerca. A hundred yards or so to the left, on the opposite side of the street, is a tiny park with a strange column, the **Cruceiro de Bonoval** (4), an attraction for numerous pilgrims. Behind it, up a hill and

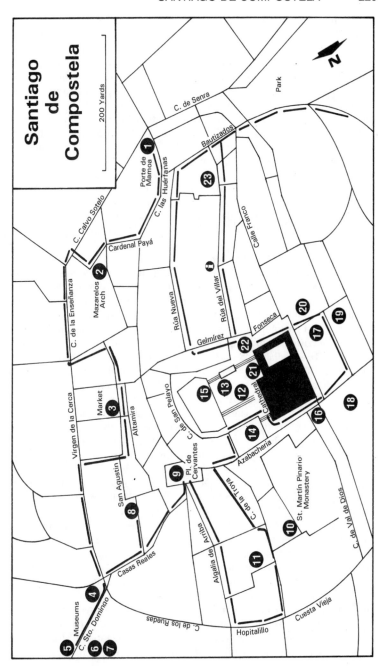

Santiago de Compostela

200 Yards

Park

C. de Senra

Bautizados

Porte de Mamoa

C. Calvo Sotelo

Cardenal Payá

C. las Huérfanas

Calle Franco

Mazarelos Arch

C. de la Enseñanza

Rúa Nueva

Rúa del Villar

Fonseca

Gelmírez

Virgen de la Cerca

Market

Altamira

C. de San Pelayo

Cathedral

Azabacheria

San Agustín

Pl. de Cervantes

C. de la Troya

St. Martín Pinario Monastery

C. de Val de Dios

Casas Reales

Algalia de Arriba

Cuesta Vieja

Museums

C. Sto. Domingo

C. de los Ruedas

Hopitalillo

then some steps, is the architecturally mixed façade of the **Convento de Santo Domingo de Bonaval** (5). Originally founded by St. Domingo de Guzmán in the early part of the 13th century, the present structure dates from the 17th and 18th centuries and was donated by the city to serve as home of the **Poblo Galego Museum** *(Museo do Poblo Galego)* (6), ☎ 58-36-20. Exhibits here are dedicated to local topics such as the sea, crafts, countryside, and the evolution of popular architecture over the centuries. These may prove of only peripheral interest to the majority of visitors, but don't let that put you off going. The very rare triple helicoidal (spiral) staircases, designed to connect all levels of the convent without any supports, are alone worth the trip. These are especially fascinating when viewed from above. *It's open Monday to Saturday from 10 a.m. to 1 p.m. and 4 p.m. to 7 p.m. Entrance free.* The adjoining church, constructed between the 14th and 16th centuries, is now home to the Pantheon of Illustrious Galicians. To the other side, and rather more incongruously, is the **Galician Center of Modern Art** *(Centro Galego de Arte Contemporánea)* (7), ☎ 54-66-29, *which is open Tuesday to Saturday from 11 a.m. to 8 p.m. and Sunday from 11 a.m. to 2 p.m., entrance free.*

Retrace your steps back down to the main road, entering back into the *Zona Monumental* through the medieval gateway of the Puerta del Camino. Follow Casas Reales where your attention may be drawn, at Rúa Traviesa the first left turning, to the façade of the **Iglesia de Santa María del Camino** (8). Of particular interest is the crown over the main window. Just around the corner from here, at Rúa Travesa, 5, is a really interesting little craft shop. The **Medialúa**, ☎ and fax 58-23-89, is named after the half-moon shaped tool to cut leather and, indeed, leather cut into objects such as bags, wallets, shoes, boots etc., etc. are on display. Really, most visitors will be hard put to leave without a sample of their own. And at the end of Casas Reales, in the Plazuela Animas, there are more attractions. The **Chapel** *(Capilla)*, to the right is, if open, well worth investigating and, opposite, are two elegant mansions, the 16th-century **Casa de Bazan**, and the 18th-century Pazo de Fondevilla. At the top of the hill glance into the **Plaza de Cervantes** (9). This is surrounded by a host of classically Compostelan-style structures, and a column supporting a bust of its namesake, the author of "Don Quixote." Unusually, it can also be reached by no less than eight different pathways.

Next turn right into Arriba, and continue along to its junction with a much busier street, Calle Hospitalillo, and a small, but nevertheless attractive little park in the Plaza de San Roque. This is a good place to sit, soothed by the splashing fountain, and relax for a moment. Continuing left down Hospitalillo you'll soon come to a set of steep steps which descend down to the the Convento de San Francisco, home of the previously mentioned Hostal Hogar San Francisco. However, avoid the temptation to follow them down and be satisfied, instead, to pause for a while and admire the contrasting, yet complementing, beauties of the ancient buildings and lush green hills unfurling below you. Make a left here, noticing that the houses in the immediate area are smaller and white-washed, and shortly afterwards the next attraction, the **St. Martín Pinario Monastery** *(Monasterio de San Martín Pinario)* (10), appears on the right. This massive structure of over 20,000 square meters was completed in the mid-17th century. Keep in mind that the entrance you see, embellished with elegantly carved figures and reached by way of a double staircase leading down to the doorway, while impressive is not the main façade. This will be passed later, and is far grander. Inside there is a particularly elaborate altarpiece.

Just to your left is the street of San Miguel, and a short diversion up to number 4 will find the unique **Pilgrim's Museum** *(Museo das Peregrinacións)* (11), ☎ 58-15-58, which, as the name states, on three floors and in eight rooms, tells the story of the cult of St. James and the associated pilgrimage. In fact, this was founded in 1951, but not opened to the public until February 1996. And the house itself is of interest too, retaining some 14th-century elements. *Open Tuesday to Friday 10 a.m. to 8 p.m., Saturday 10:30 a.m. to 1:30 p.m. and 5 p.m. to 8 p.m., and Sunday and holidays 10:30 a.m. to 1:30 p.m.   Entrance 400 ptas (EUR 2.40).* Back track down San Miguel then continue on left and take the narrow passageway that is Calle de la Troya. At the end make a right and before taking the first left there is a store that is sure to catch your eye, and one you will not leave empty handed. The windows of Requeira, ☎ 58-36-27 and fax 58-72-12, Azabachería, 9, glitter indeed, not only with a wide array of jewelry, other forms of adornment and crystal, but abound with all manner of silver clocks, watches and too many other goods to mention. What does require mentioning, though, is the absolutely fabulous array of Lladro figurines; surely the most extensive in town. Now, follow along the Via Sacra, brings you out at the top of the steps that lead down into the **Plaza de la Quintana** (12). Time, now, to take another break; so have a seat on these steps and study the architecturally contrasting scene before you. The rear of the Cathedral, with its renowned if rather unprepossessing **Holy Door** embedded in it, is to the right. Straight ahead is the 18th-century **Casa de Conga** (13), whose aesthetic lines are somewhat marred by the shops and cafés located on its lower level. Behind you is the much smaller, vine covered, **Grapevine House** *(Casa de la Parra)* (14), and covering the left side is the austerely symmetrical rectangular wall of the **San Payo Monastery** *(Monasterio de San Payo)* (15), founded by Alfonso II. The structure which now occupies this site, with two levels of metal grilled windows running the length of its Quintana façade, dates from the 17th and 18th centuries. Inside is a **Sacred Art Museum** *(Museo de Arte Sacro)*, ☎ *57-11-67, open July to September daily 10:30 a.m. to 1 p.m. and 4 p.m. to 7 p.m. Entrance 150 ptas (EUR .90).* The most important exhibit here is a small marble altar which, tradition says, was consecrated by the disciples of the Apostle James.

Exit the plaza via the steps on the left-hand side of the Casa de la Parra. This opens into the Plaza de la Immaculada, where the main face of the Monasterio de San Martín Pinario looks across to one side of the Cathedral. A downward slope leads you under the archway that supports the **Gelmírez Palace** *(Pazo de Xelmírez)* (16), ☎ 57-23-00, to the unsurpassably exquisite beauty of the **Plaza del Obradoiro** (17). There are many plazas in Spain, and most have their own particular architectural merits. None, though, has a combination as grand as this one. The Gelmírez Palace, although now wearing an 18th-century façade which adjoins the Cathedral, was commissioned by Bishop Gelmírez in 1120. Inside, its lack of ornateness serves to enhance its elegance. The most important room is the banqueting hall, the Synodal Hall, supported by lovely carved rib-vaults and a singular arch. *Visit Tuesday to Sunday 10 a.m. to 1:30 p.m. and 4:30 p.m. to 7:30 p.m., entrance 200 ptas (EUR 1.20).* Outside, and to the right, is the **Hotel Reyes Católicos** (18), which has been described under Accommodation.

On the long side of the plaza, across from the Cathedral, is the neo-classical **Ranjoy Palace** *(Pazo de Ranjoy)* (19). More modern than the other buildings here, built in the mid-18th century, its colonnaded lower level supports three more floors. The four columns at each corner support curved arches, while five central columns brace an elaborately carved tri-angular central arch. Once the Confessor's Seminary, it now has a dual role, Town hall and headquarters of the Council of Galicia. Opposite the Hotel Reyes Católicos is the more modest, but yet interesting, **St Jerónimo College** *(Colegio de San Jerónimo)* (20). Built in the 16th century as a language school for priests, so they could understand the confessions of pilgrims, it features a rather unusual portal which was, reportedly, moved here from a hostal.

Notwithstanding the merits of these preceding three structures—and there are many, they are overshadowed physically by the omnipotent spiritual presence of the towering edifice that is the focal point of any visit to Santiago de Compostela. As previously explained, construction of this ***Cathedral** *(Catedral)* (21) began in 1075. While it was not completed until 1128, some of the altars were consecrated earlier in the century by Bishop Gelmírez. Numerous additions and changes have taken place over the centuries, and it was as recently as the 18th century that the beautifully symmetrical double staircase and towers of the *Obradoiro* façade were completed. This is a brilliant sight, and especially dramatic in the fresh sunlight that follows the frequent rain showers, or when illuminated at night. You will leave Santiago de Compostela with this sight everlastingly impressed on your memory.

The interior is no less dramatic. Just inside the entrance, at the top of the stairs, is the unparalleled ***Porch of Glory** *(Pórtico de la Gloria)*, considered to be the finest example of Romanesque sculpture in the world. Pause here and observe a curious custom. Pilgrims place their right palm, and this has happened so often there is now an ingrained palm print, on a marble column and the forehead is brought down three times to touch another column. It would be impossible, and certainly presumptious, to try and detail this wondrous place in just these few lines. To fully appreciate its intricacies visitors should purchase a more detailed guide. One thing that should not be missed, though, is the incense burner, *bota-fumeiro*, so large that it takes several men to swing it, pendulum fashion, during ceremonial occasions. And, of course, the Saint's remains rest in the crypt. The **Cathedral Museum** *(Museo Catedralicio)*, ☎ 58-11-55, is as good an example of its kind as can be found. Numerous rooms, on several floors, display every possible kind of religious artwork imaginable, a prestigious collection of Flemish tapestries and, in the basement, recently excavated Roman remains. *It is open June to September Monday to Saturday 10 a.m. to 1:30 p.m. and 4 p.m. to 7:30 p.m.; and the rest of the year from 11 a.m. to 1 p.m. and 4 p.m. to 6 p.m.; all year on Sunday and holidays it opens 10 a.m. to 1:30 p.m. and 4 a.m. to 7 p.m. Entrance 400 ptas (EUR 2.40).*

Leaving the Cathedral by way of the main staircase, turn left and follow the building around to the **Silversmith's Square** *(Plaza de Platerías)* (22). From here, beyond the Fountain of the Horses, there are views of the oldest façade of the Cathedral and the immense clock tower. All around, as the name implies, silversmith's stores wait anxiously for you to purchase a souvenir. From here take either the Rúa del Villar, passing the tourist office, or the the next street, Rúa Nueva, to the constantly busy, and of course pleasing, Plaza del Toral. Just down from here is the last stop in the Monumental Zone. The **Foundation Museum Granell** *(Fundación Museo Granell)* (23), ☎ 57-63- 94, on the Praza do Toural, is housed in the charming 18th-century Pazo de Bendaña. Eugenio Granell, who was born in nearby La Coruña in 1912, but spent his childhood and youth in Santiago, began to paint surrealistically in 1941 when he lived in the Dominican Republic after his exile at the end of the Spanish Civil War. This museum not only holds many of his works, but those of other surrealist artists. *Open Monday to Saturday 11 a.m. to 9 p.m. and Sunday 11 a.m. to 2 p.m., note that, unusually, it closes on Tuesday. Entrance 300 ptas (EUR 1.80), free on Sunday.* On either street you will see excellent examples of the arcades so necessary in this city of almost certain rainfall. Leaving the *Zona Monumental* for the last time, head down Bautizados and across the main road towards the park that is the Robleda de Santa Susana. A right there, into the tree-lined Paseo de la Alameda, will soon bring you to a clearing from where, across the narrow valley, the Cathedral can be seen in all its saintly glory.

La Coruña

La Coruña, in the far northwestern corner of Spain, shares a natural harbor with its sister town across the bay, the much less attractive Ferrol. The unique natural advantages of this area were not lost on the Romans who, during their rule here, utilized the resources to great advantage. In fact, the Torre de Hércules lighthouse, the city's signature landmark, and today a prominent component on its coat-of-arms, dates from that period. Much later La Coruña belonged, initially, to the estate of the Bishop of Santiago, and it wasn't until the early 13th century that Alfonso IX, finally, granted it a law code of its own.

The 16th century saw a rapid expansion of the sea trade and a concurrent growth in the city's fortunes. In the same century, however, the ill-fated Spanish Armada sailed from the city and this brought, in its wake, substantial retaliations from the English navy. During the 18th and 19th centuries La Coruña enjoyed a period of prosperity and gracious splendor. Many of the lovely mansions and churches seen here today were constructed during that era. It was near La Coruña, during the Wars of Independence, that the English General, John Moore, suffered a mortal wound in the decisive Battle of Elvina. He is buried in the Jardín de San Carlos where a statue has been erected in his honor.

These days, though, La Coruña, the second-largest port in Spain, is better known as an administrative, trade, and industrial center than as a tourist spot. But don't let that put you off. A daytrip to this delightful city will provide an enticing contrast to the more serious splendors of Santiago de Compostela.

GETTING THERE:

Trains run frequently between Santiago and La Coruña, with a journey time of about an hour and a half.

Buses are, obviously, available, but the train service is so fast and frequent that it is the better option.

By car, La Coruña is just short of 40 miles from Santiago when travelling the N-550, and a few miles longer by way of the A-9 *autopista* tollroad.

PRACTICALITIES:

The places of interest that may be visited are all, with the exception of the Military Museum, closed on Monday. The **Dialing Code** is 981. The tourist office, **Oficina de Información**, ☎ 22-18-22, Dársena de la Marina, s/n, is open Monday to Friday 9 a.m. to 2 p.m. and 4:30 p.m. to 6:30 p.m., and on Saturday between 10:30 a.m. and 1 p.m. La Coruña has a **population** of 250,000 and is the capital of the province of the same name, one of four belonging to the autonomous region of **Galicia**.

ACCOMMODATION:

The **Hotel Finisterre** ****, ☎ 20-54-00 or fax 20-84-62, is located at Paseo de Parrote, 2. The exterior may be somewhat austere, but the interior is a delightful surprise. It has been totally renovated in an ultra modern style. Both the hotel and its extensive grounds, overlook both the harbor and city. The sports facilities are unparalleled, including no fewer than four pools. $$

The **Hotel Atlántico** ****, ☎ 22-65-00 or fax 20-10-71, Jardines de Méndez Núñez, 2, is a large hotel that was totally renovated in 1991. It offers 200 well appointed rooms and is set in lovely gardens with a marvellous location in the city center. Other facilities include a cafeteria, restaurant, disco and saunas. $$

The **Hotel Residencia Riazor** ***, ☎ 25-34-00 or fax 25-34-04, Avenida Barrie de la Maza, 29, has a bayside location on the opposite side of the narrow isthmus from the port, overlooking the beaches of Riazor and Orzán. Totally restored in 1995, it has 175 spacious, modern rooms. It also has private parking. $$

Note: As relatively few will choose to stay here overnight, I have deliberately kept to few selections. Less expensive options are available in the maze of narrow streets between the harbor and the bay.

FOOD AND DRINK:

Restaurante Coral (Estrella, 2-4), is in the side street parallel with the Jardins de Méndez Núñez, the main street alongside the harbor. Seafood, naturally, is the cuisine of choice in La Coruña, and this award-winning, classically formal, restaurant provides an elegant setting in which to taste it at its best. ☎   22-27-17. $$$

Restaurante Mesón Coral (Callejón de la Estacada, 9, just off the Avenida de La Marina), serves dishes to a standard set by its sister restaurant, the Coral (listed above). The ambiance is quite different, however. Its wooden beamed ceiling and exposed brick walls create a more informal, and relaxed, atmosphere. ☎ 20-05-69. $$

Hotel Finisterre (Paseo de Parrote, 2), has a lovely modern restaurant which specializes in local cuisine. The large picture windows allow stunning views of the harbor and the town. ☎ 20-54-00 or fax 20-84-62. $$

Restaurante Galeria (Avenida de La Marina, 3-4-5), is a strikingly modern restaurant which, as the name implies, is below the galerias. It specializes in Gallegan cuisine, with an emphasis on seafood. ☎ 22-92-35. $$

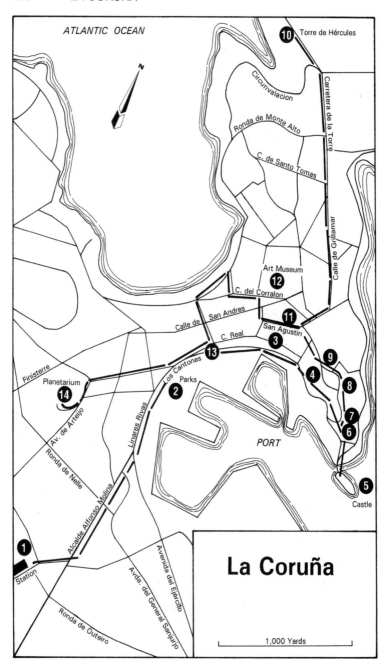

La Coruña

1,000 Yards

SUGGESTED TOUR:
Numbers in parentheses correspond to numbers on the map.

Outside of the **Railway Station** *(Estación de San Cristóbal)* (1), actually a terminal, there is a small, rather bland park. To its right you'll find the Ronda de Estaciónes, which leads diagonally down to the Plaza de Madrid, and its junction with the much busier Alcalde Alfonso Molina. A left here, onto the painfully drab Viaducto, will take you to the outskirts of the harbor. Thankfully, the journey is short and downhill, with the only thing of interest being the church of *San Pedro de Mezonzo,* to the left.

Press on, and soon a touch of greenery will enliven the horizon. This will be the beginning of a series of long, rectangular parks that run parallel to the harbor. The first two you will come to, the **Rosaleda** and **Jardíns de Méndes Núñez** (2), are pleasant indeed; enhanced by a seductive combination of fountains, statues, formal gardens, and even an English-style bandstand. Go past a row of administrative buildings to the point where the parks begin again and, soon, in the middle of one of them you'll find a tourist office. You may want to stop in, before continuing on, to avail yourself of some helpful literature. Behind the tourist office, on the city side, is a fine example of a style of architecture that, while not indigenous to La Coruña, draws more attention here than elsewhere. These apartment buildings facing the harbor have attractive **galerias** *(glassed in terraces)* (3), which not only protect them from the elements, but give off fascinating and ever-changing reflections from the sun's rays.

A short distance farther along on the left, a narrow street leads into the Plaza de María Pita, named after one of the city's most esteemed heroines. This housewife, as local folklore recounts the story, was the first citizen to spot Sir Francis Drake's advance on La Coruña in 1589, and raised an early alarm. This is the equivalent of other towns' Plaza Mayor and is dominated by the ornate and towered edifice of the Town Hall, which occupies the whole of the far side. Retrace your steps back into the main street and turn, almost immediately, onto the Calle Santiago, passing by numerous antique and art shops along the way before you reach the **Iglesia de Santiago** (4), ☎ 20-56- 96. Dating from the 12th century, this is an attractive Romanesque church. It reflects an amalgamation of architectural styles, primarily from the succeeding two centuries, but incorporating changes made during renovations in more recent years as well. *Open daily 10:15 a.m. to 1 p.m. and 6:30 p.m. to 8:30 p.m., entrance free.* Take the right fork here and follow around the church, passing the gardens along the way, to the square behind it. In fact, this is a double square, and it offers what is, most probably, the best perspective of the church.

Make your way to the right-hand corner and follow the tiny street you'll find there to its end, where it intersects with the much larger, and busier, Paseo del Parrote. The formidable looking structure directly ahead is a building that merits further investigation, the Hotel Finisterre. The interior is, in contrast, ultra modern and as you follow the street around to the left it is impossible not to be amazed at its huge grounds that abut the harbor. Tennis courts and other sports facilities abound and almost at the quayside there is a huge pool, one of four at this hotel. As you continue along the Paseo del Parrote, you'll enjoy another attribute of this area— the glorious views that unfold as the city follows the curve of the tight harbor, against the magnificent backdrop of rolling hills.

A little farther around, the city's authorities have been prescient enough to install a bench, flanked by ancient cannons, with a telescope on hand. This is a delightful place to take a rest and, while you are admiring the scenery, look left towards the **San Antón Castle** *(Castillo de San Antón)* (5), ☎ 20-59-94, that protects the harbor's entrance. It dates from the 16th century, underwent a restoration in the 18th century, and now houses the **Archaeological Museum** *(Museo Arqueológico)*, whose exhibits define Gallegan culture and include interesting displays of gold and silver work. *Open Tuesday to Saturday 10 a.m. to 9 p.m. (in the winter it closes at 7 p.m.), and Sunday and holidays 10 a.m. to 2:30 p.m. Entrance 300 ptas (EUR 1.80).*

To your back are interesting stone walls, topped by full-grown mature trees. Follow these around to the **Military Hospital** *(Hospital Militar)*, and take the steps opposite up to the **Jardín de San Carlos** (6) where you will find the **Casa de Cultura**, a house that dates from 1843 and holds the Galician archives. Take a few moments to appreciate these well-kept formal gardens, which are enhanced by a fountain and a statue of the British General, Sir John Moore, who is buried on the grounds. Retrace your way back down the steps and turn to the left where you'll come face to face with a wonderfully quaint old structure that resides in the extensive **Jardíns de la Maestranza**. This now functions as a **Regional Military Museum** *(Museo Militar Regional)* (7), ☎ 20-67-91, displaying over 1,400 military-related objects. The gardens deserve a visit on their own merit. *Open daily 10 a.m. to 2 p.m. and 4 p.m. to 7 p.m., and on holidays 10 a.m. to 2 p.m., entrance free.* The ruins of the ancient convent are a striking contrast to the wide-ranging views of the surrounding estuaries, bays, and verdant hills. Immediately below is the **Oceanographic Institute** *(Instituto Oceanográfico)*.

After leaving the museum, follow the walls of the Jardín de San Carlos to the right, and then continue under the huge brick wall on the right into the Plaza de Santa Domingo. The brick wall, you will soon see, once you read the signs posted on the gate at its end, belongs to a military barracks. The main attraction, though, is the 18th-century *Iglesia y Convento de Santo Domingo*, ☎ 20-58-50, *open daily 11 a.m. to 1 p.m. and 6:15 p.m. to 8:30 p.m., entrance free.*

Just past here is another, much smaller and rather plain, plaza. It is named, as many plazas are in Spain, in honor of its resident convent, the 15th-century **Convento de Santa Barbara** (8), ☎ 20-63-30, and also has an attractive stone cross that is powerful in its simplicity. This older part of La Coruña is known as the *Ciudad Vieja*. As a general rule, the streets here are narrow and lined with ancient houses. Follow one such street, the

Calle de Santa María, up to the **Colegiata de Santa María del Campo** (9), ☎ 20-31-86, which is perched proudly upon the highest point of the *Ciudad Vieja*. *It opens in the summer 9:30 a.m. to 1:30 p.m. and 5:30 p.m. to 8 p.m., and closes 1 hour earlier in the winter. Entrance free.* This graceful church was constructed from the 12th to the 15th centuries in an intriguing combination of Romanesque and Ojival styles. Next door, at Puerta de Aires, 23, is the small **Sacred Heart Museum** *(Museo de Arte Sacro)* (9), ☎ 20-31-86. *It is open Tuesday to Friday from 10 a.m. to 1 p.m. and 5 p.m. to 7 p.m., and on Saturday from 10 a.m. to 1 p.m. Entrance free.* The main exhibit is silverware from the 16th through 19th centuries.

Exit the *Ciudad Vieja* by way of Puerta de Aires and, crossing over at the main road, stop for a moment and admire the unusual perspective, down the steep steps of Calle Gregorio, of the side of the Town Hall. Turning your gaze back to the main road, you can not help but be struck by the extensive and formidable complex of the **Infantry Headquarters** *(Cuartel de Infantería)* across the road. Cross over to the walls of the complex and turn left, following these around until you come to the corner. Here, turn right into the Plaza de Millán Astray where you'll find the main facade of the Infantry Headquarters in all its enormity.

It is, finally, time to head for the city's most famous landmark, indeed its symbol. This is, however, some distance away and going on foot is definitely not recommended. Although bus number 3 leaves from the Calle de Orillamar, at the other corner of the Military HQ, there is a half-hour between scheduled runs. Therefore, taking a taxi both there and back, is the better option. The ***Torre de Hércules** (10), ☎ 22-37-30, has stood as a lighthouse on this promontory between the Atlantic Ocean and the estuary from early Roman times. In fact, this is the oldest working Roman lighthouse in existence today. The highly unusual and decorative exterior, though, dates from a restoration completed at the end of the 18th century. *It is open April, May, June and September daily 10 a.m. to 7 p.m.; July and August daily 10 a.m. to 9 p.m. and on Friday and Saturday until midnight; and October to March 10 a.m. to 6 p.m. Entrance 250 ptas (EUR 1.50).*

Once back at the Plaza de Millán Astray descend the steps by the side of the Town Hall and turn away towards the **Iglesia de San Jorge** (11), ☎ 20-59-45, an 18th-century church guarded by four statues. *It is open in daily 8 a.m. to 1 p.m. and 5:30 p.m. to 9 p.m., entrance free.* Round the church to the left and, next, you'll be greeted by the chatter and bustle typical of a Spanish food market, in this city the **Mercado de San Agustín**. Cross straight through the market and past another 18th-century church, the *Iglesia de San Nicolas*, before turning right into a street of the same name. The Calle de San Nicolas is a busy shopping street that ends in a curious square. The building directly in front of you, until a year or so ago, housed the ***Fine Arts Museum** *(Museo de Bellas Artes)* (12), ☎ 22-37-23. This, however, has found a new home, just 50 yards away where it proudly exhibits a collection of Spanish and European paintings and sculpture. *Open Tuesday to Friday 10 a.m. to 8 p.m., Saturday 10 a.m. to 2 p.m. and 6:30 p.m. to 8 p.m.,* *and Sunday 10 a.m. to 2 p.m. Entrance 400 ptas (EUR 2.40).*

It is time now for a change of scenery. Head across to the other side of the narrow isthmus to admire the sweeping beaches of Orzán and Riazor. Take Corralon to the, suitably named, Calle del Sol which drops you off on the promenade. You may be tempted to take a dip here, so take your swimsuit in case the temptations get the better of you. Or you may be content to just admire the views, or possibly sunbathe a little. In any event one sight that will certainly attract your attention, as you begin your walk around the bay, is the futuristic soccer stadium, the **Estadio de Riazor**, home of *Deportivo La Coruña*. Continue on and, upon arriving at the first traffic circle, cross back to the city side making a left on Rúa Alta, which soon changes its name to Nueva. In this, the narrowest part of the isthmus, the tiny side streets constitute the city's main shopping area. At its end, and once again across from the harbor, you will be greeted by a strange clock tower, the **El Obelisco** (13). This is reminiscent of Nelson's Column in Trafalgar Square, minus the surrounding lions and, of course, Nelson. At its summit, instead, is a decorative ball with four clock faces, topped by an intricate weather vane.

Across from here you'll recognize the pretty parks, also the site of the Hotel Atlántico and casino, that you passed on the first part of the tour. Follow these back in the direction of the railway station and, when the end of the greenery is in sight, cross the road and take Compostela, which runs diagonally away from the parks. Almost immediately, on the left, is the *Casa Enrique*, a small bar with much character where you may enjoy some refreshment before you begin the uphill climb along this street. It changes names more than once and passes through a modern shopping area before it terminates in the Glorieta de América. Immediately ahead is a modern, colonnaded, structure, the *Palacio de Congresos y Auditorio*. Behind that is the extensive *Parque de Santa Margarita*. You'll find in here the **Planetario y Casa de las Ciencias** (14), ☎ 27-18-28, with it's permanent scientific and technological exhibitions, as well as planetarium shows. *Open daily 11 a.m. to 9 p.m. and closing at 7 p.m. in winter; entrance museum 300 ptas (EUR 1.80) and planetarium 200 ptas (EUR 1.20).*

Now you have two options. Either end the tour by taking the Avenida de Arteijo on up the hill, then turning left and following Ronda de Outeiro back to the station. Or walk back down the hill to spend some more time in La Coruña, before returning to Santiago.

Salamanca

When Salamanca was conquered in the 3rd century BC by Hannibal it became his westernmost possession. Later, and known as *Helmántica*, its strategic position at the mid-point of the Route of Silver *(Ruta de la Plata)*, which linked the northern mines and ports to the south of the peninsula, made it an important city in the Roman Empire. In 1102, after subsequent periods of rule by the Visigoths and Moors, Salamanca was re-conquered by the forces of Alfonso VI. Just over a century later, in 1218, the first university in Spain, and one that was to gain an international reputation, was founded by Alfonso IX. It was the period between the 15th and early 18th centuries, though, that was the city's golden age. Then Salamanca was the main cultural center of the Spanish Empire, and of the population of approximately 20,000 over one-third were students at the university.

During the early 19th century the city's location between France and Portugal was once again strategic, but this time to its detriment. It suffered badly during the War of Independence, and it was entered by Wellington in the summer of 1812 just prior to the Battle of Salamanca, that was actually fought just south of the city. The cultural importance of Salamanca has been recognized by UNESCO, which has declared it to be Patrimony of Humanity.

GETTING THERE:

Trains from Madrid are limited in number and fairly slow, the journey, via Ávila, taking about three and a quarter hours. Salamanca is also on the main line connecting France and Portugal and may be reached directly, by taking the one train that runs in each direction daily, from Lisbon/Oporto or Valladolid, Burgos and San Sebastián.

Buses run directly from most nearby cities and Madrid, although they aren't recommended from the latter as the journey time is far too long to allow a daytrip.

By car, Salamanca is 145 miles northwest of Madrid and stands at the crossroads of the north-to-south N630 highway that connects Oviedo to Seville; the east-to-west N620 highway connecting Burgos to Guarda, Portugal, and the northern beginning of the N501 to Ávila.

PRACTICALITIES:

In reality Salamanca is a difficult city to fully explore in just one day, although this can be managed from either Ávila or Valladolid. It is a city, though, that should not be missed and most visitors will wish to consider making a stop of at least one night here. Of the many places to visit most, unusually for Spain, are open on Mondays. Only the museums of Fine Arts, History of the City, Bullfighting, and the Casa Lis, home of the Modern Art and Art Deco museum, are closed on that day.

Easter Week *(Semana Santa)* brings important festivities, and the city's annual Fería is held in the middle/end of September.

Salamanca's **Dialing code** is 923. The **Tourist Office of the Regional Government of Castilla Y León,** ☎ 26-85-71 or fax 26-24-92, can be found in the Casa de las Conchas at C/. Rua Mayor, s/n. And, between July 1 and September 30, there is a **Tourist Office** in the railway station foyer. Salamanca has a **population** of around 111,000 and is the capital of the province of the same name, one of nine belonging to the autonomous region of **Castilla Y León.**

ACCOMMODATION:

The **Parador de Salamanca** ****, ☎ 926-87-00 and fax 21-54-38, Calle Teso de la Feria, 2, located just across the River Tormes at the end of the Puente Romano, has all the expected attributes of this government-run chain. It also has the most spectacular views back to the city, especially when it is floodlit at night. $$

The **Hotel Residencia Rector** ****, ☎ 21-84-82 and fax 21-40-08, Paseo del Rector Esparabé, 10, is a beautiful old house once owned by one of the city's greatest aristocratic families. It has now been tastefully converted into a graceful and comfortable small hotel. $$

The **Gran Hotel** ****, ☎ & fax 21-35-00, occupies a prominent building just a couple of hundred feet or so from the Plaza Mayor, and has an ambiance of old-fashioned grandeur. $

The **Hostal Residencia Orly** **, ☎ 21-61-25, is just twenty meters from the Plaza Mayor and can be found on the second floor. Clean, comfortable, and with a TV lounge. $

The **Hostal Residencia Las Infantes** **, ☎ 25-28-44, is located directly across from the railway station and, although rather modest, offers clean and comfortable rooms with either a bath or shower. $

FOOD AND DRINK:

Pork is the specialty of this region, and in the city's restaurants you'll be able to sample every type of pork dish imaginable. Some specialties you might like to try are *Chanfaina*—a rice dish made with the offal of poultry, lamb and sausage; *Hornazo*—a dry pie filled with pork and egg; *Lomo*—cured pork sausage, or *Jamón*—cured leg of pork. Of things sweet there are *Bollo Maimón*—which is a sponge cake; *Turrón*—which originates from La Alberca and is hard nougat made from almonds and honey, or *Amendras Garrapiñadas*—sugared almonds.

Parador de Salamanca (Calle Teso de la Feria, 2), is located just across the River Tormes at the end of the Puente Romano, and the traditional-styled restaurant offers the best of local cuisine and fine wines. ☎ 926-87-00 and fax 21-54-38. $$$

Rio de la Plata (Plaza del Peso, 1), is close to the Plaza Mayor and, in a small but interesting dining room, offers a good mix of typical roasts and fish dishes. ☎ 21-90-05. $$

O'Neill's—The Irish Pub (Calle Zamora, 14), is a most unusual place to find, just a hundred yards from the Plaza Mayor, in a town like Salamanca. Traditional style, sawdust on the floor and barrels etc., is mixed with traditional Irish food and, of course, Guinness. ☎ 26-35-19 or fax 21-03-97. $

Mesón de Cervantes (Plaza Mayor, 15), is a great place for snacks and sandwiches, and is noted for its Sangría. ☎ 21-72-13. $

SUGGESTED TOUR:
Numbers in parentheses correspond to numbers on the map.

This starts and ends at the fantastic *****Plaza Mayor** (1), best reached from the train station by taking bus number 1, marked Estación/Beunos Aires. Before setting out, though, take a seat at one of the many outdoor tables, and you'll be captivated by the sight before you. Construction began on this huge and very graceful plaza in 1729 during the reign of Felipe V, but it wasn't completed until 26 years later. The arched and porticoed ground floor level, illuminated by delightful lanterns, supports three additional stories. The most prominent of the buildings are the Town Hall and Royal Pavilion. Today, and (thankfully) absolutely traffic free, it is the social hub of Salamanca and is always bustling with people.

Take the steps down, on the side where the tourist office is located, which lead to a lower, and far less grand, porticoed walkway. Incidentally, this is where the bus to and from the railway station arrives and departs. The city **Market** *(Mercado)* faces you from across the road, but simply turn right and continue to the end passing a motley collection of bars and shops. Cross the street, past the façade of the imposing Gran Hotel, and continue into Calle San Pablo. Initially this is just a typical shopping street but, as you look farther on, it becomes apparent that there are a series of classical buildings await. The first of these, to the right, is the **Palacio de la Salina** (2) and, as you can see from the plaque outside, it stands exactly 796.8 meters above sea level. Next up is the **Palacio de Orellana** (3), which houses the Diputación Provincial and faces the Plaza de Colón, a rather pleasant, if tiny, little park.

As you reach the bottom of the steps that take you through the park, a most unusual tower looms to the left. This is the **Clavero Tower** *(Torre del Clavero)* (4), an octagonally-shaped 15th-century fort featuring tall, narrow, battlements that protrude from the top of each of its sides. Turn right and then left at the Iglesia de San Pablo on the corner.

This street, Juan de la Fuente, leads downhill and, near the bottom and directly across from the Pizza Hut, is the Plaza del Concilio de Trento, home to the *****Las Dueñas Convent** *(Convento de las Dueñas)* (5), ☎ 21-54-42, *which opens daily from 10:30 a.m. to 1 p.m. and 4:30 p.m. to 7 p.m. (clos-*

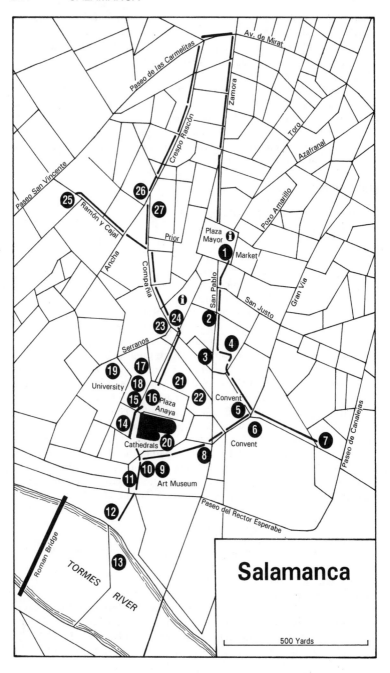

Salamanca

500 Yards

ing 1 hour earlier in winter). Entrance 200 ptas (EUR 1.20). Founded in 1419 by the wife, Doña Juana Rodríguez Maldonado, of the accountant to Juan II of Castile, this convent may not be large, but it is wonderfully charming. A small garden precedes the entrance to a beautiful and irregularly shaped patio; the upper level is particularly ornate and one side is built into a wall. Don't neglect, either, to visit the small shop in the garden where the nuns sell delicious homemade cookies and candy.

The building that dominates this immediate area, though, is diagonally across the street. Construction began on this Dominican church, the ***Convent of St. Stephen** *(Convento de San Esteban)* (6), ☎ 21-50-00, in 1524 but the ornate main Plateresque style façade, which shouldn't be missed, wasn't completed until 1610. Christopher Columbus stayed here when seeking the assistance of the Dominicans in influencing the Catholic Monarchs to sponsor his explorations. Inside, the King's Cloister with its plants and trees offers a peaceful haven, and there is a staircase of some merit. This is also the home of the Pantheon of the Theologians, the final resting place for many of the university's most renown theologians. *It can be visited daily between 9 a.m. to 1 p.m. and 4 p.m. to 8 p.m., but closes at 6 p.m. in winter. Entrance 200 ptas (EUR 1.20), free on Wednesaday morning.* Incidentally, just one block behind San Esteban, on the corner of Rosario and Escoto, is the Romanesque **Church of St. Thomas of Canterbury** *(Iglesia de Santo Tomás de Canterbury)* (7), dating from 1175. It is in the form of a Latin cross with three apses and is reputed to be the first in the world dedicated to that saint.

Cross over the pedestrian bridge back from San Esteban, go down the steps to the left, and then take a 45-degree turn into Calle de San Buena Ventura. As that joins again with San Pablo take an immediate right up a road with little steps, the Cuesta de Carvajal, which ends up in the Plaza de Carvajal. Here, above the ruins of the ancient church of San Cebrián is the **Cave of Salamanca** *(Cueva de Salamanca)* (8), one of the most secretive and mysterious sites in Salamancan history, where legend has it that necromancy, alchemy, and withcraft were practised. The tower here, the *Torre del Marques de Villena,* is named after the Marquis of Villena whose spirit is supposed to have been trapped inside forever after he reputedly tricked the devil. From the plaza one can look back to San Esteban, and directly ahead at the huge edifice that is the Cathedral.

Exit the plaza from the left-hand side and follow the narrow streets, always under the shadow of the Cathedral, to the Patio Chico and then around to Calle Gibraltar. At number 14 the metal grille gates and stained-glass windows, dating from 1905, indicate a special house indeed. Inside there are metal columns supporting a glass upper level with marvelous stained-glass walls and a similar ceiling. In fact the best view of this wonderful house, the *Casa Lis,* is from the back where the two-level wrought-iron and stained-glass façade is reached by an imposing double staircase. It is altogether fitting that this avant-garde building should be home to the **Modern Art and Art Deco Museum** *(Museo Art Nouveau y Art Decó)* (9), ☎

12-14-25, *which opens Tuesday to Friday from 11 a.m. to 2 p.m. and 5 p.m. to 9 p.m., and 11 a.m. to 9 p.m. on Saturdays, Sundays and holidays. In winter it is open in the afternoons from 4 p.m. to 7 p.m. and closes at 8 p.m.on Saturday, Sunday and holidays. Entrance 300 ptas (EUR 1.80), free Thursday morning. A joint ticket to this, the University, the Museum of Minor Schools and the Colegio del Arzobispo Fonseca is 500 ptas (EUR 3.01).*

At the end of Gibraltar is the **Masonic Lodge and National Historical Archives** *(Logia Masónica y Archivo Historico Nacional)* (10), ☎ 21-28-45, which unfortunately is not open to the public. This,.dedicated to the memory of the Civil War, holds documents siezed from the Republicans from 1937 onwards. In one room, though, disparate masonic objects have been assembled together creating a reconstruction of a perception of a lodge; the intention being of conveying a negative image of masonry. Turn left here and, after a short distance, the narrow street opens out into the **El Puerto del Rio** (11). This small plaza has a cross, a statue of Christ, and a view down to the river where there is the Moorish-influenced church of **Santiago** (12) which, as the name implies, lies on the old Pilgrims' route to Santiago de Compostela, and the **Roman Bridge** *(Puente Romano)* (13).

Retrace your steps back up the hill, and just past Gibraltar take the huge stone stairs that lead you up, and again around the Cathedral, to the Plaza de Juan XXIII. Here, across from the tower of the New Cathedral, is the rather uninteresting **City History Museum** *(Museo de Historia de la Ciudad)* (14), ☎ 21-30- 67, housed in the former Episcopal Palace, *that opens Tuesday to Saturday 9 a.m. to 2 p.m. and 4 p.m. to 8 p.m. in summer, and Tuesday to Thursday 9 a.m. to 2 p.m., and Friday and Saturday 9 a.m. to 2 p.m. and 4 p.m. to 7 p.m., in winter. Entrance free.* Just past the plaza, and underneath the huge and reddish brick doorway to the Cathedral, notice a statue of Padre Camara, a former Archbishop of Salamanca. Across from here follow the Calderon de la Barca and, at the end, await a host of surprises.

First, on the right corner, is the **House-Museum of Miguel de Unamuno** *(Casa-Museo de Unamuno)* (15), ☎ 29-44-00 Ext. 1196. He lived in this 18th-century house during his tenure as rector of the university and as well as containing his personal belongings, this now serves as a research center dedicated to his work. *Open Tuesday to Friday 9:30 a.m. to 1:30 p.m. and 4 p.m. to 6 p.m., and Saturday and Sunday 10 a.m. to 1:30 p.m. Closed July, August and September in the afternoons. Entrance 300 ptas (EUR 1.80).* Just a little farther on you'll find the *University (16), ☎ 29-44-00, and, facing it, the **Patio of Minor Schools** *(Patio de Escuelas Menores)* (17) that boasts a statue of Father Luis de León in its center. Although the University was founded in 1218, the present structure dates from the 15th century, and it is the main Plateresque façade that is its pride and joy. This elaborately stunning and beautiful creation is comprised of three parts depicting the Catholic Monarchs, Carlos V and a pope surrounded by cardinals and clergymen clad in Italian habits. Inside, there are a variety of rooms around the patio, each with their own unique character, and often marvelous ceilings. Some are still in day-to-day school use; one features a fossil/mineral display and, upstairs, there is a library with over 40,000 volumes dating from before the 19th century.

At the end of the Patio de Escuelas Menores is the small **Museum of Minor Schools** *(Museo de Escuelas Menores)* (18), ☎ 29-44-00. After perusing its clerical exhibits, furniture and busts, look up and notice the unusual and interesting split ceiling, half wooden and half domed. *The university opens Monday to Saturday 9:30 a.m. to 1:30 p.m. and 4 p.m. to 7 p.m., and Sundays and holidays from 10 a.m. to 1 p.m.; and the Museum of Minor Schools is are open Tuesday to Friday from 9:30 a.m. to 1:30 p.m. and 4 p.m. to 7:30 p.m., Saturday 10 a.m. to 1:30 p.m. and 4 p.m. to 7:30 p.m., and Sundays and holidays from 10 a.m. to 1 p.m. Entrance to both is 300 ptas (EUR 1.80), free Monday morning and May 18th. A joint ticket to these two places plus the Casa Lis and the Colegio del Arzobispo Fonseca is 500 ptas (EUR 3.01).*

Just off the Patio, and in one of its own, is the simply charming **Salamanca Museum** *(Museo de Salamanca)* (19), ☎ 21-22-35. Otherwise known as the Fine Arts museum, this is housed in the 15th-century mansion of Dr Alvárez Albarca, a physician to Queen Isabella. The exhibits are found in rooms around a unusual patio, with traditional ones located on the lower level (note an ornate ceiling in Sala 1) and more modern paintings on the upper level. *It is open Tuesday to Saturday 10 a.m. to 2 p.m. and 4:30 p.m. to 7:30 p.m., and Sunday 10 a.m. to 2:15 p.m. Entrance 200 ptas (EUR 1.20), free Saturday and Sunday in winter.*

Next stop on the trip is the *Plaza Anaya.* To get there exit the Patio de Escuelas Menores to the left, follow Libreros to the tiny La Fe, where a right followed by another right at the end will bring you to your destination. Here, on either side of a central park, are the contrasting features of the soaring elegance of the **New Cathedral** *(Catedral Nueva)* and the much more elongated and sober façade of the **Anaya Palace** *(Palacio de Anaya).* Before investigating, though, now might be a good time to sit back and be driven around town on a train. Well, not a real train of course; but a tiny sightseeing train on wheels that, between 10 a.m. and 2 p.m. and 4 p.m. to 8 p.m. during the summer months, will take you on a twenty-minute exploration.

The Cathedral itself is much more than just a Cathedral. In fact it is a combination of ***New Cathedral**, **Old Cathedral**, **Small Patio** and **Museum**, **Cloisters** and **Chapels** *(Catedral Nueva, Catedral Vieja, Patio Chico, Museo, Claustro y Capillas)* (20), ☎ 21-74-76. There is no entrance fee for the New Cathedral, which was started in 1513 because the old one had become too small and, with Renaissance and Baroque additions, is considered to be one of the last Gothic structures in Spain. Enter, at a cost this time, the Old Cathedral from the New and pass immediately into an earlier era. Work on this Romanesque structure, one of the most important in the country, was begun in 1114 and finished a century later. Its most important work is the highly intricate altar that consists of two contrasting sections and was sculptured by Nicolás Florentino, an Italian, in the first half of the 15th century. The various chapels around the cloister combine to form the museum, and are home to many fine examples of artwork and sepulchers, etc. The contrasting styles of the two cathedrals form a fascinating sight where they meet at the Patio Chico. *The New Cathedral is open from 10 a.m. to 2 p.m. and 4 p.m. to 8 p.m., and the Old Cathedral from 10 a.m. to 1:30 p.m. and 4 p.m. to 7:30 p.m. (Both close 1 hour earlier in the morning and 2 hours early in the afternoon in winter). Entrance 300 ptas (EUR 1.80).*

The **Anaya Palace** (21), of neo-classical design, dates from 1762, but the building it replaced, the Colegio Mayor, a university residence hall, pre-dated it by 350 years. There is no charge, so just walk in to view the large, and rather severe, patio. The brand-type marks around the walls, both here and throughout the city, are applied by students when they graduate. Note, also, the storks nests that adorn the towers. Next door is the smaller, and more attractive, **Hospedería** (22), that has a patio of entirely different design and gentler character.

Leave the Plaza Anaya by way of Rua Mayor, a street full of restaurants and tourist shops. At the junction of Mayor, Antigua, and Compañía are two interestingly contrasting structures. On the left is the **Clerecía** (23), that is considered to be the grandest building in the city. Work began on this huge church, now the headquarters of the Pontifical University, in 1617 and it took another 150 years to complete it. The large Baroque cloister is of particular note. The much smaller **House of Shells** *(Casa de las Conchas)* (24), ☎ 26-93-17, just across the road is considerably more unusual. It dates from the late 15th century and its owner, Dr Talavera Maldonado, a Knight of Santiago, decided to decorate the exterior with shell symbols, an idea that resonated from Santiago de Compostela. Inside, one can view the most marvelous two-level patio; gargoyles sit proudly atop marble columns that support the second floor and the railings, two on either side, are carved with differing designs. *Open Monday to Friday 9 a.m. to 9 p.m., Saturday 10 a.m. to 2 p.m. and 5 p.m. to 8 p.m., and Sunday and holidays 10 a.m. to 2 p.m. and 5 p.m. to 8 p.m. On Saturday, Sunday and holidays it opens 4 p.m. to 7 p.m. in winter. Entrance free.*

Next follow the narrow street between the two buildings and take the left fork along Compañía, and you'll be delighted by more interesting sights. Look right at the Plaza de San Benito, and the two houses at the end, the *Casas de Maldonada Rebas* and *de Celis,* differ markedly in style and are worth closer inspection. Farther along Compañía, the Plaza de las Agustinas is home to both the 17th-century **Iglesia de la Purísma,** ☎ 21-27-38, *open daily midday to 1 p.m. and 5 p.m. to 8 p.m. (7 p.m. in winter). Entrance free.* And the **Palacio de Monterrey**, which dates from 1539. The latter is a fine example of Spanish Plateresque architecture and is today owned by the Duke and Duchess of Alba.

A small diversion here, along Ramón y Cajal between the two structures, takes you to the **Fonseca College** *(Colegio Fonseca)* (25), ☎ 29-45-70. This is another Plateresque building dating from the early 16th century that was named after Archbishop Fonseca. Besides being a Gothic church from the period of the Catholic Monarchs, it today holds a collection of clocks from the period 1800 to 1925. *The chapel and cloisters open daily 10 a.m to 2 p.m. and 4 p.m. to 7 p.m. (6 p.m. in winter) and the antique clock exhibition opens Tuesday to Friday 5 p.m. to 7 p.m. (Opening and closing 1 hour earlier in the winter) and Saturday, Sunday and holidays 11 a.m. to 2 p.m. Entrance 100 ptas (EUR .60), free on Monday morning. A joint ticket to this, the University, Museum of Minor Schools plus the Casa Lis is 500 ptas (EUR 5.01).*

Return back along Compañía, which soon changes to the Calle Bordadores and opens up into a small park-like plaza. Behind the modern statue to the left is the unusual tower of the **Ursuline Convent and Museum** *(Convento y Museo de las Ursulas)* (26), ☎ 21-98-77. This Gothic church was commissioned by Archbishop Fonseca in 1512, whose remains are located here in an ornate sepulcher. *It also houses a small museum and opens every day from 11 a.m. to 1 p.m. and 4:30 p.m. to 6:30 p.m., closed last Sunday of each month. Entrance 100 ptas (EUR .60).* On the right-hand side of this small plaza are the finely sculpted features of the **House of Death** *(Casa de las Muertes)* (27).

The final leg of the journey follows straight through Bordadores into the much more modern, and bland, Crespo Rascón. Take this all the way to the end where a right turn will bring you to the most unusual of churches. The small and circular, Romanesque, *Iglesia de San Marcos,* dates from 1178 and is thought to have been one of the defensive turrets of the gateway to Zamora. Return to the Plaza Mayor by way of the slightly downhill and wide pedestrian shopping street that is Zamora. Really not that much of note here except at the Plaza de las Bandos, where there is a pleasant park and some impressive buildings, notably the one that is home to the Banco de España. Just past there be sure to continue along Zamora, by taking the left fork, and the entrance to the Plaza Mayor is directly ahead.

Trip 34

*Cáceres

A city was first founded on this site in 34 BC by the Romans, who named it *Norba Caesarina*. It is from this period that the oldest walls of Cáceres date. After the passing of Roman control, the city's fortunes declined as it endured invasions by both the Vandals and the Visigoths. The Moorish invaders brought prosperity, however, and during their nearly 400 year reign, which they called *Hizn Quazri*, the walls were rebuilt and extended. Throughout the period of the reconquest, between 1142 and 1229, control of the area changed hands several times until the latter date, when it was finally reconquered by King Alfonso IX of León. The families from León, Asturias, and Galicia who repopulated Cáceres would later become the nobility of the region.

The Order of Santiago, a brotherhood of knights, was founded here in the late 11th century. Among its chief responsibilities was to safeguard pilgrims on their journey to Santiago. To this end, the knights of Cáceres constructed houses with defensive towers. Unfortunately, many of these were destroyed by the Catholic Monarchs. It was later, in the 16th century, that the beautiful palaces and houses that give Cáceres its unique character today were constructed. The wonderful preservation of this medieval city in the "Monumental Zone" was recognized by UNESCO in 1986, when the city was declared a "Patrimony of Humanity".

GETTING THERE:

Trains arrive at Cáceres from Madrid, on their way to Mérida and/or Lisbon, Portugal. Daily, there is a single, and very slow, service between Cáceres and Seville.

Buses are best taken between Cáceres and Salamanca, where no direct train service is available; and between Cáceres and Seville where the service is not only more frequent than the train, but also faster.

By car, Cáceres, just over 187 miles slightly southwest of Madrid, is reached by taking the N-V to Trujillo, then the N-521 west to Cáceres. It is also on the main north-south highway, the N-630, just less than 45 miles north of Mérida and 130 miles south of Salamanca.

PRACTICALITIES:

Strangely, there is only one main museum here, and that is closed on Monday. This city differs from other Spanish cities in two major respects. First, the places of interest are grouped together within a very small area known as the "Monumental Zone." Second, the majority of these sites are not open to the public. Their façades, however, are most varied and, could they speak, they would most certainly recount a number of fascinating stories. Though it is not feasible, in a guide of this nature, to expound upon the virtues and the histories of these fabulous buildings in the detail they deserve, visitors who wish to explore the topic further are encouraged to purchase a copy of "Historical and Monumental Cáceres," by Antonio Rubio Rojas. This is available at most bookshops in the city.

The **Dialing Code** is 927. The main tourist office, the **Oficina de Información Turística**, ☎ 24-63-47, located in the Plaza Mayor, is open Monday to Friday from 9 a.m. to 2 p.m. and 5 p.m. to 7 p.m.; and on Saturday and holidays from 9:30 a.m. to 2 p.m. Cáceres has a **population** of about 72,000 and is the capital of the province of the same name, one of two belonging to the autonomous region of **Extremadura**.

ACCOMMODATION:

The **Parador de Cáceres** ****, ☎ 21-17-59 or fax 21-17- 29, Ancha, 6, is housed in the former 14th-century Palace of Torreorgaz, which was constructed by a Knight Commander of the Order of Santiago. It successfully blends its historical charms with the traditional style and decor of the Parador chain. \$\$

The **Meliá Cáceres** ****, ☎ 21-58-00 or fax 21-40-70, Plaza de San Juan, 11, is within a former 16th-century palace that formed a part of the ramparts of the medieval town. Completely restored in 1991, it offers a delightful combination of unusually shaped rooms, totally modern decor, and the highest level of facilities. \$\$

The **V Centenario** ****, ☎ 21-68-68 or fax 22-25-73, Manuel Pacheco, s/n, is a thoroughly modern hotel, in both design and decor, on the N-630 just to the north of the city center. Facilities include an open-air pool and a garage. \$\$

The **Hotel Extremadura** ***, ☎ 22-16-04 or fax 21-10-95, Avenida Virgen de Guadalupe, 5, is found in the modern part of the city about ten minutes walk from the "Monumental Zone." It offers all the modern amenities, a pool and parking. \$

The **Hotel Alfonso IX** **, ☎ 24-64-00 or fax 24-78-11, Calle Moret, 20, or Calle Parras, 9, is also located in modern Cáceres, and just a hundred yards from the Plaza Mayor. It is relatively small, but clean, comfortable and economical. \$

FOOD AND DRINK:

Restaurante Palacio de los Golfines (Calle Adarve Padre Rosalto, 2), serves beautifully prepared traditional regional cuisine within a marvelous ambiance of one of the traditional palaces. ☎ 24- 24-14 or fax 24-05-66. \$\$\$

Restaurante Las Indias (Plaza de San Juan, 11), is found in the Meliá Cáceres. Here, you will enjoy your choice of regional dishes or seasonal cuisine, featuring authentic Spanish produce, in an intimate dining environment. ☎ 21-58-00 or fax 21-40-70. \$\$

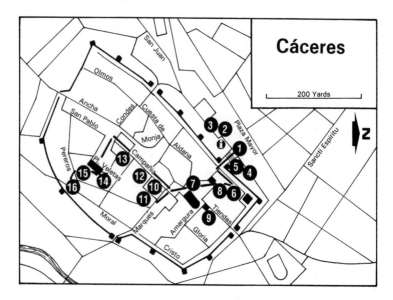

Restaurante Parador de Cáceres (Calle Ancha, 6), is a dignified restaurant noted for its local dishes which include *gazpacho extremeño,* a cold vegetable soup; *huevos fritos con migas,* fried eggs with fried bread crumbs; *la caldereta extremeña,* a lamb dish; and *la perdiz a la Alcántara,* a partridge speciality. ☎ 21-17-59 or fax 21-17-29. $$

SUGGESTED TOUR:

Numbers in parentheses correspond to numbers on the map.

Begin in the **Plaza Mayor** (1), which is not only the central meeting place of Cáceres, but also the main junction between the "Monumental Zone" (your destination) and the remainder of the city. Before continuing, though, visit the **Tourist Office** (2) and avail yourself of the many informative brochures. Then have a seat at one of the many open-air cafés to peruse the literature and admire the stretch of walls directly ahead. Though they are, at all times, impressive, these walls are absolutely spectacular first thing in the morning and in the early evening, when they seem to change their color with the moods of the sun. Behind, and to the right of, the Tourist Office is the 15th-century **Torre de los Púlpitos** (3) and, to its left, is the 12th-century **Torre de Bujaco** (4). Between the two, and to the left of the Tourist Office, are steps that will lead you through the new gate, the **Arch of the Star** *(Arco de la Estrella)* (5). Originally constructed in the 15th century, but renovated three hundred years later, this is the gateway into the "Monumental Zone".

You will discern, immediately, that this area is made up of many narrow streets. Glance towards the left down the first one, where you will see, at the end, the unusual domed tower of the 16th-century **Palacio Toledo-Moctezuma** (6). Continue on a short distance and, straight ahead, you'll find the first of the Zone's many attractive squares. Note, also, the huge storks' nests perched precariously on the towers of the church and, indeed, nearly every other building in the area. The dominant building in this, the **Plaza de Santa María**, is the church of the same name (7), ☎ 21-53-13. Although it dates from the late 13th century, a period during which many churches and cathedrals were constructed in the pure Gothic style, this one incorporates many Romanesque and Renaissance features as well. The inside is dark and rather plain. Besides the main attraction, the cedarwood altar, there are numerous tombs of prominent citizens. A small **Cathedral Museum** *(Museo de la Cathedral), is open the same hours as the church itself, Monday to Saturday 10 a.m. to 2 p.m. and 5 p.m. to 8 p.m., and Sunday and holidays 9:30 a.m. to 2 p.m. and 5 p.m. to 7:30 p.m., with an admission price of 200 ptas (EUR 1.20).* In April 1957 this church was elevated, by Papal Bull, to the status of joint cathedral in the diocese.

Directly across from the church is the **Episcopal Palace** *(Palacio Episcopal)* (8), which dates from between the 13th and 18th centuries and has a particularly handsome façade. Although the interior is not open to the public, it is possible to sneak a view of the attractive patio. To the right of the church is the unusual tower of the 15th- to 16th-century **Casa y Torres de Carvajal** (9), ☎ 25-55-97, now part of the *Patronato de Turismo,* which offers an interesting display of local arts and crafts for sale. *Open Monday to Friday 8 a.m. to 9 p.m., Saturday 9:30 a.m. to 2 p.m. and 5p.m. to 8 p.m., and Sunday and holidays 10 a.m. to 3 p.m. Entrance free.*

Retrace your steps back into the Plaza de Santa María, this time turning left past the church, passing an amazing collection of buildings boasting any number of coats-of-arms and other heraldry, along the way to the more open **Plaza de San Jorge** (10). Just around the corner from the plaza, in the Cuesta del Marques, is the rather odd private museum, the **Casa Museo Yusuf Al Burch** (11), ☎ 18-06-46. *It is supposed to open Monday to Sunday 10 a.m. to 2 p.m. and 6 p.m. to 8 p.m., but in fact these hours are flexible and on the occasions I have visited Cáceres I've never found it open. Entrance 200 ptas (EUR 1.20).*

Towering over the Plaza de San Jorge is the 18th-century **Church of San Francisco Javier** (12). Different in style from the majority of its counterparts here, its whitewashed façade is more reminiscent of those found in Portugal. Ascend the steep steps up beside the church, and make a left at the **Tower** *(Torre de las Cigüeñas),* part of the 15th-century **Casa de los Cáceres-Ovando** (13), into the Plaza de las Veletas.

Directly ahead is the **Provincial Museum** *(Museo Provincial)* (14), ☎ 24-72-34, which houses two, only mildly interesting, sections of exhibits on archaeology, arts, and popular customs. The building itself is of some interest with its 18th-century façade and 16th-century patio, but its most extraordinary feature is found below ground level. The old Arabic reservoir *(ajibe),* in the basement, has lovely graceful horseshoe-shaped arches that are typical of that period. That this is so unexpected and, seemingly, incongruous, serves to enhance its attractiveness.

Back outside, and just behind the museum, is the **Casa de los Caballos** (15), opened in 1992 to house Extramaduran Contemporary Art. The three floors of exhibits contrast vividly with their newly renovated, but very old, home. *Both this and the Provincial Museum are open Tuesday to Saturday from 9:30 a.m. to 2:30 p.m., and on Sunday and holidays between 10:15 a.m. to 2:30 p.m. Entrance 200 ptas (EUR 1.20), free for EC citizens.* A short diversion behind these two buildings leads to the **Arch of Christ** *(Arco del Cristo)* and **Tower of the Council Gate** *(Torre de la Puerta del Consejo)* (16), set into the old walls.

From here, take your choice of many routes back to the Plaza Mayor, each of which will lead you past a treasure trove of medieval architecture. Really, this is a place where most visitors will prefer to stroll, at a leisurely pace, enjoying the uniqueness of the area. It has been my experience that it is very nearly overwhelming to attempt to take in the wonders of the "Monumental Zone" in just one visit. Far better, perhaps, to wander in and out as the mood takes you. Which ever way you choose to see it, be sure to schedule a return to the Plaza Mayor at night. Then enjoy a well-earned drink, while admiring the extraordinary beauty of the floodlit medieval city.

Mérida

During the period of Roman rule, the Iberian Peninsula was divided into three: Lusitania, Tarraconensis, and Baetica. At the end of the Cantabrian Wars, Caesar Augustus chose to settle veteran legionnaires in the province of Lusitania. A search for a suitably strategic site ensued and, in 25 BC, Augusta Emerita was chosen to house veterans of the 5th and 10th legions. Soon, it was designated as capital for the province and, quickly thereafter, grew to be not only the most important city in the Iberian Peninsula, but also one of the most important in the Roman Empire.

Mérida retained a measure of importance under Visigoth control, but entered a prolonged period of decline following its conquest by the Moors in 713. The Caliphate of Córdoba disintegrated early in the 11th century and the city lost the position it had enjoyed as provincial capital of Badajoz. Even after Alfonso IX reconquered Mérida in 1230 the decline continued. During the Middle Ages the city was more or less destroyed, and most traces of its illustrious history, sadly, were lost.

It wasn't until the advent of the railroad in the 19th century that Mérida blossomed as a communications center, regaining, in the process, some prestige. Since that time, efforts have been aggressively undertaken to meticulously excavate, renovate and preserve the fantastic Roman monuments that, today, the city is famed for. These are of such historical consequence that Mérida has earned the distinction of being the only Spanish town designated a Historical Archaeological Complex (Conjunto Historico Arqueológico).

GETTING THERE:

Trains run through Mérida from Madrid, via Cáceres, on their way to Badajoz. There is also one, very slow, daily service, which stops at Mérida, between Cáceres and Seville.

Buses are a viable option only when travelling between Mérida and Seville.

By car, Mérida, 213 miles southwest of Madrid, is reached by the N-V highway, which also continues due west from Mérida to Badajoz and the Portuguese border. The city also sits astride the main north-to-south highway, the N-630, which connects Seville with the north coast.

PRACTICALITIES:

The **Dialing Code** is 924. The **Tourist Information Office**, ☎ 31-53- 53, fax 31-47-14 or e-mail otmerida@bme.es, is at Avda. José Álvarez Sáez de Buruaga, s/n. It is open Monday to Friday 9 a.m. to 2 p.m. and 4 p.m. to 6:30 p.m., and on Saturday, Sunday and holidays between 9:30 a.m. to 2 p.m. Mérida has a **population** of around 60,000 and is in the province of Badajoz, one of two provinces belonging to the autonomous region of **Extremadura**.

ACCOMMODATION:

The **Parador de Mérida** ****, ☎ 31-38-00 or fax 31-92-08, Plaza de la Constitución, 3, is found in a delightful plaza very close to the city center. It is housed within an historical building that once served as an 18th-century convent. Expect an unusual and elegant mix of history, comfort and style. $$

The **Hotel Tryp Medea** ****, ☎ 37-24-00 or fax 37-30-20, Avenida de Portugal, s/n, is in a delightfully modern structure a short distance away from the city center. The rooms are spacious and ultra modern, with amenities often including a jacuzzi. Other features include a health club an indoor and outdoor pool and ample parking. $$

The **Hotel Emperatriz** ***, ☎ 31-32-00 or fax 31-33-05, Plaza de España, 19, is housed in an historical 16th-century palace that, in its time, has played host to Carlos V, Isabel of Portugal, Felipe II and Felipe III, and a variety of other notable figures. It is centrally located and overlooks the charming Plaza de España. $$

The **Hotel Lusitania** **, ☎ 31-61-12, Oviedo, 12, located just a short walk away from the Plaza de España, past the Alcazaba is modern, clean, and reasonably priced. $

FOOD AND DRINK:

Parador de Mérida (Plaza de la Constitución, 3), offers a charming environment and the best of local cuisine, including *calderetas extremeñas* (stews), and the famous Almorahin Figs. ☎ 31-38-00 or fax 31-92-08. $$$

Restaurante El Encinar (Avenida de Portugal, s/n), is a delightfully modern restaurant in the Hotel Tryp Medea specializing in Extremaduran cuisine. ☎ 37-24-00 or fax 37-30-20. $$

Hotel Emperatriz (Plaza de España, 19), has on its medieval patio a restaurant that, besides regional gastronomy, offers a wide range of novel dishes. Be sure to sample a variety of the acclaimed local cheeses and wines. Be aware, though, some of the latter have an unusually high alcoholic content. ☎ 31-32-00 or fax 31-33-05. $$

SUGGESTED TOUR:

Numbers in parentheses correspond to numbers on the map.

Begin in the **Plaza de España** (1), Mérida's "Plaza Mayor," the center

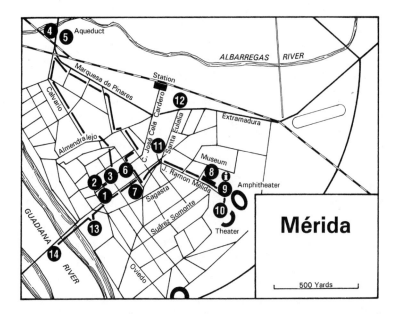

piece of which is a particularly attractive fountain. It is, generally, the hub of activity and citizens congregate at the characterful bars located both in, and around, the square. Just behind the Hotel Emperatriz, at Calle Santa Julia, 1, in the Burnay Palace, is the **Museum of Visigothic Art** *(Museo de Arte Visigodo)* (2), ☎ 30-01-06, which houses, as you most probably have surmised, exhibits of Visigothic art. *Usual opening hours are Tuesday to Friday 10 a.m. to 2 p.m. and 4 p.m. to 6 p.m., but between June 1 and September 3 the afternoon hours are 5 p.m. to 7 p.m. On Sunday and holidays, year round, the hours are 10 a.m. to 2 p.m. Entrance free.*

Next, follow the road to the right and, after a short bland stretch, another surprise awaits you in the small plaza at the end of the street. The decorative **Trajan's Arch** *(Arco de Trajano)* (3), 50 feet high and 42 feet wide, is, admittedly, out of context with its immediate environment. Previously known as the Santiago Arch, this was a monumental gate on what was then the city's most important street. At that time, this gate was the city's most well-known landmark. Go under the arch and take a right. This will lead you into the charming Plaza de la Constitución, which is dominated by the Parador hotel.

Leave the plaza by way of the narrow street to the left of the Parador, making a left into the busy Calle Almendralejo followed by a quick right onto the Calle Calvaro. This street, lined with tiny two-level houses similar to those more often seen in Andalucia, leads you, after a short distance, to the old **Roman Bridge** *(Puente Romano)* (4) over the River Alberregas. Just up from this, and accessible through a tunnel under the railroad are the extensive remains of the **Miraculous Aqueduct** *(Acueducto de los Milagros)* (5). Built just after the founding of the city, this impressive 2,700-foot-long and 80-foot-high structure was used to carry water from the Prosperina Reservoir, 3 miles away, to Mérida. Those traveling by train will get an excellent view of the aqueduct as they enter, or leave, the city.

Retrace your steps back out to the main street, Marquesa de Pinares and, after a couple of blocks, turn diagonally right into Calle Vespasiano. It's arduously uphill all the way for a while and the journey, for this stretch, is mostly uneventful. As the street comes to an end, turn left back into Calle Almendralejo. A right turn, onto Moreno de Vagos, and another onto Luis Braille, leads you back into Plaza de la Constitución.

This time depart the Plaza by way of the tiny Calle San Francisco, which will deposit you in the shopping district of town. As no Spanish town would be complete without its food market *(Mercado)*, you will find Mérida's is just at the bottom of the street. Immediately past the market is a quaint little bar, the **Casa Benito** (6), which is well worth a look. Every square inch of the walls is enveloped in bullfighting memorabilia. And, on exhibit is a very rare silk poster *(cartel)* and a corresponding ticket from the corrida in Linares, in 1949, when the extremely famous matador, Manolete, was killed in the ring.

Continue along San Francisco, making a right onto Calle Berzocana and, after about 150 yards, take the small pedestrian street to the right. This leads to the most unusual **Temple of Diana** *(Templo de Diana)* (7). Reputedly built between the 1st and 2nd Centuries AD, this imposing structure is much at odds, stylistically, with its immediate environment. It is extremely well preserved, a fact owed, rather oddly, to its subsequent use as a private mansion. Retrace your steps back to Berzocana and then follow it, towards the left, to its junction with Calle Ramón Melida. Persevere up this steep and curious little street, full of shops, small houses, and apartments and it will, at the end, bring you to three of the city's most significant monuments and the Tourist Office.

First you will come to, on the left, a rather modern looking building that was inaugurated by the King and Queen of Spain and the President of Italy on September 9, 1986, and nominated as European Museum of the Year in 1989; the ***National Museum of Roman Art** *(Museo Nacional de Arte Romano)* (8), ☎ 31-16-90. You might presuppose that the modernity of the building's design, in direct contrast to the age of the exhibits, would be unsightly. In actuality, the mixture of styles shows both off to their best advantage, and works brilliantly. It is one of the most important museums of its kind in the world, and organized tours, for a limited number of visitors, of the crypt are available. From there, also, the museum is connected to the Roman Theater and Amphitheater. *It is open Tuesday to Saturday from 10 a.m. to 2 p.m. and 4 p.m. to 6 p.m. (or 5 p.m. to 7 p.m. between June 1 and September 30), and on Sunday and holidays from 10 a.m. to 2 p.m. Entrance 400 ptas EUR 2.40, free on Saturday afternoon and Sunday morning.*

To the left of the museum is a rather large open area that encompasses the **Roman House of the Amphitheatre** *(Casa del Anfiteatro)* (9), ☎ 31-85-09. Upon best information and belief, comprising this are the remains of two houses dating from the 3rd or 4th centuries, and within the floor plans are some very interesting mosaics. Directly across from the museum is the entrance to two of the best known monuments in Mérida; the *****Roman Theater and Amphitheater** *(Teatro y Anfiteatro Romanos)* (10), ☎ 31-25-30. The **Roman Theater** is, easily, the most impressive of the Roman remains in Mérida. Originally constructed by Agrippa, son-in-law of Augustus, in 16-15 BC, it was reconstructed several times through and including a renovation in 4th century when the elegant façade, with its colonnades and statues, was added. Excavation began early in the 20th century, but it was not until the 1960s that the serious work of restoration began on this semi-circular shaped auditorium, that in its heyday seated 6,000. In addition to its historical significance it is now used each year, during the month of July, as the site for the International Festival of Classic Drama. Just a few yards away, stands the **Amphitheater**. This elliptically-shaped arena was completed in 8 BC, and had a capacity of up to 14,000. The gates, entrances and passageways are of particular interest and, although it is in a state of some disrepair, more than enough remains to feed your imagination as to the gladiatorial, and other, contests that took place here.

Exit this area, taking Calle José Ramón Melida back down towards the center of town, turning right at the bottom and walking up towards the **Santa Eulalia Monument** (11). Bear left at the fork in the road, going around a pleasant little park and continuing down the hill towards the curiously-styled **Basilica de Santa Eulalia** (12), ☎ 30-34-07. This architecturally distinctive church is dedicated to the memory of the child martyr who, Spanish legend has it, was baked in an oven as punishment for her offense of a pagan priest. Outside, you will find the **Temple of Mars**, a chapel dedicated the Saint and, inside the church, is a small museum that expounds upon the remains of the Roman houses found beneath the church. It also served, in past times, first as a Visigothic Basilica and then as 16th-century Christian chapel. Retrace your steps back up the hill towards the little park and follow Calle Santa Eulalia back to the Plaza de España. By this time you will be in need of some well-earned refreshments, so take your pick of the four bars in the square and just sit for a while enjoying the wonderful fountain.

Your next stop is just outside the plaza, on the street opposite the Hotel Emperatriz and closest to the river. The **Arab Fortress** *(Alcazaba)* (13), ☎ 31-73-09, was built by Abdel-Rahman II in AD 835, over the original Roman fortifications designed to defend the nearby bridge. Unfortunately, there is very little left besides the walls. The ramparts on these, however, offer excellent views of the Guadiana River and the bridge. Inside there are only two attractions of note, the **water cistern** *(ajibe)*, and the restored cloister of a 16th-century monastery built by the

Knights of Santiago.

The Casas Romanas del Anfiteatro y del Mithreo, Teatro y Anfiteatro Romanos, Basilica de Santa Eulalia and Alcazaba Arabe are open daily all year, 9:30 a.m. to 1:45 p.m. and 5 p.m. to 7:15 p.m. in the summer, and 4 p.m. to 6:15 p.m. in winter, with the Basilica closing on Sunday and religious festivals. Entrance to the Teatro y Anfiteatro Romanos alone is 600 ptas (EUR 3.61), but a ticket for all of these places costs just 800 ptas (EUR 4.81).

For the final leg of the tour, return to the Plaza de España. Here, take a left down the appropriately named Calle del Puente, which follows along the walls of the Alcazaba to the **Roman Bridge** *(Puente Romano)* (14). This bridge, now restricted to pedestrian traffic, has, spaced along its 866 yard length, 60 granite arches. It passes peacefully over both branches of the river and, usually, you will find numerous fishermen hopefully casting their lines into the waters below. Traffic, on the other hand, now uses the modern bridge to the right. Pause here to enjoy the restful atmosphere before returning the Plaza de España and the end of the tour.

Burgos

F ounded in AD 884 as a stronghold against the Moors, Burgos succumbed to the invaders but was re-conquered in 951 and became the
capital of Castile, an honor that it held until 1492 when the Catholic
Monarchs transferred their court to Valladolid. The city's most famous citizen, born in 1026 just 6 miles away at Vivar, was Rodrigo Diaz. He married
the cousin of King Alfonso VI, but this did not stop him falling out with the
latter and he was eventually banished from Burgos. He went on, however,
to become the renowned soldier of fortune, *El Cid*, remembered for his
conquest of Valencia in 1094. He died shortly afterwards, in 1099, following his defeat by the Moors at Cuenca. His wife returned his body to the
Monastery of San Pedro de Cardeña, where he once worked, early in the
12th century. There it remained until the beginning of the present century, when it was removed to the Cathedral in Burgos.

In 1812 Burgos, then a French garrison during the Wars of
Independence, was put under siege by Wellington's troops. It was prominent, also, during the Spanish Civil War, when Franco was declared Head
of State and Generalíssimo there in 1936. The city subsequently became
the seat of the provisional government, and it was from La Isla Palace in
Burgos, on April 1, 1939, that Franco proclaimed the cease-fire.

Located on a plateau in the Arlanzón Valley at an altitude of 900
meters (2,952 ft.), today Burgos is a quiet provincial capital that, although
its really special attractions are few, should absolutely not be missed for
sake of one alone—its magnificent Cathedral.

GETTING THERE:

Trains are a good choice when traveling to and from Burgos. It lies
midway between Madrid and the French border at Irún, and is a junction
for both the international service between Paris and Lisbon/Oporto, via
Salamanca, and the line to northwestern Spain from Barcelona, via León.
The train station is too far from the city center to walk and, as the bus service is not that convenient, it is preferable to take a taxi.

Buses are most recommended if leaving to, or arriving from, nearby
cities such as Valladolid.

By Car, Burgos is on the main N1 highway, 145 miles north of Madrid
and 142 miles southwest of San Sebastián. It is also at the junction of the
N623, running to the north and linking the city with Santander, and the
southwesterly N620 to Valladolid and Salamanca.

PRACTICALITIES:

Burgos' location precludes the realistic possibility of scheduling it as a daytrip from either San Sebastián or Madrid. Nevertheless, it should not be overlooked. The best way of incorporating this city into your tour of Spain is to designate it an overnight stop either between the above mentioned cities, or on your journey between San Sebastián and León/Santiago de Compostela. Also understand that, because of its geographical location Burgos doesn't enjoy the long, hot summers as found in most Spanish cities, and that it gets very, very cold during the winter months.

With the notable exception of the Cathedral and the San Nicolás church, all attractions here are closed on Monday. Burgos' **Dialing Code** is 947. The **Tourist Information Office**, ☎ 20-18-46 or fax 27-65-29, is found at the Plaza Alonso Martínez, 7. Ask there for the informative *Burgos Plano-Guía*, a combined plan and guide. Burgos has a **population** of 160,000 and is the capital of the province of the same name, one of nine belonging to the autonomous region of **Castilla y León**.

ACCOMMODATION:

The **Hotel Almirante Bonifaz** ****, ☎ 20-69-43 or fax 20- 29-19, Vitoria, 22-24, can be found just outside the Old Town and a couple of blocks from the imposing monument of El Cid. It has a modernly elegant style, all modern comforts and the pleasing "Los Sauces" restaurant. $$$

The **Hotel Fernán González** ****, ☎ 20-94-41 or fax 27- 41-21, Calera, 17, is located just across the river from the Old Town—closeby the Burgos Museum—and has a charmingly old-fashioned ambiance along with spacious rooms. $$

The **Hotel Mesón del Cid** ***, ☎ 20-59-71 or fax 26-94-60, Plaza Santa María, 8, has a charming ambiance and, unquestionably, the best location in the city. The front rooms, one of which you want if you stay here, have the most marvelous, and uninterrupted, views of the magnificent main façade of the Cathedral. $$

The **Hotel Cordón** ***, ☎ 26-50-00 or fax 20-02-69, Calle La Puebla, 6, is a delightful small hotel, that has just 35 rooms, all with private bathrooms, in a quiet location close to the Casa del Cordón. $

The **Hotel Residencia Norte y Londres** **, ☎ 26-41-25 or fax 27-73-75, Calle Olza Alonso Martínez, 10, is a few hundred yards from the Cathedral and is another hotel with an old-fashioned ambiance and much charm. $

FOOD AND DRINK:

Burgos is famed for its solid Castillian cuisine, with such specialties as Roast Suckling Lamb, a Sausage and Pulse Stew *(Olla Podrida)*, Spicy Minced Pork *(Picadillo)*, and red bean dishes from the local village of *Ibeas*. Its Cheese and Blood Pudding *(Queso and Morcillo de Burgos)* are popular throughout Spain. These taste better when washed down with the *Ribera de Duero* red wines.

Restaurante Mesón del Cid (Plaza Santa María, 8), is part of the hotel of the same name. It has all the character of the 16th-century palace it once was, and specializes in typically local dishes. ☎ 20-87-15 or fax 26-94-60. $$$

Restaurante Casa Ojeda (Vitoria, 5), is , after nearly 80 years, one of the oldest established restaurants in Burgos. Founded in 1912, it is run by the original proprietor's grandson, and the specialty is Castilian cuisine. Expect classic dishes such as vegetables in cream, *morcilla* with natural peppers, quail, stuffed pigeon and suckling lamb. ☎ 20-90-52 or fax 20-70-11. $$$

Restaurante Pablo Bringas (Plaza Alonso Martínez, 1, just across from the Capitánia General), offers a change from heavy Castillian cuisine by specializing in fish and shellfish. ☎ 20- 61-34. $$$

Restaurante Fernán González (Calle Calera, 17), is a traditional restaurant in the hotel of the same name, serving regional or International cuisine. ☎ 20-94-41 or fax 27-41-21. $$

Mesón de los Infantes (Right underneath the Arco de Santa María) Here you might try *Olla Podrida* or *Paella de Mariscos* (shellfish). ☎ 20-59-82. $

SUGGESTED TOUR:

Numbers in parentheses correspond to numbers on the map.

A most appropriate place to begin any tour of Burgos is at the gate that once served as the main entrance for all important visitors to the city. The riverside façade of the *Arch of St Mary (Arco de Santa María)* (1) is impressive indeed. Crenellated on multi-levels, the once-plain front was embellished, in the early 16th century, with statues of important dignitaries carved from above the arch itself to the peak, giving it a rare combination of formidableness and grace. Having once served as offices for the town hall it now sits incongruously between two rows of houses, many of which have glassed-in "galleries" to protect them from the harsh winters. Today, also, it is home of the **Historical-Artistic Cultural Center** *(Centro Cultural Histórico-Artístico)* (2). Here, on the first floor, is a video information exhibition, and on the second floor exists a small Pharmacy Museum, with exhibits from the 17th to 19th centuries. *It is open Tuesday to Saturday from 10 a.m. to 2 p.m. and 4 p.m. to 7:30 p.m., and on Sunday morning between 10 a.m. to 2 p.m.*

Before continuing on around the Old Town, cross the *Santa María* bridge, in front of the Arch, turn left onto the busy Valladolid and take the first right into Calera. This district, known as *La Vega,* was once home to many important families. Two of the mansions that survive, the *Casas Miranda* and *Iñigo Angulo,* now house the **Burgos Museum** *(Museo de Burgos)* (3), ☎ 26-58-75. The **Prehistoric and Archaeological** sections, located in the former, boasts an impressive array of exhibits, with my favorites being the unusual wooden sepulchers. Notice, also, the splendid 16th-century Renaissance patio. In the latter mansion you'll find the **Fine Arts**

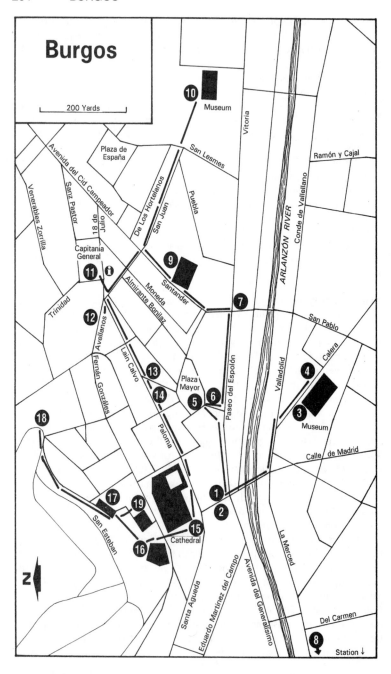

(Bellas Artes) section. *Collectively, these are open on Tuesday to Friday from 10 a.m to 2 p.m. and 4 p.m. to 7 p.m., Saturday 10 a.m. to 2 p.m. and 4:45 p.m. to 8:15 p.m., and Sunday between 10 a.m. to 2 p.m. Entrance 200 ptas (EUR 1.20), free on Saturday and Sunday.*

Those seeking a stark contrast, as well as refreshments, will delay retracing their steps to the Arch, crossing the road to the **Bar Patillas** (4). Splendid or grand it most surely isn't but, in its own right, it's full of character. Upon entering you get the impression that the world has passed it by, and the curios and bullfighting posters that cover its walls are of ceaseless interest.

Back over the Puente de Santa María, turn right and stroll down the charming Paseo del Espolón. Bordered by a double row of strangely limbed trees and a long, rectangular park that runs parallel with the River Arlanzón, this is a favorite retreat of the Burgalése. Take a moment, though, and consider the river; what you will, most likely, see can be very deceptive. Summer is usually a time of little rainfall and the river, flanked by two wide grass banks, most often looks very placid. The wide river bed is there for a reason, however. In those seasons when the rains and thaw coincide the Arlanzón can be transformed into a raging torrent, with the heights it can reach clearly evident at the next port of call.

About half way along the paseo, and to the left, three archways beckon you through to the irregularly-shaped **Plaza Mayor** (5). Like all such plazas in Spain, this is the social center of Burgos and, for me at least, it is at its best around mid-afternoon when school has just let out. Then, while mothers quietly discuss the day's events, the excited laughter of children, blissfully unconcerned with anything other than their own playfulness, echoes around the plaza. Other than a brown stone house, with columns and a statue perched proudly at the top, the only other structure of real interest is that owning the arches, the **Town Hall** *(Casa Consistorial)* (6). Prior to returning to the paseo, and venturing left, note the red lines drawn around the columns and marked with the dates June 5, 1930 and June 11, 1874. These are the high-water marks reached by the flooding river.

The recently renovated main theatre, the *Teatro Principal,* at the end of the paseo sets the stage for the city's hero, **El Cid,** who greets you, beard flowing, sword pointing defiantly towards the river, as he sits proudly astride his steed, in the adjoining Plaza de la Primo de la Rivera. This bronze **equestrian statue** (7), by Juan Cristóbal, set atop a concrete plinth, is so realistic you may recoil in anticipation.

This a good time to consider a visit to the *Las Huelgas Monastery and Fine Cloth Museum* *(Monasterio de las Huelgas y Museo de Ricas Telas)* (8), ☎ 20-16-30, which is located about a mile and a half outside of town. The Number 5 bus, marked SEDAS—BARRIO DEL PILAR, departs every 40 minutes from this plaza, and it is well worth the detour. The monastery was founded somewhere around 1180 by King Alfonso VIII and his wife, Queen Eleanor, who was the daughter of Henry II of England. The first abbess, Doña Misol, was appointed by King Alfonso and, most unusually, was granted rare privileges. In the charter of foundation she had the powers of lordship over neighboring communities and exemption from taxes, under the king's own authority. This arrangement was so lucrative that, until the end of the 14th century, no feudal lord in Castile, excepting the king himself, had more vassals. It was at one time used as a summer palace by royalty, and as well as the Gothic chapter house with its beautiful Romanesque cloister, there are numerous tombs of kings and princes. In the museum, in addition to the banner of Navas de Tolosa, won by King Alfonso VIII from the Almohads, are exhibits of cloth and jewelry recovered from the tombs. *It is open April to September on Tuesday to Saturday 10:30 a.m. to 1:15 p.m. and 3:30 p.m. to 5:15 p.m., and on Sunday and holidays 10:30 a.m. to 2:15 p.m. Between October and March it opens Tuesday to Friday 11 a.m. to 1:15 p.m. and 4 p.m. to 5:15 p.m., Saturday 11 a.m. to 1:15 p.m. and 4 p.m. to 5:45 p.m., and Sunday and holidays 10:30 a.m. to 2:15 p.m. Entrance 700 ptas (EUR 4.21), free on Wednesday.*

Back in town, there is another small adjoining plaza with two kiosks that sell English-language newspapers. This plaza leads into Santander where, almost immediately, you'll be greeted by the intricate, and original, façade belonging to the **House of Rope** *(Casa del Cordón)* (9). Notwithstanding the fact that it has been renovated over the centuries, the 15th-century mansion is one of the finest examples of its kind in Burgos. It was here, on April 23, 1497, that the Catholic Monarchs received Columbus *(Cristobal Colón)* following his second voyage to the West Indies; that the annexation of Navarra was proclaimed in 1515, and here also that Austrian kings resided when visiting Burgos. The name derives from the cordon of rope carved in stone over the entrance.

Carry back on along Santander where a right into San Juan will eventually take you through the Plaza Lesmes and to the Monastery of San Juan, impressive in its own right, and also home to the **Marcelino Santa María Museum** *(Museo de Marcelino Santa María)* (10), ☎ 20-56-87. Santa María, who lived between 1866 and 1952, was a Burgalése painter who specialized in country scenes and portraits. His paintings exhibited here, though not particulary famous, are usually in a very pleasing combination of pastel colors. *They can be seen, for a bargain-basement 25 ptas (EUR .15), on Tuesday to Saturday from 10 a.m. to 1:50 p.m and 5 p.m. to 7:50 p.m., and on Sunday mornings between 10 a.m. and 1:50 p.m.*

Now backtrack along San Juan, passing straight over Santander, and the next landmark, at the end, is the Hotel Norte y Londres. From here a glance right, towards the Plaza Alonso Martínez, will bring into view an elegant and well guarded mansion, now the residence of the **Capitánia General** (11). From the balcony of this building, on October 1, 1936, Franco had himself proclaimed Head of State and Generalíssimo. The plaza is also, incidentally, the location of the tourist office.

By now refreshments are in order, and there are numerous attractive bars tucked around the plaza waiting to oblige. The most discerning of you will, somewhat reluctantly perhaps, avoid the temptation to sit here and opt, instead, to take the tiny street across from the hotel, Calle Avellanos, and pop into the **Café/Bar Serranillos** (12), just to the left. Absolutely nothing fancy here, in truth from the outside it looks easily avoidable, but that would be a mistake indeed. In fact I never go to Burgos without paying it a visit. The reason is simple; they serve the most delicious pieces of fried fish tapas I have ever tasted in the whole of Spain. And don't stop there, you really should sample the famous Blood Sausage *(Morcillo de Burgos).*

The next step is to follow the street that runs alongside the Norte y Londres, Calle Lain Calvo which, for the most part, is unexceptional. But hold out until the end, where it transforms into the now pedestrian walkway of Paloma, a much more interesting Calle. Here you'll find a small plaza where, from a double sided **fountain** *(fuente)* (13), fresh, cool drinking water cascades from the mouths of lions. The Cathedral looms in the foreground, but a stop at Number 22, the **Casa Quintanilla** (14), might prove of interest. By American definitions this is an old-fashioned general store and, even if you don't buy anything to snack on later, it is still fun to just browse around.

Finally, it's time to visit the Cathedral, but don't be confused—the tourist entrance is in the Plaza de San Fernando, which is quite different from the main entrance up other steps, the Cadena Eleta, that lead to the main façade. The *Cathedral *(Catedral)* (15), ☎ 20-47-12 or fax 27-39-50, is considered one of the most beautiful in Spain, and is certainly my favorite. Bishop Mauricio laid the first stone in 1221, but construction of this majestic Gothic jewel, named on the World Heritage List, took another 400 years. Really, this place is simply so intricately beautiful, and its charms so multi-faceted, that a 500 ptas investment in a guide book is definitely recommended. Everything here is remarkable, not least the amazingly carved stonework—both inside and out. The Chapel of the Constables, behind the altar must be seen, also the choir and as many of the 38 altars as you wish. The oddest item sits above a clock, high to the left of the main door. The **Flycatcher** *(Papamoscas)* is a clown, dating from the 15th century, that opens and closes its mouth at each stroke of the bell. Farther along the main wall the **Golden Staircase**, built in 1519, now leads nowhere and is only used during the highly ceremonious Easter celebrations. The very interesting museum, for which there is a minimal admission charge, has numerous interesting exhibits in rooms around the Cloister. Most notable are the huge silver carriage, a golden monstrance, and the coffin of El Cid—which holds its own interesting legend. In 1921 the remains of El Cid and his wife, Ximena, were moved here. *Opening hours, for both Cathedral and museum, are 9:30 a.m. to 1 p.m. and 4 p.m. to 7 p.m., daily. Entrance 400 ptas (EUR 2.40).*

It's now time to walk around, and up, to the Plaza Santa María which has both an unusual fountain and marvelous views of the main façade. Here, also, more steps lead up to the much tinier **St. Nicholas Church**

(Iglesia de San Nicolás) (16), ☎ 30-20-95, a 15th-century church that is famous for its Gothic/Renaissance 16th century altar. *This may be seen daily during July, August and September between 9 a.m. to 2 p.m. and 4 p.m. to 8 p.m. The rest of the year it is open on Tuesday to Friday from 6:30 p.m. to 7:30 p.m, Saturday 9:30 a.m. to 2 p.m. and 5 p.m. to 7 p.m., and holidays from 9 a.m. to 2 p.m. and 5 p.m. to 6 p.m. At all times, though, it is closed to tourists during Masses.*

Turn left out of here, and left again into the narrow, cobblestoned, Pozo Seco, leading to the **Church of St. Stephen and Altar Museum** *(Iglesia de San Esteban y Museo del Retablo)* (17), ☎ 27-37-52. Found in the oldest area of the city, and one currently undergoing extensive restoration, this is a fine example of 13th-century Gothic architecture. Inside are particularly intricate altars. *It is open Tuesday to Saturday from 10:30 a.m to 2 p.m. and 4:30 p.m. to 7 p.m., and on Sunday from 10:30 a.m. to 2 p.m. Entrance 200 ptas (EUR 1.20).*

It's possible, from this point, to climb up for a visit to the castle which, although just a ruin, does offer interesting views of the city below. Alternatively, a short diversion down Calle San Esteban to the ancient Mudéjar-styled **St. Stephen's Arch** *(Arco de San Esteban)* (18), may prove of interest to some. In any event take the steps down, behind San Esteban, to Fernán González where a right turn offers different perspectives of the back of the Cathedral. Before returning to the steps back down to the Plaza Santa María you will also pass the Palacio de Maluenda, which now houses the **Municipal Archives** *(Archivos Municipal)* (19).

If you are ever in Burgos during the annual Fería, at the end of June, you'll want to stake out, early enough, a vantage point on the steps leading from the Plaza Santa María to the Plaza de San Fernando. About 11 p.m. each night fireworks are exploded from the Puente de Santa María and, traditionally, the last fusilade hangs like a multi-colored umbrella over this wonderful Cathedral. Truly a spectacular sight.

Cuenca

Cuenca is historic in the tradition of most Spanish cities, but it is not history that draws most visitors to this remote, and rather curious, city located at a point nearly equidistant between Madrid and Valencia. Cuenca is divided into two parts: the lower, modern section and, overlooking it, the Old Town, which is squeezed into a tight and very steep promontory between the Júcar and Huécar rivers. It is here that you will see, perched precariously on the edge of the cliff overlooking the Huécar river, the famous Hanging Houses *(Casas Colgadas),* which are the real tourist magnets of the city.

The city's isolated position presents a challenge for travelers. Cuenca is no longer on the main train line between Madrid and Valencia and, while the services to and from Madrid are twice as frequent as those connecting the city with Valencia, it really is not practical to make this a daytrip from either, by train. Similar difficulties plague bus travelers as well. So, definitely for those relying on public transport, and perhaps for those driving, it is sensible to make Cuenca an overnight stop. Once in Cuenca there are other practicalities to consider. While the train station, the bus station, and the majority of the hotels are found in the lower, newer, part of town, visitors will most likely be interested only in the Old Town. Taking into account the prospect of a long and very steep walk, you may want to consider staying up in the Old Town.

GETTING THERE:

Trains run through Cuenca, on a slow regional line, as they make their way to and from Madrid and Valencia. Be sure to check the schedules carefully, however, as they vary from day to day.

Buses are best used, if at all, between Cuenca and Valencia. The truth of the matter is that, on this route, the scheduling, and frequency, whether traveling by bus or train, are not that good.

By car, Cuenca, slightly over 100 miles east of Madrid, is reached by taking the N-III to Taracón, and then the N-400 to Cuenca. Just over 135 miles northwest of Valencia, it is reached by taking the N-III to Motilla del Palancar, and then joining the N-230 north to Cuenca. Cuenca and Teruel are joined by the rather tortuous N-420.

PRACTICALITIES:

The selection of museums in Cuenca is very limited, and these are closed on Monday. The **Dialing Code** is 969. The tourist office, **Información**

Turismo, ☎ 22- 22-31, Dalmacio García Izcara, 8, is in the New Town, close to the railway station. In the Old Town there is a small office in the Plaza Mayor, near the Town Hall. Cuenca has a **population** of 45,000 and is the capital of the province of the same name, one of five belonging to the autonomous region of **Castilla-La Mancha.**

ACCOMMODATION:

The **Parador de Cuenca ****, ☎** 23-23-20 or fax 23- 25-34, Paseo Hoz del Huécar, s/n, housed in the 16th-century Convent of San Pablo, has been carefully renovated to include every modern facility. Its location is fantastic as well, just across from and connected with the Old Town by a rather rickety footbridge over the Huécar river. $$

The **Hotel Torremangana ****, ☎** 22-33-51 or fax 22-96-71, Avenida San Ignacio de Loyola, 9, is a very neat modern hotel in the New Town. Contemporary decor, a delightful restaurant and pleasing terraces complete the package. $$

The **Hotel Leonor de Aquitania ***, ☎** 23-10-00 or fax 23-10-04, Calle San Pedro, 60, is in the heart of the Old Town, just a couple of hundred yards or so from the cathedral. Modern comforts have been incorporated into this historic home without compromising the character. $

The **Hostal Residencia Posada de San José **, ☎** 21-13-00 or fax 23-03-65, Julián Romero, 4, is just up the hill from the cathedral in a charming 17th-century building. Exposed wooden beams and uneven floors make for an ambiance of authenticity, and the rooms are comfortable, if a little basic. Very economical. $

FOOD AND DRINK:

Cuenca's rural position, which affords easy access to an abundance of lamb and game, colors the local cuisine a hearty flavor. Typical dishes are *morteruelo,* pork liver, chicken or game and walnuts seasoned with clover and cinnamon; *zarajos,* lamb tripe wrapped in vine shoots and fried; pijancos, meatballs and potatoes with paprika and herbs; and a variety of stews. Dishes featuring trout and crayfish, plentiful in area rivers, are also popular. A favorite dessert is *alajú,* almonds, honey and figs wrapped in a wafer; especially delicious when washed down with *resolí,* a locally produced liqueur.

Parador de Cuenca (Paseo Hoz del Huécar, s/n), housed in the old 16th-century Convent of San Pablo, features a restaurant combining the style of that era with renowned parador service. Specialities include *morteruelo* and *pisto con lomo de orza,* fried vegetables with loin. ☎ 23-23-20 or fax 23-25-34. $$$

Mesón Casas Colgadas (Canónigas, s/n), is within one of the famous Hanging Houses, affording spectacular views as a fitting accompaniment to the well-prepared and presented dishes of the region. ☎ 22-35-09. $$

Joni Cafeteria (Hermanos Becerril, 12), located near the railroad station, serves enticingly delicious shellfish. ☎ 22-60-02. $$

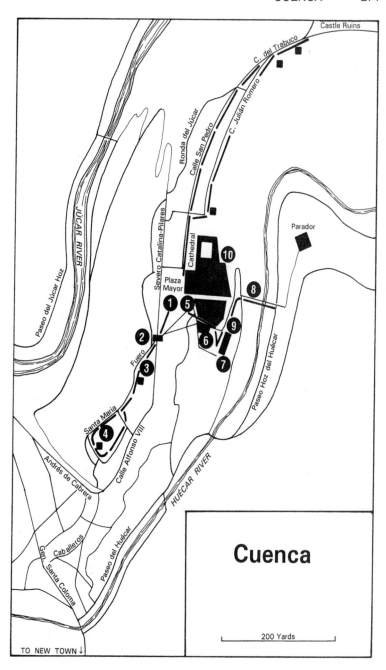

Hostal Residencia Posada de San José (Julián Romero, 4), has a restaurant that will give you hearty food at reasonable prices. ☎ 21-13-00 or fax 23-03-65. $

SUGGESTED TOUR:

Numbers in parentheses correspond to numbers on the map.

The **Plaza Mayor** (1), in the heart of the Old Town is, without doubt, the place of choice to begin a tour. You will immediately be drawn by the overpowering presence of the Cathedral, which dominates one side, but resist that temptation for now. Look back towards the lovely arched building that is the **Town Hall** *(Ayuntamiento)* (2). Heading in that direction, and just before you reach the Hall, you will come to a small tourist information office on the right hand side of the street. Capitalize on this opportunity to collect some information about Cuenca, then find a seat in one of the charming sidewalk cafés to peruse your literature and familiarize yourself with what the town has to offer.

Walk under the arch but, instead of taking the most obvious route along main road, Calle Alfonso VIII, which leads down the hill, take the right fork, Fuero, which leads into the very interesting Plaza de la Merced. To the right, is an 18th-century church named as is the plaza and, opposite the church, is an ancient building that has now been renovated to house the **Science Museum and Planetarium** *(Museo de las Ciencias y Planetario)* (3), ☎ 24-03-20 and fax 21-33-55. *Open Tuesday to Saturday 11 a.m. to 2 p.m. and 4 p.m. to 6 p.m., and Sunday 1 a.m. to 2:30 p.m., entrance free.* A bit farther along, the street fans out into an open plaza, the focal point of which is the highly unusual *Mangana Tower* *(Torre de Mangana)* (4). This tall, narrow, tower was originally constructed as a part of the Moorish fortifications, and today its strategic position, high over the New Town, has been put to good practical use. A clock, placed at its summit, can be seen from most any vantage point throughout the modern section of Cuenca.

Retracing your steps, return to the Plaza Mayor and, this time, turn right onto Obispo Valero just before you reach the Cathedral. Directly ahead, a cross, dedicated to the memory of the founder of the Falangist Party, José Antonio Primo de la Rivera, stands in close proximity to the old Episcopal Palace, which now functions as the **Diocesan Sacred Art Museum** *(Museo Diocesano Catedralico)* (5), ☎ 22-42-10. The exhibits here are mostly of a religious nature, although they do include a few works by El Greco. *Opening hours are Tuesday to Friday 11 a.m. to 2 p.m. and 4 p.m. to 6 p.m., on Saturday closing time is extended to 8 p.m., and Sunday hours are 11 a.m. to 2 p.m.* Directly across the road is the **Cuenca Museum** *(Museo de Cuenca)* (6), ☎ 21-30-69, where you will find a collection of archaeological pieces, primarily from the surrounding area, all displayed in chronological order. *Visit Tuesday to Saturday 10 a.m. to 2 p.m. and 4 p.m. to 7 p.m., and on Sunday and holidays from 10 a.m. to 2 p.m.*

Continue along the same street as it doglegs, changes its name to Canónigos, and winds down in the direction of the medieval **Hanging

Houses *(Casas Colgadas)* that are Cuenca's main attraction. One house, in particular, has been beautifully, and cleverly, renovated, masterfully combining the warmth of the original beamed ceilings and wooden floors with its very modern collection of abstract art, leaving these two seemingly incompatible styles to dwell here in harmonious contrast. This, the **Spanish Abstract Art Museum** *(Museo de Arte Abstracto Español)* (7), ☎ 21-29-83 and fax 21-22-85, *may be visited Tuesday to Friday and holidays from 11 a.m. to 2 p.m. and 4 p.m. to 6 p.m., Saturday from 11 a.m. to 2 p.m. and 4 p.m. to 8 p.m., and on Sunday from 11 a.m. to 2:30 p.m.*

As you leave, turn through the narrow arch and walk towards the rather fragile looking pedestrian footbridge, the **St. Paul's Bridge** *(Puente San Pablo)* (8). Those with a head for heights will want to walk at least part of the way across it, as it offers an unparalleled **viewpoint** back to the famous Hanging Houses (9). To avoid photographic disappointments, get your shots in here before noon, when the sun will be shining directly onto the houses. Any later, and the sunlight will be beaming directly into your lens. Also, a reminder for those staying at the parador, this bridge will be your route to and from the Old Town.

Reverse back along the route you have just taken to the Plaza Mayor where, finally, it is time to investigate the **Cathedral** *(Catedral)* (10), which has been designated a national monument. The façade of this unique 12th-century Gothic/Anglo Norman structure underwent a significant renovation in the 17th century in a style that is strikingly out of sync with its peers. Once inside, the sense of inconsistency intensifies; the modern design of the stained-glass windows does little to alleviate the plainness and austerity of the interior design. *Open Tuesday to Sunday 9 a.m. to 2 p.m. and 4 p.m. to 6:30 p.m.*

Exit and turn right, following around the cathedral to the narrow Calle de Julián Romero. This will take you up through the Old Town and all the way to the castle. Along the way you will find the charming 17th-century *Posada de San José* (see Accomodation, above), go through a small *plazuela* with lovely views across the ravine to the parador, and pass underneath the arches and houses, finally emerging near three buildings of some interest—the 17th-century *Convento Carmelitas,* a small **Electrografic Museum** *(Museo Electrografia),* ☎ 17-91-15, fax 17- 91-18 or e-mail infe@mide-cu.uclm.es, *open Monday to Saturday and holidays 11 a.m. to 9 p.m., Sunday midday to 2 p.m., free entrance,* and the **Historical Archives** *(Archivo Histórico).* Besides the latter of these, you will see a flight of steps leading up to the castle. Only the ruins of the castle remain, but the altitude of the site does offer views across the River Júcar valley and what is, most probably, the finest perspective of the curious geographical situation of Cuenca.

Stroll back down to the Calle del Trabuco which, when you reach the Iglesia de San Pedro, changes its name to San Pedro. Follow this for the short trip back to the Plaza Mayor, punctuated with attractive houses, interesting shops, and the charming *Hotel Leonor de Aquitania.*

Trip 38

León

León was founded in AD 68 by the Roman 7th legion, Gemina Pia Felix, who built their fortifications on the hill where the Cathedral now stands. In the middle of the 6th century their forces succumbed to those of the Visigoths who, in turn, were overrun by the Moors in the very early part of the 8th century. Situated on the edge of the Moors' scope of influence, the battles for control of this city were many. By the 10th century it had been repopulated by Mozarabs—Christian refugees from the south, and as the seat of the Kingdom of León was considered the most important Christian city in Spain. However, in 996, under the leadership of Almanzar, the Moors invaded once again, and it wasn't until the 11th century that the city was finally re-conquered. During that century, a strategic location on the pilgrims' road to Santiago de Compostela brought an influx of new influences and styles, in particular Romanesque. During the 12th century its prominence began to wane until, in 1235, it amalgamated with Castile.

Today, although modern and visibly affluent, it retains a somewhat old-fashioned ambiance. Perhaps this is due to an isolated geographical location, which affords it no access to the sea or proximity to another highly populated area.

GETTING THERE:

Trains run through León on either the Madrid to Oviedo/Gijón line or the lines from Barcelona or País Vasco (in the east), to Santiago de Compostela, La Coruña and Vigo (in the west).

Buses are best used between León and Salamanca, where no direct train service is available.

By car, León which is 208 miles northwest of Madrid, is reached by taking the N-VI northwest to Benavente, followed by the N-630 north to León.

PRACTICALITIES:

Be aware when planning your tour that of the four places of interest that are open to visitors, two museums, those of San Isidro and León, are closed on Monday. Its geographical location in the northern sector of the country, and just south of the Cantabrian mountain range, blesses León with a cooler summer climate than most other Spanish cities. It is, however, decidedly cold during the winter months.

The **Dialing Code** is 987. The tourist office **Oficina de Información de**

Turismo, ☎ 23-70-82 or fax 27-33-91, Plaza de Regla, 3, located directly across from the main door of the Cathedral, is open Monday to Friday from 9 a.m. to 2 p.m. and 4 p.m. to 5:30 p.m.; and Saturday from 10 a.m. to 3 p.m. León has a **population** of 137,000 and is the capital of the province of the same name, one of nine belonging to the autonomous region of **Castilla y León.**

ACCOMMODATION:

The **Parador Hotel San Marcos ***** GL,** ☎ 23-73-00 or fax 23-34-58, Plaza de San Marcos, 7, is without doubt the pride of León. This site was occupied beginning in the 12th century by a church/hospice for pilgrims to Santiago, which was demolished in the 16th century when the Catholic Monarchs decided to replace them with an architectural jewel of a monastery. Its church, completed on June 3, 1541, with palatial tower supports at either end of an elongated Plateresque façade, is among the most impressive examples from the Spanish Renaissance period. Today, the church, a small museum, and this most impressive of paradors share the San Marcos and are connected by a majestic patio. In this hotel, guests may experience the elegance of that era and enjoy all modern conveniences. $$$

The **Hotel Alfonso V ****,** ☎ 22-09-00 or fax 22-12-44, Padre Isla, 1, is a modern hotel in a central position overlooking the towering fountain of the Plaza de Santo Domingo. Opened in 1993, it has 62 rooms each with air conditioning, color TV and a private safe. $$

The **Hotel Residencia Quindos **,** ☎ 23-62-00 or fax 24- 22-01, Avenida José Antonio, 24, is found close to the San Marcos, about 15 minutes walk from the Cathedral. An ordinary exterior belies a modern avant-garde style and ambiance inside. $

The **Hotel Residencia París **,** ☎ 23-88-00 or fax 27-15- 72, Calle Generalísimo Franco, 18, (formerly the Marquis de Villasindas' palace) is located in the Monumental Zone, close to the Cathedral. Enter through a traditional stone arch, emblazoned with a coat of arms, to a surprisingly modern interior with facilities that include a restaurant, cafeteria and disco. $

The **Hostal Residencia Don Suero **,** ☎ 23-06-00, Avenida Suero de Quiñones, 15, is on a relatively bland street, halfway between San Marcos and the Monumental Zone, but the rooms are comfortable and it is a good value. $

The **Hostal Residencia Covadonga *,** ☎ 22-26-01, Avenida de Palencia, 2, is a small, and quite basic, hostal just around the corner from the railway station. $

FOOD AND DRINK:

Restaurante El Figón de Aníbal (Avenida Caboalles, 43), specializes in Trout *(Trucha)* and Pheasant *(Faisán)* with potatoes. This will invariably be busy so call ahead to book a table. ☎ 58-00-75. $$

Restaurante Ranch Chico (Plaza de San Martín, 7), is one of many restaurants in the traditional Barrio Húmedo district. Its speciality is Oxtail Stews. ☎ 25-60-47. $

Restaurante La Posada (Calle de la Rúa, 33), serves up Old World ambiance to complement typical Leónese dishes. ☎ 25-82-66. $

Restaurante El Llagar (Calle Julio del Campo, 10), is found in the new part of town close to the Plaza de Calvo Sotelo. Modern in style, it specializes in Shellfish *(Marisqueria)* and is also a Cider House *(Sidrería)*. ☎ 22-51-19. $

SUGGESTED TOUR:
Numbers in parentheses correspond to numbers on the map.

Start at the **Plaza de Santa Domingo** (1), which is on the edge of the **Old Town** *(Zona Monumental)* and is dominated by a large fountain that sprays water high into the air, and the rather run-down, but still elegant, tower of the Iglesia de San Marcelo. Just past there, along Calle del Generalísimo Franco, is the *Plaza de San Marcelo,* graced by an unusual mix of buildings. On the other side of Franco, in the tiny Plaza de Botines, is what is probably the strangest structure in León, the late-19th-century **Casa de Botines** (2). Although a long way from Catalonia, the modern neo-Gothic-style building has enough oddity about it to be, unmistakably, the work of Gaudí (see pages 92-94). It is particularly idiosyncratic when measured against its next-door neighbor.

With its clean, straight lines, elegant towers, and a main façade with a second story gallery adorned by elaborate gargoyles, the **Guzmán Palace** *(Palacio de los Guzmánes)* (3) dates from 1571. This ancestral home of the Guzmán family is the most glorious palace in the city. Nowadays it's the home of the Provincial Council and only the wonderful two-level colonnaded patio, with a glassed-in and marvelously sculpted second level, can be viewed. Back across in the San Marcelo plaza is a structure of more sober lines. The **House of la Poridad** *(Casa de la Poridad),* on which construction was begun in 1584, is considered to be the most beautiful work of Juan de Ribero Rada. It is now the **Town Hall** *(Ayuntamiento).*

Immediately across from the Town Hall take the very short Calle Teatro and then an almost immediate right along Calle de la Rúa. This is the beginning of a interesting area of small streets and narrow lanes but, for the moment, follow Rúa to its end, the Plaza de la Concepción. There is a convent, of the same name, here that can be visited if so wished, but most people will be attracted by the tower of an old church just to the left of the fork in the road. This is the Romanesque 12th-century, although later remodelled, **St. Mary of the Road Church** *(Iglesia de Santa María del Camino)* (4). Unfortunately, this fascinating church, also known as **of the Grain** *(del Grano),* that was once on the pilgrims route to Santiago, has no official opening hours but it is still worthy of a visit. To the side, in Calle Capilla, is a statue of a lion on a plinth and, at its end behind the church, is the most unusual and rustic plazas to be seen in any major city in Spain.

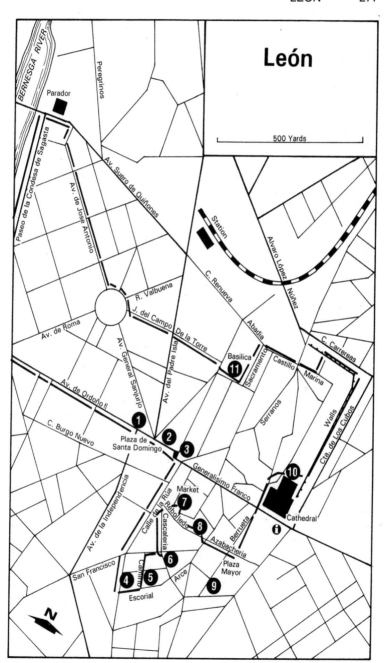

León

500 Yards

The **Plaza de Santa María del Camino** (5) has rough, cobblestoned streets that surround just two trees and an intriguing fountain, the centerpiece of which is a Doric column supported by two angels. Don't hesitate to sample the water, it is fresh and cool. The buildings around the plaza are not without contrast either. A Benedictine nuns' convent with a huge, narrow tower topped by the inevitable stork's nest and two, very different and old, colonnaded houses; one with wooden, and the other brick, columns.

To the side of these, the Calle Juan II leads to the larger Fernández Cadórniga where, immediately in front, are a series of now decrepit, but obviously once grand palaces that were home to the Quiñones de Sena y de Luna. A right turn here leads up to the *Plaza Don Gutierre,* nowadays a quiet place but, from the grace of the surrounding buildings, obviously one that has seen more splendid days. Up the steps and to the right is the façade, which boasts a splendid coat of arms, of the **Don Gutierre Palace** *(Palacio de Don Gutierre)* (6). Something though, perhaps the lines of washing hung out to dry, doesn't quite look right; and on closer inspection it'll be seen that this once-proud building is now a hovel that houses some of the city's gypsies *(gitanos).* How times change; but at least in its dying years some people are pleased to call it home, if not a palace.

On the other side of the plaza stop, perhaps, at the *Bodegas Manchegos,* a traditional old wine cellar, before departing via Cascalería, a nonentity of a street that, fortunately, soon meets with a much more interesting one. The Conde de Rebolledo is one of those narrow shopping lanes that has its origins down off the previously visited Calle de la Rúa. Take it up the hill, and a left into the Plaza del Conde Luna, home of the **Food Market** *(Mercado)* (7), throws up a colorful scene indeed. The four sides around the market are home not only to stall holders selling the most bizarre bazaar; you name it and it can be bought, anything from women's stockings, freshly killed rabbits and pheasants, live pigeons and flowers, but also ancient buildings as well.

In truth, the **Palace of the Counts of Luna**, the hereditary title of the first born of the Quiñones family, looks rather rundown, but don't be fooled. It is an architectural jewel. Home to the most prominent family of León during the Middle Ages and Renaissance periods it has, among other things, a 14th-century Gothic Porch and a 16th-century tower. In the corner diagonally opposite is the ruins of the 10th-century monastery of **San Salvador del Palat del Rey** (8). It seems strange looking at it today that, once, it was the Pantheon of the Kings before the construction of *San Isidro,* which will be visited later. Truly another example of faded grandeur.

Circumnavigate back around the plaza and leave as you entered, then turn left into Azabachería which, in fact, is a continuance of Rebolledo. The pungent smell, that will either attract you or send you a little faster up and around the Travesia de Carnicerías to the Plaza de San Martín, emanates from a wonderful shop selling mainly cheese—the Don Queso. The buildings around this elongated plaza are deceptive to the untrained eye. The boarded-up windows on the upper two floors on one side actually belongs to the acclaimed late-16th-century **House of the Butcher Shops**.

Take a left, on the side that you entered from, and Plegaria passes a small chapel built into the wall of the Iglesia San Martín before ending in the historic *Plaza Mayor*. The main building here, immediately to your right, is the hugely impressive, and sleekly elegant, **Consistorio** (9). The two towers at each end are topped by strangely shaped spires, and a small central clock tower overlooks a façade bedecked by a double level of metal grille balconies running its entire length. It dates from the late 17th century, is similar in style to others of its kind in Madrid, Segovia, and Valladolid and, from these vantage points, the town councillors, their families and friends had a grandstand view of the bullfights and other public events in the square below. The other sides are somewhat ramshackle and disheveled but, nevertheless, not lacking in charm and the center is home to yet another colorful market.

Leave the Plaza Mayor by the corner closest to the one you entered it by, and Calle Mariano Dominguez Berrueta will lead back up to Generalísimo Franco, the Plaza de Regla and the magnificent *****Cathedral** *(Catedral)* (10), ☎ 87-57-00. One of the most famous in Spain, and visible from most parts of the city, this was built between the 13th and 14th centuries and is Gothic in style. Before entering, the **Door of Our White Lady** on the western portico needs to be studied carefully. Inside, its impressiveness is enhanced by the comparative lack of elaborateness. The numerous stained-glass windows are beautiful indeed, and to see the colorful reflections in their best light it is preferable to visit, if possible, at different times of the day. Note also the many ancient sepulchers, particularly the ornate one holding the remains of King Ordoño II. *It is open for visits from 8:30 a.m. to 2 p.m. and 4 p.m. to 7:30 p.m.* The **Cathedral Museum** *(Museo Catedralicio)*, really deserves a visit also, and is housed in several rooms around the distinctive cloister. *Open July to September, Monday to Friday 9:30 a.m. to 1:30 p.m. and 4 p.m. to 7 p.m., and Saturday it closes one-half an hour earlier. The rest of the year it opens Monday to Friday 9:30 a.m. to 1:30 p.m. and 4 p.m. to 6:30 p.m., and Saturday 9:30 a.m. to 1 p.m. Entrance for the museum 600 ptas (EUR 3.61).*

A right out of the Cathedral, followed by another quick right into Cardenal Landázuri, will follow the outside walls of the cloister where, at their end, a tiny street, Cien Doncellas, leads to steps down to the Avenida de los Cubos. Walk to the left and follow the walls around. Antique shops on the right face unusual round towers, some of which have houses built in, protruding from the wall. Around the corner Carreras has plainer stretches of the wall but, before long, the **Castle Door** *(Puerta Castillo)*, an archway topped by a statue of Don Pelayo, is the entrance back into the Old Town. Before passing through, note the water fountain outside where people still fill bottles to take home.

The next stop, the *****Basilica of St Isidro** *(Basílica de San Isidro)* (11), ☎ 22-96-08, is reached by taking Santa Marina to the right and passing through the Plazas Puerta Castillo and Santo Marino before taking a left into Sacramento, which ends in the charming Plaza de San Isidro. The façade of San Isidro, a Romanesque jewel, although not grand in size, is varied and pleasing and the horseman sitting grandly atop the finely sculptured main door is that of St. Isidro himself. The original church, commissioned by Ferdinand I, was consecrated in December, 1063. It was intended to be a Royal Pantheon and the last resting place of St. Isidro himself, whose remains were brought north from Seville to avoid their being captured by the Moors. The **San Isidro Museum** *(Museo de San Isidro)* has two parts. On the lower level is the Pantheon itself, which has a series of beautiful frescoes—depicting Gospel and other scenes—on its ceilings, numerous sepulchers and a plain, if large, cloister. Upstairs, in the Chapter Treasury Room, are any number of notable exhibits. The most important of these are the **Chalice of Doña Urraca**, reportedly donated to the basilica on the day of its consecration; a chest, dating from the same year, holding the remains of St. Isidro; and the **Banner of Baeza** which, according to legend, was actually woven by the women of León on the battlefield where Alfonso VII defeated the Moors. *Open July and August Monday to Saturday from 9 a.m. to 2 p.m. and 3 p.m. to 8 p.m., and closed Sunday and holiday afternoons. The rest of the year from 10 a.m. to 1:30 p.m. and 4 p.m. to 6:30 p.m., closed Monday and Sunday afternoon. Entrance 400 ptas (EUR 2.40), free Thursday afternoon.*

Before leaving this area spend some time admiring the plaza. Besides an attractive fountain, to the right of the basilica, there is a small, two-level house embellished with a coat-of-arms and with a column in front of it honoring Gemina 7, the Roman legion that founded León. Before reaching the next destination it is necessary to pass through long, and mostly uninteresting, stretches of the modern city. Using the **Cock's Tower** (no, this is not a spelling mistake, one glance at the summit will explain the name) as a landmark, head down to the busy Ramón y Cajal. Some more of those unusual round towers *(Cubos)*, are embedded in the walls to the right and the first street opposite them, Calle de la Torre transforms into the Calle de Julio del Campo before ending in the pretty Plaza de Calvo Sotelo. Finally, a walk of four blocks along Avenida José Antonio, ninety degrees to the right, will end in the Plaza de San Marcos, and the magnificently crafted façade facing you will prove the longish walk worthwhile. The *****Hostal de San Marcos** has been described under the Accommodation section as it is the home of the parador, and it is also where the small, just one-roomed, **León Museum** *(Museo de León)* resides. *It can be visited May to September daily 10 a.m. to 2 p.m. and 5 p.m. to 8:30 p.m.; and the rest of the year from 10 a.m. to 2 p.m. and 4:30 p.m. to 8 p.m. It is closed on Monday and Sunday and holiday afternoons. Entrance 200 ptas (EUR 1.20), free on Sunday and holidays.*

Some may want to cross over the river by using the ancient **Roman Bridge** *(Puente Romano)*, and visit the relaxing Parque Quevedo on the other side. Others will be content to wander along by the side of the River Bernesga on the Paseo de la Condesa de Sagasta. Tree-lined, with attractive gardens, children's playgrounds, fountains, modern statues and banks leading down to the river, this ends at the Glorieta de Guzmán el Bueno, where its namesake statue is ringed by fountains, and is a pleasant way to be reintroduced to the modern town. From there it is just a short walk up the busy shopping street of Ordoño II, noticing the classical façade of the Banco de Santander building along the way, to end the trip back in the Plaza de Santo Domingo.

Trip 39

Málaga

Málaga, in a prime location on the Mediterranean coast, was an important trading port for the Phoenicians, the Greeks, the Carthaginians, and the Romans, long before the marauding Moors overran the Visigoths here in 712. While under Arab rule the city was controlled at first by the Caliphate of Córdoba and, following its demise early in the 11th century, by the Kingdom of Granada. Málaga was one of the last cities in Spain to be re-conquered, by the Catholic Monarchs in 1487, just five years before they entered Granada itself.

Prehistoric caves nearby give some indication as to the city's very long and rich past but, these days, Málaga's claim to fame is its position as International gateway to the world-famous Costa del Sol. Many millions of visitors jam the beaches between Málaga and Gibraltar throughout the summer, but the lesser known, and prettier, stretch of coastline to the east, towards Almería, is much more inviting. And, though most just pass blithely through on their way to the beaches, those that bother to delve beneath the surface will find Málaga to be worthy of further investigation. For many, the easy rhythm of life here is the greatest attraction. Granted major tourist attractions are few, and of those that there are the most intriguing are not always the most obvious.

One note of warning, however. Petty crime and muggings are not uncommon here; and unsuspecting, casual, tourists may become easy victims. It is, in fact, both comforting and disconcerting that the main police station employs full time interpreters.

GETTING THERE:

Trains arrive in Málaga, on the main line from Madrid, via Córdoba; and, on local lines, via Bobadilla, from Algeciras, Córdoba, Granada, and Seville. Note that many of these services require a change at Bobadilla.

Buses are best used when traveling between Málaga and Algeciras, Cádiz, Granada and, in most instances, Seville.

By car, Málaga, nearly 350 miles due south of Madrid, is reached by taking the N-IV to its junction with Bailén, then following N-323 south to Granada, via Jaén, and the N-342 west to just past Loja before heading south again on the N-321 to Málaga. It is also served by the N-340 coastal highway, which runs between Cádiz and Barcelona.

By air, Málaga's airport, constructed for Expo'92, receives scheduled flights from North America, via Madrid; from many other European destinations; and from major Spanish cities. It is also the arrival point for charter flights from all over Europe.

PRACTICALITIES:

When planning an itinerary, schedule your visit to this city on a day other than Monday, when many of the attractions are closed. The **Dialing Code** is 95. Despite Málaga's proximity to the Costa del Sol, accommodation is relatively plentiful for most of the year. There are, however, two notable exceptions; the **Easter Week** *(Semana Santa)* celebrations, and the ten days or so of the city's fair, the *(Fería de Agosto)*, which begins around August 10 every year.

There are three **tourist offices** in Málaga. Two of them belong to the **Junta de Andalucía, Oficina de Turismo,** ☎ 221-34-45 or fax 222-94-21, Pasaje de Chinitas, 4, (Just off the Plaza de la Constitución, on the Calle Larios side) or at the International Terminal at the airport ☎ 224-00-00, Ext. 2098. Hours are Monday to Friday 9 a.m. to 2 p.m., and Saturday 9 a.m. to 1 p.m. The other, the **Oficina Municipal de Turismo,** ☎ 235-00-61, Ext. 260, is located at the Bus Station *(Estación de Autobuses)*. Málaga has a **population** of about 600,000 and is the capital of the province of the same name, one of eight belonging to the autonomous region of **Andalucía**.

ACCOMMODATION:

The **Parador Málaga-Gibralfaro** ****, ☎ 222-19-02 or fax 222-19-04, Castillo Gibralfaro, s/n, is a delightfully styled hotel set high upon a hill, with panoramic views over the city, the bullring and the Mediterranean. Guests will enjoy the high level of facilities and service typical of the parador chain. $$

The **Hotel NH Málaga** ****, ☎ 207-13-23, Avda. Rio Guadalmedina, s/n, has a superb location just on the edge of the old town. Having only just opened in 1999 all the facilities are impressive and modern, it also has pleasing public areas and, importantly, private parking. $$

The **Hotel Residencia Málaga Palacio** ****, ☎ 221- 51-85 or fax 221-51-85, Cortina del Muelle, 1, has a prestigious position, between the bottom of the Paseo del Parque and the town center. It is housed in an imposing building, and has all modern comforts and a rooftop bar. $$

The **Hotel Residencia Don Curro** ***, ☎ 222-72-00 or fax 221-59-46, Sancha de Lara, 7, in the city center near the junction of the Marqués de Lario and Alameda Principal, has over 100 comfortable and well appointed rooms. $$

Note: Though accommodation here is plentiful, hotels are not. The style of accommodation weighs heavily in favor of numerous hostals and pensións, many of which are located in the narrow streets off the bottom of Marqué de Larios, or around the train station. These are, as a general rule, inexpensive and rather basic. In truth, they are all of like genre and there is not much to recommend one over another.

FOOD AND DRINK:

As would be expected, given Málaga's position on the Mediterranean, seafood and, in particular, shellfish, is the cuisine of choice. This may be enjoyed in any number of exquisite restaurants or, more casually, in one of the small bars alongside the Alameda Principal—close to Marqués de Lario. In the latter, try shrimps *(gambas)*, grilled in garlic and with a little lemon juice added. These are a real delight. And, don't forget to behave like a *Malagueño;* throw the shells on the floor. Málaga also has its own unique variety of sweet wine *(dulce)*, which is widely acclaimed, though it won't be to everyone's taste.

Parador Málaga-Gibralfaro (Castillo Gibralfaro, s/n), offers not one, but two restaurants—each with views that are among the most panoramic in town. Enjoy delightful seafood cuisine and exemplary service either indoors, surrounded by large picture windows or, in the usually cooperative weather, on the terrace. ☎ 222-19-02 or fax 222-19-04. $$$

Restaurante Antonio Martín (Paseo Marítimo, s/n), is a perpetual favorite in Málaga. Its prime beachfront location, not far from the bullring, is the first hint that the house speciality is seafood. ☎ 222-21-13. $$$

Bar Orellana (Moreno Monroy, 5), is one of the smallest bars in Málaga, but also the most popular, especially at weekends. The reasons are simple: a great atmosphere and an absolutely amazing array of *tapas.* Certainly, a place not to be missed. ☎ 222-30-12. $

SUGGESTED TOUR:
Numbers in parentheses correspond to numbers on the map.

Begin the tour at the **Plaza de la Marina** (1) which, as the name implies, is just outside the impressive gates of the docks *(Estación Marítima).* You will certainly notice the ferry boats (to Ibiza), liners, and huge yachts moored in the harbor. The focal point, though, is in the plaza itself, where a rather large fountain propels walls of water upwards to imposing heights. This is particularly attractive at night, when floodlit. Looking away from the harbor, turn left and head in the direction of the statue of the Marqués de Larios. You will come to realize, very quickly, that the Larios name figures prominently in this area. The city's predominant shopping street, which runs at a tangent to the statue, and bottles of gin and other spirits all carry it. Cross Alameda Principal, moving away from the harbor, and note the many small restaurants and bars scattered along this street as well as the side streets radiating from it. These may not look like much, but they are famous. Return here, preferably at night, but perhaps even at lunchtime, to sit at one of the outdoor tables and, if you can manage not to be too pestered by the persistence of the local beggars, enjoy a selection (or more) from among the delicious shrimp *(gambas)* dishes on offer.

Continue on a few blocks farther, then turn right at Torregorda. Immediately ahead, you will see the square metal configuration which houses the food market **Mercado Central** (2). Either pass through it, or skirt around to the left, and follow Plaza Arriola to the Pasillo Santa Isabel along the, often mostly dry, river bed. A word to the wise: Most will prefer to avoid this market area after dark, when it transforms into a rather seedy "Red Light" district. It's in the Pasillo, though, that you will find, at number

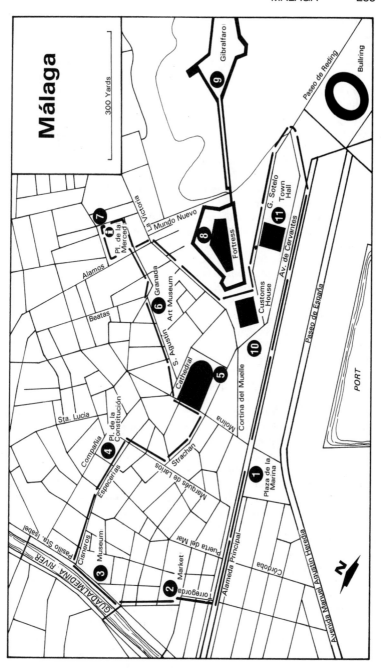

Málaga

10, one of the most unusual and charming museums you are ever likely to see. The beautiful old 17th-century house, home to the *Museum of Popular Arts* (Museo de Artes Populares) (3), ☎ 221-71-37 or www.sopde.es/malaga/museo13.html, is without doubt incongruous with its immediate surroundings. Inside, around a patio full of huge plants, are rooms containing an eclectic cross section of items of all things pertinent to life in Málaga for generations past. Look for, among other delights, crafts, carriages, paintings, wine making utensils, and even a fishing boat—to name a few. A visit here truly will enhance your understanding of the city and really should not be missed. *Opening hours are Tuesday to Saturday 10 a.m. to 12:30 p.m. and 4 p.m. to 7 p.m., and Sunday 10 a.m. to 1 p.m. Entrance 200 ptas (EUR 1.20).*

Walking away from the Mediterranean, turn right into Cisneros and follow first this, then Especerías through a shopping district to the **Plaza de la Constitución** (4). A fountain decorates the center of this plaza as well but, as with many places in Málaga, it is at its best when dressed with the vibrantly colored decorations and temporary bars of the August Fair. Next, stroll down Marqués de Lario, past a mix of upmarket stores, bars, and quaint little grocery shops, until you reach Strachan, where a left will lead you on to the **Cathedral** (Catedral) (5), ☎ 221-59-17. Erected between the 16th and 18th centuries, construction on the large, and rather unattractive, façade seems to have been suspended, leaving one tower still unfinished. The expansive interior is rather formal and, with the exception of some fine stained-glass windows, there is not much of note. *Open Monday to Saturday 10 a.m. to 12:45 p.m. and 4 p.m. to 5:30 p.m.*

Going around behind the Cathedral follow San Agustín, where you will find, at number 8, its most distinguished occupant, the building, interesting in its own right, has two patios, dates from the 16th century and, in late 1999, was still in the process of being converted into the new **Picasso Museum** (6). Continue from this point along Granada, and past the *Iglesia de Santiago,* to the **Plaza de la Merced**. On first impression, the most visible point of interest is the *Monumento Torrijos,* dominating the center, but a house in the far corner, at number 14, draws the most visitors here. The birthplace of Pablo Picasso in 1881, today the **Picasso Foundation** (Fundación Pablo Ruiz Picasso) (7), ☎ 221-50-05, doubles as a research center and small museum. *Visit Monday to Saturday 11 a.m. to 2 p.m. and 5 p.m. to 8 p.m., and Sunday 10 a.m. to 2 p.m.*

Leave the plaza, via the corner opposite Picasso's house, and follow Alcazabilla down to a paradoxical collection of sights. Near the bottom you will catch a glimpse of an old Roman theater, which may be seen from a closer perspective farther on where it joins as one of a trio of attractions: the **Fortress**, **Roman Theater**, and **Archaeological Museum** (Alcazaba, Teatro Romano y Museo Arqueológico) (8), ☎ 222-04-43. In truth, the Roman Theater is not overly impressive but the fortress, which dates from the 11th century and has recently undergone an extensive renovation, is architecturally arresting and offers lovely views out over the harbor and the Mediterranean. Some of its rooms are utilized by the museum which features, among others, exhibits from the Neolithic, Eneolithic, and Roman eras. *In late 1999 the Theatre was under renovation, the Fortress opened Tuesday to Friday 9:30 a.m. to 1:30 p.m. and 4 p.m. to 7 p.m., Saturday 10 a.m. to 1 p.m., and Sunday and holidays from 10 a.m. to 2 p.m.; and the museum opened daily 9:30 a.m. to 7 p.m.*

Behind this complex, and high up on a hill, with amazing views of the city, the surrounding countryside and the Mediterranean, is the **Gibralfaro** (9). This was originally a Phoenician fortification, but you will also find here the remains of a Moorish castle. There is a catch, however. To say the walk up, and even down, the narrow pathway is arduous is a vast understatement. Those determined to visit are advised to take a taxi, at the least for the trip up. If the journey exhausts you, the parador is closeby. Another tip, if you happen to be visiting on a day when a bullfight *(corrida)* is being held, you will have a "free" birds-eye view of the action in the plaza below.

If you opt to forego this treat, then leave the Alcazaba by turning left onto Alcazabilla. Soon you will be met by the memorable façade of the 18th-century **Customs House** *(Aduana)* (10), where another left will bring you out to the broad, park-lined, avenue that stretches from the Plaza de la Marina to the fountain, the *Fuente Genovesa,* at its other end, close to the bullring. This is a charming area indeed. The Spanish Renaissance-style **Town Hall** *(Ayuntamiento)* (11) presides over a series of delightful parks where duck-filled ponds, fountains, and statues, nestled in the shade of towering palms, are dotted with quaint little bars. Have a seat at the one that takes your fancy and refresh yourself before wandering back down to the Plaza de la Marina to end the tour.

Trip 40

Ronda

Ronda, and its immediate environs, has a long and fascinating history. Prehistoric relics such as the famous wall-paintings of the *Cueva de la Pileta* and the *Dolmen de Chopo*, are evidence of the earliest eras. Ancient Iberians followed them, but it was the Romans who established a headquarters here. The main attraction was the strange geographical features; a high promontory divided into two by a huge gorge now known as *El Tajo*. This, of course, made the place a natural fortress, a fact that didn't go unnoticed after the Moorish invasion of 711. Ronda, then known as *Madinat Runda,* soon became one of the their most important towns in the newly conquered Spain. Indeed, beautiful examples of their creations are still to be seen around town. In the very early 11th century Abu Nur displaced the then government, making Ronda an emirate in the process. Moorish rule lasted much longer here than many places, Sevilla was retaken some 200 years earlier, and it was one of the last bastions of the Kingdom of Granada when, in 1485, it was subjected to a seven-day siege by the forces, some 12,000 mounted and 25,000 on foot, of the Catholic Monarchs.

It finally succumbed on the 24th May of that year, and was soon given a City Council with the same rights as those in Sevilla and Toledo. By the 18th century the old town, *La Ciudad,* was becoming too small, and the city needed to expand. And after an earlier bridge had collapsed a new one, the *Puente Nuevo,* was built over the El Tajo connecting La Ciudad with the new quarter of town known as *El Mercadillo.* Taking around forty years to construct, it is now the symbol of the city. In the same era, in 1784 in fact, Ronda's emblamatic, neoclassical style, Plaza de Toros, was also built in El Mercadillo. And the *Escuela Rondeña,* bullfighting school, was founded by Pedro Romero, the legendary matador who is credited with creating the rules for the modern bullfight. Not long after the city was largely destroyed by Napoleon's forces during the Wars of Independence and, of course, gained notoriety by the vivid descriptions in Ernest Hemingway's "For Whom The Bell Tolls." Set in the Spanish Civil War, it details how priests, still alive, were thrown off the Puente Nuevo by the Republican forces.

These days, however, Ronda is far less turbulent but no less dramatic, and the town attracts many visitors anxious to see its unique attractions.

GETTING THERE:
Trains are most probably the best way of getting to Ronda given the

mountainous terrain. Ronda is on the line that carries long distance trains between Madrid and Algeciras. However, travelers going from other Andalucian cities such as Córdoba, Granada, Málaga and Sevilla will have to take a local service and these, more often than not, call for a change at Bobadilla, an important junction.

Buses are best used by those based on the Costa del Sol, nearby Marbella and Estepona.

By car, the only direct and straightforward road is the new one from San Pedro de Alcantara on the coast. Most all other roads make for hard going through the mountains.

PRACTICALITIES:

The **Dialing Code** is 95. The **Oficina de Turismo**, ☎ 287-12-72, Plaza de España, 1, is open Monday to Friday 9 a.m. to 7 p.m., and Saturday, Sunday and holidays 10 a.m. to 2 p.m. Ronda is in the province of Málaga, on of eight belonging to the autonomous region of **Andalucía**.

ACCOMMODATION:

The **Hotel Reina Victoria** ****, ☎ 287-12-40, fax 287-10-65 or e-mail reinavictoriaronda@husa.es, dates from 1906, has its own extensive gardens and an English ambiance. Expect 90 rooms, all renovated to include modern facilities and panoramic views over the Serrania de Ronda. $$

The **Hotel-Restaurant Alavera de los Baños**, ☎ and fax 287-91-43 or e-mail alavera@ctv.es, Hoyo San Miguel, s/n, is found in the San Miguel quarter under the eastern city walls and close to the Arab baths. Which is how it came by its name "by the baths". $

The **Hotel San Gabriel** ***, ☎ 219-03-92, fax 219-01-17 or e-mail sangabriel@ronda.net, is a charming small hotel that was opened in late December 1998. It is also the only one located in the historical and artistic area of Ronda. A nice blend of history and modern amenities. $

FOOD AND DRINK:

Restaurante Pedro Romero (Virgen de la Paz, 18), has a name that is symbolic of the city, and is considered one of the most typical restaurants in Ronda. Found next to the Post Office, it has won many awards, specializes in Spanish wines and is somewhat of a small Bullfighting museum in its own right. ☎ 287-11-10 or fax 287-10-61. $$

Restaurante Doña Pepe (Plaza del Socorro, 10), is found just a block or so away from the Plaza de Toros, in a very typical Rondeña style house/palace. Expect typical Andalucian and regional cuisine and a great selection of wines. ☎ 287-47-77 or fax 287-53-80. $$

SUGGESTED TOUR:

As most visitors will be arriving by train the **Railroad Station** *(Estación de Ferrocarril)* (1) , even though it is some distance from the historical quarter, is the best place to start. A right out of there, onto Avenida de

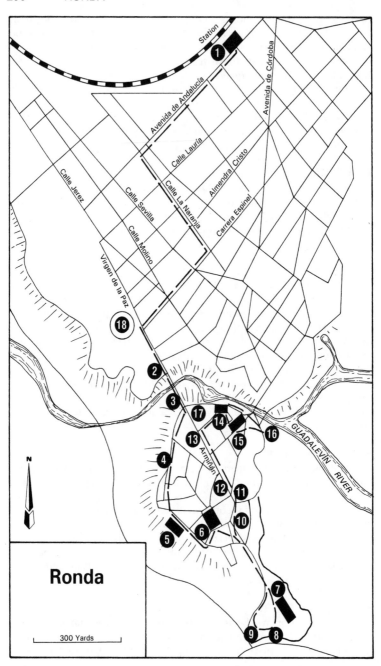

Ronda

300 Yards

Andalucía, leads to the Plaza Concepción García Redondo, home of the bus station. The next stretch or four or five blocks, left along La Naranja, is rather bland, but that soon changes when turning into Espinel, one of Ronda's main shopping streets. At the bottom of this busy street the famous *Plaza de Toros* looms to the right, but leave that for later and make a left towards the **Plaza de España** (2) home to both the Oficina de Turismo and the impressive façade of the parador hotel.

Ronda is built upon an impressive promontory, which made it difficult for the Christian armies to reconquer it, and this, itself, is cut into two parts by a hugely deep gorge. Known as *The Cliff *(El Tajo)* (3) this, in itself, and the **New Bridge** *(Puente Nuevo)* that crosses it, have become symblomatic with Ronda. Notwithstanding the fact that it was largely developed in the 18th century, this side of Ronda is known as **El Mercadillo**. To get a better view of both El Tajo and the **Medieval Quarter** *(El Ciudad)* across the gorge, take a walk around the parador to the viewpoint *(mirador)*, that will also give you a better perspective of this geographical oddity. Time, now, to cross the bridge, constructed entirely of stone between 1751 and 1793, and infamous for the fact that Roman Catholic clergy were thrown from it, still alive, during the Spanish Civil War. Few will resist the opportunity to peer over the railings at the waters of the Guadalevín river flowing 98 meters (321.5 ft) below. Interestingly, the middle of the bridge used to hold a small prison *(carcel)*. It is intriguing, also, to note the houses clinging to the sides of the cliff; reminiscent, indeed, of the Casas Colgadas in Cuenca.

Once across the bridge make a right turning into Tenorio and there, at number 20, is the **Don Juan Bosco House** *(Casa de Don Juan)* (4), ☎ 287-16-83. This is a really distinguished old house filled with a beautiful array of furniture, antiques and books, and has a pretty terrace with a fountain that allows tremendous views over the Serrania de Ronda. *Open daily 9 a.m. to 7 p.m., entrance 100 ptas (EUR .60)*. Continuing along Tenorio you will soon come to the Plaza del Campillo, an attractive little square with another mirador with great views. After this a small lane leads around to one of the most distinguished houses in Ronda. The **Mondragon Palace** *(Palacio de Mondragon)* (5), ☎ 287-84-50, was originally built in 1314 by Abomelic, the Moorish King of Ronda. Since then, obviously having undergone transformations, it has been the home of kings and governors and, these days, serves the less glamorous role of host to the city's **Municipal Museum**. *Open Monday to Friday 10 a.m. to 7 p.m., and Saturday, Sunday and holidays 10 a.m. to 3 p.m. Entrance 250 ptas (EUR 1.50)*.

The next stop, just a little further around Manuel Montero, is the very attractive, and multi-faceted, *Plaza Duquesa de Parcent*. At its center is a pleasing small park, and it is surrounded by an eclectically interesting array of buildings. Small palaces adorned with their coats-of-arms; a tiny church; the elongated, classical lines of the **Town Hall** *(Ayuntamiento)* and, dominating, the historic **Santa Maria La Mayor Church** *(Iglesia Santa María La Mayor)* (6), ☎ 287-22-46. Originally built as Ronda's main mosque in the

13th century, it was consecrated after the reconquest. However, considered too small, it was replaced by this church that was constructed in two phases. The first, Gothic in style, in the late 15th to early 16th centuries, and a later extension after the earthquake of 1580, which lasted until the 18th century. Signs of the mosque still exist inside in the form of the *mihrab,* and the minaret is now the bell tower. *Open daily 10 a.m. to 7 p.m. Entrance 200 ptas (EUR 1.20).*

Leave the plaza on the street opposite from the church, Imágenes, which will lead you to three more attractions close by each other. First is the **Church of the Holy Spirit** *(Iglesia del Espiritu Santo)* (7). Sobre and austere, this was constructed by the order of Ferdinand the Catholic in 1505, the same year as the death of his wife, Queen Isabel. *Open daily 10 a.m. to 6 p.m., entrance 100 ptas (EUR .60).* Then, just past there, are two gates; the **Puerta de Almocabar** (8) and **Puerta de Carlos V** (9). The first was originally built in the 13th century, but has been completely restored since then and the latter dates from the 16th century and has the coat-of-arms of the House of Austria over the entranceway.

Return, now, back to the Plaza Duquesa and turn right at the street at the far end of the Town Hall and there, on the rather busier Armiñán, you will find the **Bandit Museum** *(Museo del Bandolero)* (10), ☎ 287-77-85. *Open daily 10 a.m. to 8 p.m., entrance 350 ptas (EUR 2.10).* However, this and the **Hunting Museum** *(Museo de Caza)* (11), ☎ 87-78-62, open the same hours but costing 200 ptas (EUR 1.20) admission, just up the street, may not be to everyone's taste. Continuing along Armiñán the next stop is the rather unusual **San Sebastian Minaret** *(Minaret de San Sebastián)* (12). This rather rundown-looking tower is thought to originate from the 13th century, when it was a small mosque. However, after the reconquest it was converted into a church of the name it retains to this day. Clearly, it has two influences; the lower section obviously Moorish instyle, while the upper part—as often is the case—formed the bell tower of the church. Another museum, and one with more attractions than the previous two, is next on the itinerary. The **Lara Art and Antique Museum** *(Museo Lara Arte & Antigüedades)* (13), Armiñán, 29. This has clock, weapons, scientific, romantic and archeological rooms as well as a few other collections, including popular art. *Open daily 10 a.m. to 8 p.m., entrance 500 ptas (EUR 3.01).*

Just past here, on the right, a tiny street, S. Antonio, leads down to the very curious **House of the Moorish King** *(Casa del Rel Moro)* (14). Actually, this consists of two, quite different, parts. Tradition has it that King Abomelic constructed what is known as **The Mine** *(La Mina)* as a defensive measure against attacks by the Christians. It actually consists of a zigzaging staircase of 365 steps cut into the rock and leading down to the river, enabling water to be carried back up in skin jugs *(zagues)* by a human slave chain. Various chambers were also being cut into the rock at the same time. The other aspect are **Forestier's Gardens**, constructed by the famous French landscaper, Jean Claude Nicolas Forestier in 1912, having been commissioned by the house's owner, the Duchess of Parcent. Forestier also claimed fame for his creations of the Parque María Luisa in Sevilla, in Montjüic in Barcelona and at the Líria Palace in Madrid. *Open daily 10 a.m. to 7 p.m., entrance 600 ptas (EUR 3.61).* A short distance farher down the street finds the handsome outline of the **Palace of the Marquis of Salvatierra** *(Palacio del Marqués de Salvatierra)* (15). Dating from the 18th century, this has a distinguished Baroque façade featuring a wonderful coat-of-arms and wrought-iron balconies in the traditional Ronda style.

By here, also, is a vantage point that offers panoramic vistas of the east side of Ronda, and the countryside under the walls. In the distance to the right, south, the tall and elegant features of the *Iglesia del Espiritu Santo* dominate above and beyond the walls. Immediately below, from south to north, are the *Puerta de Felipe V* built in 1742, the *Puente Arabe* and the Old Bridge dating from 1616. Just to the south of these are the **Arab Baths** *(Baños Arabes)* (16), ☎ 287-38-39. Built at the end of the 13th and beginning of the 14th centuries, these have three separate chambers and are extremely well preserved. *Open Tuesday 9:30 a.m. to 1:30 p.m. and 4 p.m. to 6 p.m., and Wednesday to Saturday 9 a.m. to 3:30 p.m. Entrance free.*

Time now to head back up the steep hill that is Santo Domingo, towards the *Puente Nuevo*. At the top is the **Convent of Santo Domingo** (17), of the Dominican Order, notable for its architecturally strange combination of Gothic, Renaissance and Mudejar styles. It is, also, one of two founded by the Catholic Monarchs here after the Reconquest in 1485. Later, in the 16th century, the Tribunal of the Inquisition had its headquarters here, and after the religious order gave up the building in 1836 it was utilized as a jail, barracks and market, amongst other things.

The last stop of the tour, the **Bullring* *(Plaza de Toros)* (18), ☎ 287-41-32, is found back across the bridge in the El Mercadillo quarter, just past the Plaza de España. Actually, this is not the oldest in Spain; there are others that were built earlier, but this is far and away the largest and most elegant of the early plazas. In fact, it was inaugurated in 1785, but a *corrida* held the previous year resulted in a partial collapse of the arena, killing ten spectators. Besides being of particular beauty in its architectural style, it is also considerably different from more modern plazas in its technical layout. And with a diameter of 66 meters (72 yards) it is one of the widest rings in the world. Francisco Romero, a Rondeña, is considered to be the originator of the modern rules of bullfighting in the 18th century, and another famous local family, the Ordonez's, were, and are, prominent matadors in the 20th and early 21st century. The museum here is of real interest, and on the the first weekend of September a *"Corrida Goyesca"* is traditionally held here, in which the participants dress in colorful Goyesque costumes. *Open daily 10 a.m. to 7 p.m., entrance 400 ptas (EUR 2.40).*

It is easy from here to cross into Calle Espinel, and retrace the route back to the train station.

Valladolid

Valladolid is more often that not overlooked by visitors to Spain. But this once-royal city, which for a time was also the country's capital, has an interesting mix of attractions, and visitors will certainly not be disappointed.

Home of the Castillian kings between the 12th and 17th centuries; it was here, in 1469, that Ferdinand wed Isabella, joining the kingdoms of Aragón, Catalonia, Naples, Castile, and León into a united Spain. Valladolid was the capital of the empire during the reigns of Felipe II and Felipe III; the birthplace of several kings; the last home of Christopher Columbus and, much later in 1809, it served as a headquarters for Napoleon.

This illustrious history has left the city, otherwise a bland modern sprawl, with a legacy of beautiful buildings and several small, but very interesting, museums.

GETTING THERE:

Trains serve Valladolid well. Although not a junction, the city's recently renovated Campo Grande station is on the fast InterCity train route serving Madrid and the French border at Irún/Hendaye. It is also on the Madrid-to-Santander and Madrid-to-León lines as well as the International route between Paris and Lisbon or Oporto.

Buses do not run nearly as frequently as trains to and from the other cities included in this guide.Therefore, bus travel is not recommended.

By car, Valladolid, an important road junction, is 120 miles northwest of Madrid and reached by the N-430, passing close to Segovia along the way. The N-620 runs northeast to Burgos and southwest to Salamanca; the N-122 runs east to Aranda de Duero and the N-601 runs north-west to León.

PRACTICALITIES:

It might just be feasible to make Valladolid a daytrip from either Madrid, Burgos, León or Salamanca. But, the reality is that, given train or bus timetables, and the opening hours of the monuments (most have long lunch times and are closed on Monday), a daytrip would not allow enough time to explore Valladolid with the thoroughness it deserves. If possible, therefore, I recommend making this city an overnight stop on your itinerary.

The **Dialing Code** is 983. The main **Tourist Office**, ☎ 34-40-13 or fax 35-

47-31, is at C/. Santiago, 19, by the Plaza de Zorrilla, and open Monday to Friday 10 a.m. to 2 p.m. and 5 p.m. to 8 p.m., and on Saturday between 9 a.m. and 2 p.m. Valladolid has a **population** of over 330,000 and is the capital of the province of the same name, one of nine belonging to the autonomous region of **Castilla y León**.

ACCOMMODATION:

The **Hotel Felipe IV ****, ☎ 30-70-00 or fax 30-86-87, Gamazo, 16, is a large, modern hotel with a private garage, that was completely renovated in 1992. It has a convenient location between the train station and the town center. $$

The **Hotel Lasa ****, ☎ 39-02-55 or fax 30-25-61, Acera de Recolotos, 21, across from the city center park, Campo Grande, has an elegant façade and a classical ambiance. $$

The **Hotel Mozart ****, ☎ 29-77-77 or fax 29-21-90, Menéndez Pelayo, 7, is located in the heart of the city, and housed in a beautiful late-19th century home that was totally remodeled in 1987. It has a lovely modern style, all modern conveniences and private parking. $$

The **Hotel Imperial ****, ☎ 33-03-00 or fax 33-08-13, Peso, 4, is in the main shopping center very close to the Plaza Mayor. There are 100 traditionally styled rooms, each with a private bath and color TV. $

The **Hostal Residencia Campo Grande ****, ☎ 30-15-60, Acera Recoletos, 12, has clean, basic rooms and a good location near to the train station. $

The **Hostal Residencia Paris ****, ☎ 37-06-25 or fax 35-83-01, Especeria, 2, is a very pleasant, middle ranking hostal. The 36 modern rooms offer full facilities, and public parking is just 50 meters away. $

FOOD AND DRINK:

Restaurante Santi (Calle Correos, 1), is located around the beautiful patio of a 16th-century Renaissance building, the *Posada El Cabalto de Troya*. Diners may eat on the terrace in summer, at which time there is also on offer a selection of six set-price meals for 2,500 ptas. ☎ 33-93-55 or fax 35-00-31. $$

Parrillo de San Lorenzo (Calle Pedro Niño at its corner with Calle San Lorenzo), is on the walking tour and could, actually, merit inclusion as a sight to see as well as a restaurant. International and Casteliana cuisine are served in this castle-like atmosphere, that features solid brick walls, knights in armor, majestic columns and numerous artifacts. ☎ 33-50-88. $$

Mesón Restaurante Asturiano *(Calle Pasión, 13)*, is a particular favorite of mine. In fact I wouldn't visit Valladolid without eating here. Exposed brick walls and wooden beamed ceilings complement the delicious home made cooking. Get here early, particularly on a Saturday night or Sunday lunchtime. ☎ 37-54-37. $$

Restaurante Portobello (Calle Marina Escobar, 5), found close to the House of Cervantes, is a seafood lover's delight. The large tank in the front window sets the tone, and port holes behind the bar clearly hold aquariums as well as wine and food. ☎ 30-95-31. $$

Bar/Restaurante Zamora (Correos 5-7), is a good place for a quick snack. One of the house specialities is *Patatas Bravas,* baked potatoes with a spicy sauce. ☎ 33-00-71. $

SUGGESTED TOUR:

Numbers in parentheses correspond to numbers on the map.

Start at the **Tourist Office** (1), which also happens to be on the point of the triangle that is formed by the *Campo Grande,* the city's lovely central park. This, the most attractive corner of the Campo Grande, is graced by the huge **Monument to the Alcantara Hunters** *(Monumento A Los Cazadores de Alcantara)* and a fountain. On either side are two impressive buildings, the **Academia de Caballeria** and the **Casa Mantilla,** which is just to the left of the tourist office. Before venturing on into the Old Town, take a leisurely stroll back through the Campo Grande, taking care not to disturb the geese floating gracefully on the pond. Soon you'll come to the massive edifice of the 18th-century **Royal College of the Agustinian Fathers** *(Real Colegio de los Padres Agustinos Filipinos)* (2). No doubt you will find this impressive, but the adjoining **Oriental Museum** *(Museo Oriental),* ☎ 30-68-00, whose collection is considered the best of its kind in Spain, is of more interest. Inaugurated on October 12, 1980, by the King and Queen of Spain, it has fourteen rooms. One is an introduction to the museum, nine are dedicated to Chinese art, and the remainder exhibit art from the Phillippines. *Open Monday to Saturday from 4 p.m. to 7 p.m., and on Sunday and holidays from 10 a.m. to 2 p.m. Entrance 300 ptas (EUR 1.80).*

Retrace your steps back through the Campo Grande and take Calle Maria de Molina, along the side of the tourist office. On first impression this is a typical shopping street, but once past the elaborately tiled **Lope de Vega Theater** *(Teatro Lope de Vega)* look for a colonnaded house, that meets you head on. This isn't your destination though; that's the rather plain-looking building to the left, but don't be fooled by the apparent blandness. Once inside the 18th-century **Convent of Saints Joaquin and Ana** *(Convento San Joaquin y Santa Ana)* (3), ☎ 35-76-72, you'll find a wonderful collection of important religious art, including a collection of Christ-child figures, extensive enough to fill six rooms. The unusual church has a large dome, wooden floor, numerous paintings including works by Goya, and an entirely separate room for the choir. Note the curious little wooden opening at the reception, this has a circular apparatus making it possible for the nuns to take in money and dispense tickets without appearing in person. *Open Monday to Thursday and Saturday, from 10:30 a.m. to 1 p.m. and 4 p.m. to 7 p.m., and on Sunday and holidays 10 a.m. to 1 p.m. Entrance 300 ptas (EUR 1.80).*

Exiting from the church, take a left along the much narrower San Lorenzo, and almost immediately in front of you is a very strange structure. The ancient tower of the Church of San Lorenzo has been blended, at its base, into an architecturally contrasting modern church. Farther

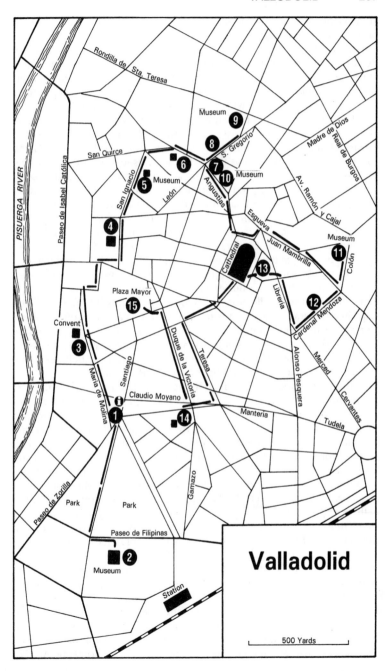

Valladolid

along is the Plaza de la Poniente, which is actually a small park. Round the rather austere building in the right-hand top corner and a surprise awaits, the immense and rather peculiar double-arched façade of the **Iglesia San Benito** (4), founded by Juan I of Castile in 1388. A walk along the side of this church will lead to San Ignacio where, at Number 9, there is an unusual little shop, **The Black Sheep** *(La Oveja Negra)*. It specializes in local products ranging from souvenirs to wine and cheese, and is well worth a look.

Just past this, and to the left in a small plaza bearing the same name, is the 16th century Palacio de Fabio Nelli. This is now home to the **Provincial Archaeological Museum** *(Museo Arqueológico Provincial)* (5), ☎ 35-13-89, otherwise known as the Valladolid Museum. Inside, an unusual three-sided patio has a graceful staircase leading to the archaeological exhibits, which are displayed in chronological order, and the sections for fine arts and the history of Valladolid. *Open Monday to Friday 9:45 a.m. to 2 p.m. and 4 p.m. to 8 p.m. (closing one hour earlier in winter), and on Saturday and Sunday, throughout the year, from 9:45 a.m. to 2:15 p.m. Entrance 200 ptas (EUR 1.20), free on Saturday and Sunday.*

The next leg of the tour, thankfully not too long, is bland but that certainly cannot be said of the destination. A left along San Lorenzo, followed by a right onto the much busier San Quirce, leads to the small Plaza de San Pablo, host to a collection of wonderful buildings. To the right is the **Capitánia General** (6), which was once the royal palace. Diagonally across from this is the **Pimentel Palace** *(Palacio de los Pimentel)* (7), the birthplace in 1527 of Felipe II — it is his statue that adorns the center of the plaza. Next is the double-towered, and beautifully sculptured, Isabelline-Gothic façade of the **Church of St. Paul** *(Iglesia de San Pablo)* (8).

The most important building, though, lays just back from the plaza along the pedestrian walkway of San Gregorio, between the Church of San Pablo and the palace. Founded in the late 15th century by Fray Alonso de Burgos, the Confessor to Isabella, the ***College of St. Gregory** (Colegio de San Gregorio)* (9) is, inside and out, simply stunning. Elaborate crenellations protect an ornately carved archway. Inside are unusual ceilings and what is considered to be one of the most beautiful patios in Spain. Since 1933 this has been the home of the ***National Sculpture Museum** (Museo Nacional de Escultura)* (9), ☎ 25-03-75, whose exhibits, mostly from the 16th to 18th centuries, are primarily of a Spanish religious nature. *It is open Tuesday to Saturday, 10 a.m. to 2 p.m. and 4 p.m. to 6 p.m., and on Sunday from 10 a.m. to 2 p.m. Entrance 400 ptas (EUR 2.40), free on Saturday and Sunday morning.*

Next take the tiny Calle de Fray Luis de Granada, across from the museum and behind the Pimentel Palace, which is the pathway to another museum. Though far less grand, it is nevertheless of interest. At Number 2 Fray Luis de Granada, where the poet José Zorrilla was born in 1817, the rather unprepossessing exterior hides a surprisingly large number of rooms containing furniture and other memorabilia that show the gracious lifestyle of a man of his standing during the "Romantic Age" of the 19th century. The *Zorrilla House-Museum (Casa-Museo de Zorrilla) (10), ☎ 42-62-55, is open Tuesday to Saturday 10 a.m. to 2 p.m. and 5 p.m. to 7 p.m., and on Sunday 10 a.m. to 2 p.m. Entrance free.

From here take La Torrecilla to the busy Agustias, turn left and follow it around and then onto the small Calle Solanilla, again on the left. Here, at the end, the most unusual tower of the **Iglesia de Santa Maria La Antigua** beckons. The next destination, the **Columbus House-Museum** (Casa-Museo de Colón) (11), ☎ 29-13-53, is a bit complicated to find, but persevere. Take Calle Antigua from the Plaza de Solanilla, turn right along Juan Membrilla and a left up Colón to the museum. This is located on the site where Columbus, by that time a broken man, spent the years immediately preceding his death on May 19, 1506. This has exhibits related to his travels, and a large map of the world which traces each voyage. Open Tuesday to Saturday 10 a.m. to 2 p.m. and 5 p.m. to 7 p.m., and Sunday 10 a.m. to 2 p.m. Entrance free.

Return back down Colón, crossing the junction into Cardenal Mendoza. The large building at the end is the **Santa Cruz Palace** (Palacio de Santa Cruz) (12), now part of the university. The elegant, but quite plain, façade fronts an attractive three-level patio. A right here, and a stroll along Libreria, brings you into the interesting plaza behind the Cathedral. Surrounding a central statue of Cervantes are the **University**, the ruins of the 14th-century Santa Maria La Mayor church, and the **Cathedral** (Catedral) (13), ☎ 30-43-62, itself. Felipe II commissioned construction in the late 16th century and Juan de Herrera, of El Escorial fame, worked on this project until the king's death 18 years later, at which time work came to halt. It was subsequently continued under a new architect, which accounts for the rather contrasting architectural styles evident on the exterior. The highlight of the structure, and a focal point for the entire city, is the statue of Christ that stands tall at its pinnacle. The interior, far plainer and more sober than many of its kind, does have an impressive altarpiece. And the museum should not be missed. It has ten rooms of noteworthy religious art, including a 13th-century sepulcher and another of Juan de Arfe's famous monstrances, this one dating from 1587. Open Monday to Friday from 10 a.m. to 1:30 p.m and 4:30 p.m. to 7 p.m., and on Saturday, Sunday and holidays from 10 a.m. to 2 p.m. Entrance 350 ptas (EUR 2.10).

Follow Regalado Cascajares away from the front steps of the Cathedral. Stop briefly to look left down Castelar to the tower of the Salvador church, then turn left into the much smaller Teresa Gil, which heads into the Plaza de España. This is notable for its curious mix of buildings; modern banks, an old-fashioned and characterful hotel, and even the Art Deco-style arch of a church. A right out of the plaza, on to Duque de la Victoria, takes you along a modern, and often upmarket, shopping street to the Plaza Mayor, and the end of the tour.

First, though, take a moment or two to wander down Miguel Iscar for a real surprise. On the left, between and around the modern shops and offices, is an impressive small garden. Behind this is a delightful ivy-covered old house, the **Cervantes House-Museum** *(Casa-Museo de Cervantes)* (14), ☎ 30-88-10, which is absolutely incongruous with its surroundings. The furniture and artifacts are typical of those a nobleman might have owned in the early 17th century. *Open Monday to Saturday 9:30 a.m. to 3:30 p.m., and on Sunday from 10 a.m. to 3 p.m. Entrance 400 ptas (EUR 2.40), free on Sunday.*

By this time you'll be more than ready to sit at one of the many sidewalk cafés surrounding the **Plaza Mayor** (15), enjoying some refreshments and taking in the scene in front of you. The sound of traffic making its way around the plaza is distracting, but this is still the social center of Valladolid as well as home of the twin-towered **Town Hall** *(Casa Consistorial)*. In the center, which is dominated by a statue of Count Ansurez, there are frequent exhibitions, meetings and even demonstrations.

Zaragoza

Zaragoza likes, rightly, to proclaim itself as a city with a 2,000-year history, and many traces of that can be found today. In 19 BC the Roman Emperor, Caesar Augustus, founded a colony on this site, naming it *Caesaraugusta,* and urban growth began. It is interesting to note that the layout of the original Roman town remains more or less intact in the old part of the city, even today. This, in fact, was one of only five Augustan cities on the Iberian Peninsula; Lugo, Mérida, Astorga, and Braga in Portugal being the others. The period of Roman rule came to an end in 472, when they were defeated by the Visigoths, although the style of life remained, essentially unchanged throughout the ensuing era.

In 714 the spreading Arab invasion of the Iberian Peninsula reached the city and the Moors entered, with little resistance, ultimately establishing an extraordinary cultural center resplendent with magnificent buildings and monuments. Following the fall of the Emirate of Córdoba, at the beginning of the 11th century, the Benihud dynasty took control and it was during this period that the glorious Palace of La Aljafería was constructed.

Re-conquest came in 1118 when, after a seven-month siege, Alfonso I, "The Fighter," defeated the Moors. The 14th century saw the construction of the exterior walls and, in 1473, the first printing press in Spain was set up in Zaragoza. During the Wars of Independence the city suffered badly. Napoleons's initial siege, between June and August of 1808, was lifted following the French defeat at the Battle of Bailén. Relief, however, was short lived. Over 20,000 French troops effected another siege beginning on December 21, and continuing until the city finally surrendered on February 20, 1809. In that short time over half the citizens, 55,000, sacrificed their lives from a combination of the hostilities, epidemics and starvation, and large areas of the city were leveled.

Much of Zaragoza, therefore, is quite modern, having been rebuilt over the course of the last century. But the authorities here have succeeded, where many other localities have failed, in creating an extremely harmonious juxtaposition of the old and new—and the result is delightful.

GETTING THERE:

Trains run through Zaragoza in five different directions. It is very nearly at the midway point on the main line that runs between Madrid and Barcelona. It is also on the main line between Barcelona and País Vasco, via Logroño or Pamplona; or the far northwestern region via Burgos, and

León. Zaragoza also has a place on two lesser routes, one of which runs north to Huesca and the French border at Canfranc, and the other of which runs south to Teruel and Valencia.

Buses need not be considered unless they are your transportation of choice.

By car, Zaragoza, 203 miles northeast of Madrid, is connected to that city by the N-II. Barcelona, 185 miles to the east, is reached by either the N-II or A-2 *autopista* toll road. Bilbao is accessible on the A-68 *autopista* toll road; Pamplona on the A-15 *autopista* toll road; Huesca on the N-123, and Valencia, via Teruel, on the N-330 and N-234.

PRACTICALITIES:

Of the attractions in Zaragoza, the three museums are closed on Monday. The **Dialing Code** is 976. Accommodation in Zaragoza is readily procurable except in the middle of October, during the city's annual fair *(Fería)*, when it is scarce. The tourist office, **Oficina de Turismo, Diputación General de Aragón**, ☎ 39-35-37, fax 35-20-06 or www.zaragoza-turismo.com, is located inside the *Torreón de la Zuda* on the Glorieta Pio XII, at the end of the Plaza del Pilar. Opening hours are Monday to Friday 8:15 a.m. to 2:45 p.m. and 4 p.m. to 7:45 p.m., Saturday from 10 a.m. to 1:30 p.m., and on Sunday from 9 a.m. to 2 p.m. The **Bus Turístico**, ☎ 20-12-00 or 902-20-12-12, operates between July 1st and October 15th from 10 a.m. to 1 p.m. and 5 p.m. to 8 p.m., with tickets costing 250 ptas (EUR 1.50) each. There are two circular itineraries, both starting at the Plaza del Pilar near the La Lonja, the blue route lasting half an hour and the red route taking one hour. Zaragoza has a **population** of nearly 600,000 and is the capital of the province of the same name, one of three belonging to the autonomous region of **Aragón**.

ACCOMMODATION:

The **Hotel Palafox** *****, ☎ 23-77-00 or fax 23- 47-05, Casa Jiménez, s/n, is the only five-star hotel in Zaragoza. Situated in a centrally located private street, it has every comfort you would expect. In addition, guests have the use of a rooftop pool, small health club with massage facilities available, and a private garage. $$

The **Gran Hotel** ****, ☎ 22-19-01 or fax 23-67- 13, Joaquín Costa, 5, opened in 1929 by King Alfonso XIII, has always been considered the city's most elegant and stylish hotel. It has recently been extensively renovated to include every modern facility. $$

The **Hotel Reino de Aragón** ****, ☎ 46-82-00 or fax 46-82-11, Coso, 80, is found in a very central part of town, just behind the Plaza España. Constructed in 1997, it is in a modern building with equally modernly eqipped rooms and a charming inside garden. $$

The **Hotel Via Romana** ***, ☎ 39-82-15 or fax 29-05-11, Don Jaime I, 54-56, centrally located next to the Plaza del Pilar, is a modern hotel with a pleasing style, and very comfortable rooms. $

The **Hotel Oriente** ***, ☎ 39-80-61 or fax 39- 83-02, Coso, 11-13, has a advantageous location close to the Plaza de España and on the edge of the Old Town. The rooms have good facilities, and there is an excellent restaurant with an very reasonably priced *menú del dia*. $

The **Hotel Conde Blanco** **, ☎ 4-14-11 or fax 28-03-39, Predicadores, 84, offers a pleasant ambiance and comfortable rooms in a quiet part of Zaragoza between the Old Town and the Palacio de la Aljafería. $

The **Hostal Ambos Mundos** **, ☎ 29-97-04, Plaza del Pilar, 16, has a fantastic location on this wonderful plaza. Some rooms overlook the Basílica del Pilar, La Lonja and the La Seo Catedral. Translated "Both Worlds," this is clean and comfortable. $

FOOD AND DRINK:

The cuisine of this area can best be described as simple and fortifying, which could similarly describe many of the local wines.

Restaurante Montal (Torre Nueva, 29), is near the Plaza de San Felipe within a Renaissance mansion that features a classical 16th-century patio. The Montal family oversees the preparation and service of fine local cuisine in wonderfully decorated private dining rooms. ☎ 29-89-98 or fax 39-10-60. $$$

Restaurante Coral (Avenida de las Torres, 28), is located within the Boston Hotel, which is just behind the Fine Arts Museum. Following in the tradition of the hotel, it has an intimate, yet very modern, ambiance, and serves beautifully prepared International or regional dishes. ☎ 59-91-92 or fax 59-04-46. $$$

Taberna Tragantua (Plaza Santa Marta, s/n), is an elegant restaurant where many dishes are sold by weight. A set meal is about 3,500 ptas. ☎ 29-91-74. $$

Restaurante Puerta Cineja *(Mártires, 7)*, is in the El Tubo district just off the Plaza de España. It specializes in regional cuisine served in a delightful open and airy atmosphere. ☎ 29-08-02. $$

Hotel Oriente (Coso, 11-13, near the Plaza de España), boasts an excellent restaurant and very affordable prices. In fact, on a recent trip, I dined here and I enjoyed one of the very best value-for-money meals I have ever had. ☎ 39-80-61 or fax 39-83-02. $

Casa Lac (Mártires, 12), is found just off the Plaza de España in a maze of narrow lanes known as El Tubo. The house dates from 1825 and has a superb ambiance created by exposed wooden beams, glowing chandeliers and an enticing bar. The *menú del dia* is priced at 1,500 ptas (EUR 9.02). ☎ 29-90-25. $

Taberna Domino (Plaza Santa Marta, s/n), was opened in 1982, and is the place to go for *tapas*. Make your selection, served up on wooden platters, from a vast array of mouth-watering choices. You most likely will not want a proper meal after your visit here. ☎ 39-80-51. $

Cafetería Trevi (Plaza de La Seo, 2-3), offers a choice of menus for 1,100 ptas, which you may enjoy at one of the outdoor tables in this charming plaza. ☎ 20-20-00. $

SUGGESTED TOUR:

Begin the tour of Zaragoza in the **Plaza de España** (1), the main link between the new and old parts of the city. This is, usually, quite a busy place as many of the bus routes originate and terminate here. On my first visit to Zaragoza I stayed in a small *pension* here, which has long since gone out of business. At that time a double room was priced at 80 ptas (EUR 0.48), a meal for two people cost 45 ptas (EUR 0.27), two bottles of sparkling water went for 14 ptas (EUR .08) and a liter of wine was just 7 ptas (EUR .04). All your heart could desire, well almost, for a grand total of 146 ptas; how times change!

Before exploring the older part of the city, take a short detour up the broad Avenida de la Independencia, turn left into Zurita and head in the direction of the **Plaza de Sitios** (2). *Sitios* is the Spanish word for siege, and the monument in the center of the plaza stands in honor of the tens of thousands of Zaragozan citizens who died in the siege of 1808/1809. Also in this plaza you will find a very graceful building dating from 1908, that was built in conjunction with the Hispano-French Exhibition. Nowadays it is home to the ***Zaragoza Mueum** (Museo de Zaragoza)* (3), ☎ 22-21-81 or fax 22-23-78, which features archaeological exhibits from prehistoric times to the Muslim era on the ground floor, and fine arts of the 12th to 20th centuries on the upper level. Of most interest is a room dedicated to works by Goya, including his self-portrait. *Visit Tuesday to Saturday from 10 a.m. to 2 p.m., and Sunday and holidays 10 a.m. to 2 p.m. Entrance 200 ptas (EUR 1.20), free for EC citizens.*

Return back to the Plaza de España, and attractions of an entirely different kind. Entering Mártires and the maze of narrow streets and lanes known as El Tubo, you'll come to an area of bars, restaurants and tiny shops. When you reach the end of Mártires, make a right into Cuatro de Agosto, followed by a left into Cinegio. At the first tiny crossroads, bear left along Estebanes and, very soon, you will find yourself at Number 15, home to the **Bodegas Almau** (4). To forego a stop here would be a mistake. Although not a traditional tourist spot, this is a microcosm reminiscent of a gentler age. One half is a liquor store, where one could browse endlessly through a fascinating maze of thousands of bottles and barrels. The other half is a tiny traditional bar, which presents an excellent opportunity to sample a glass of Aragónese wine.

Continue on as Estebanes leads into the Plaza de Sas, whose farther side abuts Alfonso I. A right into that street will give you a first glance of the huge Basilica at its end. But, before going that far, take another right, into Espoz y Mina, where you will find the **Camón Aznar Museum** *(Museo Camón Aznar)* (5), ☎ 39-73-28 or fax 39-73-87. Don José Camón Aznar was a distinguished academic who made his home in Zaragoza. This museum contains the art collection he donated to Aragón. *Open to the public Tuesday to Friday 10 a.m. to 2:15 p.m. and 6 p.m. to 9 p.m., Saturday 10 a.m.*

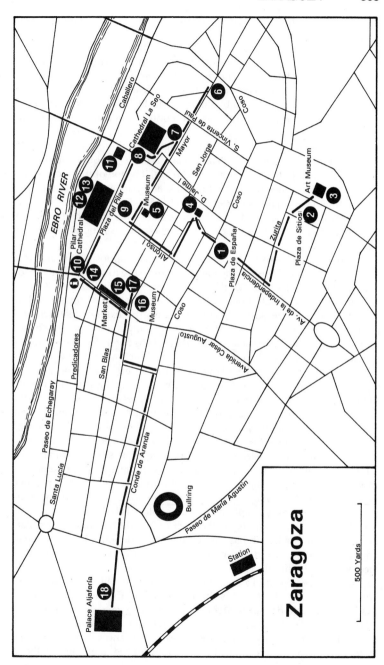

Zaragoza

500 Yards

to 2 p.m. and 6 p.m. to 9 p.m., and Sunday from 11 a.m. and 2 p.m. Entrance 100 ptas (EUR .60).

Press on, taking Espoz y Mina, crossing the more important Don Jaime I, where the name changes to Mayor, and following all the way to the **Plaza de Magdalena** (6). The highlight here is a wonderful Mudéjar tower belonging to La Magdalena Church. You will come to realize that towers of the Mudéjar style, a blending of Moslem and Western architecture, are found throughout the city and contribute greatly to its unique character.

Return back along Mayor and turn right into the narrow Argensola Cedro, making your way to the **Plaza Santa Marta** (7). Although there is not much of interest to tourists in this small plaza, it is one of the social spots of Zaragoza. Its center is filled with tables, and bars and restaurants line the perimeter. Two have been detailed in the Food and Drink section, but another will be of special interest to those interested in bullfighting. The *Cervecería Marty* is literally filled with posters *(carteles),* and other taurine items.

Best to leave here by the corner diagonally opposite the one you entered by, winding through the narrow lanes to the tower directly ahead, and the Plaza de La Seo. On the right is the ***Cathedral La Seo** (La Seo Catedral)* (8). Constructed over an old mosque, this was consecrated in 1119, but not completed until centuries later. The exterior features one huge single tower and, inside, there is, reportedly, a fine tapestry collection. But, don't expect to see it! The Cathedral has been closed for restoration for many years, and no one can predict when it will reopen.

The Cathedral is at one end of the highly impressive **Plaza del Pilar** (9), which leads all the way to the **Torreón de Zuda** (10). This was once a part of the palace of the same name that served as the residence of the Muslim governors, and now is home to the tourist office. Plazas, of all shapes and sizes, often surrounded by historical buildings, abound throughout Spain; but, in my experience, this one is unique. From one end to the other this very long and narrow plaza is home, on three of its sides, to an array of interesting and historical structures. For its elongated shape, alone, it would be considered highly unusual, but an adventurous city planner must have decided, somewhere along the line, to throw something more into the mix. It was an experiment that could easily have backfired. In actuality, however, the strategic placement of modern fountains and statues throughout its length has added an eclectic dimension to its appeal. The juxtaposition of old and new makes for an unusual ambiance that most will find highly attractive.

Moving away from La Seo, the places of note will be to your right. The first building of interest is the **La Lonja** (11). Considered the finest example of civil Renaissance architecture in Zaragoza, this was constructed between 1541 to 1551 as a commercial exchange. It functioned as a theater in the 18th century and is now used for art and other exhibitions. Unfortunately, its interesting interior may only be seen during those times. Next door is the **Town Hall** *(Ayuntamiento)* and, just past that, is the *****Pilar Cathedral** *(Basílica del Pilar)* (12), far and away the largest and most dramatic building in the plaza, and in all of Zaragoza for that matter. According to legend it was on this site that the Virgin Mary appeared, in January of AD 40, to St. James. Dating from 1677, the design of the current structure features a thin tower at each of the four corners protecting a series of colorful cupolas that encircle the central dome. The edifice dominates the city's skyline and is visible from miles around. The interior is grand and formal and boasts numerous items of architectural and artistic interest. Tucked into one small hollow in a pillar is a shrine dedicated to the Virgin, which pilgrims pay homage to with a kiss. During the annual fair, consecrated to the memory of Pilar, the façade of this church is literally blanketed with banks of flowers, a vibrantly colorful tribute placed here in her honor by citizens of the city. *Visit daily, in summer from 5:45 a.m. to 9:30 p.m., and in winter from 5:45 a.m. to 8:30 p.m.* Here also is the **Pilar Museum** *(Museo de Pilar)* (13), ☎ 39-74-97, which is, in truth, rather small and exhibits, among other things, mementoes of Pope John Paul's visit to Zaragoza. *It is open daily from 9 a.m. to 2 p.m. and 4 p.m. to 7 p.m., entrance 150 ptas (EUR .90).*

Leave the plaza now, by the end next to the *Torreón de Zuda,* taking note of the gargantuan fountain that all but blocks that end. Turn left into Avenida César Augusto and, appropriately, you will be greeted by a stretch of the **Roman Walls** *(Murallas Romanas)* (14). These stretched, at one time, for over 3,000 meters and were guarded by in excess of 200 fortified towers, and were renovated in the 3rd century. The remains of the walls, diminished in size considerably, are today embellished with fountains and a statue of a Roman Legionnaire.

You may be allured by the bustling emanating from an old-fashioned, narrow metal structure which, you will later find, houses the **Food Market** *(Mercado Central)* (15). Resist that, though, and turn left, just prior to it, into Manifestación and follow this to the Plaza de Justicia. Take a moment to admire the interesting statue/fountain in its center, before heading up Temple to the Plaza de San Felipe. This is yet another charming square where, although accomplishing it in a fashion divergent from that of the Plaza del Pilar, manages to successfully harmonize a mix of the old and the new. The imposing modern statues here are the work of Pablo Gargallo. The 17th-century Argillo Palace, interesting in its own right, houses the **Pablo Gargallo Museum** *(Museo Pablo Gargallo)* (16), ☎ 39-20-58 or fax 39-20-76, a small museum which compensates for lack of space with its interesting exhibits. These, obviously works of the artist Pablo Gargallo, consist of imaginative modern sculptures and fascinating face marks. *Opening hours are Tuesday to Saturday from 10 a.m. to 2 p.m. and 5 p.m. to 9 p.m.; and on Sunday and holidays from 10 a.m. to 2 p.m. Entrance free.* You'll note also, in a corner of the square, another Mudéjar tower, the **Tower of Forte** *(Torreón de Forte)* (17). This dates from the 15th century, and is considered the finest example of its kind in the city.

It is time now to depart the Old Town. Take Torre back out, crossing the Avenida César Augusto and following San Pablo along to a plaza, and church, of the same name. The latter is particularly impressive, although it is unlikely to be open unless you are visiting on a Sunday morning. This isn't the most salubrious of neighborhoods, so you may feel more comfortable taking the next left turning, and continuing up to the busy shopping street of Conde de Aranda. Make a right here, expecting a rather uneventful journey until you reach the **Bullring** *(Plaza de Toros)*, whose exterior plays host to a fascinating **Flea Market** *(Rastro)* on Sunday mornings. To your the left and in front of the Bullring is the Plaza del Portillo where you will find a monument to Agustina of Aragón. Just past here is the busy junction with the Paseo de María Agustín, where the narrow Calle Castillo on the opposite side, leads to one of the cities oldest monuments.

The **Palace of Aljafería* *(Palacio de la Aljafería)* (18) was originally constructed by the Moorish governor, Abu Jafar Ahamed Almoctadir, between 1047 and 1081. Following the re-conquest it was used as a residence by the Christian monarchs. It has, of course, been renovated numerous times over the centuries, the most important of which effected the addition of a palace by the Catholic Monarchs in 1492. This is now designed to resemble a small castle, and its entrance is even protected by a moat. It is unfortunate that the most interesting part, the palace of the Catholic Monarchs, and its distinguished Throne Room, have been closed for many years for restoration. The Aljafería is also home to the **Aragón Parliament** *(Cortes de Aragón). It is open daily, in the mornings from 10 a.m. to 2 p.m. In summer, afternoon hours are 4 p.m. to 7:45 p.m., in winter they are 4:30 p.m. to 6:30 p.m.*

This brings the tour to a close. The more energetic may opt to walk back to the Plaza de España along the Conde de Aranda and Coso, and this really isn't too far. If your legs need a rest, take a bus back.

Section III

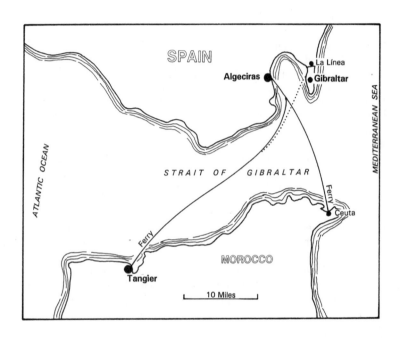

DAYTRIPS BEYOND SPAIN: FROM ALGECIRAS TO
TANGIER and
GIBRALTAR

Algeciras, strategically positioned on the Strait of Gibraltar just nine miles from Africa, has throughout the ages served as an important seaport for a succession of civilizations. Most notably it was colonized by the Phoenicians and the Romans, but it was while under Moorish control that it fully blossomed as a prominent maritime center. It was reconquered by Alfonso XI in 1344.

Today, it is the principal port in Andalucía, and home to a thriving fishing industry. There is nothing of any particular interest in the way of attractions here. And it is not even a pretty place; but, then again, that is fairly typical of a working port. It is, though, the gateway for two unique and disparate daytrips. From here, you may cross the Straits for the colorful, exotic, experience of African volatility in Tangier, or take a bus around the bay to Gibraltar, and experience the tranquility of a little bit of England on the Iberian Peninsula.

Most likely a long while before you reach Algeciras, if you travel by car or bus, and most certainly immediately upon your arrival, it will become obvious that the singular tourist attraction for this city is the proliferation of ferry services to Africa. From store window signs and shopfront placards, vendors implore you to buy, from their particular establishment, your ferry tickets to either Tangier or Ceuta. While visitors are, more often than not, familiar with Tangier, many do not realize that Spain has, in fact, retained two small territories, enclaves technically, on the North African coast. Ceuta is just across the Strait of Gibraltar, and Melilla, much farther to the east and close to Algeria. It will be of little consequence, to you at least, whether you purchase a ticket at one of these places, or in the port itself; the price will be the same. You will find that a number of companies operate services, with the only real difference being the sizes of the vessels. If your itinerary allows for a choice, I'd recommend using Trasmediterranea, especially if you can get to sail on their newer, and larger vessels. If your schedule is tight, this is really not a critical consideration and you may just want to take the next ferry. These, generally, run quite frequently, for the two-and-a-half-hour sailing to Tangier.

GETTING THERE:
Trains arrive at the Algeciras station, a terminal, from Madrid, via Córdoba and Bobadilla. There are also services from Barcelona, via Valencia, Alcázar de San Juan, Córdoba and Bobadilla, but these are very slow. Regional services link Granada, Málaga, and Seville, all via Bobadilla, with Algeciras, but the journey from the latter two is rather convoluted.

Bus is the better choice from Málaga and Seville, and the only realistic choice from Cádiz and Jerez de la Frontera.

By Car, Algeciras is 480 miles south of Madrid and, of the two options, one route is really no better than the other. Both use the N-IV from Madrid to Bailén. From there either continue on the N-IV to Cádiz, via Córdoba and Seville, and then take the N-340 south to Algeciras; or take the N-323 south to Granada, the N-342 west to its junction with the N-321, then south to Málaga and finally travel southwest from that point along the coastal N-340 to Algeciras.

PRACTICALITIES:
Algeciras has its annual fair (fería) in the last week of June. If you are traveling by car and plan a jaunt to Tangier, be careful where you leave it

in Algeciras. The safest place is at the car parks in the port itself. My preference is the tiny open-air one at the entrance to the port, just in front of
the main ticket office. The **Dialing Code** is 96. The **Tourist Office**, ☎ 57- 26-
36 or fax 57-04-75, Calle Juan de la Cierva, s/n, is in a strange glass building
between the station and the port, and much closer to the latter. Algeciras
has a **population** of 100,000 and is in the province of Cádiz, one of eight
belonging to the autonomous region of **Andalucía**.

ACCOMMODATION:

Algeciras really is not a place visitors plan to stay overnight, but if you
get stuck try one of these:

The **Hotel Al-Mar** ***, ☎ 65-46-61 or fax 64-45-01, Avenida de la Marina,
2-3, is a large, modern, hotel. Most of its 192 rooms have views over the
port and Bay of Algeciras. It has all modern facilities, private parking and
is handicapped accessible. $

The **Pensión Nuestra Señora de la Palma** *, ☎ 63-24-81, Plaza de la
Palma, 12, is a nice, clean, value-for-money place, located in the market
square. $

FOOD AND DRINK:

There really is nothing special here and, in any case, most visitors will
not be here long enough to worry. If you need a quick snack before you
sail, there are any number of bars along the Avenida de la Marina, or in the
port itself.

Trip 43
A Daytrip From Algeciras

Tangier

There are few countries in the world, let alone cities, that have drawn as much international attention to themselves as has Tangier. Undoubtedly, its commanding strategic position at the western end of the Strait of Gibraltar, just 17 miles from the Spanish coast, has much to do with that.

Known to the Greeks as *Tingi*, it has been established that the Phoenicians and Carthaginians also visited the area. It became a Berber kingdom when affiliated with Mauretania. During the period of Roman control it was, first, an autonomous state and, subsequently, in the 3rd century, enjoyed the status afforded a full colony. Control changed hands as the Vandals cut a swath of conquest in the 5th century and, under such control, the city's fortunes declined dramatically. This trend was reversed when, in the very early 8th century, the Muslims overcame the current inhabitants in their sweep across North Africa. Tangier blossomed under Muslim control and, over the next 750 years, it grew to become an important Mediterranean port, and was fought over by any number of Muslim dynasties. In 1471, it was conquered by the Portuguese and they, in concert with the Spanish, controlled the area until 1662 when, as part of a dowry, it was given to Charles II. Tangier was, at that time, granted a charter making it the equal of an English town. Less than a quarter of a century later, however, the English had ignominiously departed, leaving Tangier to the control of Morocco.

Morocco, in time, became a French Protectorate, but political machinations were such in the early 20th century that, in the early 1920s Tangier was placed under the control of an International Commission, with representatives from many European nations. The Second World War caused a brief hiatus in this arrangement, during which time Tangier was controlled solely by Spain. Finally, in 1956, independence arrived, and Tangier became a part of the new Kingdom of Morocco.

Its international connections have made Tangier more cosmopolitan than most other Moroccan cities, a facet of its character that is enhanced by the number of tourists that visit yearly; either on the cruise lines or on daytrips from Spain.

GETTING THERE:

By Boat, ferries run to and from Algeciras on a very frequent, daily, basis. There is also a ferry service to and from Gibraltar. As of January 1997, these left Gibraltar on Monday, Tuesday and Friday, returning from Tangier on Sunday, Tuesday and Friday. For further information about this service contact Tourafrica, ICC Building, Main Street, Gibraltar, ☎ (350) 77666.

PRACTICALITIES:

The most interesting day to visit Tangier is on a Friday, the Muslim Holy Day, when there is always extra activity in, and around, the Casbah. The official language is Arabic, but expect that everyone will also speak French, and that almost everyone can converse in Spanish and English as well. The *Dirham* is the official currency of Morocco, and you may purchase it in any one of the travel agents-cum cambios in Algeciras, in the harbor there, on the ferry or, of course, in Tangier. Do not, however, expect to change it back so easily; outside of Morocco, even on the ferry, no one will touch it. I would recommend that you change only as much, or even a little less, than you anticipate spending. And, the reality is that this is not the problem you might imagine. You can shop in Tangier, indeed almost anywhere in Morocco, with whatever currency, or credit card, you might have to hand. Although this is convenient you will, most likely, not get favorable rates; the vendors here are consummate traders.

The **Country Code** for Morocco is 212, and the **Dialing Code** 09. There is a small **tourist office** on Boulevard Pasteur, one of the main streets above the Casbah, but it really does not have too much on offer. Tangier has a **population** of about 500,000, and the king appoints its governor.

ACCOMMODATION:

There are numerous high-rise and fancy hotels around the bay from the city that cater, mostly, to the cruise market. But, nice as they are, these don't really have a convenient location. On the city's popular street, by the port and railway station, there are a number of hotels, hostals and pensions whose generally low rates are commensurate with their facilities. For those that intend to spend one night, and one night will, under most circumstances, be enough, I strongly recommend:

The **El Minzah Hotel ******, ☎ 93-58-85 or fax 93-45-46, 85, Rue de la Liberté, not only has a fantastic location, just a block from the Casbah and overlooking the city, harbor and Strait of Gibraltar, but much style as well. Built by Lord Bute in 1930, it features a traditional Moorish character, lovely private gardens, a terrace restaurant and a pool. This is a real haven in the hustle and bustle of Tangier. $$$

FOOD AND DRINK:

Most everyone will have heard stories of the horrendous stomach upsets the food and water may cause here and I can, unfortunately, attest to those personally. Really, you should exercise good judgment, and it is certainly wise to drink only bottled water and/or internationally-known soft drinks. And, take equal care with your food. It may be somewhat more expensive, but it's certainly safer and very enjoyable to eat at:

El Minzah Hotel (85, Rue de la Liberté) Surround yourself with a Moroccan ambiance while enjoying classical French cuisine and wines. ☎ 93-58-85 or fax 93-45-46. $$$

SUGGESTED TOUR:

First, I would be remiss not to clarify a most important point; this is not a tour, it is an adventure. And, as with all adventures, a degree of uncertainty goes hand-in-hand with the surprises. Those that have never ventured past the borders of the USA and Europe will be in for a drastic culture shock. And those that have been to this part of North Africa in the past will, undoubtedly, be feeling both excited and apprehensive.

In reality it becomes clear back in Algeciras, and on the ferry, that you are on the edge of a new world, where, perhaps for the first time, you come face-to-face with an entirely different culture. The faces, clothes, and language of some of those around you are as colorful as they are unfamiliar, a fact that can not help but command your attention.

All of these sensations will be heightened as the ferry pulls slowly into Tangier—as strange, slightly erotic, aromas drift towards you from the tightly packed jumble of whitewashed buildings tumbling down the hillside, and coming to an abrupt halt on the edge of the harbor. Once alighted, though, it is the utter sense of chaos that is most striking. To help guide you safely through it there will be no shortage of help at hand. Even if you do not want assistance, and in truth for first-time visitors it is most helpful, you are going to be pestered so much that it is inevitable you will end up having it.

From out of nowhere expect to find a new "friend." One that only, perhaps, wants to practice his English and then direct you to a store in the Casbah owned by a brother, uncle, or cousin. All of this may well be true, but if you are not interested then the challenge begins. And, the challenge is telling him—it certainly won't be a her—no! You will learn very quickly indeed that these guys just will not take no for an answer. Wherever you go your new "friend" will follow, and no matter how many protestations you offer he will stay by your side. If, by some fluke, you manage to wear his patience thin, he will quickly be replaced by another. If for no other reason, and most cannot help but admire their linguistic abilities, you will most definitely be impressed by their vicidic determination. It is a determination, though, driven by poverty; and it is economic hardship that makes them so persistent.

The bottom line is that you're going to be stuck with one anyway, whether you agree or not, and after following you around he will still demand to be paid. So you may as well make the most of it and take one of your choice, I usually find the middle-aged to be somewhat less aggressive than the younger ones, and let him guide you around. After all, you do have the advantage of being able to ask questions, and he will, no doubt, make sure you aren't bothered by others. And, in reality, it won't cost too much; I certainly would never pay more than $10 for a morning or afternoon.

Having settled on your guide, it is now time to visit the Casbah, really the highlight of any trip to Tangier. Although there are interesting museums in Tangier, most notably the Museums of Moroccan Arts and Antiquities and the Forbes Museum, I certainly do not recommend spending precious time visiting them. For me, and I am sure most visitors as well, the sights you see around you on the streets, most especially in the Casbah, are of far more interest than inanimate objects in any museum. It is in the Casbah that your guide will prove most helpful, providing you use him solely as a guide and interpreter. Whatever you do, though, you should not take his advice on purchasing anything. What little he makes directly from you will be supplemented by commissions from store owners. That is why he will always try and take you to specific stores, and will never help drive the price down to what it should be; that is simply not in his best interest. Although not as confusing as some, the Casbah really is an intricate maze of tiny streets and back alleys, and even those with the very best of sense of directions would have problems extricating themselves from it. Certainly, there will be no map to assist you.

The moral is stay close to your guide and enjoy an unparalled adventure in the most interesting, colorful, noisy, aroma-filled and exotic market you are ever likely to have seen. But don't expect the sights and sounds to always be pretty. Poverty, and sometimes extreme poverty at that, is never far away. It can be disconcerting, to say the very least, to see that the source of the wailing and screaming you might hear is an old man with his a leg literally devoured by some manner of disease. But these things, as disturbing as they can be, are part and parcel of any visit to Morocco. And, in any event, as cynical as it may sound, such sights will be temporarily overwhelmed, though they will surely return to haunt you later, by everything else going on around you.

Your eyes will be drawn back, again and again, to the small shops that cover every space available in the Casbah. Their colorful array of goods is mind boggling indeed, and include about everything you might want, along with plenty you won't. Prevalent are the leather goods, and particularly popular are bags and jackets. At every doorway the proprietor will be waiting to tempt you in but, in truth, there are many more shops than prospective shoppers, so it is definitely a buyer's market. But it is not quite that simple, and that is what makes a trip to Tangier so interesting. Finding the goods you want, and no two stores have the same products, is difficult enough; but, actually paying for them, is an adventure in itself.

The first, and most vital, piece of advice is that there is no such thing as a fixed price. The initial price you are going to be quoted, no matter how cheap it may appear, is much, much more than you really need to pay. Remember, too, that these vendors are probably the most astute traders you have ever met, and that they are all linguistically fluent. What comes next is nothing less than a battle of wits, especially if you have really set your heart on what you want. Make it plain that you think the price way too high. You will then be asked for your "best price." As a rule of thumb, counter with a figure between one-third and one-quarter of the quoted price. Of course, expect this to be met with exclamations of incredulity, which are quickly followed by how impossible it is for him to sell it to you at that price. Do not believe a word of it, no matter the apparent sincerity. Take this process through another round of similar negotiations and, if you still really want that prized bag or jacket, begin to walk out of the store. The protestations will be immediate, and the proprietor will do what he possibly can to keep you in the store. Some of the hard-luck stories you will be told stretch credibility; my favorite one is that "that taxes are due in the next day or so, and that he must sell to you; even at a loss." In a country as chaotic as Morocco it is difficult to imagine an Internal Revenue officer being that efficient! The thing to remember is that you set the rules. If you want the goods, persevere; and continue playing the game. Eventually, after more threatened walkouts on your part, and strenuous arguments on his, you will have raised your offer a little and his price will have been lowered dramatically, to something approaching yours.

You must be aware that pride will prevent him from actually matching your figure. So it's now time to resort to the subtleties of haggling. Walk around the store pretending you are deep in thought considering the deal. Really, though, you should be looking for something else you fancy. Something smaller, and whose cost, you think, when combined with that of the original item, will be something more than the merchant's last price. Having agreed, after another haggling session, on the cost of the new item, then tell the trader you'll take them BOTH for his original price. Of course, be prepared for outrageous, and sometimes theatrical, denials, which are a sure sign that the game is nearing its climax. To clinch the deal, and save his sensibilities, now raise your price a little. More often than not, it is a compromise that will, ever so reluctantly, be accepted. And, just to assuage any guilt you may be feeling, be aware that you have most probably still paid over the odds anyway!

Having gotten what you wanted, and a story you can relate for many years after as well, it is time just to wander around, absorbing the immense cultural differences. From men sitting in cafés drinking mint tea, possibly a colorful water seller; to the inevitable Berber women in their traditional dress and strange hats, who come down from the mountains each day with their fresh vegetables and fruit. Wherever you go, however, you never will be able to escape the grinding poverty of the majority of these people. It is this image, among many others, that will remain with you as a permanent reminder of Morocco.

The contrast will be even more evident if you decide to stay overnight at the El Minzah. Literally just a moment or two from the Casbah, it is an oasis of wealth in a desert of destitution. To enter its doors, opened by attendants in traditional dress, is to leave one world for another. Here you may relax in sophistication, and with a calmness of peace and tranquility impossible to find in the streets. Be sure to request a room, though, overlooking the town and harbor, with the Strait of Gibraltar in the background. The panoramic views are stunning in their own right, but when combined with the sounds and smells of the old city, immediately beneath your window, the effect is nothing if not mesmerizing.

A trip to Tangier, especially for the first time, is a travel experience that should not be missed. Most, though, will not be unhappy to arrive back in Spain. Although the way of life there is still different from home, it is, at least, familiar. A stark contrast to Tangier where, apart from the ubiquitous Coca-Cola symbol, little is familiar.

Trip 44
A Daytrip From Algeciras

Gibraltar

When most people think of Gibraltar, the images that come to mind are the Rock itself, the Barbary apes, and quaint British customs. While these things are all an integral part of the Crown Colony, they are only a small portion of what makes up the wonder of Gibraltar.

The ever-so-prominent Rock is, geologically speaking, anomalous to its immediate surroundings. The fact that it is formed of limestone, which is, in simplest terms, a compaction of small fossils, indicates that at one time the Rock was a seabed. It is also known that the geological formations in this area have altered on many occasions. One such change, caused by a seismic movement, brought the Rock westward to roughly the position it occupies today. Another, later, disruption joined together the continents of Europe and Africa, and subsequently the Mediterranean evaporated. Approximately five million years ago, a fissure developed allowing the Atlantic to pour in, filling the empty sea bed and creating what is now known as the Strait of Gibraltar. This natural water passageway is flanked by two mountains: The Rock, "Jbel Turik" or "Mons Calpe;" and the "Jbel Musa" or "Mons Abyla", in Africa. The Roman legend, which recounts the story of Hercules, dubbed these "The Pillars of Hercules," by which name they are still known today.

Scientists have ascertained that Gibraltar was a home for pre-historic man. Neanderthal skulls were found first in 1848 and again in 1928, and it seems likely that Gibraltar was one of the last bastions for this early species of man.

Though there is evidence that the Phoenicians, Greeks, and Carthagenians were aware of Gibraltar, none of these civilizations developed any settlements on The Rock. Even during the prolonged period of Roman rule in the area, from about 500 BC to AD 475, a town was never built on this particular site. The next people to arrive in the area, the Visigoths and Vandals, destroyed virtually all traces of culture in the immediate vicinity. It was, therefore, left to the next invaders, the Moors in 711, to establish the first city at Gibraltar. But, even they were in no hurry—a settlement was not founded until 1160, more than four hundred years later! The next three hundred years brought internecine squabbles between the many Moorish kingdoms and with Christian forces, made up of English Knights, the French, and a variety of others who had joined forces with Iberian crusaders in an effort to oust the Moors from Western

Europe. The Christians did actually win control of Gibraltar in 1309 but managed to maintain it only until 1333. Few people wanted to live here, however, and to entice his citizens to reconsider, the king of Castile, Ferdinand, offered freedom from justice to anyone who would live in Gibraltar for a year and a day. Another siege by the Moors followed but finally, in 1462, Gibraltar was definitively reconquered.

Unfortunately, this was not the end of unrest in this area and, in fact there followed a series of attacks by other Spanish factions. Isabel the Catholic, by then queen, was so distressed by these attacks that, on December 22, 1501, she signed a decree declaring Gibraltar a crown property. The very next year Gibraltar received the Royal Warrant which granted its coat-of-arms consisting of, as it does today, a castle and a key.

With the 16th century came a new breed of raiders, in the form of Barbary and other Mediterranean pirates. In order to protect the area, the Spanish monarchs built, and later extended, defensive walls. At the beginning of the 18th century, political machinations over who should succeed to the Spanish throne led an Anglo-Dutch force, on behalf of Charles of Austria, to lay siege to, and eventually capture, Gibraltar in 1704. This series of events was a precursor to Spain's ceding of Gibraltar to Britain, which was accomplished through the Treaty of Utrecht in 1713. Given all of this, the Spanish were not through fighting for Gibraltar yet. In 1727 they instigated a siege that failed and, in 1779, combined Spanish and French forces totaling over 50,000 troops laid the final, Great Siege, against a mere 5,000 defenders. This continued for nearly four years, and caused havoc and much hardship to the citizens of Gibraltar before finally failing in 1783.

Although the 19th century was comparatively peaceful, this era still saw some notable events. Nelson made it his headquarters and, in 1805, his body was returned, some say in a barrel of rum, following his death in the nearby Battle of Trafalgar. When Napoleon's troops invaded Spain during the Wars of Independence, Gibraltar became an important British base. In 1830 Gibraltar was granted the rights of a Crown Colony.

The beginning of the 20th century brought the opening of the massive new docks, which were put to good use during the two World Wars that were to follow. During the second of these conflicts all but those most essential citizens were evacuated to the United Kingdom, and to other colonies. Also in the Second World War, General Eisenhower conducted the Allied invasion of North Africa from one of the tunnels in The Rock.

During the 1960s new problems arose with Spain. In 1963/64 Gibraltar's future was debated at the United Nations, leading to renewed Spanish claims on the colony. In 1967 the question was put to those it would most affect, the citizens themselves, and in a referendum on their future 99.9% of Gibraltarians voted to remain a part of Britain. This decision was followed, in 1969, by the drafting of a new constitution which granted fully responsible self-government. These events severely provoked General Franco and he closed the frontier that same year. Franco's death, in 1975, opened the way for diplomatic activity which ended in an agreement to re-open the border in 1982. This was delayed, however, until February 5, 1985, as Britain's war with Argentina over the Falkland Islands, and its use of Gibraltar as a staging post, scuttled the diplomacy. The significance of Gibraltar's strategic position for assisting in far-flung military actions was proved, yet again, in 1991 during the Gulf War.

This eventful history, on its own merits, attracts many visitors to Gibraltar, and when they arrive they are pleasantly surprised to find that the city has many other, some surprising, activities. You can try, for example, guided fishing trips, dolphin-watching expeditions, safaris, scuba diving, or even flying-boat sightseeing excursions over the Rock, Strait of Gibraltar, and North Africa. And, you can add to this mix, the undeniable attraction of duty-free goods. On first consideration, you may think of setting aside just one day in your itinerary to explore "The Rock", but think again, as most discerning travelers will plan to stay for at least one, and preferably two, nights.

GETTING THERE:

Trains do not run into Gibraltar, nor do they service La Linea de la Concepción on the Spanish side of the border. The nearest train station is in Algeciras and, hence, it will be necessary to take a bus (the bus station is, conveniently, directly across from the train station) from there to La Linea, where the bus station is just a couple of hundred yards from the border.

Bus services from Algeciras have been detailed above. Buses also operate from a variety of other Spanish towns to the bus station in La Linea.

By Car, it is perfectly possible to cross the border by car. However, there can be delays during the rush hours, and it is not unknown for border disputes to cause slowdowns and other problems.

By Air, there are direct daily flights from the UK to Gibraltar.

By Sea, there is a limited ferry service between Gibraltar and Tangier. In January 1997 this left Gibraltar on Monday, Wednesday and Friday, with return sailings from Tangier were scheduled Sunday, Tuesday and Friday. For current schedules contact Tourafrica, ☎ 77666.

PRACTICALITIES:

The **Dialing Code** is 350. In Gibraltar the legal tender, currency, is Gibraltar Government notes and coins, although UK notes and coins are equally accepted. Most vendors also accept Spanish currency, but do not expect a good rate of exchange. The tourist office, **Gibraltar Information Bureau**, ☎ 48395, Duke of Kent House, Cathedral Square, is open Monday to Friday 9:30 a.m. to 5:30 p.m. Gibraltar has a **population** of 31,000, and is a self-governing Crown Colony of the United Kingdom. It has its own House of Assembly, with fifteen elected members and two nominated members, but the UK is responsible for defense, foreign affairs, financial stability, and internal security.

ACCOMMODATION:

The **Rock Hotel Gibraltar** *****, ☎ 73000 or fax 73513, Europa Road, sits nestled under The Rock, just above the Alameda Gardens and a short walk away from the busy town center. It epitomizes the highest of English standards, in both the habitations and the spacious public rooms. There are also spectacular views of the Bay of Gibraltar and the Strait, and of Africa in the distance. The gardens cover over nine acres, and include a salt water swimming pool with a separate bar. $$$

The **Caleta Palace Hotel** ****, ☎ 76501 or fax 71050, Catalan Bay, is located in a dramatic setting—literally overhanging the Mediterranean—underneath the massive east wall of the Rock. And, given the size of Gibraltar, it is relatively isolated. The rooms are comfortable and well equipped, and guests will enjoy use of the private pool and terraces overlooking the sea. $$

FOOD AND DRINK:

For such a small place Gibraltar offers an amazing array of places to eat, and they cater to just about any style you fancy. Of course, priding itself on its connections, you may enjoy typical English fare, from pub grub eaten at the bar to fish-and-chips, wrapped in paper and eaten wherever you fancy. Expect to find, also, many Chinese and Indian restaurants.

Rib Room Restaurant (Europa Road), following the precedent set by The Rock Hotel in which it is located, is internationally acclaimed for its standard of excellence. The cuisine is delectable, the service is exemplary, and the ambiance of style and sophistication is enhanced by the glittering views of The Bay of Gibraltar. ☎ 73000 or fax 73513. $$$

The Kemmel's Restaurant (in the Caleta Palace house, directly overlooking the Mediterranean). Its menu has an International flavor, as does the wine list. ☎ 76501 or fax 71050. $$

SUGGESTED TOUR:

Gibraltar's diminutive size might cause people to think that it is an easy place to get around. But this would be a serious miscalculation. Many of the places of interest are on, or in, the Upper Rock Nature Reserve and, besides a lack of public transport, the roads themselves are often twisting and in a poor state of repair. But don't despair. The authorities have recognized the problem, and come up with an innovative solution. Official taxi or mini-bus guides take visitors on **The Official Rock Tour** with the intention of whetting your appetite, and the hope that you will return later, and have a series of stops. Some stops are compulsory, drivers are required to stop at these during the initial ninety-minute tour. Others are optional, and prices may be negotiated with the driver if you wish to see them. The tour costs a total of £10 per person; £5 per person for transportation, plus another £5 per person admission fee to the Nature Reserve in the Upper Rock Area. The latter, though, also includes entrance to all the attractions.

Although the tour may be started at any one of six locations, I would suggest beginning at the frontier, which is crossed by over 4,000,000 people each year. But expect a delay on your journey into town if a plane is taking off or landing; the runway cuts across the main road. The first two stops are on the east side of the rock. First is the attractive **Catalan Bay**, and second is a look at the unusual sheets on the side of the rock. These were, at one time, used to collect rainwater, which was subsequently stored in reservoirs inside the rock. These days, though, freshwater is provided by desalinating the Mediterranean's water.

Next on the agenda is the **Lighthouse**, standing 156 ft. above the high-water mark, at the southernmost tip of Gibraltar. It is the only one outside of Great Britain that is regulated by Trinity House. When the weather permits, this is a thought-provoking spot. How many other places are there in the world where two continents and two seas meet? Unfortunately, you can not count on the weather being cooperative; Gibraltar is regularly shrouded by sea mist.

It is time now to climb to the **Upper Rock Nature Reserve**, which is open daily 9:30 a.m. to 7:30 p.m. Your first destination is the **Jew's Gate** which affords spectacular views across the Strait to Morocco. On the way up, however, take time to notice the yellow patches with their iron rings that are found all around the Upper Rock. These were used to haul the heavy guns up the Rock.

Next you will come to the very dramatic ***St. Michael's Cave**, one of Europe's most amazing natural grottoes. The stalagmites and stalactites are incredible in their own right, but multicolored illuminations add yet another dimension to their beauty. The cave is so enormous that an auditorium has been situated in its interior, lending a striking background for the events that are staged here throughout the year. During the Second World War the intention was to use the cave as a hospital, and in the process of opening up a second entrance to accommodate this facility, a lower cave was excavated. This, the **Lower St. Michael's Cave**, which with the exception of the lighting is in its original condition, contains the better-known formations of the two as well as an underground lake. If you are planning on paying the caves a visit, here is a tip: Wear sturdy shoes and casual clothes as it will involve much clambering about. *The tour costs £5 per person, starts at 6 p.m. on weekdays and 2:30 p.m. on Saturday, and lasts over three hours. Reservations for this tour must be made at least three days in advance to either Mr. Walker ☎ 55829 or 40561; Mr. Pisarello ☎ 73527; or Mr. Vallejo ☎ 71871.*

An optional stop, but one highly recommended, is **O'Hara's Battery**, open daily 10 a.m. to 5 p.m., at the highest point of The Rock, 1,396 ft above sea level. Besides astounding views, you can admire the 9.2-inch gun that still commands the Strait. Probably the most popular stop on the tour, the **Ape's Den** is next, but along the way take time to study the environment here. You'll notice that there is absolutely no soil on the Upper Rock. That, however, has not precluded over 600 species of wildflower from growing into the limestone itself. By now you will have seen numerous caves; in fact there are over 150 of them inside The Rock. Over the centuries, these have yielded any number of fossil and human remains including, in 1848, the skull of a Neanderthal woman at Forbes Quarry. The area has its own unique species of wildlife as well. Most everyone has heard about the *Apes of Gibraltar, and you will, no doubt, be charmed by their antics. They will come close to you, but remember, they are not domesticated so you should not try to pet them. Also, you will be left in no doubt that theirs is a patriarchal society. The leading male dominates absolutely, and woe betide any of the others if they cross him—especially when he's feeding. But, like with grumpy grandfathers, the young babies can get away with more than the others. It is not widely known, either, that Gibraltar is the only place in Europe where monkeys roam semi-wild. Gibraltar hosts another species that is unique on mainland Europe as well. As with the apes, the British imported the Barbary Partridge in the 18th century.

The Great Siege of 1779 to 1783 presented unusual problems to those defending Gibraltar. True, the great north face of the Rock guarded the entrance to Gibraltar; but how on Earth could they mount guns upon it? The brightest military minds of the day had no answers, so General Elliott, the Commander-in-Chief, offered a reward for the best suggestion. Taking into account the characteristics of limestone, a certain Sergeant Ince came up with an answer—tunnels. This suggestion seemed to have potential, but also had one major problem—cannons are designed to fire upwards, not down. This difficulty was ingeniously circumvented as the side tunnels, branching from the main one and leading to the face itself, were dug out sloping downwards! For his efforts in defending Gibraltar, Elliott was given an annual pension of £1,500 and the Order of the Bath. A few years later he was appointed to the title Baron Heathfield of Gibraltar. Sergeant Ince wasn't ignored either. Land is one of the most treasured commodities in Gibraltar, and he was awarded a plot which he turned into a farm that bears his name to this day.

Though a visit to these *Great Siege Tunnels are listed as an optional stop on this tour; I would suggest, if your schedule will possibly permit, that you not miss them. The are inhabited by talking models and, at the very end, a gallery allows spectacular views along the eastern face of the Rock. The idea of using tunnels was not overlooked in later wars either. During the Second World War, tunnels totaling over 32 miles in combined length were excavated. These hold a fully developed power station, a hospital, and a guns division. As these are still under military control only groups can tour them, and then only by way of pre-booking through the H. M. Forces Public Relations Office, ☎ 5-4231.

Outside the Great Siege Tunnels is a viewing platform which gives a birds-eye view of the unusual runway below, and Spain in the distance. Take note, too, of the cemetery with plain, simple, Jewish graves to the left; the more elaborate Christian ones in the center; and, finally, the war graves to the right. It is as likely as not that you will be greeted here by yet another troop of amusing apes. On the way down, another optional stop is at the **Tower of Homage**. This was rebuilt in the early 14th century, and has withstood 13 sieges. Basically, it is comprised of not much more than exceedingly thick walls, and a central tower with a viewing platform.

Back at sea level you will find three more optional stops for this tour. If time does not permit on your first trip, you may want to keep these in mind for investigation at a later date. **Nelson's Anchorage** is close to the spot where Lord Nelson's body was brought ashore following the battle of Trafalgar. This spot has notable views of the Strait of Gibraltar. Nearby is the Victorian supergun, and this really is a sight to behold. With the barrel alone weighing 100 tons, it is the largest gun of its type in the world. *This may be visited Monday to Saturday 9:30 a.m. to 5 p.m.* On the opposite side of Rosia Bay is the **Parson's Lodge**, which has an interesting design and has been defending the nearby waters since the middle of the 18th century. This is being renovated, albeit slowly, and, in the process, additional guns are being added. *Visit Tuesday to Sunday 10 a.m. to 5 p.m.* The final of these attractions is one of a considerably more gentle character. The **Alameda Gardens**, prior to 1814, were used as a parade ground. In 1816 the then Lieutenant-Governor decided to redefine the use of this area, and today it is being upgraded into the Gibraltar Botanical Gardens.

Your next stop, and one that is a "must see," is the *****Gibraltar Museum**, housed in a building containing what are considered the best preserved Moorish Baths in Europe. A fifteen-minute movie, the "Story of Gibraltar," gives an overview of Gibraltar's history and other pertinent facts that will enhance your understanding and appreciation of the museum exhibits which consist, mainly, of numerous artefacts relating to the colony's history.

If you have been perceptive enough to schedule a couple of days in Gibraltar, and find yourself with some time on your hands at the end of this tour, the following are a few more worthwhile options for you to consider. On Casemates Square, in what used to be an army barracks, you'll find the **Glass Factory**. Here you may watch as artisans practice skills developed over the centuries, and then purchase your favorite from among these exquisite hand-blown glass ornaments as a souvenir—at a nice discount, of course. *Opening hours are Monday to Friday 9:30 a.m. to 7 p.m., and Saturday 9:30 a.m. to 2 p.m.* You may wish to further explore the Upper Rock Nature Reserve and, if so, you need not worry about having to walk. There is a much less taxing way up. The **Gibraltar Cable Car**, found next to the Alameda Gardens, will whisk you up to either the Middle Station—and the Apes Den, or the Top Station—which is within an easy walk of the St. Michael's Cave. *It operates, Monday to Saturday, from 9:30 a.m., and the last car up leaves at 5:15 p.m. and down at 5:45 p.m.*

Up until this point every attraction has been land-based but, considering that Gibraltar is surrounded by water and air, you should investigate the following as well. The Bay of Gibraltar, famous for its large population of dolphins, is frequently visited by whales as well. The **Dolphin Safari**, ☎ 71914, will take you out on a two-and-a-half-hour voyage to get a closer look at these fascinating creatures. On occasion, you might even get close enough to touch them! If, by the very unlikely chance, they are in hiding on the day of your voyage, you will receive, in compensation, a complimentary Dolphin Safari Book and Dolphin Safari video. If you are of the sporting sort, you will know that, where there are dolphins, the fish can not be far away—and **North Africa Safari**, ☎ 74537 and fax 74535, will know just where to find them. Their charter vessels depart Gibraltar at 6 a.m. for a day of unforgettable fishing, in the unforgettable surroundings of the Strait of Gibraltar. And, of course, where you find boats you know there will be wrecks, and divers will be intrigued to visit some of the thirty in residence around these shores and upon the surrounding reefs and pinnacles. **Rock Marine**, ☎ 73147 or fax 74754, can show you all of these and what's more, will provide an introductory trial diving lesson for novices.

How about combining the pleasures of sea and air? There can surely be no better way of seeing the "Pillars of Hercules" than from the air, and **Ocean Air**, ☎ 47333, will be more than happy to oblige. Their "flying boat" will take you on a sightseeing flight over the Rock, the Bay of Gibraltar, the Strait and Africa. And, if you are really adventurous, ask the pilot to perform a "touch and go" in the harbor or bay! Oh, one last thing; just think of the photographs you'll be able to show your friends.

Section IV

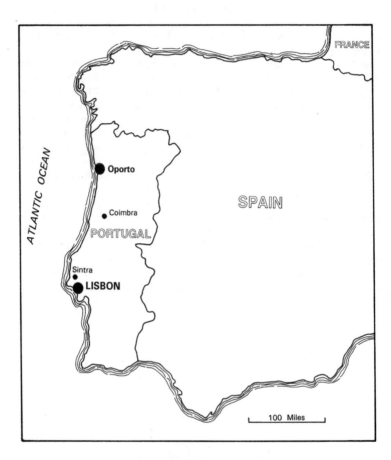

DAYTRIPS IN
PORTUGAL

The most fascinating destinations in Portugal are easily explored on daytrips from either Lisbon or Oporto. In fact, many of the best attractions are within these two cities themselves, and are covered in a series of one-day self-guided tours. For those staying overnight, hotel recommendations as well as restaurant choices are given for each destination.

Lisbon:
(Lisboa)

The Old City & Alfama

L isbon's geographical location, alongside the wide natural harbor of the Tejo river, has made it an important seaport for trade between the Mediterranean and northern Europe throughout the ages. The Phoenicians colonized the area around 1200 BC, calling it *Alis-Ubbo*; the Greeks, in their turn, called it *Olisipo*; and to the Romans, whose rule began in 205 BC, it was known as *Felicitas Julia*. Nine centuries later, in 714, the Moors overran the settlement, renaming it *Ascbouna*. Afonso I, with the assistance of northern Crusaders, reconquered the city on October 25, 1147. And, just over a century later, in 1255, Afonso III transferred the capital of Portugal from Coimbra to this city.

Portugal, taking Lisbon in its wake, became the center of the world in the 15th and 16th centuries. During this period, Vasco de Gama sailed for the Indies in 1497-1499 and Brazil was discovered in 1500. The wealth from these territories literally flowed back to Portugal. This enabled King Manuel I to build such monuments as the Monastery of Jerónimos and Tower of Belém, with the highly intricate and unusual architectural style used in this era, ultimately named in his honor; *Manueline*. In the middle of the 18th century, on November 1, 1755, an earthquake leveled much of the city. It was, however, subsequently rebuilt under the direction of the then prime minister, the Marquês de Pombal. The new style of architecture chosen became known as *Pombaline*. The best examples of this style may be seen today on the axis that runs between the magnificent Praça do Comércio, by the river, and the Praça Marquês de Pombal, which stretch features a towering statue of Pombal himself. In between these streets is the area known as Baixa, a gridded rectangle that leads into the Praça Dom Pedro IV, popularly known as Rossio, and then onto the wide, tree-lined, boulevard of the Avenida da Liberdade. The park behind the Praça Marquês de Pombal, the Parque Eduardo VII, was named in honor of King Edward VII of England, who visited Lisbon in 1902.

These days Lisbon, naturally protected from the ravages of the nearby Atlantic Ocean, is one of the premier ports of Europe and, as such, is home to miles of docks, quays and dry docks capable of servicing even the largest of oil tankers.

GETTING THERE:

Trains arrive in Lisbon on internal main lines from Oporto and Coimbra in the north, and Faro in the south. Secondary lines serve Évora and Beja, to the east, and Figueira da Foz, in the north. International services connect Lisbon to Paris, via Salamanca, Irún and Bordeaux; and to Madrid, via Valência de Alcântara and Cáceres.

Buses arrive in Lisbon, at different bus stations, from nearly every city and town in Portugal.

By car, Lisbon is connected to Coimbra, Oporto and Braga by the *auto-estrada* tollroad, and other destinations are easily reached on roads that branch from it. To the south, and the Algarve, take the A-2 *auto-estrada* tollroad to its junction with the IP-I, and continue south.

By air, International flights arrive from every destination imaginable. Internal flights are available from both Oporto and Faro.

PRACTICALITIES:

It is safest to assume that the majority of Lisbon's monuments, museums and places of interest will be closed on Monday. Visitors will quickly realize that Lisbon is built on seven hills and, except next to the river, almost nowhere is flat. In fact, nearly everywhere you go entails a jaunt up and down one, or more, of its hills. Although the subway system is being extended, in reality there is little need, except to go out to the Parque das Nações, to use it.

The Parque das Nações was the site of Expo '98, but it is some distance from the center of Lisbon. Most probably, the only serious attraction there for tourists is the sparkling new **Oceanarium** *(Oceanário)*, ☎ 891-70-02 or fax 895-57-62. *Open summer 10 a.m. to 8 p.m., closing in winter at 7 p.m., entrance 1,500$00 (EUR 7.48).*

Those spending 2/3 days in Lisbon, and most will, should seriously consider purchasing a **Lisboa Card**, costing 1,900$00 (EUR 9.50) for 24-hours, 3,100$00 (EUR 15.50) for 48-hours and 4,000$00 (EUR 20.00) for 72-hours. Besides allowing free transportation arounf town, it also offers free admission to 26 museums, monuments and other places of interest, plus other perks.

The **Dialing Code is 21**. The tourist office **Informação Turística**, ☎ 346-63-07, is in the Palácio Foz at the Praça dos Restauradores, and opens daily from 9 a.m. to 8 p.m. The city of Lisbon has a **population** of 1,500,000.

ACCOMMODATION:

The **Hotel Tivoli Lisboa** *****, ☎ 353-01-81 or fax 357-94-61, Avenida da Liberdade, 185, grand and elegant, is affiliated with the Hotéis Tivoli chain and, as such, you may expect to enjoy exemplary service from the very minute you arrive in its expansive two-level lobby. Rooms are well appointed and decorated in a modern style and the suites are particularly spacious. The location is convenient as well—on the city's main street, halfway between the city center and the Parque Eduardo VII. $$$

The **Hotel Da Lapa** *****, ☎ 395-00-05 or fax 395- 06-65, Rua do Pau de Bandeira, 4, within the city's diplomatic area, frequently plays host to visiting dignitaries. And that is not surprising. This is a particularly gracious and charming hotel. The public rooms are exceptionally elegant and, within the Palace Wing, no two rooms are alike. Each reflects the style of a different Portuguese era, from 18th-century classical to Art Deco. This establishment is a part of the Leading Hotels of the World organization. $$$

The **Hotel Avenida Palace** *****, ☎ 346-01-51 or fax 342-28-84, Rua 1 Dezembro, 123, offers both elegance and convenience; it features an impressive classical façade and boasts an enviable central location, by Rossio. The interior decor, maintained in its original style, adds warmth and character to the list of the Avenida Palace's charms. $$$

The **Altis Apartamentos** *****, ☎ 314-24-96, fax 354-86-96 and www.maisturismo.pt/altisap.html, Rua Castilho, 13, offers 40 absolutely luxurious, and large, apartments all completely equipped and with parking facilities. Reception open 24-hours, room service and secretarial services as well as an outside pool. $$$

The **Pensão York House** ****, ☎ 396-24-35 or fax 397-27-93, Rua das Janelas Verdes, 32, is a gracious pensáo disguised as a delightful 17th-century building, formerly the Convento dos Marianos. Modern facilities have been incorporated appealingly with antique furniture, marble tiling, and warm wooden floors. Its lovely patio, shaded by lush foliage, is sure to enchant. $$$

The **Hotel Real Parque** ****, ☎ 357-01-01 or fax 357-07-50, Avenida Lués Bivar, 67, is an impressive hotel, recently constructed on a quiet side street in an appealing section of the city, between the Marquês de Pombal and Campo Pequeno. Seven of the rooms have been designed to accommodate the special needs of handicapped guests. $$$

The **Aparthotel Orion Eden** ****, ☎ 321-66-00 or fax 321-66-66, Praça dos Restauradores, 18-24, is one of the newest places to stay in the city of Lisbon, just opened in mid-1996. It offers 75 studios (for one or two guests), 59 two room apartments, and a great location nearby Rossio. Guests will also enjoy the enclosed terrace which features a pool and bar. It is easily recognizable by its very interesting neo-classical façade. $$$

The **Pensão As Janelas Verdes** ****, ☎ 396-81-43 or fax 396-81-44, Rua das Janelas Verdes, 47, housed in an 18th-century ivy-covered mansion, once owned by the Portuguese novelist Eça de Queirós, is an absolute delight. This small pensáo features an uncomplicated classical style decor and an enchantingly peaceful patio. $$$

The **Hotel Metropole** ***, ☎ 346-91-64 or fax 346- 91-66, Rossio, 30, originally constructed at the turn of the century, has been recently refurbished and remodeled in a style reminiscent of the 1920s. The effect is elegant and enchanting. And, guests here may enjoy and/or purchase the fantastic Bussaco wines, exclusively offered by the Hotéis Alexandre chain. $$

The **Albergaria Senhora do Monte** ****, ☎ 886-60-02 or fax 887-77-83, Calcada do Monte, 39, takes a bit of effort to locate. It is off the beaten path, but the views, once you are here are, without a doubt, the best in town. These are best enjoyed from the delightful rooftop bar and garden. $$

The **Hotel Eduardo VII** ***, ☎ 353-01-41 or fax 353- 38-79, Avenida Fontes P. Melo, 5, is a member of the Best Western group. It is recognizable by its peculiar shape which curves around two major streets in a busy section of Lisbon. The roof-top restaurant offers sweeping views over the city and guest rooms are both spacious and comfortable. $$

The **Hotel Alif** ***, ☎ 795-24-64 or fax 795-41-16, Campo Pequeno, 51, is ultra modern in design and decor, centrally located and convenient to the bullring. It offers all the expected amenities and some not so expected, such as soundproofing, satellite T.V. and an automated wake-up call system. $$

The **Hotel Borges** **, ☎ 346-19-51 or fax 342-66-17, Rua Garrett, 108, is one of only a handful of places to stay in Chiado, an upmarket neighborhood which consists, mostly, of pricey shops and fashionable apartment buildings. This hotel, in keeping with that environment, is quite elegantly furnished; but the pieces are cleverly incorporated to create an atmosphere of refined comfort. $$

The **Hotel Suíço Atlântico** **, ☎ 346-17-13 or fax 346-90-13, Rua da Glória, 3-19, close to Rossio, is nestled into a small side street which runs parallel to the Avenida da Liberdade. Though the decor is slightly old-fashioned, the guests rooms are sizable and the public rooms are warmly decorated with stone arches and wooden beams. $$

The **Pensão Coimbra e Madrid** ***, ☎ 342-17-16 or fax 342-32-64, Praça da Figueira, 3, is a rather plain and modest pensáo, but rooms are priced accordingly. Some offer a pleasant surprise—fantastic views over the Praça da Figueira and the castle in the distance. $

The **Pensão Castilho** **, ☎ 386-08-22 or fax 386-29- 10, Rua Castilho, 57, may well be eclipsed by its larger neighbors, but should not be overlooked. This pensáo offers clean, comfortable rooms with good facilities at a very reasonable rate. It is a good choice for families or those traveling in groups as some rooms have three or four beds. $

The **Pensão Norte** **, ☎ 887-89-41, Rua dos Douradores, 159, is a pensáo very centrally located just off the Praça da Figueiras. The rooms are neat and comfortable. This is good value for money. $

FOOD AND DRINK:

Restaurante Gambrinus (Rua das Portas de Santo Antão, 23/25), is, in a word, exceptional, and one of the most famous in Portugal. The service is impeccable, the cuisine delectable and the wine list, which includes a selection of vintage ports, is impressive. If you are in an informal mood, you may still enjoy your gourmet meal—served at the bar. And, those who

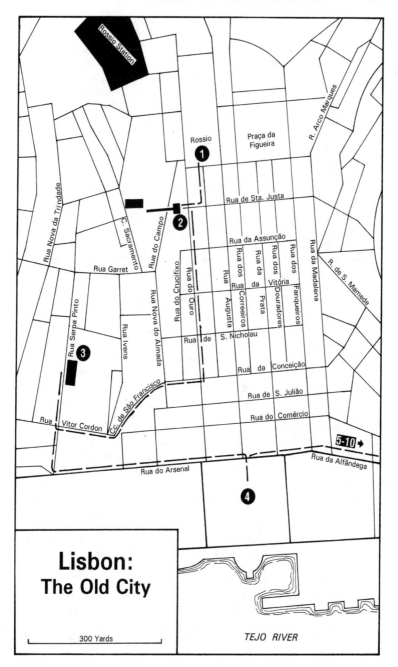

Lisbon:
The Old City

300 Yards

TEJO RIVER

prefer to dine late will be pleasantly surprised also; dinner is served until 2 a.m. ☎ 342-14-66 or fax 346-50-32. $$$

Clara Restaurante (Campo dos Mártires da Pátria, 49), is a short taxi drive from the center of Lisbon, but well worth the bother. In fact, it is one of my favorite restaurants in town. After enjoying an aperitif in the small bar, you are led into a discreet dining room which, in summer, opens on to a charming patio. The cuisine is as classical as the ambiance, with expected favorites enhanced with delicacies like Breast of Duck, Saddle of Lamb and eclectic touches including Spit of Frog-Fish and Shrimps. ☎ 885-3-53 or fax 885-2-82. $$$

Restaurante Tipico o Faia (Rua da Barroga, 56), serves traditional Portuguese cuisine in an exclusive location in the heart of the Bairro Alto. It is divided into two sections, a delightful bar and the dining room, which is charmingly decorated with wooden beamed ceilings, a multitude of archways, and beautiful *azulejos* (painted tiled pictures). You will be sere-naded by the renowned *Fado* singers. It is closed on Sunday. ☎ 342-67-42 or fax 342-19-23. $$$

Restaurante Taverna do Embuçado (Beco dos Cortumes, 10), named the "Tavern of the Hooded Man" is situated at the end of a small passageway in the ancient district of Alfama. An elegant ambiance is created by exposed wooden beams, brick archways and tiled floors. The fare is typi-cally Portuguese and, again, you will be entertained by *Fado* singers. It has generous opening hours—dinner is served until 2:30 a.m., but it is closed Sunday. ☎ 886-50-88 or fax 886-50-78. $$

Restaurante Pap'açòrda (Rua da Atalaia, 57), in the heart of the Bairro Alto, offers cuisine that is best described as eclectic and cosmopolitan. In fact, its advertising logo—the caricature of a gentleman in coattails sport-ing a cane who peers at you from beneath the brim of his top-hat, is most certainly reflective of the ambiance. Specialties include such delights as Roasted Black Blood Sausage with Turnips, Mixed Small Fried Fish, "Alioli" Sauce with Sole, Eel, Whitebait, Fillet of Angler, Squid and Shrimp, and Fried Marinated Kid. It is closed on Sunday, at Monday lunchtime, for the middle two weeks of July and for two weeks in the month of November. ☎ 346-48-11 or fax 342-97-05. $$

Restaurante Conventual (Praça das Flores, 45), is most appropriately named. This dignified restaurant is decorated to resemble a convent and serves dishes from historical convent menus. Selections are many and include such delicacies as Baby Eels Fried in Oil, Garlic and Chilli Peppers; Ox Tongue in an Egg Sauce and Country Pheasant, in addition to the more traditional dishes. It is closed on Saturday at lunchtime and there is no ser-vice on Sunday. ☎ and fax 60-91-96. $$

Restaurante Massima Culpa (Rua da Atalaia, 35-37), found in the Bairro Alto and, as the name would indicate, the cuisine on offer is Italian. A tempting array of antipasta and pasta dishes are served in a neat and uncluttered decor, at a reasonable price. It is closed on Wednesday. ☎ 342-01-21. $

Restaurante Espalha Brasas (Armazén, 12, Doca de Santo Amara, Alcântara), is in the trendy Alcântara area of the city, literally in the shadow of the magnificent April 25 suspension bridge. It is one among many in a row of modern restaurants. The building is architecturally interesting and the whimsical menu includes specials of the day and a nice selection of cocktails. During the summer months there is live entertainment. It is open until 1 a.m. daily except during the month of August, when it is closed. ☎ 396- 20-59 or fax 396-91-77. $

SUGGESTED TOUR:
Numbers in parentheses correspond to numbers on the maps.

Begin the tour in **Rossio** (1), choosing any one of the narrow streets leading from of it, in the area known as Baixa, and running towards the Tejo river. At the first crossing street, Rua de Santa Justa, turn right and continue to the end where there is an unusual iron structure. Upon closer inspection you will realize that this is an elevator, **Elevador Santa Justa** (2), which was constructed in the 19th century. And, the next logical step is to try it out. Once you reach the top climb the two levels of a tight, spiraling, metal stairs to the open-air bar at the top. This is an ideal place have some refreshments, and enjoy the panoramic views out over this intriguing town to the castle on the opposite hill.

It used to be that you could then cross a ramp to visit the **Archaeological Museum** *(Museu Arqueológico)* that was housed in the dramatic ruins of the Senhora do Monte de Carmo church, overlooking Lisbon. Originally dedicated in 1423, it was largely destroyed in the earthquake of 1755. This small museum, renown for its tombs and macabre skeletons, was within one of the sections that had been restored. However, as of late 1999, the construction of another subway line had caused subsidence on this hillside, so this is no longer an option. So, instead, go back down to Baixa and wander around these streets, the only ones in Lisbon with a grid layout, and enjoy the numerous shops in the area. Many of these are somewhat touristic but one, in particular, shouldn't be missed. **Augusta Joalheiros**, ☎ or fax 342-23-33, Rua Augusta, 106, not only has a magnificent array of plates and boxes, a wonderful range of watches, Italian jewelry and pretty glass pieces but a beautiful collection of Filligree, handcrafted gold and silver pieces from very small factories in northern Portugal that make excellent souvenirs.

Time, now, to head for one of Lisbon's finest museums, so leave Chiado by way Conceição and up São Francisco, Vitor Cordon before turning right into Serpa Pinta where you will arrive at the *****Chiado Museum** *(Museu do Chiado)* (3), ☎ 343-21-48. This museum boasts one of the most important collections of Portuguese contemporary art in the world, which includes paintings by such artists as Malhoa, Columbano and sculptures by Soares dos Reis, among others. *Opening hours are Tuesday 2 p.m. to 6 p.m. and Wednesday to Sunday 10 a.m. to 6 p.m.*

Turn left upon exiting and follow down to Arsenal where a left will lead to the Praço do Município; note that it was from the balcony of the Paços do Conselho here, dating from 1774 but renovated since then, that Portugal was declared a republic in 1910. Continue on and, soon, you will arrive at the impressive neoclassical Arco da Vitória, the gateway to the large **Praça do Comércio** (4). This graceful and expansive square, colonnaded on three sides, is home to the mustard and white colored government offices. The equestrian statue in the center is of King Jose I, who was monarch when his minister, the Marquês de Pombal, rebuilt the city following the earthquake of 1755. Before continuing on to Alfama this is the perfect spot to take a break from walking, and see some of Lisbon by way of two very different forms of transportation. The area immediately in front of the Arco is a busy bus and tram stop, but it is, most definitely, the latter that will prove more attractive. The larger, newer, ones, usually emblazoned with advertising certainly catch the eye, but it is the old-fashioned ones that captivate the mind. They can be used as a way of getting around the city, but between March and September three circular tours begin and end here, and allow you to get on and off around town. The schedules for these vary, as do the months they operate; expect a ticket to be either 2,000$00 (EUR 9.98) or 2,800$00 (EUR 13.97). The remaining side of the square is open to the river and just across and to the left you will see the dock *Terreiro do Paço*, from which the ferry boats depart, crossing the Tejo to Barreiro. It is also the home of boat cruises on the Tejo operated by **Transtejo**, ☎ 882-03-48 or fax 882-03-65. *These set sail daily, between April and October, at 11 a.m. and 3 p.m. and cost 3,000$00 (EUR 14.96).*

Suitably refreshed, leave the Praça do Comércio by taking a right turn in the top corner, and following Alfândega to the much smaller square a few hundred yards ahead. In addition to excellent views of the Cathedral towers, there is one other attraction here. The entire exterior of the **Casa dos Bicos** (5), built in the 16th century, is decorated with diamond-shaped stones. This was destroyed in the earthquake of 1755 and used as a codfish warehouse until its most recent renovation in 1982. Oddly, there is a similar house, the *Casa de los Picos*, in Segovia, Spain.

Exit the plaza by another route, the Rua dos Bacalhoeiros, a street lined with all manner of restaurants, following this to Magdalena. Take a right here and, after two blocks, you will come upon the twin, fortress-like towers of the **Cathedral** *(Sé)* (6). Originally constructed in the 12th century this, also, was renovated extensively after the 1755 earthquake. The interior is rather plain, but, in the cloisters, excavations have exposed some interesting traces of the Roman and Visigothic eras. *Open Monday to Saturday 10 a.m. to 5 p.m.*

Continue on, following the steep hill to the left of the cathedral, up to the **Largo Sta. Luzia** (7). On the right is a charming little park that affords marvelous views out over the busy Tejo waterway, where all manner of vessels are passing by. Next, and still within the park, if you look carefully you will find a small pond and a wall with two *azulejos* where a vine-cov-

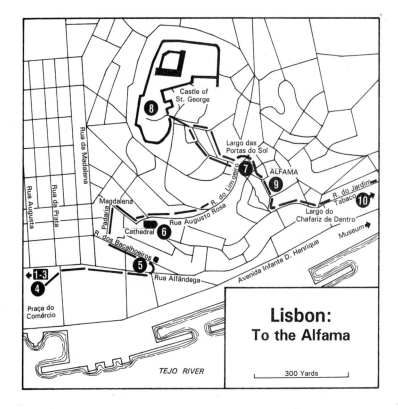

Lisbon:
To the Alfama

300 Yards

TEJO RIVER

ered area shelters old men who pass their time playing cards. This is altogether a pleasant place to recover from the exertions of the hill, and to
gather strength for those that are to come.

Press on, taking Limoeiro, again uphill, and following the signs that
direct you through a maze of narrow streets to a large gate. This is the
entrance to the ancient *Castle of St. George and Olissipónia* (Castelo de
São Jorge e Olissipónia) (8), ☎ 887- 72-44. The Romans, Visigoths, and
Moors all had fortifications on this site, and Afonso I, the first king of
Portugal, expanded upon these after his reconquest of Lisbon in 1147. Not
much of that structure remains today, but it still merits a visit. It has
enchanting flower gardens with several ponds, a limited number of animals on exhibit, and the views are absolutely magnificent. You may walk
around the ramparts to get what is virtually a birds-eye perspective of the
city. And, from a vantage point near the gate, you will glean a true appreciation for the immensity of Lisbon's natural harbor, with the giant suspension bridge looming in the distance. As you wander around you are
almost directly above the *Baixa* and the *Bairro Alto,* on the opposite hill,

seems almost within reach. Going a little farther on, there is a perfect opportunity to see, from above, the complicated layout of *Rossio* and *Restauradores*. *The castle is open daily 9 a.m. to 9 p.m. and the Olissipónia, a multimedia exhibition detailing the city's history, is open 10 a.m. to 6 p.m.*

Return back to the gate and follow along, downhill for this leg of the tour, until you reach the *Largo das Portas do Sol*. This offers more excellent views as well as the starting point for investigating *Alfama (9), the oldest section of Lisbon. This area was developed during the Visigothic era and, subsequently, the Moors built many fine mansions here. Unfortunately, very little escaped the wrath of the earthquake and, in its deteriorated state, it became the quarter for fishermen and seamen. These days this veritable maze of very steep and very narrow lanes is a colorful sight indeed. Many of the tiny houses are decorated with *azulejos* tile work and embellished with cheerful flower boxes. This is also the origin of *Fado*, the traditional folksong of Lisboa. Alfama is famous for its proliferation of restaurants, where seafood and *Fado* predominate. This is truly a place for a relaxing stroll and, therefore, I have outlined no suggested route through here. Just wander as your fancy takes you and, sooner or later, you will end up at the **Largo do Chafariz de Dentro.**

A left here, along the Rua Terreiro do Trigo, will lead you to the Largo do Museu, and the **Military Museum** *(Museu Militar)* (10), ☎ 888-23-00. The museum was founded by King Manuel I in the 16th century, and a valuable collection of military paraphernalia is now housed in this elegant 18th-century structure, which is worth seeing in its own right. *Visit Tuesday to Saturday 10 a.m. to 4 p.m. and Sunday 11 a.m. to 5 p.m.*

Immediately across from the museum is the *Santa Apolónia* railroad station and, as you have by now had quite a workout, I would recommend that you treat yourself and catch either a 39 or 46 bus back to Rossio. If you have any energy left, follow the main road, Avenida Infante D. Henrique, on what is not a very salubrious walk, back to the Praça do Comércio.

Lisbon:
(Lisboa)

*Belém

S ome of Lisbon's most appealing sights lie west of the Old City, in the
waterfront neighborhood of Belém.

GETTING THERE:
PRACTICALITIES:
ACCOMMODATION:
FOOD AND DRINK:
See pages 328-333 for all of the above.

SUGGESTED TOUR:
Numbers in parentheses correspond to numbers on the map.

Begin this tour at **Rossio**, wandering down through Baixa to the Praça
do Comércio, where a right along the riverfront will bring you to the railway terminal of **Estação Cais de Sodré**. Take one of the frequent trains that,
on its way to Belém station, passes along the waterfront and under the
massive **Ponte 25 Abril** suspension bridge.

Exit **Belém station** (1) by way of the footbridge over the road and head
for the riverside. You will see to your left the electrical generating plant
Central Tejo, which supplied electricity to Lisboa during the first half of
the 20th century. It is now the **Electricity Museum** *(Museu da Electricidade)*.
A ferry station is on the quay, but the views are dominated by the bridge
and, on the far bank, the majestic statue of **Christ in Majesty**, a smaller version of the one found in Rio de Janeiro.

Pressing on, turn right and, as you approach a small marina, your
attention will be drawn to a most unusual monument on the opposite
side, which appears even more surreal when viewed through the masts of
the moored yachts. The **Descobertas Monument** *(Monumento das
Descobertas)* (2), ☎ 301-62-28, is reached by walking around the marina
until you come to the plaza that fronts the monument, easily recognizable
by the large compass embedded there and two world globes. It is most
difficult to adequately describe this attraction and an understatement to
call it unique. It was built in 1960 to celebrate the 500th anniversary of the

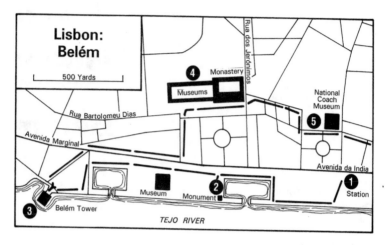

death of Prince Henry the Navigator, and, at its core, is a thin, elongated, windowless, concrete tower with an elevator inside that will whisk you to the observation tower at the top. In point of fact, it is not all that high. Nonetheless, the effect produced by its shape might make those without a head for heights a little wary, though there is no denying that it certainly has the best vantage point from which to see the area of Belém. In the age of maritime exploration sailors would stop at Belém before their departure to pray for a safe voyage and, upon returning, would come here to offer their prayers of thanksgiving. Upon the site of the original chapel built by Prince Henry the Navigator for this purpose, Infante D. Enrique, King Manuel I, subsequently constructed a monastery. The full scope of that structure may be seen clearly from the pinnacle of this modernistic monument. *Visit Tuesday to Sunday 9:30 a.m. to 6:30 p.m.* From the viewing platform it is also possible to see the distant hills of Sintra, but it is the small tower, within your view a few hundred yards away and jutting out into the Tejo, that is your next destination.

Back outside, and to the left, is a man-made lake with restaurants in its center and, beyond is rather unattractive building housing the **Museu de Arte Popular**. In truth, this will not be of interest to most visitors, so I would suggest you just continue along, rounding another marina to reach a sizable park. Within this park, actually sitting in the river and reached by a rickety footbridge, is what can truly be called the trademark symbol of not only Lisboa, but of Portugal as well. The ***Belém Tower*** *(Torre de Belém)* (3), ☎ 362-00-34, was built by King Manueline I between 1515-1520 as part of the defensive lines of Lisbon. Later, during the Spanish occupation of Portugal, it functioned as a prison and was fully restored in the middle of the 19th century. The exterior is a really marvelous example of that peculiarly intricate style of architecture known as *Manueline*. The interior, however, is, in complete contrast, bland and austere. *It is open Tuesday to*

Sunday 10 a.m. to 5 p.m.

Now cross back through the park, taking the footbridge over the railroad and road and turning back towards Lisbon at the bottom. The next few hundred yards will be noisy and uninspiring, but persevere. Suddenly, across the road from the *Museu de Arte Popular*, a huge white stone façade resembling a modern-day fort springs from nowhere. Follow on to its far end facing the beautiful gardens of the *Praça do Império*. Here you will learn that this building is the new **Cultural Center of Belém** *(Centro Cultural de Belém)*. Still, this is not the most impressive monument here. That privilege belongs to the elongated structure at the back of the square, the ****Monastery of Jerónimos** *(Mosteiro dos Jerónimos)* (4), ☎ 362-00-34, which would better be described as a complex than a building. At its end nearest to the Cultural Center is the entrance to the **Maritime Museum** *(Museu da Marinha)*, ☎ 362-00-19. Originally founded by King Luís I in 1863, this museum camped, throughout the years, in several locations before finding an appropriate home here in 1962. The exhibits reflect Portugal's famous maritime achievements, and include, among others, the plane used for the first crossing of the South Atlantic by air in 1922. *Visit Tuesday to Sunday mid-June to mid-September from 10 a.m. to 6 p.m.; and it closes an hour earlier during the rest of the year.* Farther along the façade you will come to the **National Museum of Archaeology** *(Museu Nacional de Arqueologia)*, ☎ 362-00-00, which houses notable collections of ceramics, sculpture, mosaics, glassware, and gold and silver jewelry. *It is open Tuesday 2 p.m. to 6 p.m. and Wednesday to Sunday 10 a.m. to 6 p.m.*

As interesting and significant as these last two places are, they are of just ancillary interest compared to the main attraction in Belém, which is, possibly, the main attraction in all of Lisbon as well. The entrance to the monastery, towards the far end of the façade, is the finest example of *Manueline* architecture in Lisbon. King Manuel I received Papal authorization in 1496, and construction began four years later. This endeavor was financed by the wealth generated by the new territories, and the trade monopolies granted by the Holy See. Nevertheless, following the king's death, in 1521, financial problems beset the project, which was finally completed, though not as originally planned, in the late 16th century. To the right as you enter is the ornate church of **Our Lady of Bethlehem**. Six massive and intricately carved columns lead to the altar and, beside that, doors lead to a beautiful double-level cloister. *It is open Tuesday to Sunday 10 a.m. to 5 p.m.* Note that on that part of the façade fronting the church, the complexity of the stonework around the archways is simply stunning.

As you move away from the monastery another square comes into view. Head in that direction, keeping to the left and following the pink walls, and soon you will be in the presence of the ceremonial armed guards who protect the Palace of the President of the Republic. Press on to the crossroads at the end of the pink walls, and your the next destination. The **National Coach Museum** *(Museu Nacional dos Coches)* (5) housed within the old royal riding school, is an extraordinary museum, considered to be one of the best of its genre in the world. Not only are there a wide variety of coaches, in every shape and size imaginable, from the 18th and 19th centuries, but the rooms themselves are of great artistic interest. *Opening hours are Tuesday 2 p.m. to 6 p.m., and Wednesday to Sunday 10 a.m. to 6 p.m.*

A fun way to get around this area, which is quite widespread, is to take the **Belém Train** *(Comboio de Belém),* ☎ 393-19-85, which leaves from in front of the monastery every hour on the hour from 10 a.m. *A ticket costs 500$00 (EUR 2.49), but includes discounts on some attractions.*

It is time now to end your tour, back in the center of Lisbon. But, rather than take the train again, or even a mundane bus, travel by one of Lisboa's most endearing attractions; the **old-fashioned *tramcars**. A Number 15 will take you directly to the Praça da Figueira.

Sintra and Queluz

S intra is twice blessed, first with an environment of stunning beauty, and second with a uniquely advantageous geographical location. This fact has been recognized and capitalized upon throughout the ages. The Moors took full advantage of both attributes, building two castles here; one on the lower slopes of the mountain surrounded by the splendidly lush vegetation and hillsides cascading with natural waterfalls, and the other strategically encircling the mountain peak.

Following the re-conquest in the 12th century, the Portuguese monarchs became aware of the charms of Sintra, and established a summer residence here. Towards the end of the 14th century King João I built, upon the foundations of the lower of the two Moorish castles, the *Palácio Nacional de Sintra*. This structure was enlarged by King Manuel I in the early 16th century, with further additions made at various times throughout the ensuing centuries. Today, this sprawling palace, recognizable by its two strange conical towers, fairly dominates the town of Sintra.

In like manner, the mountain of Sintra dominates the surrounding countryside, and can be seen clearly from as far away as Lisbon. From its peak there are simply amazing views of the Atlantic Ocean and the Lisbon Coast. And, this is the wonderfully romantic site of Sintra's other palace, the *Palácio Nacional da Pena*. Although lacking the historical connections of its lower counterpart, the quixotic style of this palace will be more appealing to the majority of visitors.

The town of Sintra is, in a word, charming—and inundated with tourists on weekends. Unfortunately, the buses that transport them, standing in line one after another around the main road, do little to augment Sintra's natural beauty. On the second and fourth Sunday of each month the town hosts the *Feira de São Pedro de Sintra,* a huge and intriguing outdoor market, and, on these days, the crowds are even larger. The area is also extremely congested from mid-June to mid-July during the Sintra Music Festival, when concerts are given in the palaces.

Queluz, on the other hand, is a town of few charms, but the one it does have should not be missed. Yet again, it is a palace, but one with an entirely different character to those in Sintra. And, as it is conveniently located halfway between Lisbon and Sintra, it makes for an ideal stop on the return trip.

GETTING THERE:

Trains are easily the best option, with scheduled services departing Rossio four times each hour. The journey time to Sintra is 44 minutes and to Queluz-Belas just 23 minutes. You will want to note that the train station here is also a terminal.

PRACTICALITIES:

The timing of this trip is critical as there is no co-ordination between the three palaces regarding the day of the week they have chosen to close. The *Palácio Nacional da Pena* closes on Monday, the *Palácio Nacional de Queluz* closes on Tuesday, and the *Palácio Nacional de Sintra* closes on Wednesday. Add to the mix that the museums in Sintra close on Monday. Therefore, arranging your itinerary to place you here near week's end is highly recommended. The **Dialing Code** is 21. Sintra has two **tourist offices**: the Main Office, ☎ 923-11-57 or fax 923-51-76, Praça da República; and the Railway Office, ☎ 924-16-23. Both of these are open daily from 9 a.m. to 7 p.m.

ACCOMMODATION:

The **Hotel Palácio de Setais** *****, ☎ 923-32-00 or fax 923-42-77, Avenida Barbosa du Bocage, 10, is an impressive hotel affiliated with the prestigious Hotéis Tivoli chain. You will find a more detailed description of the lovely 18th-century palace it occupies in the Suggested Tour Section, below. It is located just a short distance outside of the town of Sinatra. $$$

The **Lawrence's Hotel** *****, ☎ 910-55-00 or fax 910-55-05, Rua Consiglieri Pedroso, 38-40, is one of the most beautiful and interesting hotels that you are likely to find anywhere. It also claims to be one of the oldest hotels on the Iberian Peninsula, having first opened in 1764. In 1989 it was purchased by a Dutch couple, who oversaw a complete renovation that saw it reopen in 1999. With just 16 rooms, five of which are suites, it offers a rare combination of style and comfort, and a fine restaurant to match. $$$

The **Hotel Tivoli Sintra** ****, ☎ 923-35-05 or fax 923-15-72, Praça da República, is located in a peaceful corner of Sinatra's town center. It is also a part of the Hotéis Tivoli chain. The amenities are many and luxurious, as one would expect of a Tivoli, and the views across the valley are magnificent. $$

The **Pensão Sintra** ***, ☎ or fax 923-07-38, Travessa dos Avelares, 12, São Pedro, is housed in one of many lovely private homes in an area just outside Sintra. This pleasing pensão is clean, neat and tidy and features a large garden with a private pool. $

The **Hotel D. Maria I** ****, ☎ 435-61-58 or fax 435-61-89, Largo Palácio Nacional de Queluz, is within a very beautiful structure, once known as the "Clock Tower", which has been tastefully transformed into a marvelous pousada. In days gone by it housed the staff of the fabulous 18th-century Queluz National Palace which stands just opposite. $$

FOOD AND DRINK:

Restaurante Hotel Palácio de Setais (Hotel Palácio de Setais, Avenida Barbosa du Bocage, 10), changes its menu daily to entice diners with a variety of International and traditional Portuguese dishes. The ambiance is reflective of the character of the late 19th-century palace in which it is housed. ☎ 923-32-00 or fax 923-42-77. $$$

Restaurante Cozinha Velha (Pousada D. Maria I, Largo Palácio Nacional de Queluz), is quite unique. It is, appropriately, housed in what were once the old kitchens for the Queluz Royal Palace, situated just across the road. Its lofty wooden-beamed ceiling and simple decor provide a tantalizing glimpse of past centuries. It is acclaimed for its old-fashioned preparation of the more traditional Portuguese dishes such as Fried Squid and Boiled Potatoes or Clams with Pork Chunks. Adding to your enjoyment will be live entertainment, by a pianist on Wednesdays and Saturdays and by a harpist on Tuesday, Thursday and Friday evenings. ☎ 435-07- 40 or fax 436-22-34. $$$

Restaurante Panorâmico (Hotel Tivoli Sintra, Praça da República), overlooks the lush and verdant Sintra valley. A different speciality of the week is on offer as the main dish each evening, or you may select from a rather small general menu. ☎ 923-35-05 or fax 923-15-72. $$

SUGGESTED TOUR:

Numbers in parentheses correspond to numbers on the map.

This tour begins at the classical railway station, *Rossio,* the very center of Lisbon. It's best to leave early, and you need not worry about catching a train; they depart every fifteen minutes. The journey is pleasantly short, lasting under 45 minutes, but it does not foretell the delights to come.

Leaving the train station, turn left and then wind around to the right. You will be greeted, immediately, by the elegant outline of the Town Hall. Here take a left, into the *Volta do Duche,* where you will get your first true impressions of the uncommon geographical features of Sintra. You will also see directly ahead, past a steeply lined ravine and in the shadows of the towering mountain, the distinctive conical towers of the palace. To get to it, and the town, continue following the *Volta* around. When you reach Liberdade Park, which rises to the left, take the steps leading down into the ravine to the **Museum House of Anjos Teixeira** *(Museu-Casa da Anjos Teixeira)* (1). Here you'll find an important collection of sculptures, plaster-of-paris studies and other works by Artur Anjos Teixeira, who lived from 1884 to 1935. Also on display are works by his son, Pedro, who still lives and works in Sintra. *Visit Tuesday to Friday 9:30 a.m. to noon and 2 p.m. to 6 p.m., and Saturday, Sunday and holidays 2 p.m. to 6 p.m.*

Back up on the *Volta* refresh yourself, like the locals do, by partaking of the fresh spring water from the fountains to your left. As you approach the town center the enormity, and complexity, of the *National Palace of Sintra* *(Palácio Nacional de Sintra)* (2), ☎ 910-68-40, becomes more evident,

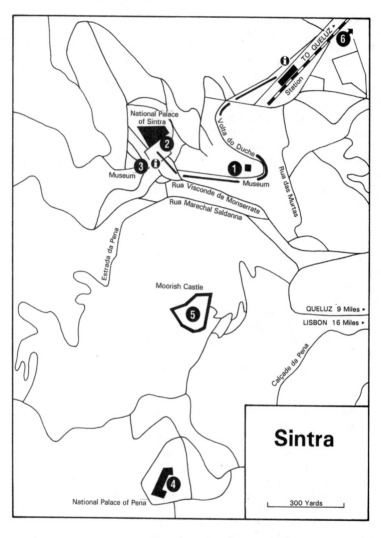

completely overshadowing all other structures in town. The contrasting architectural styles from the many different eras represented in its construction, and its subsequent reconstructions and renovations have combined, not always harmoniously, to produce a most unusual façade. The result is not entirely aesthetically pleasing, although the *Manueline* windows are of some interest, and transitions between the various sections are not always accomplished smoothly. Bits and pieces seem to appear from everywhere. Nevertheless this, also called the *Paço Real* or *Palácio da*

Vila, is the most important royal palace in Portugal.

The interior is equally disparate, and not particularly luxurious. Most notable among its rooms are the **Hall of the Coats of Arms** *(Sala dos Brazoes);* the **Hall of the Magpies** *(Sala das Pêgas),* whose ceiling displays 136 magpies, a decoration that, legend has it, was inspired by a royal scandal involving one of the 136 ladies-in-waiting; and the **Hall of the Swans** *(Sala dos Cisnes),* the largest of the rooms, which is embellished with painted and ornamental swans. The palace also boasts a most important collection of Mudéjar *azulejos.* The building is presently used to host official receptions, concerts, pageants, and the like. *Opening hours are daily, except Wednesday, 10 a.m. to 1 p.m. and 2 p.m. to 5 p.m., with the last ticket sold one half-hour prior to closing time. Entrance 400$00 (EUR 2.00).*

For a change of pace, as you pace between palaces, indulge the child who still lives inside of you with a visit to the **Toys Museum** (3), ☎ 910- 60-16, located in the Largo Latino Coelho. Revisit fantasy land as you investigate the exhibits, which contain no less than 20,000 toys; ranging from toy soldiers, of course, to dolls, puppets, and Meccano sets. *It is open Tuesday to Sunday 10 a.m. to 6 p.m.*

It is now time to visit the *National Palace of Pena *(Palácio Nacional da Pena)* (4), ☎ 910-53-40, totally different in character, at the top of the hill. There is, however, one question; how do you get there? Walking is definitely not recommended unless, that is, you are of a mind to have a workout. Even for the physically fit, in the summer it's sure to be an uncomfortable climb. Luckily, during that season a bus operates a service to the top but, failing that, opt for a taxi; you will most certainly not regret it. As you climb the hill and enter into the *Parque da Pena,* you would be remiss not to take a moment to survey the variety of foliage present here. These have their origins from all over the world. At the beginning of the 16th century, 1503 to be exact, the Monastery of Nossa Senhora da Pena was constructed on this fantastic site. And, if the astounding views out over the surrounding plains and ocean were not conducive to contemplation, then nothing would be. Religious orders were, however, expelled from Portugal in 1832, and this small monastery was allowed to fall into a state of disrepair.

Seven years later Ferdinand of Saxe-Coburg-Gotha, husband of Queen Maria II, realized its indisputable potential and purchased what could, then, be best described as partial ruins. Not content to leave matters as they were and inspired by the Bavarian castles of his homeland, he commissioned a German architect, Baron Eschewege, to construct the castle of his fantasies. And now, sitting proudly at the pinnacle of the hill and visible for many, many, miles around, is the most tantalizingly fascinating creation you will ever likely chance upon. A multitude of architectural styles combine with brilliant colors to challenge all known concepts of harmony; and the result is so outrageously outlandish that you cannot fail to be charmed.

That is, just on the exterior. The interior has been left more or less undisturbed, and the message that comes across loud and clear is that this nobleman was not keen to be without his creature comforts. Well, let me clarify that; it is evident that he was content with nothing short of absolute luxury. You have to admire his tastes; it is the kind of place anyone would want to live in, even these days. The impact of this splendor is heightened as you consider that Portugal is not the most affluent of countries even now, let alone then. It is little wonder, given its extravagance, that the monarchy in Portugal only lasted another seventy years. *Visit Tuesday to Sunday 10 a.m. to 1 p.m. and 2 p.m. to 5 p.m., with the last ticket sold half an hour prior to closing time. Entrance 400$00 (EUR 2.00).*

The path back down the mountain to Sintra is a little rough at times but, overall, it is not too bad. And it does afford you an opportunity to explore the ruins of the 8th-century **Moorish Castle** *(Castelo dos Mouros)* (5), ☎ 923-51-16. Once the rough path comes to an end, the tarmacked road leads down into São Pedro, and, if you pass this way on the second or fourth Sunday of the week, you are in for a wonderful surprise. The *Feira de São Pedro de Sintra* is an open-air market where you can find just about anything you might, or might not, want; clothes, household sup- plies, furniture, fish and animals—even a flea market. A variety of delicious foods are on offer as well. Particularly tasty is a bread roll with a sausage in the middle, which is baked in a brick oven. From here it is a very pleas- ant stroll, past more verdant foliage, back down to Sintra proper or, those who so choose, may take a diversion through the Liberdade Park.

There is yet another palace in Sintra—just a mile outside of the town to be exact—and this is one where you can share in the luxury. Originally constructed in the late 18th century by the Dutch Consul, the *Palácio de Seteais* was sold, not too long afterwards, to the 5th Marquis of Marialva. In 1802 he added a wing and, uniquely, connected the two buildings with a monumental arch. Today, it houses a majestic hotel.

Head back to the station now, and take the next train to **Queluz-Belas**. Come out of its station, turn left and follow the Avenida António Enes, past the public gardens of the Avenida da República and through the Rua da República to the Largo do Palácio. In truth this downhill walk is less than inspiring, but you definitely will not be disappointed at the end. Here, the narrow, crowded streets suddenly open out to reveal, directly ahead, the delightful pink façade of the *National Palace of Queluz (Palácio Nacional de Queluz)* (6), ☎ 435-00-39. Complementing that, and in the same style, to your left, is the tower and accompanying building that are now home to the pousada. Before its conversion, however, this elegant "Clock Tower" was the residence for those who served in the palace across the road. Construction on the palace itself was initiated by the future King Pedro III in 1747, but it was decades later before the structure was completed. The resulting building is what most people envision a royal palace should be, and its splendid formal gardens are more than reminiscent of the Palace of Versailles. The interior is just as sumptuous, graced by every kind of artistic work imaginable. Confirming its stature is the fact that it serves as the official residence of guests of the Portuguese State. At other times it is a fitting setting for concerts and pageants. *Opening hours are daily, except Tuesday, from 10 a.m. to 1 p.m. and 2 p.m. to 5 p.m., with entrance of 500$00 (EUR 2.49). The ornamental gardens are open in summer from 10 a.m. to 6:30 p.m. and close at 5 p.m. in the winter months (November to April), admission 100$00 (EUR .50).* It is worthwhile scheduling a visit here on Thursdays betwen May and October (except August) when, at 11 a.m., the Portuguese Cavalry School puts on an interesting equestrian show, for a 1,200$00 (EUR 5.99) admission price.

Oporto:
Tour #1

Oporto's history has been inextricably linked to its strategic position; high on the banks of the Douro river, within eyesight of the Atlantic Ocean. This had attracted the Phoenicians long before the Romans, in the 3rd century BC, expanded upon the existing settlement on the north bank. They called it *Portus,* and founded a new one on the opposite side, naming it *Cale.* The twin towns of *Portus Cale* grew to become major cities within the Roman Empire and, much later, were to be the derivation of the name and language for the country of Portugal.

Although the Moors invaded and conquered Oporto, they were expelled in the 9th century, much earlier than in most any other town on the Iberian Peninsula. In 1095 the daughter of King Alfonso VI of Castile, Princesa Dona Teresa, wed Henry of Burgundy, and *Portucale* was transferred to him as a portion of her dowry. It was their son, D. Afonso Henriques, who, subsequently, proclaimed himself the first King of Portugal.

With the 15th century came Prince Henry the Navigator, Oporto's most famous citizen. It was he who equipped the fleet that, eventually, wrested control of Cuenta from the Moors in 1415, and went on to lead the famous explorations that led to a Portuguese overseas empire. Another period of affluence ensued during the 18th century following the signing of the Treaty of Methuen, in 1703, between England and Portugal. This facilitated a reciprocal trade procedure, under which English cloth and Portuguese wine received favorable trading conditions in one anothers' countries. The names of British wine merchants who, consequently, opened businesses in Oporto are, even today, in much evidence upon the rooftops of the Port Lodges in Gaia.

Conversely, the 19th century brought with it much turmoil. In response to the capture of Oporto by Napoleon's troops in 1808, the British dispatched Arthur Wellesley, later better known as the Duke of Wellington, to restore order. The whole exercise had to be repeated just one year later, however, in the wake of a second French attack. An internal attempt to curtail the powers of the crown gave rise to a conflict between King Miguel I, and his brother Pedro of Brazil, which was known as the "War of the Two Brothers." During the hostilities the former, ruling as an absolute dictator, besieged Oporto for a full year, in the process reducing the citizens to a state of near starvation, before Pedro returned to Portugal to defeat his brother.

In the latter part of the century two intricate metal bridges were constructed to span the Douro. One of these, the railway bridge *Ponte Dona Maria Pia,* was designed by Eiffel. Early in the 20th century, with the demise of the monarchy, came a period of renewed economic expansion that continues today.

The people of Oporto, *Portuenses,* are stubbornly proud of their reputation as being a serious, hard working, independently spirited people. And this is immediately evident to visitors to this city. Its population is decidedly working class and, not coincidently, it is much more dour than its sister city of Lisbon. Should you wander through the maze of narrow, steep streets directly below the Cathedral, you will see a degree of poverty that is not always so obvious in other Portuguese cities. Few will fail to notice, either, the city's passion for soccer. Everywhere you go, even on the steepest of steps, you are sure to come upon some aspiring player delicately and skillfully maneuvering a ball with his feet. Few things are guaranteed to encite more excitement in the Portuenses than a victory won by their favorite Porto team, especially if the losing team hails from their arch rival Lisbon.

Even given the facts that there are no major tourist attractions here, and that the city may, at times, appear somewhat grey and drab, this is a place with a unique charm. Few visitors will leave regretting their stay in Oporto.

GETTING THERE:

Trains arrive at Oporto on the mainline from Lisbon; and on International services from Vigo, Spain, via Valença do Minho; and from Paris, via San Sebastián, Burgos, Salamanca and Pampilhosa.

Buses are a viable option from either Lisbon or Coimbra, but do not expect that they will be faster or more frequent.

By Car, Oporto, 200 miles north of Lisbon, is reached on the A-1 *auto-estrada* toll road. From Oporto, A-4 *auto-estrada* runs as far west as Amarante, from where regular highways continue on to Vila Real and then either Chaves or Bragança.

By Air, Oporto's Francisco Sá Carneiro airport is a short distance north of the city, and receives a limited number of International flights. Internal flights connect the city to Lisbon and Faro.

PRACTICALITIES:

Lisbon is built on seven hills, more than Oporto it's sure, but those in Oporto are definitely steeper. Be aware: it is impossible to go anywhere in this city without a stiff walk. The **Dialing Code** is 22. The tourist office **Centro Informação Turística ICEP,** ☎ 205-75-14 or fax 205- 32-12, is at Praça D. João I, a tiny street just off Rua do Bonjardim, and opens Monday to Friday 9 a.m. to 7 p.m., and Saturday, Sunday and holidays 9:30 a.m. to 3:30

p.m. While there consider purchasing a **Passe Porto** that offers free transport on the buses and trams, free entrance to eight museums and discounts to others as well as discounts in certain stores. A one day pass costs 800$00 (EUR 3.99) and a two day one 1,100$00 (EUR 5.49). Oporto has a **population** of over 400,000.

ACCOMMODATION:

The **Hotel Infante de Sagres** *****, ☎ 200-81-01 or fax 31-49-37, Praça D. Filipa de Lencastre, 62, is a beautifully appointed hotel in the city center. The public rooms are furnished with fine antiques and the guest rooms offer all the amenities a discerning traveler would expect. $$$

The **Porto Palácio Hotel** *****, ☎ 608-66-00, fax 609-14-67 or e-mail pto.palaciohotel@mail.telepac.pt, Avenida de Boavista, 1269, located in an affluent suburb of Oporto, is an elegant 19-story hotel that, until recently, used to be the Sheraton. Since being taken over a complete refurbishment has taken place incorporating all the expected modern facilities and guests will be able to choose from Classic or Business Rooms, with the latter having a desk and a second phone line for modem connections. Look, also, for the extensive Solinca Health Club, that has facilities for massage and other treatments. $$$

The **Hotel Dom Henrique** ****, ☎ 200-57-55 or fax 201-94-51, Rua Guedes de Azevedo, 179, is right in the heart of the city, convenient to the shopping district and to attractions. Of the 22 floors in this hotel, one is reserved for non-smoking guests. There is also a bar with a panoramic view. $$

The **Grande Hotel da Batalha** ****, ☎ 200-05-71 or fax 200-24-68, Praça de Batalha, 116, is a recently remodeled, charming, hotel, located a short walk from the city center. Features include room designed to accommodate the special needs of handicapped guests, rooms for women and non-smokers, and a terrace with panoramic views. $$

The **Grande Hotel do Porto** ***, ☎ 200-81-76 or fax 21-10-61, Rua de Santa Catarina, 197, is a pleasant and stylish hotel, located in a popular pedestrian shopping street, a few blocks away from the center of town. A spacious bar and delightful restaurant complete the package. $$

The **Hotel Internacional** ***, ☎ 200-50-32 or fax 200-90-63, Rua do Almada, 131, is just a block off the wide Avenida dos Aliados in the very center of Oporto. This hotel offers a curious, yet pleasing, blend of Baroque and modern styles. $$

The **Hotel da Bolsa** ***, ☎ 202-67-68 or fax 31- 88-88, Rua Ferreira Borges, 101, is conveniently near both the shopping districts and the tourist attractions, and closeby the Stock Exchange—from which it gets its name. It has an attractive façade, comfortable rooms, inviting public areas and a prime location. $$

The **Albergaria Miradouro** ****, ☎ 57-07-17 or fax 57-02-06, Rua da Alegria, 598, is on the upper floors of a prominent tower block which, itself, is set upon the summit of a hill behind the city center. This very unusual combination of height on height affords incredible views over Porto and the surrounding terrain. A very highly acclaimed restaurant is also found here. $$

The **Pensão dos Aliados** ***, ☎ 200-48-53 or fax 200-27-10, Rua Elísio de Melo, 27, overlooks the street from which it gets its name. Located in an impressive building which has been designated a city landmark, this pensão is one of the better of its type. $

FOOD AND DRINK:

Restaurante Dona Filipa (Hotel Infante de Sagres, Praça Filipa de Lencastre, 62), echos the ambiance of the hotel in which it is housed; highly dignified and medieval in style. Both the menu and wine list are comprehensive with many dishes prepared table side. The service, as your would anticipate, is impeccable. In cooperative weather you may choose to dine outdoors on the lovely patio. ☎ 200-81-01 or fax 31-49-37. $$$

Restaurante Portucale (Albergaria Miradouro, Rua da Alegria, 598), is located some distance from the town center at the very top of a prominent tower clock. This widely acclaimed restaurant is most unusual indeed. Specialties include a mouth-watering variety of traditional Portuguese and International meat, fish and game dishes, and the wine list is impressive. The views over Oporto and the surrounding area are a fitting accompaniment to this dining experience. ☎ 57-07-17 or fax 57-02- 06. $$$

Restaurante Don Manoel (Avenida Montevideu, 384), is within an old mansion with enticing views out over the Atlantic Ocean. As you would expect, fish and shellfish dishes dominate the menu. The choices are many; just about anything that swims is available here. The *Parrilhada mista* (Mixed Grill of Fish and Shellfish), prepared for four, is the speciality of the house. This establishment caters to more than your appetite for food, as it co-hosts a jewelers' store and an antique shop. It is closed Sundays and holidays. ☎ 537-07-17 or fax 537-02-06. $$$

Restaurante Madruga (Hotel Porto Palácio, Avenida Boavista, 1269), offers an extensive à la carte menu featuring many Portuguese and International dishes, as well as vegetarian selections. On Friday and Saturday evenings the menu is expanded to include a number of deliciously tempting dishes reflecting traditional cuisine from the various regions of Portugal. Also on the weekends you will be serenaded by folksingers. ☎ 608-66-00 or fax 609-14-67. $$

Restaurante D. Tonho (Cais da Ribeira, 13-15), is among many restaurants on the quayside, set in the shadow of Eiffel's unique bridge. Expect a modern ambiance in an ancient environment where the exposed walls, in places several feet thick, are centuries old. Fish and shellfish figure prominently on the menu, but it also includes a number of traditional and regional dishes. ☎ 200- 43-07 or fax 208-57-91. $$

Restaurante Taverna do Bebobos (Cais da Ribeira, 24-25), on the Ribeira waterfront, has lovely views out over the Douro river. If you are in the mood for a little history lesson, look carefully and you will see marks made to record the points at which the river has crested during past floods. Diners enjoy a real tavern atmosphere and scrumptious food. My favorite is their Octopus Rice. It is closed Monday and December 20 to January 10. ☎ 31-35-65. $$

Restaurante Tripeiro (Rua de Passos Manuel, 195), shares the name of a dish for which Oporto is renown; Tripe. In addition to its tourist and à la carte menus, there are nine suggested menus, for lunch or dinner, that range in price from 2,200$00 to 12,000$00. Often, of course, these feature tripe.It is closed Sunday. ☎ 200-58-86 or fax 31-59-25. $$

Restaurante Chez Lapin (Rua dos Canastreiros, 42), is another of the characterful restaurants found in the Ribeira district. It has a rustic ambiance with antiques hanging everywhere and offers a different typical Portuguese dish each day. There are some seats out on the sidewalk. ☎ 200-64-18. $

SUGGESTED TOUR:
Numbers in parentheses correspond to numbers on the map.

Begin this tour at the **Estação de São Bento** (1), a railway terminal right in the center of town. The main railway station, the *Estação d Campanhã*, is on the edge of town, and a shuttle service links the two. *São Bento*, though, is more than just a train station, it is an attraction in its own right. Visitors to Oporto would be remiss if they did not pause to admire the local scenes, so colorfully, and beautifully, depicted on *azulejos*.

Turn left out of the station and head up the hill, on Avenida D. Afonso Henriques, in the direction of the Cathedral. Just before reaching it, you will come to a small open-air market to the right, which is prefaced by an interesting plaza. The elevation here allows a panoramic perspective not only of the city below, but of the Port Lodges in Gaia and the Douro winding its way to the Atlantic. Perhaps even more dramatic, however, is the visual revelation that this city is crammed quite tightly into a steep-sided valley. The building that dominates the opposite side of the hill is the pencil-thin tower of *Clérigos*, which you will have the opportunity to explore later in the tour. Turning your attention back to the plaza, you may note that children often utilize the edge of this plaza as a soccer pitch, and it is amusing to watch the ritual played out when the ball goes over the edge and disappears down into the distance. There is no argument about who fetches it; that always falls to the last one to have touched it, even if it by way of an unfortunate deflection! You may glean from the appearance of the kids that they are not particularly well-heeled. And, as you investigate the surrounding area, you will understand the reason why.

It is time now to visit the **Cathedral** *(Sé)* (2), ☎ 220-59-02. Stylistically, the impressive exterior exhibits elements from its original construction, as a fortress/church, in the 12th and 13th centuries, as well as Baroque additions effected during the 17th and 18th centuries. On the other hand, the interior, excepting the 17th-century silver altar, a 14th-century Gothic

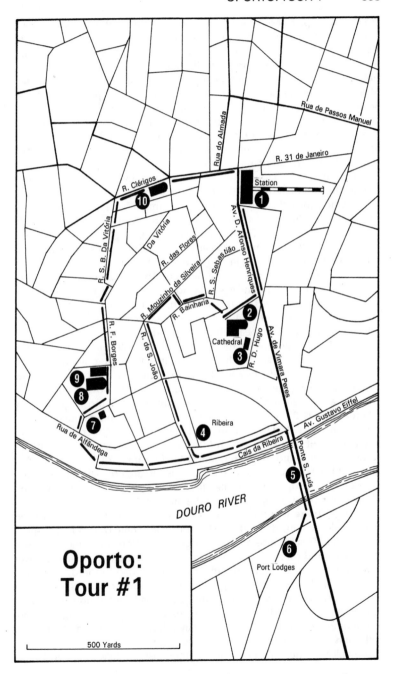

Oporto:
Tour #1

500 Yards

cloister with picturesque *azulejos,* and the 18th-century Galilé chapel, contains few splendors. *Opening hours are Monday to Saturday 9 a.m. to 12:30 p.m. and 2:30 p.m. to 5:30 p.m. Entrance 250$00 (EUR 1.25).* Before leaving the area investigate a small street, Rua D. Hugo, immediately behind the Cathedral. There, at number 32, you'll find the **House and Museum of Guerra Junqueiro** *(Casa Museu de Guerra Junqueiro)* (3), ☎ 205-36-44. In this 18th-century Baroque house are furniture and works of art collected by the famous Portuguese poet Guerra Junqueiro, who lived between 1850 and 1923. *Open Tuesday to Saturday 10 a.m. to 12:30 p.m. and 2 p.m. to 5:30 p.m., and Sunday 2 p.m. to 5:30 p.m. Entrance 150$00 (EUR .75), free on Saturday and Sunday.*

Return to the plaza and take the steps down, by the side of the equestrian statue, and a left at the bottom brings you to Rua Bainharia. As the street winds down the hill, past ancient apartment blocks tightly squeezed together and numerous small bars and stores, you will become keenly aware of the poverty. The numerous urchins running around are a reminder of Victorian times—Dickens's on the Douro, perhaps! And, pop into a bar if you get the chance. The beer will be refreshingly cool, and your entre, most certainly, will be unusual. There are no doors as such, just those swinging entrances similar to those of Wild West saloons, as seen in the movies. Next, turn right on the Rua da Ponte Nova and then, almost immediately, left out along the much busier Rua Mouzinho da Silveira. At the junction, bear left down Rua de São João.

The Douro glistens at the bottom of the hill, but the way there involves negotiating across the Rua Infante D. Enrique, arriving at the Praça da Ribeira, where, by a few bars and a fountain, a left turn will allow you to walk along the riverside in an area commonly known as **Ribeira** (4). By here, also, there are an array of boat trips of which those operated by **Douroacima,** ☎ 200-64-18 or fax 200-88-56 can be recommended. During the day the "Five Bridges" cruise is popular, but the night cruise will offer you a different perspective of Oporto. This is a popular spot with a multitude of charms, and many frequent it for its variety of restaurants, bars and, not least, its views. Across the river is the area of Gaia, home of the famous Port Lodges, whose familiar English names are displayed on almost every rooftop up and down the hill.

To get there you have to cross one of Oporto's landmarks, indeed what could be considered its symbol, the iron ***Ponte D. Luís I** (5) suspension bridge. This is a most unique bridge. In addition to the main roadway, it has a second running right across its top. When crossing via the lower level, you will most surely note the unusual sailboats moored just off the opposite bank. The barrels on their decks give you a clue as to what their original use was. In days gone by, the port was brought downriver from the estates to the lodges using these vessels, but the building of a dam brought those days to an end. These days, they mostly ornament the river, although they are actually raced on occasion.

Logically, one would assume that the most prestigious of **Port Lodges**

(6) would be on the prime real estate—closest to the river—but that is not so. The Douro has a propensity to flood, with the blue markers on the buildings along the Ribeira showing just how high the waters can rise. Consequently, the most prestigious lodges are on higher, safer ground up the hill. Of course, no visit to Oporto would be complete without a visit to one of these lodges, and you are certainly spoilt for choice. Whether you choose the nearest one or that of your favorite brand, all are, generally, open from 9 a.m. to 12:30 p.m. and 2 p.m. to 5 p.m. But a word of warning is definitely needed here. Port wine must always be drunk sensibly, as it doesn't take too many glasses to leave you considerably the worse for wear. Beware then the free samples. The wine itself comes in a multitude of different guises, all of which you'll be offered tastes of; and some houses simply leave bottles out for you to help yourselves. If you imbibe too liberally the hills that await you will look, and feel, like mountains.

Time now to cross back over that strange bridge, inaugurated in 1886, lingering a moment to take in how amazingly steeply the buildings rise away from the quayside.Stroll back along *Ribeira* and, just past the impressive iron gates, turn right into Rua de Alfândega. Halfway up this narrow street is what, at first glance, appears to be an unprepossessing house, The **Casa do Infante** (7). This is, reputedly, the house where Prince Henry the Navigator was born in 1394, and up until the 19th century served as the city's Customs House. It was rebuilt in 1677 and restored again in the present century. Today it houses the Oporto historical archive, which can only be visited by prior arrangement.

At the top of the hill, by the Praça do Infante D. Enrique, are two buildings that definitely merit a visit. Just outside the square, to the left, is the ***St. Francis Church** *(Igreja de São Francisco)* (8), ☎ 220-62-10. This is a Gothic-style Franciscan convent, dating from the 14th and 15th centuries, which boasts a substantial amount of 18th-century Baroque carving, though it suffered a considerable amount of damage during the siege of the "War of the Two Brothers." There is a small museum here as well but it is the church itself, particularly ornate with magnificent altar pieces, that is of most interest. *It is open Monday to Saturday 9:30 a.m. to 4:30 p.m., entrance 500$00 (EUR 2.49).*

Just around the corner, in the praça, is an altogether more temporal attraction. The ***Bolsa Palace** *(Palácio da Bolsa)* (9), ☎ 233-99-00, the Commercial Trading Hall, dates from the 19th century. The main attraction here is the trading hall itself, with a magnificent painting featuring the Alhambra, in Granada, Spain. *Guided tours, in Portuguese, French, and English, commence daily, 9 a.m. to 12:30 p.m. and 2 p.m. to 5:30 p.m. Entrance 750$00 (EUR 3.74).* Before continuing on the tour take a very short detour around the corner to the **Casa das Rolhas**, ☎ 205-08-37, at 13, Rua de Mouzinho da Silveira. Founded in 1850 this hardly seems that it could have changed since then, and you will find all kinds, and sizes, of wooden barrels and jugs etc., that make for excellent and most unusual souvenirs.

The next stop is some distance away and, yes, you have guessed correctly; it is steeply uphill all the way! First, take Rua F. Borges, which runs up the side of the market. Then cross Belomonte, going up the steps to Rua da Vitória, and taking a left that leads into the smaller São Bento da Vitória. This will bring you, at its end, to the Campo Mártires da Pátria. Before you have had a chance to catch your breath you will recognize, to the right, the unmistakable outline of the **Clérigos Tower** (*Torre dos Clérigos*) (10), ☎ 200-80-56. There is an 18th-century church, of Baroque and rococo style, that is of some note, but it is the tower that is the main attraction. At 246 ft., it has the distinction of being the tallest bell tower in the country, and those with any energy remaining may climb its 225 steps for the finest view in all of Oporto. *Visit the church Monday to Saturday 10 a.m. to midday and 2 p.m. to 5 p.m., and Sunday 10 a.m. to 1 p.m. and 8 p.m. to 10:30 p.m.; and the tower, daily 10 a.m. to midday and 2 p.m. to 5 p.m. Entrance to the tower 200$00 (EUR 1.00).*

From Clérigos it is a short, but, of course, up and down, journey along the Rua Clérigos, past the statue of D. Pedro IV, and back to the Estação de São Bento to end this tour.

Oporto:
Tour #2

M ore of Oporto's charms can be found on this short excursion.

GETTING THERE:
PRACTICALITIES:
ACCOMMODATION:
FOOD AND DRINK:
See pages 349-352 for all of the above.

SUGGESTED TOUR:
Numbers in parentheses correspond to numbers on the map.

A number of Oporto's attractions are a short distance away from the city center and, therefore, are difficult to incorporate into a walking tour. Also, to get a true perspective of the differing physical attributes of the city you must investigate the area in an alternative fashion. These obstacles are not insurmountable, however, and, in fact, can be overcome in the most charming of ways. This tour begins in the **Praça Gomes Teixeira** (1), just one block away from the Clérigos Tower. Here, await the arrival of a Number 18 tramcar. Upon boarding, be sure to pick a window seat on the left, then settle back and enjoy yourself. The ride may be a little bumpy, but you will soon become oblivious to that. The route travels downhill, initially, along Da Restauração, but soon flattens out and follows the river towards the west. Once under the new *Ponte da Arrábida* the Douro widens dramatically, and you will get your first views of the Atlantic Ocean in the distance. You will note that a huge sandbar obstructs most of the mouth of the river, and just past this point the road swings in a northerly direction, following the ocean.

This area is very popular with *Portuenses* and, farther along when the road changes to Avenida de Montevideu, there are one or two particulary elegant restaurants, my favorite of which is the Don Manoel. In short order, at the *Castelo do Queijo*, there is a large traffic circle and the Avenida da Boavista double backs on Montevideu, at a ninety-degree angle, running in a straight line through the heart of Oporto's upmarket area. Just past here, and on the right opposite the **City Park** *(Parque da Cidade)*, is a most unusual museum indeed. The **Paper Money Museum**

(Museu do papel Fiduciário) (2), ☎ 610-11-89, in a modern building and in its own grounds details the history of paper money and in doing so claims to be unique in Europe. *Open Monday to Friday 10 a.m. to 1 p.m. and 2:30 p.m. to 6:30 p.m. Entrance 300$00 (EUR 1.50).* A short distance further along the Avenida alight at the junction with Avenida Marechal Gomes da Costa. Then follow that street down to the park that is home to the *Fundação de Serralves*, a fine example of a 1930s house, where you will find the **National Museum of Contemporary Art** *(Museu Nacional de Arte Moderna)* (3), ☎ 617-26-94 or fax 617-38-62. Here, besides the museum there are exhibitions, concerts and other amusement activities. *The museum opens Tuesday, Wednesday and Friday 10 a.m. to 7 p.m., Thursday 10 a.m. to 10 p.m. and Saturday, Sunday and holidays 10 a.m. to 7 p.m. Exhibitions are open 10 a.m. to 7 p.m. and the park opens at 10 a.m. and closes at 8 p.m. Entrance 800$00 (EUR 3.99), free on Sunday between 10 a.m. to 2 p.m.*

Back on the tram expect to see in Boavista large, 5-Star hotels, expensive restaurants and, incongruously, the Boavista soccer stadium, home of Oporto's lesser rated team. As the tram trundles on past these it will become obvious that the area has begun to deteriorate. When you reach the Praça de Mouzinho de Alberquerque, it is time to alight and, once again, take to your feet.

Six streets radiate from this square, so be careful to take the right one; Rua de Júlio Dinis. Follow this on until you come to the park, which you will follow around to the right and into Rua Entre-Quintas. Soon, on a bluff above the river, you will come to a double delight. In the upper half of a charming 19th-century house is the **Romantic Museum** *(Museu Romântico)* (4), ☎ 609-11- 31, which allows a glimpse of the lifestyle prevalent among the rich and elegant who lived during that era. One room of particular interest is that in which the exiled Italian king, Carlos Alberto of Sardinia, died. *Visit Tuesday to Saturday 10 a.m. to midday and 2 p.m. to 5 p.m., and Sunday 2 p.m. to 5:30 p.m. Entrance 150$00 (EUR .75).*

Beneath this is a place that will appeal to subtly different tastes. The ***Institute of Port Wine*** *(Solar do Vinho do Porto)* (5), ☎ 2609-47-49, is a port-lovers delight. It is run by the Ministry of Agriculture and the menu, pages and pages of it, consists of just one offering—port; and just about everybody will be astounded at the number of variations there are available. Most of these may be purchased by the glass, but the very expensive ones, and they are expensive, must be purchased by the bottle. An unexpected bonus is the delightful garden where while sipping a glass of port, you may look out over the Douro river and, in the distance, the Atlantic Ocean. *Open Monday to Friday 10 a.m. to 11:45 p.m., and Saturday 11 a.m. to 10:45 p.m.*

It's time now to head for the last, but certainly not least, attraction on this tour. Retrace your steps back up and around the park, past Júlio Dinis, and along Rua de D. Manuel II until you come to the ***National Museum of Soares dos Reis*** *(Museu Nacional Soares dos Reis)* (6), ☎ 339-37-70 or fax 208-28-51. Here, in what was once the late 18th-century Carrancas royal

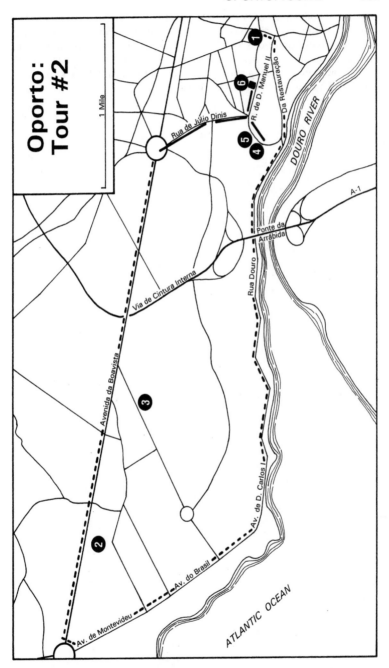

Oporto:
Tour #2

1 Mile

DOURO RIVER

A-1

Da Restauração

R. de D. Manuel II

Rua de Júlio Dinis

Ponte da
Arrábida

Via de Cintura Interna

Rua Douro

Avenida da Boavista

Av. de D. Carlos I

Av. do Brasil

Av. de Montevideu

ATLANTIC OCEAN

palace, are collections of Portuguese jewelry from the 16th century to the present, Portuguese paintings from the 19th century and, of course, works of sculpture by Soares dos Reis himself. *Opening hours are Wednesday to Sunday 10 a.m. to 12:30 p.m. and 1:30 p.m. to 6 p.m. Entrance 350$00 (EUR 1.75).* From here it is just a short walk, around the hospital, back to where the tour began at Praça da Gomes Teixeira.

Coimbra

The hill known today as the Alta was more than likely occupied by Celtic tribes as long ago as a few centuries before Christ. Its strategic dominance of the surrounding countryside was not overlooked by the Romans either, who positioned their forum here, calling the town *Aeminium*. The Visigoths, who brought Christianity to this area, were originally based at the nearby Roman town of Conímbriga, but when they in turn realized the significance of this hill they moved their settlement here. The present name, Coimbra, was derived from the name of their previous community. The Moors conquered the town in 711, and among their achievements was the encircling of the hill with fortified walls. Indeed, to this day, the most important entrance to the Alta is the Almedina gate, constructed during that era.

The city changed hands more than once during the battles for reconquest, and it was not until 1064 that Ferdinand I, King of León and Castile, definitively vanquished the Moors. Coimbra became the capital of the "reconquered" territory that lay wedged between an area in the south, still controlled by the Moors, on the one side, and the Douro River on the other. It became the capital of Portugal after Dom Afonso Henriques defeated the Spanish forces and declared Portugal an independent country. An impressive total of six kings were born in Coimbra during the Middle Ages. Three before the capital was moved to Lisbon in 1260 and, as Coimbra remained a royal court, three subsequent to that event.

The University, the oldest in Portugal, and one of the oldest in Europe, was established here in 1290. Its location vacillated, however, between this city and Lisbon until it finally settled in Coimbra in 1537. Today the influence of this institution is most evidenced by the presence of students outfitted in flowing black gowns. These are pinned together by colored ribbons that identify the student's course of study.

The 16th and 17th centuries brought an era of affluence and cultural splendor, and many of the marvelous buildings seen here today, their interiors often lavishly decorated with Brazilian gold, date from that period. A multitude of writers resided in Coimbra during this period, one of the most famous being the poet Luís de Camões, author of the acclaimed *The Lusiads*. The 19th century, unfortunately, was not so peaceful. In the course of the Peninsula War Napoleon's troops overran the city. During these battles Arthur Wellesley, the future Duke of Wellington, dispatched by England to defend the territory, made his headquarters at the Quinta das Lágrimas, now a luxury hotel just a few hundred yards from the city center. With the end of the conflict many changes came to Portugal, notably the closing of religious orders throughout the country. Over thirty were closed in Coimbra alone.

These days Coimbra is a charming provincial capital, whose alluring historical monuments should not be missed.

GETTING THERE:

Trains run through Coimbra on the mainline between Lisbon and Oporto. Be aware that you must disembark at Coimbra-B; and, from there, take another train to the Coimbra-A station, a terminal in the center of town.

Buses may be taken from Lisbon and Oporto, but the trains, fast and frequent, are a better option.

By Car, Coimbra, 127 miles north of Lisbon and 73 miles south of Oporto, may be reached, from either, via the A-1 *auto-estrada* tollroad.

PRACTICALITIES:

As the premier museum in Coimbra is closed on Monday, it is better not to schedule your tour for that day. The **Dialing Code** is 239. The correct pronunciation of the city's name is *Quim-Bra*. The tourist office for the **Central Tourist Region**, ☎ 83-30-19 or fax 82-55-76, is at Largo da Portagem, just across from the Santa Clara bridge. It is open on weekdays from 9 a.m. to 12:30 p.m. and 2 p.m. to 7 p.m.; and weekends from 9 a.m. to 12:30 p.m. and 2 p.m. to 5:30 p.m. During winter it closes at 6 p.m. on weekdays and at 1 p.m. on weekends. Coimbra has a **population** of about 100,000.

ACCOMMODATION:

The **Hotel Tivoli Coimbra** ****, ☎ 2-69-34 or fax 2-68-27, Rua João Machado, is a luxuriously modern hotel located just outside the city center. The rooms are spacious, comfortable and well equipped. Guests will also enjoy use of an in-house health club. $$

The **Hotel Quinta das Lágrimas** ****, ☎ 44-16-15, fax 44-16-95 or www.supernet.pt/hotelagrimas, Apartado 5033,is within a fantastically beautiful old house across the Mondego River, but still less than half a mile from the city center. In its day it graciously received such dignitaries as General Wellington, the Emperor of Brazil and various Portuguese kings. Easily the most dignified in town, combining history with comfort and with various sporting facilities in its extensive gardens. $$

The **Hotel Astória** ***, ☎ 2-20-55 or fax 2-20-67, Avenida Emídio Navarro, 21, overlooks the Mondego River from its convenient location in the city center. The rooms are well appointed and tastefully decorated in the Art Deco style. As an affiliate of the Hoteis Alexandre chain you may enjoy the famous, and exclusive, Bussaco wines here. $$

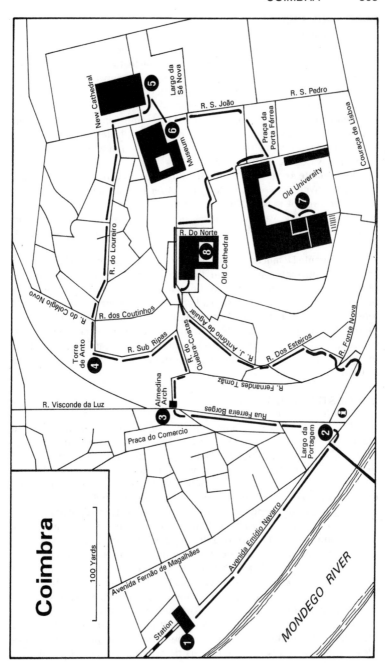

Coimbra

FOOD AND DRINK:

Restaurante Porta Férrea (Rua Joáo Machado), in the recently opened Hotel Tivoli is reflective of the character of that establishment, unaffected but elegant. A menu of International Cuisine features interesting hors d'oeuvres such as Kiwi Fruit with Smoked Ham; a variety of vegetables and salads, and tempting entrees such as Stuffed Rolls of Sole with Shrimp Sauce. ☎ 2-69-34 or fax 2-68-27. $$$

Quinta das Lágrimas (in the hotel of the same name), the restaurant here is as fistinguished as everything else in this hotel. Classical dishes such as Cod with Parma ham and Partridge braised in wine, supplemented by fine wines match the ambiance. $$$

Restaurante Adega Paço do Conde (Rua Paço do Conde, 1), is a characterful place with very reasonable prices. *Adega* is translated "wine cellar" and, as you might expect, the decor is accentuated by a proliferation of old barrels. A wide variety of meats, poultry and fish are skewered and barbequed on a large open grill in the patio. Closed on Sunday. ☎ 2-56-05. $

Restaurante Democratica (Travessa Rua Nova, 5), offers a wide ranging and surprisingly affordable menu, though finding this establishment may prove a challenge. There are two dining areas, one traditionally set with tables and chairs and a less formal back room furnished with tables and long benches. The latter is a favorite haunt of students from the city's prestigious University, recognizable by their distinctive black gowns. The house speciality is *Arroz de Polvo* (Octopus Rice). You can be assured that, except for Sunday when it is closed, this establishment will be open as late as there are customers. ☎ 2-37-84. $

SUGGESTED TOUR:

Numbers in parentheses correspond to numbers on the map.

The logical place to begin your tour of Coimbra is at the **Railroad Station** (1), which is conveniently located by the banks of the Mondego river, and close to the old town. Exit straight out and then, by the side of the river, walk along the embankment formed by the Avenida Emídio Navarro, towards the simple lines of the *Ponte de Santa Clara*. This bridge carries traffic over the river towards the rolling green hills in the distance and, on the city side, ends at the triangular shaped **Largo da Portagem** (2). Here, around a small central park are some attractive façades and, also, the beginning of the *Rua Ferreira Borges,* a pedestrian shopping street.

Follow this until it opens out a bit and there, on the right-hand side, you will find the **Almedina Arch** *(Arco de Almedina)* (3). Formerly a part of the old Moorish walls, this still serves as the main entrance to the Upper Town *(Alta)*, where the city's oldest monuments are located. This part of town is called "Upper" for a reason. The maze of tiny streets and alleyways that make up this area usually have at least one thing in common—their steepness. This reality is reflected in the name of the first, narrow, cobblestone street you will come to, Rua do Quebra-Costas, which literally means Back-Breaker street. You can, however, break up the climb by stopping now again at any number of the many antique and *azulejo* shops along the way.

Before you reach the top, turn left into Rua Sub Ripas, but do not expect a respite from the steepness. Pass the Sub Ripas palace and arch, which has a lovely *Manueline* doorway dating from very early in the 16th century, and follow the signs to the **Torre de Anto** (4). This, at last, provides a perfect opportunity to stop for a moment or two, and catch your breath. Originally a part of the old walls, and home of the poet António Nobre, its ramparts are an ideal place to sit and admire the views, looking down over the kaleidoscopic jumble of rooftops and out over the river and the hills beyond. Before you leave you may wish to purchase a souvenir from the **Coimbra Region House of Handicrafts** *(Casa de Artesanato da Região de Coimbra)*, now on this site.

It is time to press on and, yet again, it's uphill all the way. Follow the street around from the *Torre*, after which the Rua do Loureiro takes you, relentlessly, to the very top of the hill. Once you arrive, you will immediately see why all this effort was worthwhile. The University buildings tower majestically above you, the first one, strangely, incorporating the **New Cathedral** *(Sé Nova)* (5), ☎ 89-21-38. This was founded by the Jesuits at the very end of the 16th century, but construction was not completed for another 100 years. Its façade reflects Classical and Baroque styles, and has a host of notable features inside. *Visit Tuesday to Saturday 9 a.m. to midday and 2 p.m. to 6:30 p.m., entrance free.*

Directly across the road is the biggest attraction in the immediate area, and one of the most highly acclaimed museums in all of Portugal. In addition, the building in which it is housed is notable on its own merits. From the 12th century until the country became a republic in 1910, it served as the Bishop's Palace. Today, named after a very significant 18th-century Portuguese sculptor, the *****Machado de Castro National Museum** *(Museu Nacional de Machado de Castro)* (6), ☎ 82-37-27, boasts one of the country's premiere collections of sculpture, and gold and silver work. Also displayed are such items as a sarcophagus, *azulejos*, crockery, and even carriages. All these are shown to marvelous advantage in this elegant building with its beautiful wooden ceilings, and a patio with an unusual veranda. Be sure to allow a few minutes to visit the veranda where you get a true birds-eye view of the Alta and, particularly, the Old Cathedral. From this angle only the dome appears prominently, and you can clearly see how cramped and crowded this ancient area really is. Before leaving, investigate one more surprise, this time found beneath the museum. Here, dating from the 1st century, is the Roman Cryptoportic, an amazing, and intriguing, series of underground passages of huge proportions. The museum's collection of Roman artifacts aside, it is worth the entrance fee to see this ancient wonder. *Opening hours are Tuesday to Sunday 9:30 a.m. to 12:30 p.m. and 2 p.m. to 5:15 p.m., entrance 250$00 (EUR 1.25).*

Coming out, turn right and follow in the shadow of the sober

University buildings to the left. Not far along you will arrive at the Praça de Porta Férrea, where, to your right, is the entrance to the *Old University (7), ☎ 85-98-41. This is one of the oldest seats of higher learning in Europe, having been created, on March 1, 1290, by a royal decree from King Dom Dinis. In August of the same year, the Pope, by order of Papal Bull, confirmed its foundation. The University functioned alternatively in Lisbon and Coimbra until, in 1537, at the instigation of King João III, who donated his palace to house the institution, it made Coimbra its permanent home. In the 18th century, under the guidance of the Marqués de Pombal, a number of renovations were undertaken and many new buildings were constructed. Today, the distinctively different buildings from these diverse periods occupy three sides of an immense patio, which is accessed through a rectangular gateway, set into the façade, and known as the **Iron Gate** *(Puerta Férrea)*. It is so named because the imposing gates, and frame, are made of metal. Both the decorative and intricate portals, exterior and interior, are basically identical.

Once inside, your eyes will feast on a host of differing architectural styles. To the left is the long, three story, whitewashed façade of the St. Peter's College. Immediately to the right, and announced by three staircases, is the largest part of the palace donated by King João III, whose statue dominates the center of the square. The central, and unusually elegant, staircase, rises in harmony with the three high arches which support a triangular pediment embellished with Portugal's coat-of-arms. The lower level, reached by the staircases at either end, is colonnaded and supports a balconied upper level. This ensuing covered walkway is known as the **Latin Way** *(Via Latina)*, supposedly because, at one time, the scholars who strolled its length conversed in Latin. The interior of the palace contains two contrastingly interesting rooms. The **Sala de Capos**, Room of Cardinal's Hats, served in the early 16th century as the Grand Hall of the *Manueline* palace. This is where the most important University ceremonies are conducted. Next door is the elaborately decorated Private Examination Room, which was fully restored in 1701.

In the far corner of the *Via Latina* is the symbol of the University and, indeed, of Coimbra itself. Soberly Baroque, the Clock Tower, construction of which began in 1728, rises over 100 ft to dominate the city skyline. One of its bells, whose tolling helped to order the schedules of students and citizens alike, is nicknamed The Goat *(Cabra)*.

To its left, and long the opposite side, is the Museum of Sacred Art, which adjoins the St. Michael's Chapel. It features four rooms exhibiting religious items donated to the Chapel. Original construction of the structure began in 1517, but extensive renovations were made in the 17th and 18th centuries. Nearly every square inch is decorated in some fashion with, surprisingly, many *azulejos*. Look, also, for the resoundingly imposing Baroque altar.

Though the preceding attractions are quite engaging, it is the next, and last, building that will be most fascinating to the majority of visitors.

In my opinion it is, also, the highlight of this tour. The ***King John Library** *(Biblioteca Joanina)* was built of timber and gold brought from Brazil, on the 1717 order of King João V. Enter through an imposing Baroque portal crowned by an impressive three-dimensional coat-of-arms. Inside are three rooms, all interconnected by arches similar in style to the exterior portal, that seemingly compete to outshine the others in their Baroque splendor. In each room, a small balcony, supported by delicate columns, separates two levels of absolutely beautiful wooden bookshelves. These contain in excess of 300,000 volumes from the 16th, 17th and 18th centuries. *Open daily 9:30 a.m. to midday and 2 p.m. to 5 p.m. Entrance to the library, Room of the Doctors and Museum of Arts 500$00 (EUR 2.49).* It is nearly time to leave the University for now but, before doing so, wander over to the balcony on the open side of the patio. From this vantage point you can see the Mondego river meandering through the verdant hills, an altogether relaxing, and pleasing, sight.

Retrace your steps back through the *Porte Férrea,* and take the stairs which descend to your immediate left. Passing the wrought-iron gate of the **Pharmacy Faculty** *(Faculdade de Farmacia),* and turning left yet again, you will immediately come upon the ***Old Cathedral** *(Sé Velha)* (8), ☎ 82-52-73. Construction began on this Romanesque church in 1162, during the reign of Afonso Henriques, Portugal's first king, making this the oldest Cathedral in the country. It has, obviously, been modified since that time, most particularly in the 16th century, and it was completely refurbished three centuries later, leaving it with an intriguing mix of styles. The interior is dominated by a wood altarpiece from the early 16th century. And, though there is a small entrance charge, the peaceful solitude of the charming Gothic cloister alone, is worth the price. *Open daily, except Friday mornings and holidays, 10 a.m. to midday and 2 p.m. to 7:30 p.m. Entrance 150$00 (EUR 0.75).*

From the Largo da Sé Velha, outside the Cathedral, take the sloping Rua João António de Aguiar, which changes its name in the process, downhill to the corner dominated by the Civil Governor's office. Make a sharp right and follow that street, downhill again, all the way back to the Largo da Portagem, to end the tour.

Index

Special interest attractions are also listed under their category headings.

Daytrips

OTHER AMERICAN & EUROPEAN TITLES

Daytrips

HOLLAND, BELGIUM *and* LUXEMBOURG

40 *one day adventures by rail, bus or car*

EARL STEINBICKER

Daytrips

OTHER AMERICAN & EUROPEAN TITLES

Daytrips FRANCE

By Earl Steinbicker. Describes 48 daytrips — including 5 walking tours of Paris, 24 excursions from the city, 5 in Provence, and 14 along the Riviera. Expanded 5th edition, 304 pages, 60 maps, and a menu translator. ISBN: 0-8038-2006-2.

Daytrips ITALY

By Earl Steinbicker. Features 40 one-day adventures in and around Rome, Florence, Milan, Venice, and Naples. Walking tours of the main cities are included. 4th edition, 288 pages, 45 maps, and a menu translator. ISBN: 0-8038-2004-6

Daytrips LONDON

By Earl Steinbicker. Explores the metropolis on 10 one-day walking tours, then describes 45 daytrips to destinations throughout southern England, with excursions to the Midlands, West Country, and Wales — all by either rail or car. Expanded 6th edition, 352 pages, 62 maps. ISBN: 0-8038-9443-0.

Daytrips GERMANY

By Earl Steinbicker. 60 of Germany's most enticing destinations can be savored on daytrips from Munich, Frankfurt, Hamburg, and Berlin. Walking tours of the big cities are included. Expanded 5th edition, 352 pages, 67 maps, and a menu translator. ISBN: 0-8038-9428-7.

Daytrips SWITZERLAND

By Norman P.T. Renouf. 45 one-day adventures in and from convenient bases including Zurich and Geneva, with forays into nearby Germany, Austria, and Italy. 320 pages, 38 maps. ISBN: 0-8038-9417-7.

Daytrips HOLLAND, BELGIUM & LUXEMBOURG

By Earl Steinbicker. Many unusual places are covered on these 40 daytrips, along with all the favorites plus the three major cities. 3rd edition, 272 pages, 45 maps, and a bilingual menu translator. ISBN: 0-8038-2009-7

Daytrips IRELAND

By Patricia Tunison Preston. Covers the entire Emerald Isle with 55 one-day self-guided tours both within and from the major tourist areas, plus sections on shopping. Expanded 2nd edition, 400 pages, 57 maps. ISBN: 0-8038-2003-8.

Daytrips ISRAEL

By Earl Steinbicker. 25 one-day adventures by bus or car to the Holy Land's most interesting sites. Includes Jerusalem walking tours. 2nd edition, 206 pages, 40 maps, 40 B&W photos. ISBN: 0-8038-9374-4.

Daytrips

• AMERICAN TITLES •

Daytrips NEW ENGLAND

By Earl Steinbicker. Discover the 50 most delightful excursions within a day's drive of Boston or Central New England, from Maine to Connecticut. Includes Boston walking tours. Revised 2nd edition, 320 pages, 60 maps. ISBN: 0-8038-2008-9.

Daytrips WASHINGTON, D.C.

By Earl Steinbicker. Fifty one-day adventures in the Nation's Capital, and to nearby Virginia, Maryland, Delaware, and Pennsylvania. Both walking and driving tours are featured. 368 pages, 60 maps. Revised 2nd edition. ISBN: 0-8038-9429-5.

Daytrips PENNSYLVANIA DUTCH COUNTRY & PHILADELPHIA

By Earl Steinbicker. Completely covers the City of Brotherly Love, then goes on to probe southeastern Pennsylvania, southern New Jersey, and Delaware before moving west to Lancaster, the "Dutch" country, and Gettysburg. There are 50 daytrips in all. 288 pages, 54 maps. ISBN: 0-8038-9394-9.

Daytrips SAN FRANCISCO & NORTHERN CALIFORNIA

By David Cheever. Fifty enjoyable one-day adventures from the sea to the mountains; from north of the wine country to south of Monterey. Includes 16 self-guided discovery tours of San Francisco itself. 336 pages, 64 maps. ISBN: 0-8038-9441-4.

Daytrips HAWAII

By David Cheever. Thoroughly explores all the major islands — by car, by bus, on foot, and by bicycle, boat, and air. Includes many off-beat discoveries you won't find elsewhere, plus all the big attractions in detail. 288 pages, 55 maps. ISBN: 0-8038-9401- 5.

Daytrips NEW YORK

Edited by Earl Steinbicker. 107 easy excursions by car throughout southern New York State, New Jersey, eastern Pennsylvania, Connecticut, and southern Massachusetts. 7th edition, 336 pages, 44 maps, 46 B&W photos. ISBN: 0-8038-9371-X.

Daytrips FLORIDA

By Blair Howard. Fifty one-day adventures from bases in Miami, Orlando, St. Petersburg, Jacksonville, and Pensacola. From little-known discoveries to bustling theme parks; from America's oldest city to isolated getaways — this guide covers it all. 320 pages, 47 maps, 28 B&W photos. ISBN: 0-8038-9380-9.

HASTINGS HOUSE
Book Publishers

2601 Wells Ave., Suite 161, Fern Park, FL 32730
☎ orders toll-free (800) 206-7822
Internet: www.daytripsbooks.com
e-mail: Hhousebks@aol.com

ABOUT THE AUTHOR

ABOUT THE AUTHOR:

Although now living in Richmond, Virginia, Norman Renouf was born in London and educated at Charlton Central School, Greenwich. From 1962 to 1989 he worked for a variety of financial institutions both in the United States and the UK, the last eight of those years being spent in the Insurance industry in London. The economic recession of that era, and a subsequent redundancy, allowed him to work professionally as a freelance travel writer and photographer on what, previously, had been a lifelong hobby.

During the above period he traveled frequently, and widely, in the USA and Europe, and developed a lifelong passion for Spain. Since 1989 besides numerous newspaper and magazine articles, this is the fourth full length guide book he has written about the countries of the Iberian Peninsula. Besides that he has criss-crossed Europe updating the Berlitz Pocket Guides and, in collaboration with his wife Kathy, has begun a "Romantic Weekends" series of guides to attractive locations in America.